INTERNET
PROGRAMMING
WITH VISUAL BASIC 5

Steven Holzner

M&T
BOOKS

Henry Holt & Co., Inc. • New York

M&T Books
A Division of MIS:Press, Inc.
A Subsidiary of Henry Holt and Company, Inc.
115 West 18th Street
New York, New York 10011
http://www.mispress.com

Limits of Liability and Disclaimer of Warranty

First Edition—1997

ISBN 1-55851-558-5

MIS:Press and M&T Books are available at special discounts for bulk purchases for sales promotions, premiums, and fundraising. Special editions or book excerpts can also be created to specification.

For details contact: Special Sales Director
                           MIS:Press and M&T Books
                           Subsidiaries of Henry Holt and Company, Inc.
                           115 West 18th Street
                           New York, New York 10011

10 9 8 7 6 5 4 3 2 1

Associate Publisher: *Paul Farrell*

Managing Editor: *Shari Chappell*   **Production Editor:** *Anthony Washington*
Editor: *Michael Sprague*   **Copy Edit Manager:** *Karen Tongish*
Copy Editor: *Betsy Hardinger*

CONTENTS-IN-BRIEF

CONTENTS

CHAPTER 1

HANDLING HTML

Welcome to *Internet Programming with Visual Basic 5*. In this book, you'll learn how to create super Internet applications—applications that display more than static information: applications that ask questions, change appearance, and support many unique interactions with users. *Internet Programming with Visual Basic 5* offers the best of two worlds: Internet programming that is both powerful and simple to create. In this book, we'll explore what Visual Basic has to offer to developers who are writing applications for the Internet, and we'll see it all at work.

It's no secret that Microsoft has embraced the Internet with great enthusiasm. And Visual Basic is a big part of its Internet strategy. With Visual Basic and Visual Basic Script (VBScript), you can create Web browsers, send and receive email, and create ActiveX controls to embed in Web pages. (In fact, Visual Basic is now the easiest way to create ActiveX controls.) These two tools also let you work with Internet protocols such as HTTP, the World Wide Web protocol—including secure Web transactions, as we'll see—as well as FTP and others. You can create and work with ActiveX documents—much like running a Visual Basic program right in a Web browser—and even handle databases over the Internet. You'll learn all this and more in this book. A tremendous amount of Visual

Basic Internet programming is possible right now, and there's more to come.

Visual Basic has always had the reputation of enabling simple yet powerful programming. When it comes to Internet programming, it's still true. You'll see, for example, how to add an entire Web browser to a Visual Basic application with a single click of the mouse when you create the application. The user can browse the Web from your application as easily as opening a document.

Much Visual Basic Internet programming is aimed at the World Wide Web, and Chapter 2 shows you how to create a Web browser in Visual Basic. Because so much Internet programming is aimed at Web pages, we'll use Web pages for VBScript, Web browsing, embedding ActiveX controls and documents, database handling, and more, and we will start with a review of working with Web pages in this chapter. Here, we'll review Hypertext Markup Language (HTML), the language of Web pages. This information will be important when you create your own Web pages, as you will throughout the book, embedding ActiveX controls, VBScript, and even database tables.

After we review HTML, we'll proceed to Visual Basic in Chapter 2. If you're an HTML expert, there's no reason that you can't skip to the next chapter immediately. If you're not an HTML expert, however, you might want to read through the following material to brush up.

Our First Web Page

Our first task is to see what goes into a Web page. At its most basic, a Web page is really just text that can be interpreted by a Web browser. You can open many types of files, such as **.avi** movie files or **.zip** compressed files, with Web browsers, especially if you take advantage of the available helper applications. But Web pages themselves are written in text, even though they include HTML statements. With all the different possible formats, how does a Web browser know what kind of file it is working on? That's based on the file's extension. If the extension is **.html**, such as **review.html**, the Web browser expects a file written in HTML. Note that because of

MS-DOS's three-letter file extension limit, many Web browsers also assume that files with the extension **.htm** are written in HTML.

The Shortest Web Page

Because the text in a Web page is interpreted based on the file's **.html** extension, we can write a Web page that is extraordinarily short. It might contain only a single line:

```
Hello, world!
```

We need only give the Web page's file the extension **.html**. In this case, we might put the text into a file named **hello.html**, and Web browsers would treat it as a Web page:

Hello.html file

```
Hello, world!
```

We could have a Web page as short as a single character, as long as we gave the file containing it the extension **.html**. (This also assumes that you install the Web page in your Internet service provider (ISP), as discussed later.) The text in a Web page's **.html** file is straight text, and on PCs that usually means ASCII text. If you are using a word processor such as Microsoft Word for Windows 95, you must save your files in plain text format (as text that can be displayed on the screen with the **TYPE** command). That's all it takes to write a Web page.

We'll assume that you are familiar with the basic steps of installing a Web page on the Web. That usually means uploading your Web page properly to an ISP with a computer that can run day and night so that your Web page is always accessible. The uploading details vary from machine to machine. It can mean using special uploading software that uploads Web pages at the click of a mouse button or using an FTP (file transfer protocol) program to transfer the Web page and any included graphics files to a specially designated area of your ISP, using UNIX commands to set the page's protections so that only you can modify them. The default name for a Web page is **index.html**, which is what a Web browser looks for at a given Web site if you do not specify the name of a file to open.

Our "Hello, world!" Web page isn't very exciting (unless you want to prove to your friends how easy it is to create a Web page), so let's design a more typical Web page. We'll build it up part by part during the rest of this chapter until we get a functional Web page at the end. We'll start our example Web page with the <HTML> tag:

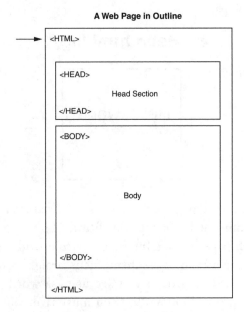

The <HTML> Tag

Usually, Web pages include text that you want to display and HTML commands that are read by Web browsers. These commands are enclosed in *tags*, which are surrounded by the < and > characters. For example, the usual first line in a Web page indicates that it is written in HTML with an HTML tag:

```
<HTML>
   .
   .
   .
```

In this way, a Web browser can tell that what is to follow is written in HTML, although that information is usually obtained from the Web page file's **.html** extension.

The <!> Comment Tag

Because we want to make it clear what's going on in our first Web page, we will add comments by using comment tags, which begin with a !. Web browsers will ignore the comments that follow. (You have to be careful. Early versions of some browsers had problems when you included a tag, such as <HTML>, inside a comment. That's why we enclose the tags in quotes in our comments here.)

```
<HTML>
<!-START THE PAGE with an HTML tag (a tag is an HTML command, and
    HTML tags appear between angle brackets) We use "HTML" to indicate
    this document is in HTML, which is the language of Web pages.>
   .
   .
   .
```

Here, our comment indicates what the <HTML> tag is all about. Adding comments can help you recall what's going on in your own Web pages and help you understand what's going on in other people's Web pages. But keep in mind that your entire Web page must be downloaded into someone's Web browser, and that means the comments will be downloaded as well. For that reason, comments (which most people surfing the Web will never see) should probably be kept to a minimum. Some professional Web page writers keep a commented version of Web pages and run software to strip the comments from the copy they install. In our example, however, we'll comment our first page heavily.

The <HEAD> Tag

Web pages consist of both a head and a body:

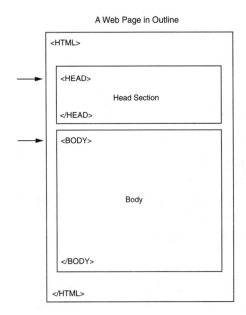

A Web Page in Outline

The head section, defined with the <HEAD> tag, is where we place text that explains more about the Web page. In the past, the head section was used more often. These days, this section usually has only the title of the Web page (see the <TITLE> tag, coming up next). It is worth noting, however, that certain advanced tags, such as <BASE> and <RANGE>, can function only in the head section of a Web page. (<BASE> is an interesting and unusual tag. It allows you to specify a page's *base location*, from which all other references to subdirectories and so on will be taken. This arrangement allows you to move a page to another directory to work on it, while any embedded images and so on will still be found properly.) We start our page's head section with the <HEAD> tag:

```
<HTML>

<!-The HEAD section of the Web page includes text about the page,
    although usually this section only includes the title.>
```

```
<HEAD>                <-
       .
       .
       .
```

The <TITLE> Tag

Although Web page programmers often skip the <HEAD> tag, they rarely skip <TITLE>. That's because a Web page's title counts; it's the text that most Web browsers will enter into the list of favorites or bookmarks when someone likes your page and marks it to return to later. Also, this text usually appears in the title bar of the Web browser when it's displaying your page, like this: "THIS IS THE TITLE OF MY PAGE!–Microsoft Internet Explorer." We'll give our new Web page the title "BUILD YOUR OWN WEB PAGE!" using the <TITLE> tag. HTML tags come in pairs. We "turn off" the title using the tag </TITLE> and finish the head section using </HEAD>:

```
<HTML>

<!-A PAGE'S TITLE is how a browser will refer to it if visitors save
    it in their Favorites or Bookmarks menu. Note that we also indicate
    we are finished defining the title with "/TITLE." This second tag
    matches the first tag, "TITLE." HTML tags
    always come in pairs, such the following one, which indicates that
    we are finished with the page's header.>

<HEAD>                                        <-
<TITLE>BUILD YOUR OWN WEB PAGE!</TITLE>       <-
</HEAD>                                       <-
       .
       .
       .
```

Usually, for each tag <TAG>, there is a corresponding closing tag, </TAG> (although that is not true for some tags, such as the line break, <BR>, tag). Making sure you have as many </TAG>s as <TAG>s may not be necessary in HTML (Web browsers are very forgiving), but it is good form to make sure you do. In fact, this is one of the first things that Web page *validators* check for. (Validators are programs on the Web that will check your page for errors. Just do a Web search for "validator.")

Now we've completed the head section of our Web page, and we're ready to turn to the body:

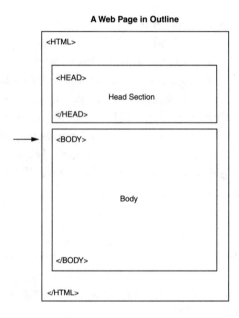

A Web Page in Outline

The <BODY> Tag

The body follows a Web page's head section and makes up the remainder of the document. This is where the action is. We declare the body with the <BODY> tag:

```
<HTML>

<HEAD>
<TITLE>BUILD YOUR OWN WEB PAGE!</TITLE>
</HEAD>
```

```
<BODY>   <-
    .
    .
    .
```

We set up options in the body section that indicate how we want the entire Web page to appear, including the color of the text, the hyperlinks, the hyperlinks that have been visited, and so on.

In this example, let's make the text yellow, the hyperlinks red, and the visited hyperlinks yellow to blend in with the rest of the text. Although they will still appear underlined, hyperlinks that have already been visited will no longer stand out in red. This brings up the question, how do we define colors in HTML?

Setting Web Page and Text Colors

Recent Web browsers (such as the Microsoft Internet Explorer and Netscape) include a set of predefined colors: aqua, black, blue, fuchsia, gray, green, lime, maroon, navy, olive, purple, red, silver, teal, yellow, and white. However, older Web browsers have no idea what these color names mean and ignore them, so we will not use them either (there are many people out there with older Web browsers). Instead, we will specify color using color values: a six-digit number in hexadecimal.

Color values are expressed as rrggbb, where rr is the red color value, gg the green color value, and bb the blue color value. Each of these color values is a two-digit hexadecimal value from 0 to ff—that is, from 0 to 255 in decimal. (Hexadecimal digits go from 0 to f.) In this way, we specify pure red as #ff0000, pure blue as #0000ff, bright yellow (a combination of red and green) as #ffff00, and bright white as #ffffff. Black is simply #000000. We can express intermediate values as well, such as a muted green, which might look like #00aa00; gray is #888888. We can also use combinations of colors, such as a powder blue, which is set up as #aaaaff.

Now let's add some color values to our <BODY> tag. We intend to make the text yellow (using the TEXT keyword), hyperlinks red (using the LINK keyword), and visited hyperlinks yellow (using the VLINK keyword). In addition, we'll specify that as the user clicks a link, it should be displayed momentarily in white (using the ALINK keyword) to indicate that we are jumping to that location. All that looks like this in our <BODY> tag:

```
<HTML>

<HEAD>
<TITLE>BUILD YOUR OWN WEB PAGE!</TITLE>
</HEAD>

<!—BODY OF PAGE starts with the following "BODY" tag. COLOR VALUES
   are "#rrggbb" (red, green, and blue) in hexadecimal (0-255 = 0-ff);
   for example, pure red is "#ff0000," pure green is "#00ff00," and
   yellow is "#ffff00." Here we start the Web page's body, indicating
   we want yellow text, hyperlinks to be red, hyperlinks to turn white
   when pushed, and links that the user has already clicked to be
   yellow.>
<BODY TEXT  = "#ffff00" LINK  = "#ff0000" ALINK = "#ffffff" VLINK =
"#ffff00">

   .

   .

   .
```

In addition, we could specify the background color of the Web page using the BGCOLOR keyword. For example, we could make the background color white this way: <BODY BGCOLOR = "#ffffff">. For this example, however, let's use a graphics file for the background; the Web browser will use this graphics file to tile the background of our Web page, a technique that produces pleasing effects. You may have seen backgrounds that mimic various cloth or paper textures or even look like marble. We'll use a graphics file named **back.gif** to show how this works (see Figure 1.1). This image is a white dot on a black background.

Figure 1.1 Our first Web page's graphics background.

We install **back.gif** as our Web page's background using a new <BODY>
tag and the BACKGROUND keyword:

```
<HTML>

<HEAD>
<TITLE>BUILD YOUR OWN WEB PAGE!</TITLE>
</HEAD>

<BODY TEXT  = "#ffff00" LINK  = "#ff0000" ALINK = "#ffffff" VLINK =
"#ffff00">

<!—BACKGROUND PICTURE (which is optional) is tiled on the page's
   background. Here, we indicate we want the Web browser to use the
   graphics file back.gif, which is in our www/gif directory>
<BODY BACKGROUND = "gif/back.gif">      <—
   .
   .
   .
```

Because **back.gif** is a small file, Web browsers will use it repeatedly to tile
the background of our Web page. The background will appear as a series
of white dots.

Speaking of graphics, how did we produce **back.gif**? Where do we
store it? Let's take a look at that topic, because graphics is a large part of
Web page programming.

A Little About Graphics

The usual graphics file formats used in Web pages are the **.gif** format and the **.jpg** (or **.jpeg**) formats. (Internet Explorer can handle **.bmp** format, but many other browsers can't.) Which is better? That depends on your needs. **.jpg** files can be smaller, and that means faster download times, but compared with **.gif** format, there is some loss of data and images can look less sharp. The best thing to do is to give it a try both ways: Microsoft Internet Explorer can load and save images in **.bmp**, **.gif**, and **.jpg** format, so you can easily convert images this way. You can even use the Windows Paint program to design your graphics (although there are far more powerful graphics programs), save it in **.bmp** format, and then use Internet Explorer to save the file in **.gif** or **.jpg** format.

In addition to graphics you draw, there are other sources of graphics files, such as scans of photos. If you don't have your own scanner, you can often get it done commercially at a copy center. Ask for the standard 72 dots per inch (dpi) resolution, which is as good as screens get, and make your graphics file a reasonable size. (If you expect people to download your file and print it on very high resolution laser printers, you can ask for better scan resolution. Web pages are another possible source of graphics, and that can be tempting. However, before simply copying what someone else has done, you should be aware that the work may be copyrighted. Ask first.

When we insert graphics into a Web page such as the one we're designing, we usually need to know the width and height of the image in pixels (the background **.gif** or **.jpg** file is an exception) so that the Web browser can fit the page together while leaving space for the image. If you have a photo scanned, you can ask the operator what the image size is in pixels; otherwise, you can use a program such as Windows Paint, which will tell you the dimensions. Paint displays the current location of the mouse in pixels, so you need only move the mouse cursor to the lower-right corner of the image to get its height and width.

Where do we store images? It is customary to set up a separate directory for image files in your ISP. If you store your HTML files in a directory named www, you might want to create and store your images in a subdirectory named www/gif; you can create such a directory using the **mkdir** command on UNIX machines. We will store **back.gif** in a subdirectory named gif. When we want to reference a file, we indicate the correct path to that file: gif/back.gif. Because the files reside in the ISP's computer, we follow the UNIX convention of separating directories with forward slashes. We don't use backward slashes, which is the IBM PC convention.

```
<HTML>

<HEAD>
<TITLE>BUILD YOUR OWN WEB PAGE!</TITLE>
</HEAD>

<BODY TEXT  = "#ffff00" LINK  = "#ff0000" ALINK = "#ffffff" VLINK =
"#ffff00">

<!—BACKGROUND PICTURE (which is optional) is tiled on the page's
   background. Here, we indicate we want the Web browser to use the
   graphics file back.gif, which is in our www/gif directory.>
<BODY BACKGROUND = "gif/back.gif">       <—
   .
   .
   .
```

Note, however, that it is not necessary to use a separate directory for your image files, and many Web sites do not.

At this point, we've installed our background image. The next step is to add text to our Web page. For example, we might add a heading that says "BUILD YOUR OWN WEB PAGE!" This is the first time we see what our new Web page will look like:

```
BUILD YOUR OWN WEB PAGE!
```

The <Center> and Header Tags

To add a header to our Web page, we use the header tags <H1> to <H6>.
<H1> creates the largest-font header:

```
<HTML>

<HEAD>
<TITLE>BUILD YOUR OWN WEB PAGE!</TITLE>
</HEAD>

<BODY TEXT  = "#ffff00" LINK  = "#ff0000" ALINK = "#ffffff" VLINK =
"#ffff00">

<BODY BACKGROUND = "gif/back.gif">

<!—HEADERS. Now we are going to place a header of the largest size in
    our page, so we use the "H1" tag, as well as the "CENTER" tag.
    "CENTER" simply makes sure the following text or image is
    centered. Note that all HTML tags come in pairs — to turn off
    centering, we use "/CENTER" at the end of our header's
    specification.>
<H1>BUILD YOUR OWN WEB PAGE!</H1>        <—
    .
    .
    .
```

Now our header will appear in the text color we have chosen, yellow, in the largest header style. In addition, we center the header using the <CENTER> and </CENTER> tags:

```
<HTML>

<HEAD>
<TITLE>BUILD YOUR OWN WEB PAGE!</TITLE>
</HEAD>

<BODY TEXT  = "#ffff00" LINK  = "#ff0000" ALINK = "#ffffff" VLINK =
"#ffff00">

<BODY BACKGROUND = "gif/back.gif">

<!-HEADERS. Now we are going to place a header of the largest size in
    our page, so we use the "H1" tag, as well as the "CENTER" tag.
    "CENTER" simply makes sure the following text or image is centered.
    Note that all HTML tags come in pairs — to turn off centering, we
    use "/CENTER" at the end of our header's specification.>
<CENTER>                                <-
<H1>BUILD YOUR OWN WEB PAGE!</H1>
</CENTER>                               <-
    .
    .
    .
```

Our header will appear in large yellow letters, centered in our Web page, as shown in Figure 1.2. Note that we did not have to use the <CENTER> tag; instead, we could have specified an alignment for our header in the <H1> tag this way: <H1 ALIGN = alignment>, where alignment can be LEFT, RIGHT, or CENTER.

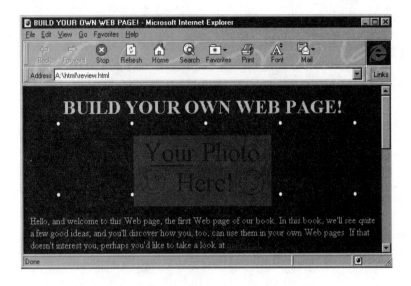

Figure 1.2 Our first Web page.

At this stage, we've just begun our Web page. We've set up the background image and the header text. Next, we review how to space things appropriately.

The
 Tag

The next step is to leave some space after the header and before adding any images. We do that using the line break tag, <BR>:

```
<HTML>

<HEAD>
<TITLE>BUILD YOUR OWN WEB PAGE!</TITLE>
</HEAD>

<BODY TEXT  = "#ffff00" LINK  = "#ff0000" ALINK = "#ffffff" VLINK =
"#ffff00">
<BODY BACKGROUND = "gif/back.gif">

<CENTER>
```

```
<H1>BUILD YOUR OWN WEB PAGE!</H1>
</CENTER>

<!-LINE BREAKS. To space things vertically, we use "BR" and "/BR"
    to skip a line.>
<BR>                              <-
    .
    .
    .
```

Let's add some graphics next. For example, this page might hold a photo of you, **yourgif.gif**:

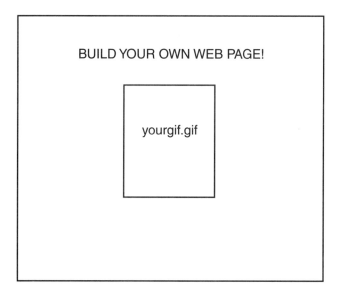

We insert graphics images with the <IMG> tag, which we'll review next.

The <IMG> Tag

Now we will insert the image file **yourgif.gif**. We'll center the image using the <CENTER> tag and perform the insertion using the <IMG> tag. We'll indicate the dimensions of the image using the WIDTH and HEIGHT keywords. We also indicate the path of the image file as well as its name using the SRC (for "Source") keyword, making our <IMG> tag look like this:

```
<HTML>

<HEAD>
<TITLE>BUILD YOUR OWN WEB PAGE!</TITLE>
</HEAD>

<BODY TEXT  = "#ffff00" LINK  = "#ff0000" ALINK = "#ffffff" VLINK =
"#ffff00">
<BODY BACKGROUND = "gif/back.gif">

<CENTER>
<H1>BUILD YOUR OWN WEB PAGE!</H1>
</CENTER>

<BR>

<!—IMAGES. We display an image, which will appear centered because of
    the "CENTER" tag, with the "IMG" tag, adding the width and height
    in pixels. Here, we display our GIF file yourgif.gif from the GIF
    directory, but this is where a photo of you could go.>
<CENTER>                                                      <—
<IMG WIDTH=236 HEIGHT=118 SRC="gif/yourgif.gif"></IMG>        <—
</CENTER>                                                      <—
    .
    .
    .
```

If you want to have text appear in the image space while the image is being loaded, you can add the ALT keyword to the <IMG> tag. This text is all that will appear in text-only Web browsers.

```
<IMG WIDTH = 236 HEIGHT = 118 ALT = "A photo of the Web page
    author as a young man." SRC="gif/yourgif.gif">
```

And that's how **yourgif.gif** appears in the Web page, as shown in Figure 1.2. It's easy to add images to a Web page using the <IMG> tag.

Now that we've added a picture, let's add text to our developing Web page:

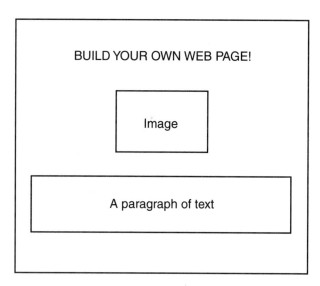

The <P> Tag

To start our text, which will introduce the Web page to the user, we use the <P> paragraph tag. This tag moves us to the next line and starts a paragraph of text. (Note that it is not necessary to use the <P> tag when inserting text.) We can place this text in our Web page by typing it to follow the <P> tag; note that we will set up a hyperlink to microsoft.com at the end of the paragraph:

```
Hello, and welcome to this Web page, the first Web page of
ourbook. In this book, you'll see quite a few good ideas, and
you'll discover how you, too, can use them in your own Web pages.
If that doesn't interest you, perhaps you'd like to take a look
at [microsoft.com].
```

In our Web page, we simply place the text directly into the **.html** file like this:

```
<HTML>
```

```
<HEAD>
<TITLE>BUILD YOUR OWN WEB PAGE!</TITLE>
</HEAD>

<BODY TEXT  = "#ffff00" LINK  = "#ff0000" ALINK = "#ffffff" VLINK =
"#ffff00">
<BODY BACKGROUND = "gif/back.gif">

<CENTER>
<H1>BUILD YOUR OWN WEB PAGE!</H1>
</CENTER>

<BR>

<CENTER>
<IMG WIDTH=236 HEIGHT=118 SRC="gif/yourgif.gif"></IMG>
</CENTER>

<!-PARAGRAPHS of text start with "P".>
<P>
-> Hello, and welcome to this Web page, the first Web page of our
-> book. In this book, you'll see quite a few good ideas, and you'll
-> discover how you, too, can use them in your own Web pages. If
-> that doesn't interest you, perhaps you'd like to take a look at
                            .

                            .

                            .
```

And that's it—now our paragraph of text appears as shown in Figure 1.2.

The <P> tag has one keyword: ALIGN. You can align text using these keywords: ALIGN = LEFT, ALIGN = RIGHT, and ALIGN = CENTER. In this way, you have some modest control over the formatting of your text paragraph. In addition, you can use the <B> tag to make displayed text bold, and the <I> tag to make it appear italicized.

We have not yet activated the hyperlink to microsoft.com at the end of the paragraph. Let's do that next, introducing a link into our **.html** file with the <A> tag.

The <A> Tag

We add hyperlinks using the <A> (for "anchor") tag, used together with the HREF keyword. To add a link to microsoft.com's Web page, we need the page's World Wide Web address, or URL (which stands for universal resource locator): http://www.microsoft.com. We don't want to give the URL as the name of the link, however; we'll display this link as "microsoft" in the hyperlink color we've chosen (which is red). Here's the <A> tag in our Web page:

```
<HTML>

<HEAD>
<TITLE>BUILD YOUR OWN WEB PAGE!</TITLE>
</HEAD>

<BODY TEXT  = "#ffff00" LINK  = "#ff0000" ALINK = "#ffffff" VLINK =
"#ffff00">
<BODY BACKGROUND = "gif/back.gif">

<CENTER>
<H1>BUILD YOUR OWN WEB PAGE!</H1>
</CENTER>

<BR>

<CENTER>
<IMG WIDTH=236 HEIGHT=118 SRC="gif/yourgif.gif"></IMG>
</CENTER>

<!-PARAGRAPHS of text start with "P".>
<!-LINKS. We add a hypertext link with the "A" tag, using the HREF
   keyword. In particular, we add a link to microsoft.com's Web page
   at http://www.microsoft.com below. This means that the text
   "microsoft" will appear underlined and in the standard link color
   (which we've set to red); when the user of your page clicks that
   text, the user will jump to Microsoft's home page.>
<P>
```

```
    Hello, and welcome to this Web page, the first Web page of
    ourbook. In this book, you'll see quite a few good ideas, and
    you'll discover how you, too, can use them in your own Web pages.
    If that doesn't interest you, perhaps you'd like to take a look
    at <A HREF="http://www.microsoft.com">microsoft</A>.    <-
<BR>
<BR>
</P>
    .
    .
    .
```

When someone takes a look at our Web page, this paragraph of text will appear in yellow, and the word "microsoft" at the end will appear in red and underlined, indicating it is a hyperlink. When clicked, this hyperlink will take visitors to microsoft.com. If we wanted to use an image as a hyperlink, we would simply use an <IMG> tag instead of the text "microsoft."

Now we've added text and hypertext to our Web page. Let's take a look at formatting the page. So far we've placed text or images into our page and centered them. There is much more we can do. Next, we'll take a look at the process of setting up text and images to be displayed right next to each other:

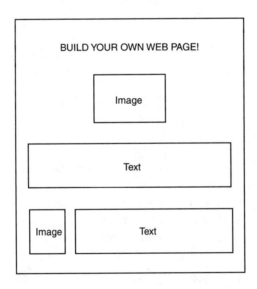

Aligning Images and Text

We've reviewed how to handle images and text separately; now we will combine them, placing an image on the left and text on the right. All we have to do is to use the ALIGN keyword in the <IMG> tag. To add a new image named **sidebar.gif**—which appears in Figure 1.3—on the left of our page, we specify that its alignment be LEFT (as opposed to CENTER or RIGHT):

```
<HTML>

<HEAD>
<TITLE>BUILD YOUR OWN WEB PAGE!</TITLE>
</HEAD>

<BODY TEXT  = "#ffff00" LINK  = "#ff0000" ALINK = "#ffffff" VLINK =
"#ffff00">
<BODY BACKGROUND = "gif/back.gif">

<CENTER>
<H1>BUILD YOUR OWN WEB PAGE!</H1>
</CENTER>

<BR>

<CENTER>
<IMG WIDTH=236 HEIGHT=118 SRC="gif/yourgif.gif"></IMG>
</CENTER>

<P>
   Hello, and welcome to this Web page, the first Web page of our
   book. In this book, you'll see quite a few good ideas, and you'll
discover how
   you, too, can use them in your own Web pages. If that doesn't
   interest you, perhaps you'd like to take a look at
   <A HREF="http://www.microsoft.com">microsoft</A>.
<BR>
<BR>
</P>
```

```
<!—ALIGNING PICTURES AND TEXT is done with the ALIGN keyword used in
    the "IMG" tag. In this case we just have to indicate that we want the
    graphics to appear on the left with ALIGN = LEFT. We also change
    the text color to green temporarily with a "FONT" tag ("FONT"
    works only in recent browsers).>
<IMG WIDTH=141 HEIGHT=126 SRC="gif/sidebar.gif" ALIGN=LEFT>      <—
```

Figure 1.3 Sidebar.gif, the image that appears next to text in our Web page.

Now we're ready to add text to the right of the image. We just type it; we don't need to align the text RIGHT or anything. Because the image is on the left, the text will automatically fill the space on the right. To make it a little more interesting, let's switch the color of our text from our default of yellow to green. We do that with the <FONT> tag.

The <FONT> Tag

The <FONT> tag is not supported in early versions of Web browsers such as Netscape (for example, in the 1.n versions), so you must be careful when relying on <FONT> tags. Nonetheless, most Web browsers support it now, so we'll put it to work here. To switch the color of our text to green, we use the <FONT> tag with the COLOR keyword:

```
<IMG WIDTH=141 HEIGHT=126 SRC="gif/sidebar.gif" ALIGN=LEFT>
<FONT COLOR = "00ff00">            <—
    We can even do green text next to graphics. This text appears next
    to the graphics on the left, allowing you to intersperse your words
    with pictures. When you take a look at the HTML for this Web page,
    you'll see how this and more is done.
```

```
</FONT>                          <-
</IMG>
   .
   .
   .
```

Note that to restore the text's default color, we use a </FONT> tag. Now our text appears next to the sidebar image we used, as shown in Figure 1.4.

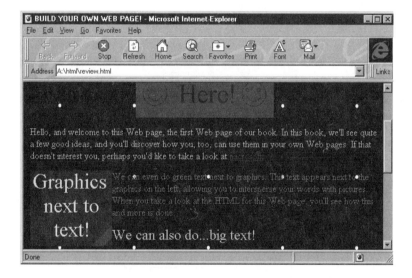

Figure 1.4 Setting up text next to images.

In addition to changing the text's color, we can change its size with the <FONT> tag and the SIZE keyword. Let's increase the size of our text temporarily so that it appears larger, as shown in Figure 1.4. We use this line in our **.html** file:

```
<IMG WIDTH=141 HEIGHT=126 SRC="gif/sidebar.gif" ALIGN=LEFT>
<FONT COLOR = "00ff00">
   We can even do green text next to graphics. This text appears next
   to the graphics on the left, allowing you to intersperse your words
   with pictures. When you take a look at the HTML for this Web page,
   you'll see how this and more is done.
</FONT>
```

```
</IMG>

<!-FONT SIZE is also done with the "FONT" tag; here, we set the
    size of our text temporarily to 5, a large size.>
<FONT SIZE = 5>                    <-
We can also do...big text!       <-
</FONT>                           <-
<BR>
<BR>
    .
    .
    .
```

The result appears in Figure 1.4. In addition, using the <FONT> tag with the FACE keyword, you can set the typeface used for your text, such as Courier or Arial, assuming that the typeface is installed on the machine running the Web browser. (If you list a number of typefaces, the first available one will be used.)

Now let's take a look at how to put up a table in our page:

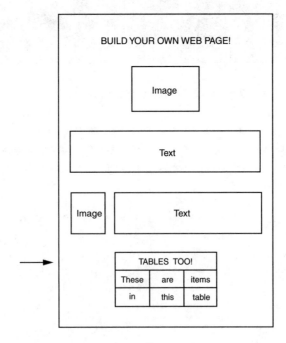

Making Tables

Setting up a table is not very difficult, even though the resulting HTML is not very readable. Let's create this table, which has three rows (one of which is the table's header), three columns, text centered in each table cell, and a header reading "TABLES TOO!" that spans all three columns:

TABLES TOO!		
These	are	items
in	this	table

We start our table with the TABLE tag. Here, we use the BORDER keyword to indicate that our table should have a border. In addition, we'll use the CELLPADDING keyword to add some padding (four pixels) around our text to improve its appearance and readability:

```
<TABLE BORDER CELLPADDING = 4>
        .
        .
        .
```

In setting up a table, we work row by row. To set up a row, we use the <TR> tag. Here, we align the text in our table's rows using the ALIGN keyword:

```
<TABLE BORDER CELLPADDING = 4>
<TR ALIGN = CENTER>                <—
        .
        .
        .
```

We want our table's header, which we set up with the <TH> tag, to span all three columns and to read "TABLES TOO!" We use the COLSPAN keyword:

```
<TABLE BORDER CELLPADDING = 4>
```

```
<TR ALIGN = CENTER>
<TH COLSPAN = 3>TABLES TOO!        <-
</TH>                              <-
      .
      .
      .
```

That finishes this row, so we use the </TR> tag:

```
<TABLE BORDER CELLPADDING = 4>
<TR ALIGN = CENTER>
<TH COLSPAN = 3>TABLES TOO!
</TH>
</TR>    <-
      .
      .
      .
```

To start the next row, we use the <TR> tag, aligning text in the center again, like this: <TR ALIGN = CENTER>. Now we set up our data for the three columns in this row, and we do that with the <TD> tag. We want to set up the columns like this:

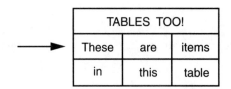

TABLES TOO!		
These	are	items
in	this	table

To do that, we use <TD> and </TD> pairs, one for each column:

```
<TABLE BORDER CELLPADDING = 4>
<TR ALIGN = CENTER>
<TH COLSPAN = 3>TABLES TOO!
</TH>
</TR>
<TR ALIGN = CENTER>
<TD>These</TD>              <-
<TD>are</TD>                <-
<TD>items</TD>             <-
```

```
</TR>                    <-
    .
    .
    .
```

Note that at the end, we use </TR> to finish the table row. The last step is to set up the third and final row:

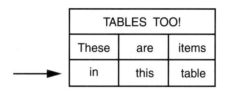

We do that as we did with the previous row:

```
<TABLE BORDER CELLPADDING = 4>
<TR ALIGN = CENTER>
<TH COLSPAN = 3>TABLES TOO!
</TH>
</TR>
<TR ALIGN = CENTER>
<TD>These</TD>
<TD>are</TD>
<TD>items</TD>
</TR>
<TR ALIGN = CENTER>        <-
<TD>in</TD>                 <-
<TD>this</TD>               <-
<TD>table!</TD>            <-
</TR>                      <-
```

At the end of the table specification, we include the </TABLE> tag to indicate we are finished:

```
<HTML>

<HEAD>
<TITLE>BUILD YOUR OWN WEB PAGE!</TITLE>
</HEAD>
```

.

.

.

```
<!—TABLES. Tables are not so hard; just use the "TABLE" tag.
    we indicate we want our table to have a border and to add space
    "padding" around the text in each cell. You don't have to worry
    about cell widths or heights — that's done automatically by Web
    browsers. The "TH" tag sets up a table's header (and here we
    indicate we want that header to span all three columns of our
    table). The "TR" tag sets up a table row, and we just include
    entries for each column with the "TD" tag — if you want more
    columns, just add more "TD" tags in each table row.>
<CENTER>
<TABLE BORDER CELLPADDING = 4>
<TR ALIGN = CENTER>
<TH COLSPAN = 3>TABLES TOO!
</TH>
</TR>
<TR ALIGN = CENTER>
<TD>These</TD>
<TD>are</TD>
<TD>items</TD>
</TR>
<TR ALIGN = CENTER>
<TD>in</TD>
<TD>this</TD>
<TD>table!</TD>
</TR>
</TABLE>            <—
</CENTER>
```

.

.

.

That completes our table. Tables enable us to organize our data in one
way, but there are other ways. For example, we can set up a list, which
displays items vertically, this way:

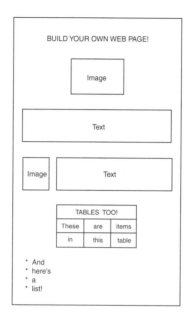

Figure 1.5 shows our Web page with a table and list. Next, let's review the process of setting up a list.

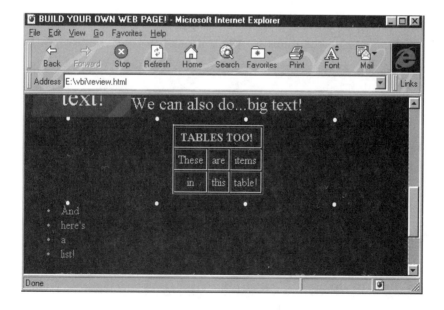

Figure 1.5 Our Web page with a table and list.

Making Lists

Our list will have four items:

```
* And
* here's
* a
* list!
```

There are four kinds of lists: unordered (bulleted) lists, ordered (numbered) lists, directory lists (can be arranged into columns), and menu lists (plain lists without bullets or numbers). Here we'll set up a bulleted—unordered—list using the <UL> tag. To make it a little more interesting visually, we'll first change the color of our list to light blue with a <FONT> tag. Next, we start the list with <UL>:

```
<FONT COLOR = "#aaaaff">
<UL>
       .
       .
       .
```

Now we indicate the items we want in our list using the list item, <LI>, tag:

```
<FONT COLOR = "#aaaaff">
<UL>
<LI> And              <-
<LI> here's           <-
<LI> a                <-
<LI> list!            <-
       .
       .
       .
```

Finally, we finish our list with </UL>:

```
<FONT COLOR = "#aaaaff">
<UL>
<LI> And
<LI> here's
<LI> a
<LI> list!
</UL>
</FONT>
     .
     .
     .
```

The result of adding the list appears in Figure 1.5.

Another popular feature is to allow your Web page visitors to email you, and that will be the last item in our HTML review.

Enabling Email

To enable email, we use an anchor tag with the HREF keyword, but instead of referencing an URL here, we use the MAILTO keyword. For example, to let the person viewing your Web page email the address username@server.com, you would do this:

```
<!—EMAIL. We let the user of our Web page email us by using an HREF
    tag with the MAILTO keyword. When users of your page click on
    the underlined MAILTO address, their email program will open and
    they can write email directly to you.>
E-mail username: <A HREF="MAILTO:username@server.com">  <—
    username@server.com</A>                              <—
```

It was simple to enable email. It's as shown in Figure 1.6.

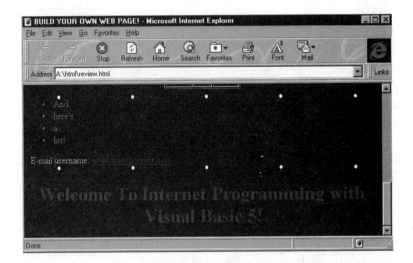

Figure 1.6 Our first Web page, with email capability.

And That's It

That's it for our review, and that's it for our first Web page. We finish it with the message "Welcome to Internet Programming with Visual Basic!" in large type:

```
<!—EMAIL. We let the user of our Web page email us by using an HREF
    tag with the MAILTO keyword. When users of your page click on
    the underlined MAILTO address, their email program will open and
    they can write email directly to you.>
E-mail username: <A HREF="MAILTO:username@server.com">
    username@server.com</A>
<BR>
<BR>

<BR>
<FONT COLOR = "#ff0000">
<CENTER>
<H1>Welcome To Internet Programming with Visual Basic!</H1>          <—
</CENTER>
</FONT>
```

.
.

The last step is to finish the body of our Web page with the </BODY> tag and finish the HTML file itself with the </HTML> tag:

```
<!-EMAIL. We let the user of our Web page email us by using an HREF
    tag with the MAILTO keyword. When users of your page click on
    the underlined MAILTO address, their email program will open and
    they can write email directly to you.>
E-mail username: <A HREF="MAILTO:username@server.com">
    username@server.com</A>
<BR>
<BR>

<BR>
<FONT COLOR = "#ff0000">
<CENTER>
<H1>Welcome To Internet Programming with Visual Basic 5!</H1>
</CENTER>
</FONT>

</BODY>                                  <-
</HTML>                                  <-
```

That's it—now our Web page is ready to be installed in our ISP. The result appears in Figure 1.6. Our first Web page is a success, and we've included many popular HTML items. The HTML for our review Web page, **review.html**, appears in Listing 1.1.

Listing 1.1 review.html

```
<!-START THE PAGE with an HTML tag (a tag is an HTML command, and
    HTML tags appear between angle brackets). We use "HTML" to indicate
    this document is in HTML, which is the language of Web pages.>
<HTML>

<!-The HEAD section of the Web page includes text about the page,
    although usually this section includes only the title.>
```

```
<!—A PAGE'S TITLE is how a browser will refer to it if visitors save
    it in their Favorites or Bookmarks menu. Note that we also indicate
    we are finished defining the title with "/TITLE." This second tag
    matches the first tag, "TITLE." HTML tags
    always come in pairs, such as the following one, which indicates
    that we are finished with the page's header.>
<HEAD>
<TITLE>BUILD YOUR OWN WEB PAGE!</TITLE>
</HEAD>

<!—BODY OF PAGE starts with the following "BODY" tag. COLOR VALUES
    are "#rrggbb" (red, green, and blue) in hexadecimal (0-255 = 0-ff);
    for example, pure red is "#ff0000," pure green is "#00ff00," and
    yellow is "#ffff00." Here we start the Web page's body, indicating
    we want yellow text, hyperlinks to be red, hyperlinks to turn
    white when pushed, and links that the user has already clicked to
    be yellow.>
<BODY TEXT  = "#ffff00" LINK  = "#ff0000" ALINK = "#ffffff" VLINK =
"#ffff00">

<!—BACKGROUND PICTURE (which is optional) is tiled on the page's
    background. Here, we indicate we want the Web browser to use the
    graphics file back.gif, which is in our www/gif directory.>
<BODY BACKGROUND = "gif/back.gif">

<!—HEADERS. Now we are going to place a header of the largest size in
    our page, so we use the "H1" tag, as well as the "CENTER" tag.
    "CENTER" simply makes sure the following text or image is centered.
    Note that all HTML tags come in pairs — to turn off centering, we
    use "/CENTER" at the end of our header's specification.>
<CENTER>
<H1>BUILD YOUR OWN WEB PAGE!</H1>
</CENTER>

<!—LINE BREAKS. To space things vertically, we use "BR" and "/BR"
    to skip a line.>
<BR>

<!—IMAGES. We display an image, which will appear centered because of
```

```
    the "CENTER" tag, with the "IMG" tag, adding the width and height
    in pixels. Here, we display our GIF file yourgif.gif from the GIF
    directory, but this is where a photo of you could go.>
<CENTER>
<IMG WIDTH=236 HEIGHT=118 SRC="gif/yourgif.gif"></IMG>
</CENTER>

<!-PARAGRAPHS of text start with "P".>
<!-LINKS. We add a hypertext link with the "A" tag, using the HREF
    keyword. In particular, we add a link to microsoft.com's Web page
    at http://www.microsoft.com below. This means that the text
    "microsoft" will appear underlined and in the standard link color
    (which we've set to red); when the user of your page clicks that
    text, the user will jump to Microsoft's home page.>
<P>
    Hello, and welcome to this Web page, the first Web page of our
    book. In this book, you'll see quite a few good ideas, and you'll
    discover how you, too, can use them in your own Web pages. If
    that doesn't interest you, perhaps you'd like to take a look at
    <A HREF="http://www.microsoft.com">microsoft</A>.
<BR>
<BR>
</P>

<!-ALIGNING PICTURES AND TEXT is done with the ALIGN keyword used in
    the "IMG" tag. In this case we just have to indicate that we want
    the graphics to appear on the left with ALIGN = LEFT. We also
    change the text color to green temporarily with a "FONT" tag (
    "FONT" works only in recent browsers).>
<IMG WIDTH=141 HEIGHT=126 SRC="gif/sidebar.gif" ALIGN=LEFT>
<FONT COLOR = "00ff00">
    We can even do green text next to graphics. This text appears next
    to the graphics on the left, allowing you to intersperse your words
    with pictures. When you take a look at the HTML for this Web page,
    you'll see how this and more is done.
</FONT>
</IMG>
<BR>
<BR>
```

```
<!—FONT SIZE is also done with the "FONT" tag; here, we set the
    size of our text temporarily to 5, a large size.>
<FONT SIZE = 5>
We can also do...big text!
</FONT>
<BR>
<BR>

<!—TABLES. Tables are not so hard; just use the "TABLE" tag. Here
    we indicate we want our table to have a border and to add space
    "padding" around the text in each cell. You don't have to worry
    about cell widths or heights — that's done automatically by Web
    browsers. The "TH" tag sets up a table's header (and here we
    indicate we want that header to span all three columns of our
    table). The "TR" tag sets up a table row, and we just include
    entries for each column with the "TD" tag — if you want more
    columns, just add more "TD" tags in each table row.>
<CENTER>
<TABLE BORDER CELLPADDING = 4>
<TR ALIGN = CENTER>
<TH COLSPAN = 3>TABLES TOO!
</TH>
</TR>
<TR ALIGN = CENTER>
<TD>These</TD>
<TD>are</TD>
<TD>items</TD>
</TR>
<TR ALIGN = CENTER>
<TD>in</TD>
<TD>this</TD>
<TD>table!</TD>
</TR>
</TABLE>
</CENTER>

<!—LISTS. Bulleted lists are also easy, using the "UL" tag. Just
    use the "LI" tag for each list item as follows.>
<FONT COLOR = "#aaaaff">
```

```
<UL>
<LI> And
<LI> here's
<LI> a
<LI> list!
</UL>
</FONT>

<!-EMAIL. We let the user of our Web page email us by using an HREF
    tag with the MAILTO keyword. When users of your page click
    the underlined MAILTO address, their email program will open and
    they can write email directly to you.>
E-mail username: <A HREF="MAILTO:username@server.com">
    username@server.com</A>
<BR>
<BR>

<BR>
<FONT COLOR = "#ff0000">
<CENTER>
<H1>Welcome To Internet Programming with Visual Basic 5!</H1>
</CENTER>
</FONT>

</BODY>
</HTML>
```

That completes our first Web page and our review of HTML. If you don't feel comfortable with what we've done so far, you should turn to a book on writing Web pages before proceeding. On the other hand, if all this is old hat to you, it's time to dig into Visual Basic itself, as we turn to the next chapter.

CHAPTER • 2

CREATING A WEB BROWSER

In this chapter, we'll get right to work, creating a working Web browser in Visual Basic. Our Web browser will be fully functional, supporting forward and back functions (*history* functions, in browser terminology), images, text, hyperlinks, and even a default home page. What's more, programming this Web browser will be extraordinarily simple, thanks to Visual Basic.

This chapter introduces our first Visual Basic programs, so we'll review Visual Basic itself. Because this book takes familiarity with Visual Basic for granted, we'll spend some time reviewing Visual Basic programming in this chapter to make sure you have the fundamentals. This review is especially important if you haven't programmed in Visual Basic 5 very much, because we'll use the Visual Basic Application Wizard a great deal in this book. The Application Wizard creates a powerful skeleton program for you, writing the code you'll need. Our Web browser will be an Application Wizard–written program. For these reasons, we will take the time to dissect an Application Wizard program and to become familiar with its parts so that we can modify it in coming chapters.

Programming in Visual Basic is a joy, especially if you know what you're missing. In most C or C++ packages, you must create your visual objects in code and hope they'll look the way you want them to. (By "visual objects," I mean controls such as buttons and text boxes. We will not use the word *object* in the C++ sense here.) In Visual Basic, by contrast, you simply draw what you want and then add perhaps a few lines of code. What could be easier or more appropriate?

Visual Basic provides an enormous, powerful set of resources and tools for us to explore. We'll begin our review of Visual Basic with a look at Windows.

An Overview of Windows

You may be surprised to learn that Microsoft started working on Windows in 1983, when the PC was all of two years old. The original version, Windows 1.01, didn't ship until 1985. With this version, you could only tile windows on the screen; you couldn't overlap them. Anyone who's seen the original Windows knows that Microsoft still had far to go; the interface felt very flat (both in perceived depth on the screen and in power) and lost few opportunities to crash. Critics said it would never amount to anything.

Next came Windows 2, but that product could run only in 80x86 real mode, hobbling it in a total of 1MB of memory. For a while, Windows even split into two products—Windows 386 and Windows 286—to take advantage of the new memory modes offered by the new 80386.

By May 1990, Microsoft introduced the first product that people usually think of as Windows: Windows 3.0. This step was truly revolutionary. Not only was the feel of the program far stronger, but also it could handle as much as 16MB of real memory and a total of 64MB if virtual memory was enabled (allowing sections of memory to be stored on disk). Next came Windows 3.1, with TrueType fonts and a common set of dialog boxes that helped unify the user interface. By this time, Windows had already become the fastest-selling software package in history. Three million copies of Windows 3.0 were sold in the first nine months.

But, predictably, the memory boundaries began to chafe as computers became more powerful. At last, Microsoft introduced its Windows NT and

Windows 95 products. Now the limits were off, and true 32-bit programming had arrived. Windows 95 has been a tremendous success; the Task Manager of Windows 3 has become the Taskbar in Windows 95. The cumbersome File Manager has been replaced by the Explorer. Windows 95 is also much more robust—resistant to crashing—than Windows 3, and it supports true multitasking. The successor to DOS has finally come into its own.

The original programs for Windows were written exclusively by Microsoft. After Windows caught on, however, other programmers wanted to write Windows programs. Microsoft evidently saw the wisdom in this, and it released the Windows Software Development Kit (SDK)—but programmers were dismayed. The SDK was a mass of uncoordinated functions, thousands of them, interacting in unpredictable and inconsistent ways. The C programming techniques used in Windows programs were also questionable.

The core problem was the amount of material Windows programmers had to master before putting a single window on the screen. It took a five-page C program to simply place a blank window in front of the user. The programmer had to select from hundreds of options and initialize many mysterious parts of the Windows program in unexplained ways. And Windows programs got larger quickly. As soon as programmers wanted to add, say, text reading or file handling, they found themselves working with pages and pages of code. In other words, in C, Windows programming was unwieldy.

Introducing Visual Basic

The first major breakthrough in Windows programming was Visual Basic. (The second was the serious application of C++ to Windows programming, which also solved many of the problems.) Visual Basic came on the scene like a thunderbolt. Here was Windows programming as it should be: visually oriented—like the Windows programs developers were creating—easy to use, and even fun. If you want a window a certain size, just stretch it that way. If you want a listbox, just draw it in. Visual Basic was an overnight success. And with it, Windows programming truly became popular, no longer the esoteric pursuit of a few.

Our First Program

Let's see Visual Basic in action. Start it up, and Visual Basic presents you with the New Project dialog box. Double-click the entry marked **Standard EXE** (we'll examine the other options throughout the book). This action creates the display shown in Figure 2.1. As you can see, we already have a window, called a *form*, ready for us to design.

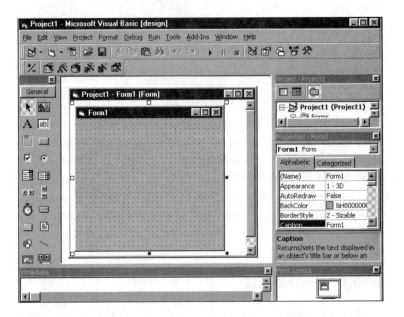

Figure 2.1 The Visual Basic environment.

We can actually run this program as it stands, simply by selecting the **Start** item in the Run menu. If we do so, we'll get the blank window shown in Figure 2.2. Nothing appears in this window, but the maximize and minimize buttons are active, as is the system menu. You can resize this window with the mouse by dragging the lower-right corner to the new position. You can move the window around the screen and use it to cover other windows.

Figure 2.2 Running the default Visual Basic form.

Obviously, our program offers us a lot of support—but there's not much of interest here. Let's start by personalizing our window. End the running program by selecting **Close** in its system menu.

Let's begin our first Visual Basic program by printing the phrase "No problem." in our window. That's easy enough—simply return to Visual Basic and double-click the main form to open the associated subroutine, Form_Load(), as shown in Figure 2.3. That's the way we reach code in Visual Basic: double-clicking the form opens the code window. Form_Load() is an event handling subroutine. Because this event occurs when the form is first loaded, Form_Load() is called then. Inside Form_Load() is where we will perform the initialization associated with the form. In this case, we add our text to the Form_Load event by adding this code (as shown in Figure 2.3):

```
      Private Sub Form_Load()
->         Print "No problem."
      End Sub
```

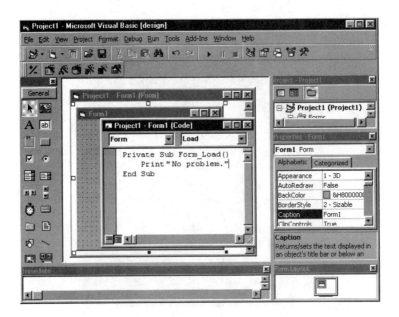

Figure 2.3 Adding code to the Form_Load() event.

In addition, we must set the form's AutoRedraw property to True in the properties window. Find the line labeled **AutoRedraw** in the properties window, click it, and set it to **True** using the drop-down listbox that appears. AutoRedraw handles the following situation: when you've placed your window on the screen and filled it with the graphics you want, it becomes vulnerable. The user may place another window on top of yours or may minimize your window. When your window is reopened or uncovered, it must once again reproduce the graphics that it originally held. This is quite a bother in C or C++ programs, where you must redraw everything in that window yourself. In Visual Basic, however, we have the AutoRedraw event to handle this chore. If we set AutoRedraw to True, our program will automatically redraw the window whenever such redrawing is required. It turns out that our window will not display the initial text we place in it ("No problem.") unless we set the AutoRedraw property to True, so we set it to True as shown in Figure 2.4.

In addition, we can give our program's window the caption "No Problem" simply by setting the form's Caption property to that string in the properties window. Click the line labeled **Caption** and type in the new caption: **No Problem**. That's all it takes. Now we run our program, as shown in Figure 2.5.

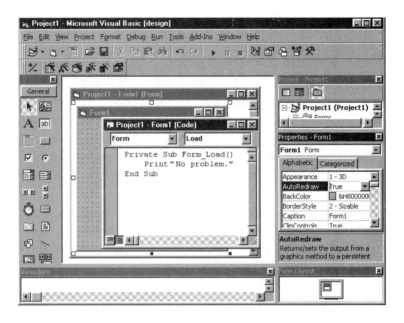

Figure 2.4 Setting a form's AutoRedraw property to True.

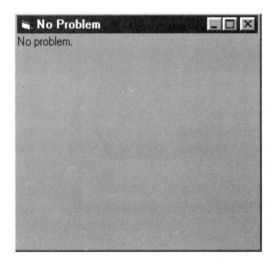

Figure 2.5 Our first program at work.

This window can be resized, closed and opened, covered and uncovered, and so on. It's fully functional.

Visual Basic Projects

Now that we've created our first program, let's store it and its code on disk. We will store this program in a directory named Noprob. Visual Basic programs under development are stored as *projects*. After you create a directory named Noprob, select the **Save Project As...** item in the File menu. This action causes Visual Basic to open the Save File As dialog box. It will automatically display one such dialog box for each file in the project, including the project file itself, which stores the names and locations of the other files. Using this dialog box, save the form as **Noprob\Form1.frm** (the default name for Form1). Next, save the project file as **Noprob\Noprob.vbp** (.vbp = Visual Basic project). That's it—now we've stored our project on disk. The code for **Form1.frm** appears in Listing 2.1, and for **Noprob.vbp** in Listing 2.2.

Listing 2.1 (Noprob) FORM1.FRM

```
VERSION 5.00
Begin VB.Form Form1
    AutoRedraw      =   -1  'True
    Caption         =   "No Problem"
    ClientHeight    =   3195
    ClientLeft      =   60
    ClientTop       =   345
    ClientWidth     =   3705
    LinkTopic       =   "Form1"
    ScaleHeight     =   3195
    ScaleWidth      =   3705
    StartUpPosition =   3   'Windows Default
End
Attribute VB_Name = "Form1"
Attribute VB_GlobalNameSpace = False
Attribute VB_Creatable = False
Attribute VB_PredeclaredId = True
Attribute VB_Exposed = False
Private Sub Form_Load()
    Print "No problem."
End Sub
```

Listing 2.2 Noprob.vbp

```
Type=Exe
Form=Form1.frm
Reference=*\G{00020430-0000-0000-C000-000000000046}#2.0#0
#C:\WINDOWS\SYSTEM\STDOLE2.TLB#OLE Automation
Startup="Form1"
Command32=""
Name="Project1"
HelpContextID="0"
CompatibleMode="0"
MajorVer=1
MinorVer=0
RevisionVer=0
AutoIncrementVer=0
ServerSupportFiles=0
CompilationType=-1
OptimizationType=0
FavorPentiumPro(tm)=0
CodeViewDebugInfo=0
NoAliasing=0
BoundsCheck=0
OverflowCheck=0
FlPointCheck=0
FDIVCheck=0
UnroundedFP=0
StartMode=0
Unattended=0
ThreadPerObject=0
MaxNumberOfThreads=1
```

Visual Basic Controls

This is fine as far as it goes, but what about something interactive, something the user can click or type? Let's add a text box and a command button (the kind of button you click) to our No Problem program so that it looks like this:

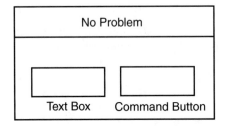

We might give the button the caption **Click Me** like this:

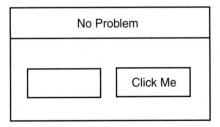

When the user clicks this button, we'll place the "No Problem." message in the text box:

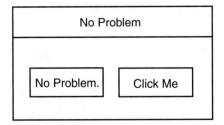

Items such as text boxes and buttons are called *controls*, and we'll put them to work as we review how Visual Basic controls operate and how to use them in our programs.

Return to our Noprob project in Visual Basic and double-click the text box button in the Visual Basic toolbox; the toolbox is the window full of icons at the left in the Visual Basic display. (If you don't know which control is which in the toolbox, rest the mouse cursor over a tool icon. A tooltip—a little yellow window—will appear, telling you which tool the icon corresponds to.) A new text box, with the text **Text1** already in it, appears in the center of the form, surrounded by small black squares called *sizing handles*. Using the mouse, move the text box to the left of the form and stretch it to roughly the size shown in Figure 2.6; to stretch it, press the mouse button when the mouse cursor is over a sizing handle and drag the sizing handle until the textbox is the desired size.

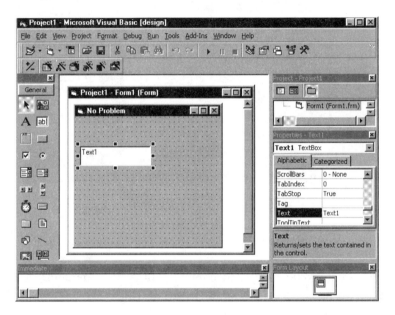

Figure 2.6 We create and position a new text box.

Next, erase the text in the text box: select the text box with the mouse (click the text box, making sure the sizing handles appear) and delete the text in its Text property in the properties window (select the line labeled **Text** in the properties window and delete the text there). Now create a new command button by selecting the command button tool in the toolbox and clicking it twice. A new button appears on the form; move it to the right of the form, as shown in Figure 2.7. Set the new button's Caption property to **Click Me** in the properties window; that string appears in our button, as shown in Figure 2.7. In addition, set the button's TabIndex property to **0** in the properties window; this ensures that this button has the input focus (is surrounded by a black border and responds to keyboard input) when we start our program. This step is optional, but it gives the program a nicer feel.

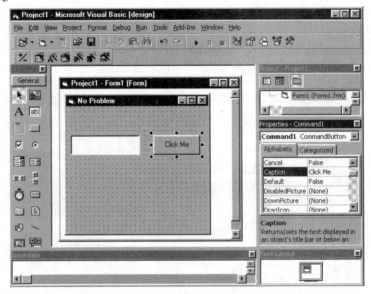

Figure 2.7 We create and position a new command button.

When the user clicks this new command button, Command1, we want to display the string "No Problem." in the text box Text1. Double-click the command button, opening the subroutine Command1_Click(), as shown in Figure 2.8. That subroutine now looks like this:

```
Private Sub Command1_Click()

End Sub
```

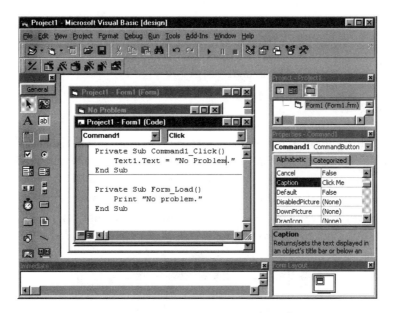

Figure 2.8 Opening the Command1_Click() subroutine.

Our program will call this subroutine when the user clicks the command button. To display the string "No Problem." in the text box, we set the text box's Text property to that string in our code.

Visual Basic Properties in Code

As far as Visual Basic is concerned, our program is made up of a collection of *objects*. The form itself is a program object, the text box is an object, and so is the command button. (In fact, there is also an Application object representing the entire program.) Each of these objects has associated with it both *properties* and *methods*. A property holds data (such as the string "No Problem."). A method is either a function or a subroutine built into the object (such as the Move method, which allows you to move windows and controls around when your program runs). You refer to a property like this: object.property; you refer to a method like this: object.method(). (Although the use of the word *object* here does not correspond exactly to the idea of an object in object-oriented programming, it is pretty close.) To set the Text property of the text box to the string "No Problem." we execute this code in Command1_Click():

```
        Private Sub Command1_Click()
->          Text1.Text = "No Problem."
        End Sub
```

Place this line of code into the subroutine Command1_Click(). When you type **Text1.**, Visual Basic pops up a handy window that indicates all the possible properties of the text box, allowing you to select **Text** from that window if you like. Otherwise, just type **Text**. Now run the program. When you click the button, our text string is placed into the text box's Text property, and that's how we display it, as shown in Figure 2.9.

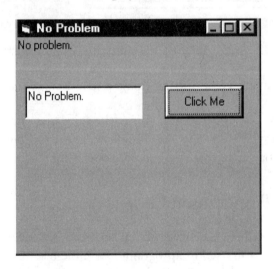

Figure 2.9 Our Noprob program with working button and text box.

Note that the text in the text box is now vulnerable; users can change it any way they want too. If you want to avoid this, you should use a label control instead of a text box. Label controls allow you to display text without letting the user change it.

This is getting better—we've been able to let the user interact with our program. The new version of **Form1.frm** appears in Listing 2.3. But that's just the beginning. What if we wanted to display a dialog box when the user clicked the **Click Me** button? It's easy to do that in Visual Basic, and it will be our next review topic.

Listing 2.3 (Noprob Version 2) FORM1.FRM

```
VERSION 5.00
Begin VB.Form Form1
   AutoRedraw      =   -1  'True
   Caption         =   "No Problem"
   ClientHeight    =   3195
   ClientLeft      =   60
   ClientTop       =   345
   ClientWidth     =   3705
   LinkTopic       =   "Form1"
   ScaleHeight     =   3195
   ScaleWidth      =   3705
   StartUpPosition =   3  'Windows Default
   Begin VB.CommandButton Command1
      Caption      =    "Click Me"
      Height       =    495
      Left         =    2280
      TabIndex     =    0
      Top          =    720
      Width        =    1215
   End
   Begin VB.TextBox Text1
      Height       =    495
      Left         =    120
      TabIndex     =    1
      Top          =    720
      Width        =    1815
   End
End
Attribute VB_Name = "Form1"
Attribute VB_GlobalNameSpace = False
Attribute VB_Creatable = False
Attribute VB_PredeclaredId = True
Attribute VB_Exposed = False
Private Sub Command1_Click()
```

```
        Text1.Text = "No Problem."
End Sub

Private Sub Form_Load()
        Print "No problem."
End Sub
```

Multiple-Form Visual Basic Programs

Let's redesign our program so that when the user clicks the **Click Me** button, a dialog box opens. We start with the program as it stands now:

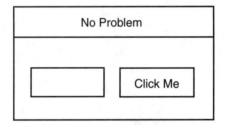

But when the user clicks the **Click Me** button, a dialog box opens with a new button that holds the caption **Click Me Too**:

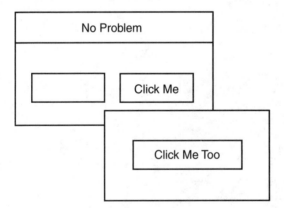

When the user clicks this new button, the program places our text message into the text box in the main window and removes the dialog box from the screen:

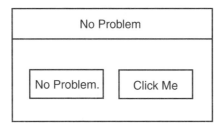

Let's see this in action. Open the Noprob project. To add the new dialog box to our program, select the Project menu's **Add Form** item and click the **Form** entry in the Add Form dialog box that opens. This action creates a new form, as shown in Figure 2.10. This new form has the name Form2 (just as our text box was named Text1, our command button Button1, and so on). Give this form a new caption by selecting the **Caption** property in the properties window; set the caption to **Click Me Too**, as shown in Figure 2.10.

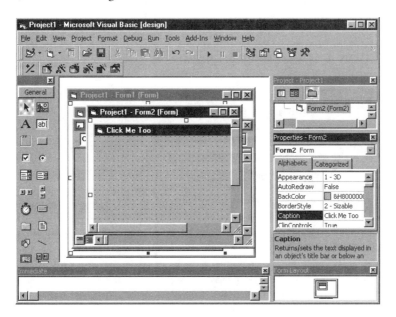

Figure 2.10 Creating a new form in Visual Basic.

Now return to Form1, the main form. When the user clicks the **Click Me** button, we used to place our message directly into the text box Text1:

```
      Private Sub Command1_Click()
-->       Text1.Text = "No Problem."
      End Sub
```

Now we want to display our new dialog box, Form2, instead. We display it with the Show method this way: Form2.Show. Place that line into Command1_Click(), replacing the earlier code:

```
      Private Sub Command1_Click()
-->       Form2.Show
      End Sub
```

When the user clicks the **Click Me** button, then, the dialog box will appear on the screen. Return to the dialog box, Form2, now. Add a new command button to that form, giving it the caption **Click Me Too** by setting its Caption property in the properties window, as shown in Figure 2.11. You can alternate between code and the visual appearance of the form by clicking the code and form buttons at the top of the Project window, which appears right above the Properties window; you can also select a form to work on by clicking its entry in the Project window.

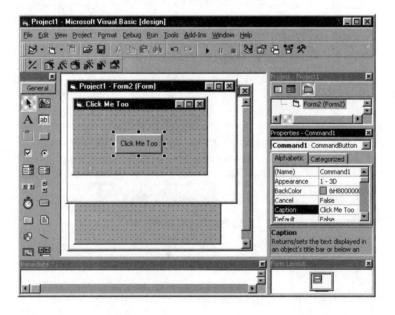

Figure 2.11 Adding a button to our dialog box.

Now double-click this new button, opening the associated click event handler, which looks like this:

```
Private Sub Command1_Click()

End Sub
```

When the user clicks the **Click Me Too** button, we want to display our message in the text box Text1 (in Form1) and to hide the dialog box again. We start by placing the string "No Problem." into the Text property of the control Text1 in Form1. We've already seen that properties can be reached like this: object.property. If the object is a control, such as Text1, we can elaborate that reference: form.object.property. We usually skip the first part, the name of the form, when we refer to a property, because the controls we deal with are usually on the same form that we're working with. Here, however, the property we want to access—Text1.Text—is connected to a form on another form, so we reach it this way: Form1.Text1.Text. We set that property to our string by adding this code to Command1_Click():

```
       Private Sub Command1_Click()
->         Form1.Text1.Text = "No Problem."
                   .
                   .
                   .

       End Sub
```

Next, we make sure that the dialog box disappears from the screen. We use the Hide method (which applies to forms) by adding this code:

```
       Private Sub Command1_Click()
           Form1.Text1.Text = "No Problem."
->         Form2.Hide
       End Sub
```

That completes the code for our **Click Me Too** button. To make Form2 into a dialog box, we remove its maximize button by setting its MaxButton property to **False**, the minimize button by setting its MinButton property to **False**, and its system menu by setting its ControlBox property to **False**.

We give it a rigid, nonsizable border by setting its BorderStyle to **3, Fixed Double**.

Now run the program. First, our main window appears by itself:

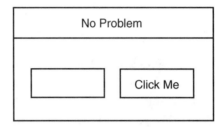

When the user clicks the **Click Me** button, our dialog box opens with the **Click Me Too** button in it, as shown in Figure 2.12:

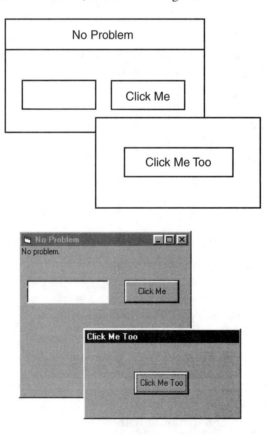

Figure 2.12 Our dialog box in operation.

When the user clicks the dialog box's button, we place our text message into the text box in the main window and hide the dialog box:

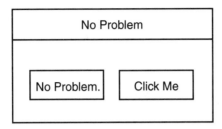

Our dialog box program is fully functional, and we've seen how to handle multiple forms in our programs. The new version of **Form1.frm** appears in Listing 2.4, **Form2.frm** appears in Listing 2.5, and the new **Noprob.vbp** appears in Listing 2.6.

Listing 2.4 (Noprob Version 3) FORM1.FRM

```
VERSION 5.00
Begin VB.Form Form1
    AutoRedraw      =    -1  'True
    Caption         =    "No Problem"
    ClientHeight    =    3195
    ClientLeft      =    60
    ClientTop       =    345
    ClientWidth     =    3705
    LinkTopic       =    "Form1"
    ScaleHeight     =    3195
    ScaleWidth      =    3705
    StartUpPosition =    3   'Windows Default
    Begin VB.CommandButton Command1
        Caption     =    "Click Me"
        Height      =    495
        Left        =    2280
        TabIndex    =    0
        Top         =    720
        Width       =    1215
    End
    Begin VB.TextBox Text1
        Height          =    495
```

```
        Left            =    120
        TabIndex        =    1
        Top             =    720
        Width           =    1815
     End
End
Attribute VB_Name = "Form1"
Attribute VB_GlobalNameSpace = False
Attribute VB_Creatable = False
Attribute VB_PredeclaredId = True
Attribute VB_Exposed = False
Private Sub Command1_Click()
     Form2.Show
End Sub

Private Sub Form_Load()
     Print "No problem."
End Sub
```

Listing 2.5 (Noprob Version 3) FORM2.FRM

```
VERSION 5.00
Begin VB.Form Form2
   Caption         =    "Click Me Too"
   ClientHeight    =    1575
   ClientLeft      =    60
   ClientTop       =    345
   ClientWidth     =    3405
   LinkTopic       =    "Form2"
   ScaleHeight     =    1575
   ScaleWidth      =    3405
   StartUpPosition =    3   'Windows Default
   Begin VB.CommandButton Command1
      Caption      =    "Click Me Too"
      Height       =    495
      Left         =    1080
      TabIndex     =    0
      Top          =    600
```

```
       Width            =    1215
    End
End
Attribute VB_Name = "Form2"
Attribute VB_GlobalNameSpace = False
Attribute VB_Creatable = False
Attribute VB_PredeclaredId = True
Attribute VB_Exposed = False
Private Sub Command1_Click()
    Form1.Text1.Text = "No Problem."
    Form2.Hide
End Sub
```

Listing 2.6 (Noprob Version 3) Noprob.vbp

```
Type=Exe
Form=Form1.frm
Reference=*\G{00020430-0000-0000-C000-
000000000046}#2.0#0#C:\WINDOWS\SYSTEM\STDOLE2.TLB#OLE Automation
Form=Form2.frm
Startup="Form1"
Command32=""
Name="Project1"
HelpContextID="0"
CompatibleMode="0"
MajorVer=1
MinorVer=0
RevisionVer=0
AutoIncrementVer=0
ServerSupportFiles=0
CompilationType=-1
OptimizationType=0
FavorPentiumPro(tm)=0
CodeViewDebugInfo=0
NoAliasing=0
BoundsCheck=0
OverflowCheck=0
FlPointCheck=0
```

```
FDIVCheck=0
UnroundedFP=0
StartMode=0
Unattended=0
ThreadPerObject=0
MaxNumberOfThreads=1
```

We've taken another important step by reviewing dialog boxes. Now let's turn to the topic of adding a new menu system to our program.

Menus

We can add a menu to our program and let the user display our message by making a selection from that menu. Let's add a File menu to our program. (The File menu has become so common that even programs that do not handle files often have one.)

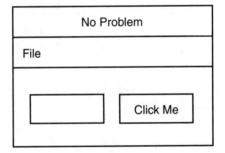

Let's give the menu one item—**Show Message**—so that users see it when they open the menu:

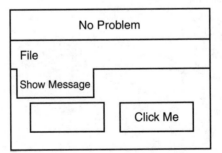

After they select the **Show Message** item, we display our message in the text box:

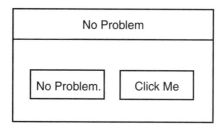

In fact, let's add a second item to the File menu: an **Exit** item. Users expect **Exit** to be the last item in the File menu (which is why the File menu is popular, even in programs that don't handle files):

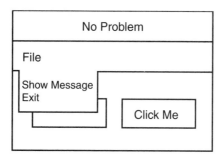

Let's see this in action. Load the Noprob project into Visual Basic. Next, select **Form1** with the mouse (we will add our menu to Form1) and select the **Menu Editor** item in the Visual Basic Tools menu. The Visual Basic Menu Editor opens, as shown in Figure 2.13.

We begin the creation of our new menu by typing the name of that menu, **File**, into the box labeled **Caption** at the top of the Menu Editor. That's the name that will appear in the menu bar. (Although Visual Basic does not limit you to one-word menu names, it's a good practice. Menus with two or more words in the menu bar sometimes look as if they represent two or more separate menus, one belonging to each word). In addition to the caption, we need a way of referring to our menu in code. We specify that name by typing it into the **Name** box, just below the Caption box in the Menu Editor. We will use the name **File**, as shown in Figure 2.14.

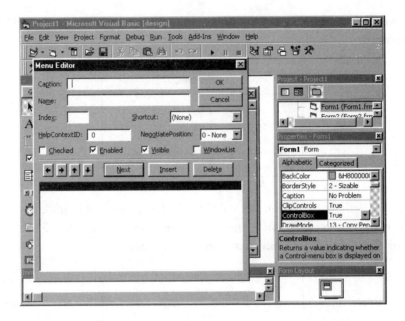

Figure 2.13 We use the Visual Basic Menu Editor to create and modify menus.

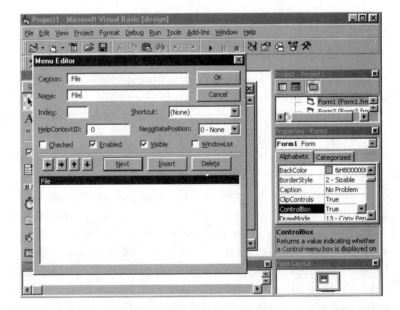

Figure 2.14 Creating a new menu is as easy as typing its name.

Now we have specified the name of our new menu in the Menu Editor. If we were to quit the Menu Editor now, we'd have that menu in our program:

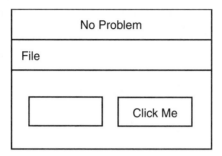

However, we also want two menu items in that menu: **Show Message** and **Exit**.

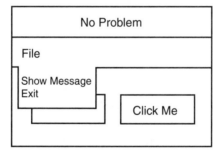

Let's add the **Show Message** menu item now. First, click the button in the Menu Editor marked **Next** to indicate that we want to create another entry in the menu system. The highlighted bar in the large box below the **Next** button moves to the next line, indicating that the Menu Editor is ready for the next entry. Type the caption **Show Message** for this new menu item, and give it the name **ShowMessage**, as shown in Figure 2.15.

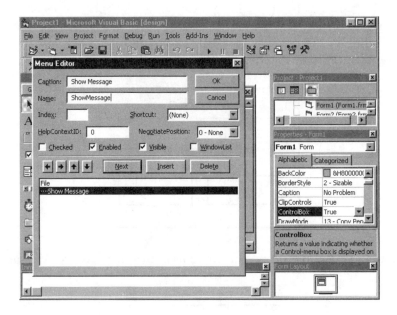

Figure 2.15 Creating a menu item is as easy as typing it into the Menu Editor.

We're not finished yet. If we left our new entry, **Show Message**, as it is, it would be a new menu and not a new menu item. **Show Message** is supposed to be the first item in the File menu, and we indicate that by *indenting* **Show Message** underneath the entry for **File**. That's done by clicking the arrow that points to the right (in the group of four such buttons near the **Next** button). When you click the arrow button, the entry for the menu item **Show Message** appears indented under the entry for the File menu, as shown in Figure 2.15, and four dots appear before this new menu item:

```
File
....Show Message
```

In a nutshell, you create a menu system in the Menu Editor by placing a new entry in it corresponding to a new menu; follow that with indented entries corresponding to the menu items. Now we'll add the **Exit** item. Click the **Next** button in the Menu Editor again, moving the highlighted bar down one level, indicating that the editor is ready for a new entry. Give this new item the name Exit and the caption **Exit**, and indent it under the File menu using the right-pointing arrow button. Our menu system appears like this, as shown in Figure 2.16:

```
File
....Show Message
....Exit
```

Our menu system is complete. Click **OK** to close the Menu Editor and to install the new menu system in our form, as shown in Figure 2.17.

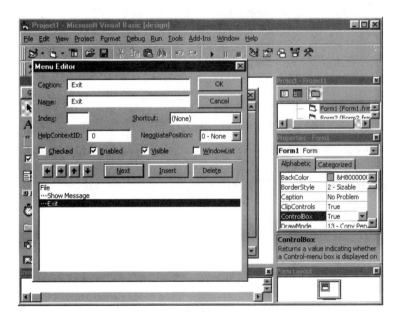

Figure 2.16 We add an **Exit** item to our File menu.

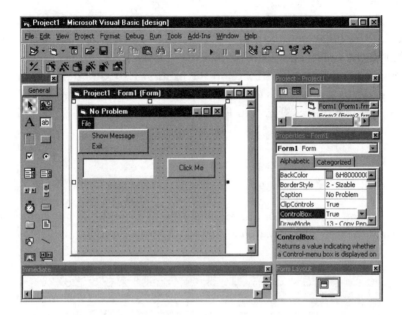

Figure 2.17 A form can display its associated menu system
while under design.

The next step is to add the code that will make these menu items active.
Visual Basic treats menu items as controls just it does text boxes. Click the
Show Message item in the File menu, opening the corresponding event
handler, ShowMessage_Click(), which is called by our program when the
user clicks that item:

```
Private Sub ShowMessage_Click()

End Sub
```

When the user clicks this item, we want to display the message "No
problem." in the text box Text1. As we've done before, we add this code:

```
Private Sub ShowMessage_Click()
    Text1.Text = "No problem."           <-
End Sub
```

That's it for ShowMessage_Click(). The next step is to make the **Exit** item active. Click that item, opening the associated event handler, Exit_Click():

```
Private Sub Exit_Click()

End Sub
```

If the user clicks **Exit**, we want to end the program. We use the Visual Basic End command:

```
Private Sub Exit_Click()
    End                         <—
End Sub
```

And that's it—our program is ready to run. Select **Start** in the Run menu to execute the program. Our menu appears as in Figure 2.18, with both menu items active.

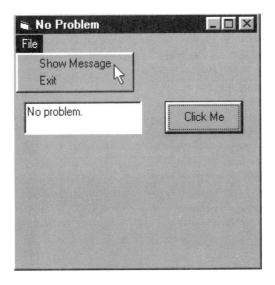

Figure 2.18 Our first working Visual Basic menu.

When you click **Show Message**, our message is displayed in the text box as before. Our program is a success. The new version of **Form1.frm** appears in Listing 2.7, and **Noprob.vbp** appears in Listing 2.18.

Listing 2.7 (Noprob Version 4) FORM1.FRM

```
VERSION 5.00
Begin VB.Form Form1
    AutoRedraw      =    -1  'True
    Caption         =    "No Problem"
    ClientHeight    =    3195
    ClientLeft      =    165
    ClientTop       =    735
    ClientWidth     =    3705
    LinkTopic       =    "Form1"
    ScaleHeight     =    3195
    ScaleWidth      =    3705
    StartUpPosition =    3   'Windows Default
    Begin VB.CommandButton Command1
        Caption         =    "Click Me"
        Height          =    495
        Left            =    2280
        TabIndex        =    0
        Top             =    720
        Width           =    1215
    End
    Begin VB.TextBox Text1
        Height          =    495
        Left            =    120
        TabIndex        =    1
        Top             =    720
        Width           =    1815
    End
    Begin VB.Menu File
        Caption         =    "File"
        Begin VB.Menu ShowMessage
            Caption         =    "Show Message"
        End
        Begin VB.Menu Exit
            Caption         =    "Exit"
        End
    End
End
```

```
Attribute VB_Name = "Form1"
Attribute VB_GlobalNameSpace = False
Attribute VB_Creatable = False
Attribute VB_PredeclaredId = True
Attribute VB_Exposed = False
Private Sub Command1_Click()
    Form2.Show
End Sub


Private Sub Exit_Click()
    End
End Sub


Private Sub Form_Load()
    Print "No problem."
End Sub


Private Sub ShowMessage_Click()
    Text1.Text = "No problem."
End Sub
```

Listing 2.8 (Noprob Version 4) Noprob.vbp

```
Type=Exe
Form=..\Noprob3\Form1.frm
Reference=*\G{00020430-0000-0000-C000-000000000046}#2.0#0
#C:\WINDOWS\SYSTEM\STDOLE2.TLB#OLE Automation
Form=..\Noprob3\Form2.frm
Startup="Form1"
Command32=""
Name="Project1"
HelpContextID="0"
CompatibleMode="0"
MajorVer=1
MinorVer=0
RevisionVer=0
AutoIncrementVer=0
ServerSupportFiles=0
```

```
CompilationType=-1
OptimizationType=0
FavorPentiumPro(tm)=0
CodeViewDebugInfo=0
NoAliasing=0
BoundsCheck=0
OverflowCheck=0
FlPointCheck=0
FDIVCheck=0
UnroundedFP=0
StartMode=0
Unattended=0
ThreadPerObject=0
MaxNumberOfThreads=1
```

In addition to menus, we can use toolbars in Visual Basic. The Application Wizard programs we write in this book will automatically include toolbars, so we'll review them now.

Toolbars

So far, our Noprob program looks like this:

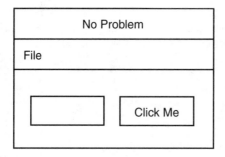

Let's add a toolbar to Noprob that holds a button with the caption **Click Here**:

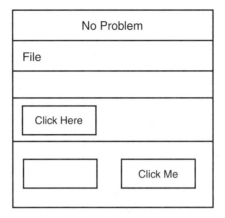

To add a toolbar to Noprob, we first add a Toolbar tool to the Visual Basic toolbox. Select the **Components** item in the Project menu, opening the Components dialog box, as shown in Figure 2.19. Click the box labeled **Microsoft Windows Common Controls 5.0** and close the Components dialog box by clicking **OK**.

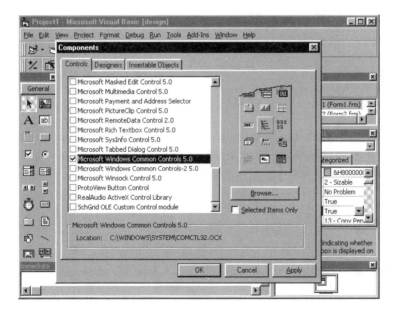

Figure 2.19 Adding a new control type to the toolbox.

Now the Toolbar tool appears in the toolbox, as shown in Figure 2.20. (Later you'll learn more about adding new controls to the toolbox.) Double-click the Toolbar tool to create a new toolbar, and set the toolbar's border style to single and fixed by selecting the entry marked **ccFixedSingle**.

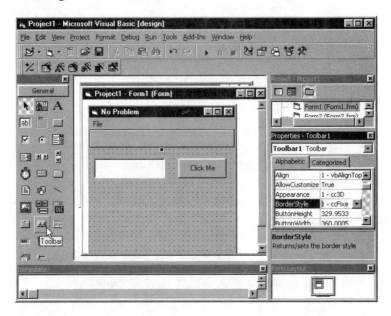

Figure 2.20 Using the Toolbar tool.

Now right-click the new toolbar and select the **Properties** item in the popup menu that appears, opening the Properties dialog box, as shown in Figure 2.21.

Click the **Buttons** tab and then the **Insert Button** button that appears. This action creates a new button in the toolbar; give it the caption **Click Here**, as shown in Figure 2.21, and set its Key value to **ClickHere**. Click the **Apply** button followed by **OK** to close the Properties window. Our new toolbar contains one button, **Click Here**, as shown in Figure 2.22.

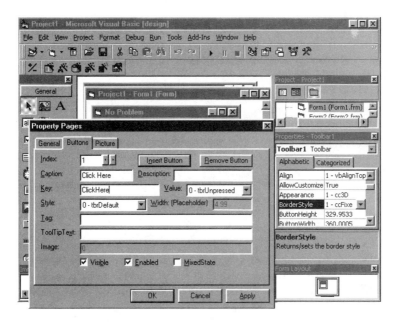

Figure 2.21 The toolbar Properties window.

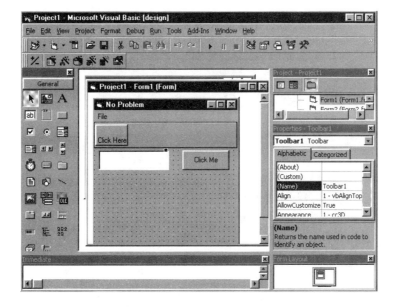

Figure 2.22 Our new toolbar.

Double-click the button to open its code window:

```
Private Sub Toolbar1_ButtonClick(ByVal Button As
ComctlLib.Button)
    End Sub
```

We determine which toolbar button was clicked by checking the Button object's Key property this way, using a Select Case statement:

```
Private Sub Toolbar1_ButtonClick(ByVal Button As
ComctlLib.Button)
        Select Case Button.Key
            .

            .

        End Select
    End Sub
```

We have only one button, and its Key value is "ClickHere," so we display our text when that button is clicked:

```
Private Sub Toolbar1_ButtonClick(ByVal Button As
ComctlLib.Button)
        Select Case Button.Key

            Case "ClickHere"
                    Text1.Text = "No Problem."
        End Select
    End Sub
```

Now run the program. Our new toolbar is active, as shown in Figure 2.23. Our toolbar program is a success.

Figure 2.23 Our new toolbar at work.

The new version of **Form1.frm** appears in Listing 2.9.

Listing 2.9 (Noprob Version 5) FORM1.FRM

```
VERSION 5.00
Object = "{6B7E6392-850A-101B-AFC0-4210102A8DA7}#1.1#0";
"COMCTL32.OCX"
Begin VB.Form Form1
    AutoRedraw      =   -1  'True
    Caption         =   "No Problem"
    ClientHeight    =   3195
    ClientLeft      =   165
    ClientTop       =   735
    ClientWidth     =   3705
    LinkTopic       =   "Form1"
    ScaleHeight     =   3195
    ScaleWidth      =   3705
    StartUpPosition =   3  'Windows Default
    Begin ComctlLib.Toolbar Toolbar1
        Align       =   1  'Align Top
        Height      =   660
```

```
         Left              =    0
         TabIndex          =    2
         Top               =    0
         Width             =    3705
         _ExtentX          =    6535
         _ExtentY          =    1164
         ButtonWidth       =    1482
         ButtonHeight      =    953
         Appearance        =    1
         BeginProperty Buttons {7791BA41-E020-11CF-8E74-00A0C90F26F8}
            NumButtons     =    1
            BeginProperty Button1 {7791BA43-E020-11CF-8E74-00A0C90F26F8}
               Caption          =    "Click Here"
               Key              =    "ClickHere"
               Description      =    ""
               Object.ToolTipText    =    ""
               Object.Tag            =    ""
            EndProperty
         EndProperty
         BorderStyle       =    1
         MouseIcon         =    "Form1.frx":0000
      End
      Begin VB.CommandButton Command1
         Caption           =    "Click Me"
         Height            =    495
         Left              =    2280
         TabIndex          =    0
         Top               =    720
         Width             =    1215
      End
      Begin VB.TextBox Text1
         Height            =    495
         Left              =    120
         TabIndex          =    1
         Top               =    720
         Width             =    1815
      End
      Begin VB.Menu File
         Caption           =    "File"
```

```
        Begin VB.Menu ShowMessage
            Caption         =   "Show Message"
        End
        Begin VB.Menu Exit
            Caption         =   "Exit"
        End
    End
End
Attribute VB_Name = "Form1"
Attribute VB_GlobalNameSpace = False
Attribute VB_Creatable = False
Attribute VB_PredeclaredId = True
Attribute VB_Exposed = False
Private Sub Command1_Click()
    Form2.Show
End Sub

Private Sub Exit_Click()
    End
End Sub

Private Sub Form_Load()
    Print "No problem."
End Sub

Private Sub ShowMessage_Click()
    Text1.Text = "No problem."
End Sub
```

Now that we're up to speed, let's create the main program of this chapter: our Web browser. This browser program includes all the Visual Basic features we've reviewed, so we have a good start.

Our Web Browser

We should first note that this example depends on having Microsoft Internet Explorer 3.0 installed; if you haven't installed it, you'll find it on your Visual Basic 5.0 CD-ROM or at http://www.microsoft.com.

Creating a Web-browsing program in Visual Basic is incredibly easy. Start Visual Basic, as shown in Figure 2.24. This time, select **VB Application Wizard** in the New Project dialog box (instead of Standard EXE), as shown in Figure 2.24. Click **OK**.

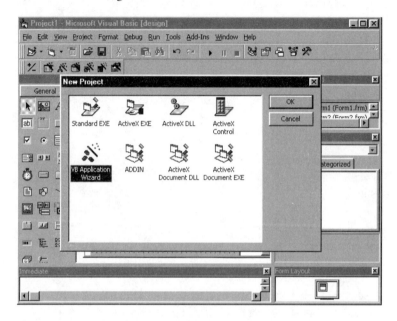

Figure 2.24 Selecting the type of Visual Basic project.

This action opens the Application Wizard, as shown in Figure 2.25.

Click the **Next>** button to close the Introduction dialog box, bringing us to the Application Wizard–Interface Type dialog box. Here, we select from three types of applications: **Multiple Document Interface (MDI)**, **Single Document Interface (SDI)**, and **Explorer** (like the Windows Explorer, with a tree of nodes displayed in a window on the left). MDI is the default, and we'll accept that by clicking the **Next>** button.

The next screen asks which menus we want; click **Next>** again, accepting the defaults: File, Edit, Window, and Help. The following dialog box asks about resource files; we won't use any here, so click **Next>** again. This brings us to the Application Wizard–Internet Connectivity dialog box, as shown in Figure 2.26.

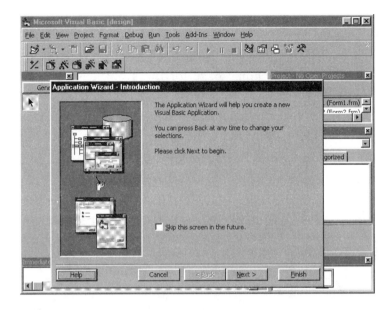

Figure 2.25 The VB Application Wizard.

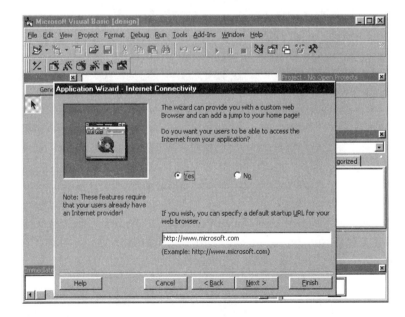

Figure 2.26 The Application Wizard–Internet Connectivity dialog box.

Here's where we create our Web browser—with a single click. In response to the question "Do you want your users to be able to access the Internet from your application?", just click the **Yes** button, as shown in Figure 2.26. We also set a default home page for the Web browser; leave that at http://www.microsoft.com (the default), as shown in Figure 2.26.

Now click **Next>** to get to the Standard Forms dialog box, which allows you to add standard forms such as an About box. Click **Next>** again to get to the Data Access dialog box (you can create forms from databases here), and click **Next>** again to get to the Finished! dialog box, as shown in Figure 2.27.

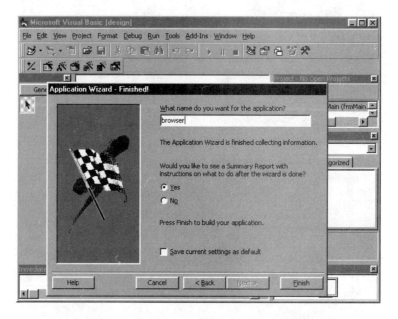

Figure 2.27 The Application Wizard–Finished! dialog box.

Here we set the name of our application to browser, in the box labeled **What name do you want for your application?**. Then click the **Finish** button to create our browser application.

Running Our Web Browser

Now run the browse program by selecting **Start** in the Visual Basic Run menu. This new program presents us with a document that we can type into, as shown in Figure 2.28.

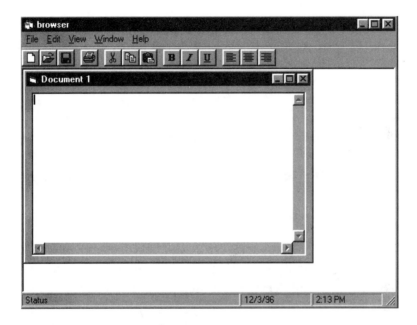

Figure 2.28 Our Browser program's default document.

To run the Web browser, select the **Web Browser** item in the View menu. This action opens a new window, and it connects to http://www.microsoft.com, as shown in Figure 2.29. Note that this assumes you have an Internet provider and have set up a connection to it; in Windows 95, that means setting up a connection to your ISP in the Windows Dial-Up Networking folder of the My Computer icon.

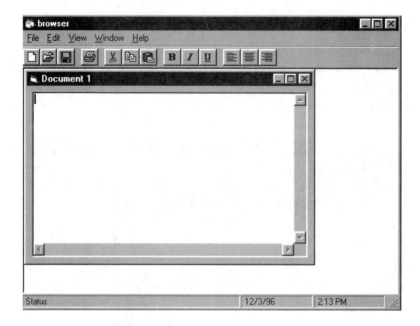

Figure 2.29 Our new Web browser at work.

We now have a working Web browser, and it really works. It was remarkably easy, thanks to the WebBrowser control, which is really the guts of Internet Explorer. Our browser program is really just a shell for that control, as we'll see.

Our next step is to dissect this program that the Application Wizard wrote for us. We'll write Application Wizard programs throughout the book, and we'll have to know their structure in order to work with and adapt them.

Dissecting Our Web Browser

The browser program is an MDI (multiwindow) program because we accepted the default settings of the Application Wizard. (To avoid long listings, most of the programs we write in this book will be SDI—that is, single window—programs.) Like other Application Wizard programs, ours starts with a Main() subroutine in the **Module1.bas** module:

```
Sub Main()
    Set fMainForm = New frmMain
    fMainForm.Show
End Sub
```

If a Visual Basic program has a Main() subroutine, that's what runs first (you don't need a Main() subroutine at all in Visual Basic). Our Main() subroutine's only task is to create a new MDI window (which will contain MDI child windows such as our browser) using the Set and New keywords and to display it on the screen. The code for the main MDI window, stored in **frmMain.frm**, takes over when we execute the fMainForm.Show statement.

When it starts, the main MDI window positions and sizes itself using values stored from the last time it appeared, if it has appeared before on the screen. (In Windows 95, these values are stored in the registry.) Then it calls the subroutine LoadNewDoc():

```
Private Sub MDIForm_Load()
    Me.Left = GetSetting(App.Title, "Settings", "MainLeft", 1000)
    Me.Top = GetSetting(App.Title, "Settings", "MainTop", 1000)
    Me.Width = GetSetting(App.Title, "Settings", "MainWidth", 6500)
    Me.Height = GetSetting(App.Title, "Settings", "MainHeight", 6500)
-> LoadNewDoc
End Sub
```

LoadNewDoc() creates a new document of the type we saw when we first started the browser (a generic document we could type in, as shown in Figure 2.28). The name of this form is frmDocument, and it's a form of type MDIChild, so it will appear in the larger MDI window when we show it. (The code for this form is in **frmDocument.frm**.) Here's how the default document is set up and shown in the main MDI window. (Note that the program uses the variable lDocumentCount to keep track of the number of windows in the MDI window.)

```
Private Sub LoadNewDoc()
    Static lDocumentCount As Long
    Dim frmD As frmDocument

->  lDocumentCount = lDocumentCount + 1
->  Set frmD = New frmDocument
->  frmD.Caption = "Document " & lDocumentCount
->  frmD.Show
End Sub
```

We display the Web browser by clicking the **WebBrowser** item in the program's View menu. This item's name in code is mnuViewBrowser, and its associated click event is mnuViewBrowser_Click():

```
Private Sub mnuViewBrowser_Click()
    Dim frmB As New frmBrowser
    frmB.StartingAddress = "http://www.microsoft.com"
    frmB.Show
End Sub
```

Here, the program simply creates and displays a new MDI child window of the frmBrowser type (the code for this form appears in **frmBrowser.frm**). You can see this form in Figure 2.30; this form contains the WebBrowser control stretched across its face. (This control is really Internet Explorer 3.0 in disguise.)

You add a control of type WebBrowser to your Visual Basic project using the **Components** item in the Project menu. This opens the Components dialog box, as shown in Figure 2.31.

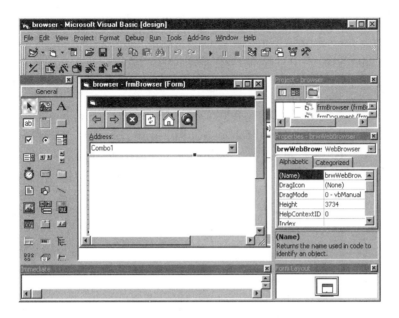

Figure 2.30 The frmBrowser form.

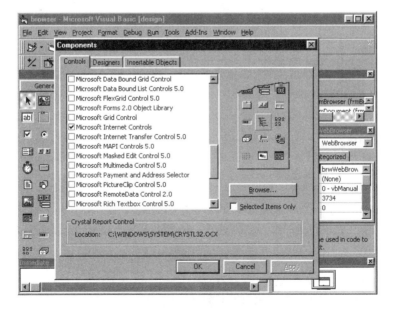

Figure 2.31 Inserting a new control into Visual Basic.

As we saw earlier when we added a toolbar to our review application, to insert a new control you just click it in the Components dialog box and then click **OK**. In this case, the WebBrowser control is part of the package called Microsoft Internet Controls, as shown in Figure 2.31. After you click **OK**, the WebBrowser control appears in the toolbar (its icon looks like a folder being scrutinized by a magnifying glass), and you can add it to your program. The WebBrowser control in the browser program is called brwWebBrowser, and the combo box control that holds the URL to navigate to is called cboAddress. The main MDI window stores the starting URL for the Web browser in the variable StartingAddress. When the Web browser form is loaded, we use the WebBrowser Navigate method to display the URL in StartingAddress:

```
Private Sub Form_Load()
    On Error Resume Next
    Me.Show
    tbToolBar.Refresh
    Form_Resize

    cboAddress.Move 50, lblAddress.Top + lblAddress.Height + 15

    If Len(StartingAddress) > 0 Then
        cboAddress.Text = StartingAddress
        cboAddress.AddItem cboAddress.Text
        'try to navigate to the starting address
        timTimer.Enabled = True
->      brwWebBrowser.Navigate StartingAddress
    End If

End Sub
```

That's literally all it takes—now the URL is displayed. If the user clicks a new address in the Web browser's combo box, we navigate to that new selection in the cboAddress_Click() subroutine:

```
Private Sub cboAddress_Click()
    If mbDontNavigateNow Then Exit Sub
    timTimer.Enabled = True
```

```
-> brwWebBrowser.Navigate cboAddress.Text
End Sub
```

The user can also type a new address into the browser's combo box and then press the **Enter** key. To implement that, we check to see whether the **Enter** key was pressed in the subroutine cboAddress_KeyPress(). If it was, we call cboAddress_Click() to navigate to the new URL:

```
Private Sub cboAddress_KeyPress(KeyAscii As Integer)
    On Error Resume Next
-> If KeyAscii = vbKeyReturn Then
->     cboAddress_Click
-> End If
End Sub
```

Note all the buttons in the Web browser's toolbar; these buttons allow you to go forward or backward just as in the Internet Explorer, to refresh the visible Web page, to go to the home or search page, and to stop the current online operation. These functions are handled in frmBrowser's tbToolBar_ButtonClick() subroutine, which functions much as the toolbar subroutine we developed for our Noprob application. Here, however, we use the GoBack(), GoForward(), Refresh(), GoHome(), GoSearch(), and Stop() methods of the brwWebBrowser control:

```
Private Sub tbToolBar_ButtonClick(ByVal Button As Button)
    On Error Resume Next

    timTimer.Enabled = True

    Select Case Button.Key
        Case "Back"
->          brwWebBrowser.GoBack
        Case "Forward"
->          brwWebBrowser.GoForward
        Case "Refresh"
->          brwWebBrowser.Refresh
        Case "Home"
->          brwWebBrowser.GoHome
```

```
        Case "Search"
->          brwWebBrowser.GoSearch
        Case "Stop"
            timTimer.Enabled = False
->          brwWebBrowser.Stop
            Me.Caption = brwWebBrowser.LocationName
    End Select

End Sub
```

And that's all there is to it—the WebBrowser control does all the work for us. That's all we need to create our own Web browser. The code for **Module1.bas** appears in Listing 2.10, **frmMain.frm** in Listing 2.11, **frmDocument.frm** in Listing 2.12, and **frmBrowser.frm** in Listing 2.13.

Listing 2.10 Module1.bas

```
Attribute VB_Name = "Module1"
Public fMainForm As frmMain

Sub Main()
    Set fMainForm = New frmMain
    fMainForm.Show
End Sub
```

Listing 2.11 frmMain.frm

```
VERSION 5.00
Object = "{F9043C88-F6F2-101A-A3C9-08002B2F49FB}#1.1#0";
"COMDLG32.OCX"
Object = "{6B7E6392-850A-101B-AFC0-4210102A8DA7}#1.1#0";
"COMCTL32.OCX"
Begin VB.MDIForm frmMain
    BackColor       =   &H8000000C&
    Caption         =   "browser"
    ClientHeight    =   3195
    ClientLeft      =   165
    ClientTop       =   735
    ClientWidth     =   4680
```

```
LinkTopic        =    "MDIForm1"
StartUpPosition =    3  'Windows Default
Begin ComctlLib.Toolbar tbToolBar
   Align            =    1  'Align Top
   Height           =    420
   Left             =    0
   TabIndex         =    1
   Top              =    0
   Width            =    4680
   _ExtentX         =    8255
   _ExtentY         =    741
   ButtonWidth      =    635
   ButtonHeight     =    582
   Appearance       =    1
   ImageList        =    "imlIcons"
   BeginProperty Buttons {7791BA42-E020-11CF-8E74-00A0C90F26F8}
      NumButtons    =    17
      BeginProperty Button1 {7791BA43-E020-11CF-8E74-00A0C90F26F8}
         Key              =    "New"
         Object.ToolTipText      =    "New"
         Object.Tag              =    ""
         ImageIndex       =    1
      EndProperty
      BeginProperty Button2 {7791BA43-E020-11CF-8E74-00A0C90F26F8}
         Key              =    "Open"
         Object.ToolTipText      =    "Open"
         Object.Tag              =    ""
         ImageIndex       =    2
      EndProperty
      BeginProperty Button3 {7791BA43-E020-11CF-8E74-00A0C90F26F8}
         Key              =    "Save"
         Object.ToolTipText      =    "Save"
         Object.Tag              =    ""
         ImageIndex       =    3
      EndProperty
      BeginProperty Button4 {7791BA43-E020-11CF-8E74-00A0C90F26F8}
         Key              =    ""
         Object.Tag              =    ""
         Style            =    3
```

```
    EndProperty
    BeginProperty Button5 {7791BA43-E020-11CF-8E74-00A0C90F26F8}
        Key             =    "Print"
        Object.ToolTipText     =    "Print"
        Object.Tag          =     ""
        ImageIndex      =    4
    EndProperty
    BeginProperty Button6 {7791BA43-E020-11CF-8E74-00A0C90F26F8}
        Key             =     ""
        Object.Tag          =     ""
        Style           =    3
    EndProperty
    BeginProperty Button7 {7791BA43-E020-11CF-8E74-00A0C90F26F8}
        Key             =    "Cut"
        Object.ToolTipText     =    "Cut"
        Object.Tag          =     ""
        ImageIndex      =    5
    EndProperty
    BeginProperty Button8 {7791BA43-E020-11CF-8E74-00A0C90F26F8}
        Key             =    "Copy"
        Object.ToolTipText     =    "Copy"
        Object.Tag          =     ""
        ImageIndex      =    6
    EndProperty
    BeginProperty Button9 {7791BA43-E020-11CF-8E74-00A0C90F26F8}
        Key             =    "Paste"
        Object.ToolTipText     =    "Paste"
        Object.Tag          =     ""
        ImageIndex      =    7
    EndProperty
    BeginProperty Button10 {7791BA43-E020-11CF-8E74-00A0C90F26F8}
        Key             =     ""
        Object.Tag          =     ""
        Style           =    3
    EndProperty
    BeginProperty Button11 {7791BA43-E020-11CF-8E74-00A0C90F26F8}
        Key             =    "Bold"
        Object.ToolTipText     =    "Bold"
        Object.Tag          =     ""
```

```
        ImageIndex      =    8
    EndProperty
    BeginProperty Button12 {7791BA43-E020-11CF-8E74-00A0C90F26F8}
        Key             =    "Italic"
        Object.ToolTipText      =     "Italic"
        Object.Tag              =     ""
        ImageIndex      =    9
    EndProperty
    BeginProperty Button13 {7791BA43-E020-11CF-8E74-00A0C90F26F8}
        Key             =    "Underline"
        Object.ToolTipText      =     "Underline"
        Object.Tag              =     ""
        ImageIndex      =    10
    EndProperty
    BeginProperty Button14 {7791BA43-E020-11CF-8E74-00A0C90F26F8}
        Key             =     ""
        Object.Tag              =     ""
        Style           =    3
    EndProperty
    BeginProperty Button15 {7791BA43-E020-11CF-8E74-00A0C90F26F8}
        Key             =    "Left"
        Object.ToolTipText      =     "Left Justify"
        Object.Tag              =     ""
        ImageIndex      =    11
    EndProperty
    BeginProperty Button16 {7791BA43-E020-11CF-8E74-00A0C90F26F8}
        Key             =    "Center"
        Object.ToolTipText      =     "Center"
        Object.Tag              =     ""
        ImageIndex      =    12
    EndProperty
    BeginProperty Button17 {7791BA43-E020-11CF-8E74-00A0C90F26F8}
        Key             =    "Right"
        Object.ToolTipText      =     "Right Justify"
        Object.Tag              =     ""
        ImageIndex      =    13
    EndProperty
    EndProperty
EndProperty
MouseIcon       =     "frmMain.frx":0000
```

```
End
Begin ComctlLib.StatusBar sbStatusBar
   Align          =    2   'Align Bottom
   Height         =    270
   Left           =    0
   TabIndex       =    0
   Top            =    2925
   Width          =    4680
   _ExtentX       =    8255
   _ExtentY       =    476
   SimpleText     =    ""
   BeginProperty Panels {2C787A52-E01C-11CF-8E74-00A0C90F26F8}
      NumPanels    =    3
      BeginProperty Panel1 {2C787A53-E01C-11CF-8E74-00A0C90F26F8}
         AutoSize      =    1
         Object.Width        =    2619
         MinWidth      =    2540
         Text          =    "Status"
         TextSave      =    "Status"
         Key           =    ""
         Object.Tag          =    ""
      EndProperty
      BeginProperty Panel2 {2C787A53-E01C-11CF-8E74-00A0C90F26F8}
         Style         =    6
         AutoSize      =    2
         Object.Width        =    2540
         MinWidth      =    2540
         TextSave      =    "11/30/96"
         Key           =    ""
         Object.Tag          =    ""
      EndProperty
      BeginProperty Panel3 {2C787A53-E01C-11CF-8E74-00A0C90F26F8}
         Style         =    5
         AutoSize      =    2
         Object.Width        =    2540
         MinWidth      =    2540
         TextSave      =    "2:32 PM"
         Key           =    ""
         Object.Tag          =    ""
```

```
            EndProperty
        EndProperty
        BeginProperty Font {0BE35203-8F92-11CE-9DE3-00AA004BB851}
            Name            =   "MS Sans Serif"
            Size            =   8.25
            Charset         =   0
            Weight          =   400
            Underline       =   0   'False
            Italic          =   0   'False
            Strikethrough   =   0   'False
        EndProperty
        MouseIcon       =   "frmMain.frx":001C
    End
    Begin MSComDlg.CommonDialog dlgCommonDialog
        Left            =   1740
        Top             =   1350
        _ExtentX        =   847
        _ExtentY        =   847
        FontSize        =   1.28424e-37
    End
    Begin ComctlLib.ImageList imlIcons
        Left            =   1740
        Top             =   1350
        _ExtentX        =   1005
        _ExtentY        =   1005
        BackColor       =   -2147483643
        ImageWidth      =   16
        ImageHeight     =   16
        MaskColor       =   12632256
        BeginProperty Images {8556BCD2-E01E-11CF-8E74-00A0C90F26F8}
            NumListImages   =   13
            BeginProperty ListImage1 {8556BCD3-E01E-11CF-8E74-00A0C90F26F8}
                Picture         =   "frmMain.frx":0038
                Key             =   ""
            EndProperty
            BeginProperty ListImage2 {8556BCD3-E01E-11CF-8E74-00A0C90F26F8}
                Picture         =   "frmMain.frx":038A
                Key             =   ""
            EndProperty
```

```
BeginProperty ListImage3 {8556BCD3-E01E-11CF-8E74-00A0C90F26F8}
    Picture         =   "frmMain.frx":06DC
    Key             =   ""
EndProperty
BeginProperty ListImage4 {8556BCD3-E01E-11CF-8E74-00A0C90F26F8}
    Picture         =   "frmMain.frx":0A2E
    Key             =   ""
EndProperty
BeginProperty ListImage5 {8556BCD3-E01E-11CF-8E74-00A0C90F26F8}
    Picture         =   "frmMain.frx":0D80
    Key             =   ""
EndProperty
BeginProperty ListImage6 {8556BCD3-E01E-11CF-8E74-00A0C90F26F8}
    Picture         =   "frmMain.frx":10D2
    Key             =   ""
EndProperty
BeginProperty ListImage7 {8556BCD3-E01E-11CF-8E74-00A0C90F26F8}
    Picture         =   "frmMain.frx":1424
    Key             =   ""
EndProperty
BeginProperty ListImage8 {8556BCD3-E01E-11CF-8E74-00A0C90F26F8}
    Picture         =   "frmMain.frx":1776
    Key             =   ""
EndProperty
BeginProperty ListImage9 {8556BCD3-E01E-11CF-8E74-00A0C90F26F8}
    Picture         =   "frmMain.frx":1AC8
    Key             =   ""
EndProperty
BeginProperty ListImage10 {8556BCD3-E01E-11CF-8E74-
                          00A0C90F26F8}
    Picture         =   "frmMain.frx":1E1A
    Key             =   ""
EndProperty
BeginProperty ListImage11 {8556BCD3-E01E-11CF-8E74-
                          00A0C90F26F8}
    Picture         =   "frmMain.frx":216C
    Key             =   ""
EndProperty
```

```
        BeginProperty ListImage12 {8556BCD3-E01E-11CF-8E74-
                            00A0C90F26F8}
            Picture         =   "frmMain.frx":24BE
            Key             =   ""
        EndProperty
        BeginProperty ListImage13 {8556BCD3-E01E-11CF-8E74-
                            00A0C90F26F8}
            Picture         =   "frmMain.frx":2810
            Key             =   ""
        EndProperty
    EndProperty
End
Begin VB.Menu mnuFile
    Caption         =   "&File"
    Begin VB.Menu mnuFileNew
        Caption         =   "&New"
        Shortcut        =   ^N
    End
    Begin VB.Menu mnuFileOpen
        Caption         =   "&Open"
        Shortcut        =   ^O
    End
    Begin VB.Menu mnuFileClose
        Caption         =   "&Close"
    End
    Begin VB.Menu mnuFileBar1
        Caption         =   "-"
    End
    Begin VB.Menu mnuFileSave
        Caption         =   "&Save"
        Shortcut        =   ^S
    End
    Begin VB.Menu mnuFileSaveAs
        Caption         =   "Save &As..."
    End
    Begin VB.Menu mnuFileSaveAll
        Caption         =   "Save A&ll"
    End
    Begin VB.Menu mnuFileBar2
```

```
         Caption          =    "-"
End
Begin VB.Menu mnuFileProperties
         Caption          =    "Propert&ies"
End
Begin VB.Menu mnuFileBar3
         Caption          =    "-"
End
Begin VB.Menu mnuFilePageSetup
         Caption          =    "Page Set&up..."
End
Begin VB.Menu mnuFilePrintPreview
         Caption          =    "Print Pre&view"
End
Begin VB.Menu mnuFilePrint
         Caption          =    "&Print..."
         Shortcut         =    ^P
End
Begin VB.Menu mnuFileBar4
         Caption          =    "-"
End
Begin VB.Menu mnuFileSend
         Caption          =    "Sen&d..."
End
Begin VB.Menu mnuFileBar5
         Caption          =    "-"
End
Begin VB.Menu mnuFileMRU
         Caption          =    ""
         Index            =    0
         Visible          =    0    'False
End
Begin VB.Menu mnuFileMRU
         Caption          =    ""
         Index            =    1
         Visible          =    0    'False
End
Begin VB.Menu mnuFileMRU
         Caption          =    ""
```

```
         Index          =   2
         Visible        =   0    'False
      End
      Begin VB.Menu mnuFileMRU
         Caption        =   ""
         Index          =   3
         Visible        =   0    'False
      End
      Begin VB.Menu mnuFileBar6
         Caption        =   "-"
         Visible        =   0    'False
      End
      Begin VB.Menu mnuFileExit
         Caption        =   "E&xit"
      End
   End
   Begin VB.Menu mnuEdit
      Caption           =   "&Edit"
      Begin VB.Menu mnuEditUndo
         Caption        =   "&Undo"
         Shortcut       =   ^Z
      End
      Begin VB.Menu mnuEditBar1
         Caption        =   "-"
      End
      Begin VB.Menu mnuEditCut
         Caption        =   "Cu&t"
         Shortcut       =   ^X
      End
      Begin VB.Menu mnuEditCopy
         Caption        =   "&Copy"
         Shortcut       =   ^C
      End
      Begin VB.Menu mnuEditPaste
         Caption        =   "&Paste"
         Shortcut       =   ^V
      End
      Begin VB.Menu mnuEditPasteSpecial
         Caption        =   "Paste &Special..."
```

```
            End
        End
        Begin VB.Menu mnuView
            Caption         =   "&View"
            Begin VB.Menu mnuViewToolbar
                Caption         =   "&Toolbar"
                Checked         =   -1  'True
            End
            Begin VB.Menu mnuViewStatusBar
                Caption         =   "Status &Bar"
                Checked         =   -1  'True
            End
            Begin VB.Menu mnuViewBar2
                Caption         =   "-"
            End
            Begin VB.Menu mnuViewRefresh
                Caption         =   "&Refresh"
            End
            Begin VB.Menu mnuViewOptions
                Caption         =   "&Options..."
            End
            Begin VB.Menu mnuViewBrowser
                Caption         =   "&Web Browser"
            End
        End
        Begin VB.Menu mnuWindow
            Caption         =   "&Window"
            WindowList      =   -1  'True
            Begin VB.Menu mnuWindowNewWindow
                Caption         =   "&New Window"
            End
            Begin VB.Menu mnuWindowBar1
                Caption         =   "-"
            End
            Begin VB.Menu mnuWindowCascade
                Caption         =   "&Cascade"
            End
            Begin VB.Menu mnuWindowTileHorizontal
                Caption         =   "Tile &Horizontal"
```

```
      End
      Begin VB.Menu mnuWindowTileVertical
         Caption        =    "Tile &Vertical"
      End
      Begin VB.Menu mnuWindowArrangeIcons
         Caption        =    "&Arrange Icons"
      End
   End
   Begin VB.Menu mnuHelp
      Caption         =    "&Help"
      Begin VB.Menu mnuHelpContents
         Caption        =    "&Contents"
      End
      Begin VB.Menu mnuHelpSearch
         Caption        =    "&Search For Help On..."
      End
      Begin VB.Menu mnuHelpBar1
         Caption        =    "-"
      End
      Begin VB.Menu mnuHelpAbout
         Caption        =    "&About browser..."
      End
   End
End
Attribute VB_Name = "frmMain"
Attribute VB_GlobalNameSpace = False
Attribute VB_Creatable = False
Attribute VB_PredeclaredId = True
Attribute VB_Exposed = False
Private Declare Function OSWinHelp% Lib "user32" Alias "WinHelpA"
(ByVal hwnd&, ByVal HelpFile$, ByVal wCommand%, dwData As Any)
Private Sub MDIForm_Load()
    Me.Left = GetSetting(App.Title, "Settings", "MainLeft", 1000)
    Me.Top = GetSetting(App.Title, "Settings", "MainTop", 1000)
    Me.Width = GetSetting(App.Title, "Settings", "MainWidth", 6500)
    Me.Height = GetSetting(App.Title, "Settings", "MainHeight",
6500)
    LoadNewDoc
End Sub
```

```
Private Sub LoadNewDoc()
    Static lDocumentCount As Long
    Dim frmD As frmDocument

    lDocumentCount = lDocumentCount + 1
    Set frmD = New frmDocument
    frmD.Caption = "Document " & lDocumentCount
    frmD.Show
End Sub


Private Sub MDIForm_Unload(Cancel As Integer)
    If Me.WindowState <> vbMinimized Then
        SaveSetting App.Title, "Settings", "MainLeft", Me.Left
        SaveSetting App.Title, "Settings", "MainTop", Me.Top
        SaveSetting App.Title, "Settings", "MainWidth", Me.Width
        SaveSetting App.Title, "Settings", "MainHeight", Me.Height
    End If
End Sub


Private Sub mnuViewBrowser_Click()
    Dim frmB As New frmBrowser
    frmB.StartingAddress = "http://www.microsoft.com"
    frmB.Show
End Sub


Private Sub mnuHelpAbout_Click()
    'To Do
    MsgBox "About Box Code goes here!"
End Sub


Private Sub mnuViewOptions_Click()
    'To Do
    MsgBox "Options Dialog Code goes here!"
End Sub


Private Sub mnuViewStatusBar_Click()
    If mnuViewStatusBar.Checked Then
        sbStatusBar.Visible = False
        mnuViewStatusBar.Checked = False
```

```
    Else
        sbStatusBar.Visible = True
        mnuViewStatusBar.Checked = True
    End If
End Sub

Private Sub mnuViewToolbar_Click()
    If mnuViewToolbar.Checked Then
        tbToolBar.Visible = False
        mnuViewToolbar.Checked = False
    Else
        tbToolBar.Visible = True
        mnuViewToolbar.Checked = True
    End If
End Sub

Private Sub tbToolBar_ButtonClick(ByVal Button As ComctlLib.Button)

    Select Case Button.Key

        Case "New"
            LoadNewDoc
        Case "New"
            mnuFileNew_Click
        Case "Open"
            mnuFileOpen_Click
        Case "Save"
            mnuFileSave_Click
        Case "Print"
            mnuFilePrint_Click
        Case "Cut"
            mnuEditCut_Click
        Case "Copy"
            mnuEditCopy_Click
        Case "Paste"
            mnuEditPaste_Click
        Case "Bold"
            'To Do
            MsgBox "Bold Code goes here!"
```

```vb
            Case "Italic"
                'To Do
                MsgBox "Italic Code goes here!"
            Case "Underline"
                'To Do
                MsgBox "Underline Code goes here!"
            Case "Left"
                'To Do
                MsgBox "Left Code goes here!"
            Case "Center"
                'To Do
                MsgBox "Center Code goes here!"
            Case "Right"
                'To Do
                MsgBox "Right Code goes here!"
        End Select
    End Sub


    Private Sub mnuHelpContents_Click()

        Dim nRet As Integer

        'if there is no helpfile for this project display a message to
        'the user you can set the HelpFile for your application in the
        'Project Properties dialog
        If Len(App.HelpFile) = 0 Then
            MsgBox "Unable to display Help Contents. There is no Help
            associated with this project.", vbInformation, Me.Caption
        Else
            On Error Resume Next
            nRet = OSWinHelp(Me.hwnd, App.HelpFile, 3, 0)
            If Err Then
                MsgBox Err.Description
            End If
        End If
    End Sub


    Private Sub mnuHelpSearch_Click()

        Dim nRet As Integer
```

```
        'if there is no helpfile for this project display a message to
        'the user you can set the HelpFile for your application in the
        'Project Properties dialog
        If Len(App.HelpFile) = 0 Then
            MsgBox "Unable to display Help Contents. There is no Help
            associated with this project.", vbInformation, Me.Caption
        Else
            On Error Resume Next
            nRet = OSWinHelp(Me.hwnd, App.HelpFile, 261, 0)
            If Err Then
                MsgBox Err.Description
            End If
        End If
End Sub


Private Sub mnuWindowArrangeIcons_Click()
    Me.Arrange vbArrangeIcons
End Sub


Private Sub mnuWindowCascade_Click()
    Me.Arrange vbCascade
End Sub


Private Sub mnuWindowNewWindow_Click()
    'To Do
    MsgBox "New Window Code goes here!"
End Sub


Private Sub mnuWindowTileHorizontal_Click()
    Me.Arrange vbTileHorizontal
End Sub


Private Sub mnuWindowTileVertical_Click()
    Me.Arrange vbTileVertical
End Sub


Private Sub mnuViewRefresh_Click()
    'To Do
    MsgBox "Refresh Code goes here!"
End Sub
```

```
Private Sub mnuEditCopy_Click()
    'To Do
    MsgBox "Copy Code goes here!"
End Sub

Private Sub mnuEditCut_Click()
    'To Do
    MsgBox "Cut Code goes here!"
End Sub

Private Sub mnuEditPaste_Click()
    'To Do
    MsgBox "Paste Code goes here!"
End Sub

Private Sub mnuEditPasteSpecial_Click()
    'To Do
    MsgBox "Paste Special Code goes here!"
End Sub

Private Sub mnuEditUndo_Click()
    'To Do
    MsgBox "Undo Code goes here!"
End Sub

Private Sub mnuFileOpen_Click()
    Dim sFile As String

    With dlgCommonDialog
        'To Do
        'set the flags and attributes of the
        'common dialog control
        .Filter = "All Files (*.*)|*.*"
        .ShowOpen
        If Len(.filename) = 0 Then
            Exit Sub
        End If
        sFile = .filename
    End With
```

```
    'To Do
    'process the opened file
End Sub

Private Sub mnuFileClose_Click()
    'To Do
    MsgBox "Close Code goes here!"
End Sub

Private Sub mnuFileSave_Click()
    'To Do
    MsgBox "Save Code goes here!"
End Sub

Private Sub mnuFileSaveAs_Click()
    'To Do
    'Set up the common dialog control
    'prior to calling ShowSave
    dlgCommonDialog.ShowSave
End Sub

Private Sub mnuFileSaveAll_Click()
    'To Do
    MsgBox "Save All Code goes here!"
End Sub

Private Sub mnuFileProperties_Click()
    'To Do
    MsgBox "Properties Code goes here!"
End Sub

Private Sub mnuFilePageSetup_Click()
    dlgCommonDialog.ShowPrinter
End Sub

Private Sub mnuFilePrintPreview_Click()
    'To Do
    MsgBox "Print Preview Code goes here!"
End Sub
```

```
Private Sub mnuFilePrint_Click()
    'To Do
    MsgBox "Print Code goes here!"
End Sub

Private Sub mnuFileSend_Click()
    'To Do
    MsgBox "Send Code goes here!"
End Sub

Private Sub mnuFileMRU_Click(Index As Integer)
    'To Do
    MsgBox "MRU Code goes here!"
End Sub

Private Sub mnuFileExit_Click()
    'unload the form
    Unload Me
End Sub

Private Sub mnuFileNew_Click()
    LoadNewDoc
End Sub
```

Listing 2.12 frmDocument.frm

```
VERSION 5.00
Begin VB.Form frmDocument
    Caption         =   "frmDocument"
    ClientHeight    =   3195
    ClientLeft      =   60
    ClientTop       =   345
    ClientWidth     =   4680
    LinkTopic       =   "Form1"
    MDIChild        =   -1  'True
    ScaleHeight     =   3195
    ScaleWidth      =   4680
    Begin VB.TextBox txtText
```

```
        Height        =    2000
        Left          =    100
        MultiLine     =    -1   'True
        ScrollBars    =    3    'Both
        TabIndex      =    0
        Top           =    100
        Width         =    3000
     End
  End
  Attribute VB_Name = "frmDocument"
  Attribute VB_GlobalNameSpace = False
  Attribute VB_Creatable = False
  Attribute VB_PredeclaredId = True
  Attribute VB_Exposed = False
  Private Sub Form_Load()
      Form_Resize
  End Sub

  Private Sub Form_Resize()
      On Error Resume Next
      txtText.Move 100, 100, Me.ScaleWidth - 200, Me.ScaleHeight - 200
  End Sub
```

Listing 2.13 frmBrowser.frm

```
VERSION 5.00
Object = "{6B7E6392-850A-101B-AFC0-4210102A8DA7}#1.1#0";
"COMCTL32.OCX"
Object = "{EAB22AC0-30C2-11CF-A7EB-0000C05BAE0B}#1.0#0";
"SHDOCVW.DLL"
Begin VB.Form frmBrowser
   ClientHeight     =    5130
   ClientLeft       =    3060
   ClientTop        =    3345
   ClientWidth      =    6540
   LinkTopic        =    "Form1"
   MDIChild         =    -1   'True
   ScaleHeight      =    5130
   ScaleWidth       =    6540
```

```
ShowInTaskbar   =   0    'False
Begin SHDocVwCtl.WebBrowser brwWebBrowser
   Height            =    3734
   Left              =    50
   TabIndex          =    0
   Top               =    1215
   Width             =    5393
   Object.Height         =    249
   Object.Width          =    360
   AutoSize          =    0
   ViewMode          =    1
   AutoSizePercentage=    0
   AutoArrange       =    -1   'True
   NoClientEdge      =    -1   'True
   AlignLeft         =    0    'False
End
Begin VB.Timer timTimer
   Enabled           =    0    'False
   Interval          =    5
   Left              =    6180
   Top               =    1500
End
Begin ComctlLib.Toolbar tbToolBar
   Align             =    1 'Align Top
   Height            =    420
   Left              =    0
   TabIndex          =    3
   Top               =    0
   Width             =    6540
   _ExtentX          =    11536
   _ExtentY          =    741
   ButtonWidth       =    635
   ButtonHeight      =    582
   Appearance        =    1
   ImageList         =    "imlIcons"
   BeginProperty Buttons {7791BA42-E020-11CF-8E74-00A0C90F26F8}
      NumButtons     =    6
      BeginProperty Button1 {7791BA43-E020-11CF-8E74-00A0C90F26F8}
         Key              =    "Back"
```

```
        Object.ToolTipText    =    "Back"
        Object.Tag            =    ""
        ImageIndex    =    1
    EndProperty
    BeginProperty Button2 {7791BA43-E020-11CF-8E74-00A0C90F26F8}
        Key           =    "Forward"
        Object.ToolTipText    =    "Forward"
        Object.Tag            =    ""
        ImageIndex    =    2
    EndProperty
    BeginProperty Button3 {7791BA43-E020-11CF-8E74-00A0C90F26F8}
        Key           =    "Stop"
        Object.ToolTipText    =    "Stop"
        Object.Tag            =    ""
        ImageIndex    =    3
    EndProperty
    BeginProperty Button4 {7791BA43-E020-11CF-8E74-00A0C90F26F8}
        Key           =    "Refresh"
        Object.ToolTipText    =    "Refresh"
        Object.Tag            =    ""
        ImageIndex    =    4
    EndProperty
    BeginProperty Button5 {7791BA43-E020-11CF-8E74-00A0C90F26F8}
        Key           =    "Home"
        Object.ToolTipText    =    "Home"
        Object.Tag            =    ""
        ImageIndex    =    5
    EndProperty
    BeginProperty Button6 {7791BA43-E020-11CF-8E74-00A0C90F26F8}
        Key           =    "Search"
        Object.ToolTipText    =    "Search"
        Object.Tag            =    ""
        ImageIndex    =    6
    EndProperty
    EndProperty
    MouseIcon       =    "frmBrowser.frx":0000
End
Begin VB.PictureBox picAddress
    Align          =    1  'Align Top
```

```
            BorderStyle    =    0   'None
            Height         =    675
            Left           =    0
            ScaleHeight    =    675
            ScaleWidth     =    6540
            TabIndex       =    4
            TabStop        =    0    'False
            Top            =    420
            Width          =    6540
            Begin VB.ComboBox cboAddress
                Height         =    315
                Left           =    45
                TabIndex       =    2
                Text           =    "Combo1"
                Top            =    300
                Width          =    3795
            End
            Begin VB.Label lblAddress
                Caption        =    "&Address:"
                Height         =    255
                Left           =    45
                TabIndex       =    1
                Tag            =    "&Address:"
                Top            =    60
                Width          =    3075
            End
        End
    End
    Begin ComctlLib.ImageList imlIcons
        Left           =    2670
        Top            =    2325
        _ExtentX       =    1005
        _ExtentY       =    1005
        BackColor      =    -2147483643
        ImageWidth     =    24
        ImageHeight    =    24
        MaskColor      =    12632256
        BeginProperty Images {8556BCD1-E01E-11CF-8E74-00A0C90F26F8}
            NumListImages   =    6
            BeginProperty ListImage1 {8556BCD3-E01E-11CF-8E74-00A0C90F26F8}
```

```
                    Picture          =     "frmBrowser.frx":001C
                    Key              =     ""
                 EndProperty
              BeginProperty ListImage2 {8556BCD3-E01E-11CF-8E74-00A0C90F26F8}
                    Picture          =     "frmBrowser.frx":072E
                    Key              =     ""
                 EndProperty
              BeginProperty ListImage3 {8556BCD3-E01E-11CF-8E74-00A0C90F26F8}
                    Picture          =     "frmBrowser.frx":0E40
                    Key              =     ""
                 EndProperty
              BeginProperty ListImage4 {8556BCD3-E01E-11CF-8E74-00A0C90F26F8}
                    Picture          =     "frmBrowser.frx":1552
                    Key              =     ""
                 EndProperty
              BeginProperty ListImage5 {8556BCD3-E01E-11CF-8E74-00A0C90F26F8}
                    Picture          =     "frmBrowser.frx":1C64
                    Key              =     ""
                 EndProperty
              BeginProperty ListImage6 {8556BCD3-E01E-11CF-8E74-00A0C90F26F8}
                    Picture          =     "frmBrowser.frx":2376
                    Key              =     ""
                 EndProperty
           EndProperty
        End
End

Attribute VB_Name = "frmBrowser"
Attribute VB_GlobalNameSpace = False
Attribute VB_Creatable = False
Attribute VB_PredeclaredId = True
Attribute VB_Exposed = False
Public StartingAddress As String
Dim mbDontNavigateNow As Boolean
Private Sub Form_Load()
    On Error Resume Next
    Me.Show
    tbToolBar.Refresh
    Form_Resize
```

```vb
        cboAddress.Move 50, lblAddress.Top + lblAddress.Height + 15

        If Len(StartingAddress) > 0 Then
            cboAddress.Text = StartingAddress
            cboAddress.AddItem cboAddress.Text
            'try to navigate to the starting address
            timTimer.Enabled = True
            brwWebBrowser.Navigate StartingAddress
        End If

End Sub


Private Sub brwWebBrowser_DownloadComplete()
    On Error Resume Next
    Me.Caption = brwWebBrowser.LocationName
End Sub


Private Sub brwWebBrowser_NavigateComplete(ByVal URL As String)
    Dim i As Integer
    Dim bFound As Boolean
    Me.Caption = brwWebBrowser.LocationName
    For i = 0 To cboAddress.ListCount - 1
        If cboAddress.List(i) = brwWebBrowser.LocationURL Then
            bFound = True
            Exit For
        End If
    Next i
    mbDontNavigateNow = True
    If bFound Then
        cboAddress.RemoveItem i
    End If
    cboAddress.AddItem brwWebBrowser.LocationURL, 0
    cboAddress.ListIndex = 0
    mbDontNavigateNow = False
End Sub


Private Sub cboAddress_Click()
    If mbDontNavigateNow Then Exit Sub
    timTimer.Enabled = True
```

```
        brwWebBrowser.Navigate cboAddress.Text
End Sub


Private Sub cboAddress_KeyPress(KeyAscii As Integer)
    On Error Resume Next
    If KeyAscii = vbKeyReturn Then
        cboAddress_Click
    End If
End Sub


Private Sub Form_Resize()
    cboAddress.Width = Me.ScaleWidth - 100
    brwWebBrowser.Width = Me.ScaleWidth - 100
    brwWebBrowser.Height = Me.ScaleHeight - (picAddress.Top +
picAddress.Height) - 100
End Sub


Private Sub timTimer_Timer()
    If brwWebBrowser.Busy = False Then
        timTimer.Enabled = False
        Me.Caption = brwWebBrowser.LocationName
    Else
        Me.Caption = "Working..."
    End If
End Sub


Private Sub tbToolBar_ButtonClick(ByVal Button As Button)
    On Error Resume Next

    timTimer.Enabled = True

    Select Case Button.Key
        Case "Back"
            brwWebBrowser.GoBack
        Case "Forward"
            brwWebBrowser.GoForward
        Case "Refresh"
            brwWebBrowser.Refresh
        Case "Home"
```

```
            brwWebBrowser.GoHome
        Case "Search"
            brwWebBrowser.GoSearch
        Case "Stop"
            timTimer.Enabled = False
            brwWebBrowser.Stop
            Me.Caption = brwWebBrowser.LocationName
    End Select

End Sub
```

That's it for our Web browser. Creating it was almost automatic when we used the Application Wizard. You can add a Web browser to your applications by using the Application Wizard or by adding a WebBrowser control directly.

In Chapter 3, we'll dig deeper into Visual Basic Internet programming when we start working with the FTP and HTTP protocols directly. These powerful methods account for much of the popularity of the Internet, and we'll put them to work for us.

VB ON THE INTERNET: HTTP AND FTP

In this chapter, we'll examine the powerful capabilities of Visual Basic to handle two important Internet protocols: File Transfer Protocol (FTP) and Hypertext Transfer Protocol (HTTP). FTP is usually used to transfer large files; most Internet servers have an FTP area that you can examine and upload files to or download files from. The HTTP protocol is the basis of the World Wide Web and is usually used to fetch Web pages; you get the direct HTML of a Web page using this protocol. Like the FTP protocol, HTTP can also be used to get binary files (such as images or **.zip** files). Visual Basic's built-in support for these methods makes writing programs around them almost easy. In this chapter, we'll write a program that reads the directory of an FTP site and allows us to get both binary and text data. We'll also create an HTTP program that fetches a Web page and displays its HTML. (This is unlike the WebBrowser control, which displays the Web page without the underlying HTML.)

You can also get creative with these methods. For example, you might use FTP methods in your programs to automatically download documentation for a user who clicks items in the Help menu. Or you could use HTTP methods to write a program that gets all the graphics images from a Web page without having to click each one.

Visual Basic uses the Internet Transfer control to handle these two protocols, so let's take a look at this exceptionally powerful control first.

The Internet Transfer Control

The Visual Basic Internet Transfer control implements both FTP and HTTP protocols for us. You might wonder why Microsoft didn't create two controls: an FTP control and an HTTP control. It turns out that there is no need for that: the Internet Transfer control figures out which protocol to use based on the URL we pass to it (such as ftp://ftp.microsoft.com or http://www.microsoft.com).

This is how we'll use the Internet Transfer control: first, we'll add it to a program using the Project menu's **Components** item by clicking the entry marked **Microsoft Internet Transfer Control 5.0**. After the control appears in the toolbox, we'll double-click it to create a new Internet Transfer control in our program (the default name of this control is Inet1). Then all we have to do is to use the OpenURL() or Execute() method to access the Internet. The OpenURL() method gets the data we are trying to fetch, and the Execute() method executes FTP or HTTP commands such as GET or PUT.

There is one more thing you should keep in mind before we start our FTP example: OpenURL() is a *synchronous* method, and Execute() is *asynchronous*. This means that the OpenURL() method waits until the data you are requesting is downloaded; the Execute() method returns at once, and the code that follows it in your program is executed while Execute() is working. This arrangement can save time in very long file transfers. We'll begin by creating an FTP program.

Using FTP from Visual Basic

Our first Internet Transfer control example will examine and download files from the Microsoft ftp site, ftp.microsoft.com. This site contains a great deal of free software, readily available for downloading. All we have to do is to use the ftp protocol correctly. Let's name our new program FTPer, and let's have it display the files we download. This means that we'll download text files, so we set up FTPer to display the names of the available text files:

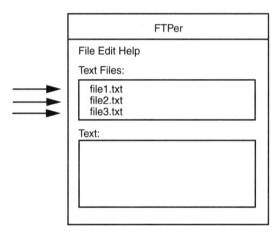

Users select from these listed text files; when they click, say, **file2.txt**, we download that file and display its contents:

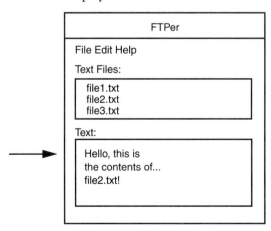

Let's put this to work now. Use the Visual Basic Application Wizard to create a new SDI project (click the **SDI** option and not the MDI option) named **FTPer**. We'll need an Internet Transfer control, so select the **Components** item in Visual Basic's Project menu. Find the entry marked **Microsoft Internet Transfer Control 5.0** and click it. We'll display the text of our text files in a rich text box, so add that control by clicking the **Microsoft Rich Textbox Control 5.0** entry; then click **OK**.

Now open the main form of the project, frmMain, and add an Internet Transfer control (Inet1), a rich text box (RichTextBox1), and a Listbox control (List1) for the names of the text files:

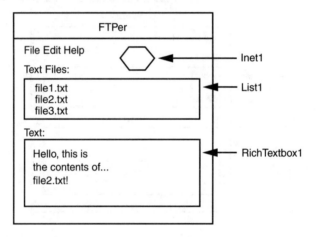

At this point, we're ready to begin coding the FTPer program.

Logging On to an FTP Server

The first step is to log on to the FTP server ftp.microsoft.com. In general, there are two types of FTP servers: public and private ones. For both types, you must provide a user name and password. In public FTP servers, such as ftp.microsoft.com, you typically use "anonymous" as your user name, and your email address as the password. The Internet Transfer control makes it easy, because it supplies this information automatically (getting your email address from the Windows registry).

To log on to a private FTP server, you must provide a password and user name, and you do that using the Internet Transfer control's UserName and Password properties. For example, if we wanted to connect to ftp.private.com, we would start by setting the Internet Transfer control's URL property to ftp.private.com. (You don't have to set the URL property if you use the OpenURL() method, because you pass the URL when calling OpenURL().)

```
Inet1.URL = "ftp://ftp.private.com"
    .
    .
    .
```

Next, set the UserName and Password properties:

```
    Inet1.URL = "ftp://ftp.private.com"
->  Inet1.UserName = "George Washington"
->  Inet1.Password = "no_lies"
    .
    .
    .
```

Then you can the Execute method to execute FTP commands such as GET; in this case, we'll download a file named **source.txt** from the FTP server and save it as **c:\target.txt**:

```
Inet1.URL = "ftp://ftp.private.com"
Inet1.UserName = "George Washington"
Inet1.Password = "no_lies"
Inet1.Execute , "GET source.txt C:\target.txt"
    .
    .
    .
```

In this way, you use the Execute method to execute FTP commands (just as you might in a command-line FTP program). Finally, we execute a CLOSE command to close the connection:

```
        Inet1.URL = "ftp://ftp.private.com"
        Inet1.UserName = "George Washington"
        Inet1.Password = "no_lies"
        Inet1.Execute , "GET source.txt C:\target.txt"
  ->    Inet.Execute ,"CLOSE"
```

That's the way to execute FTP commands: with the Execute method. You may be familiar with these commands. They are the backbone of FTP handling, although, as we'll see in a minute, you don't have to use any of these commands to download if you use the OpenURL() method. Table 3.1 shows the supported FTP commands, such as CD, GET, DELETE, PUT, and MKDIR (MKDIR creates a new directory on the Internet host if you have the privilege to do so), and describes what they do. Using these commands, we can download files from and upload files to FTP sites. For example, to change directories and upload a file named **source.txt**, renaming it to **target.txt**, you would execute this code:

```
        Inet1.URL = "ftp://ftp.private.com"
        Inet1.UserName = "George Washington"
        Inet1.Password = "no_lies"
        Inet1.Execute , "CD gifs\thegifs"
        Inet1.Execute , "PUT C:\source.txt target.txt"
        Inet.Execute ,"CLOSE"
```

Table 3.1 FTP commands of the Internet Transfer Control's Execute Method

Command	Does This
CD newdir	Changes directory (e.g., Execute , "CD gifs\thegifs").
CDUP	Changes to parent directory. Identical to "CD ..".
DELETE file	Deletes specified file (e.g., Execute , "DELETE nogood.dat").

Table 3.1 FTP commands of the Internet Transfer Control's Execute Method (continued)

Command	Does This
DIR (newdir)	Searches current directory or directory specified. Use GetChunk() to get the data (e.g., Execute , "DIR /gifs").
GET source target	Gets file "source" and creates a local file "target" (e.g., Execute , "GET source.txt C:\target.txt").
LS	List. Same as DIR.
MKDIR newdir	Creates new directory newdir (e.g., Execute , "MKDIR /newdir").
PUT source target	Copies local file "source" to remote computer as "target" (e.g., Execute , "PUT C:\source.txt target.txt").
PWD	Print Working Directory. Use GetChunk() method to get the data (e.g., Execute , "PWD").
QUIT	Close the connection (e.g., Execute , "QUIT").
RECV source target	Same as GET.
RENAME oldname oldnewname	Renames a file (e.g., Execute , "RENAME name.txt newname.txt").
RMDIR dirname	Removes directory (e.g., Execute , "RMDIR dirname").
SEND source	Same as PUT.
SIZE filename	Gets the size of specified file (e.g., Execute "SIZE filename.txt").

Controlling Asynchronous Transfers

Execute() works asynchronously, and that means that we need some way of keeping track of what it is doing. In particular, we need to know when the operation is finished (such as when the file we want is downloaded). We do that in the Internet Transfer control's StateChanged event; double-clicking the Internet Transfer control opens this event:

```
Private Sub Inet1_StateChanged(ByVal State As Integer)

End Sub
```

We can determine what is happening in this event by checking the variable passed to us: State. Table 3.2 lists the values that this variable can contain and describes what those values mean. Using this event handler, we can watch as the control connects to the Internet, downloads the data, and finishes.

Table 3.2 The Internet Transfer Control's StateChanged Values

Value	Meaning
icNone (= 0)	No state
icHostResolvingHost (= 1)	Looking up IP address of specified computer
icHostResolved (= 2)	Got the IP address of specified computer
icConnecting (= 3)	Connecting to computer
icConnected (= 4)	Connected to computer
icRequesting (= 5)	Sending request to host computer
icRequestSent (= 6)	Sent the request
icReceivingResponse (= 7)	Receiving a response from computer
icResponseReceived (= 8)	Received a response from computer

Table 3.2 The Internet Transfer Control's StateChanged Values (continued)

Value	Meaning
icDisconnecting (= 9)	Disconnecting from computer
icDisconnected (= 10)	Disconnected from computer
icError (= 11)	Error occurred
icResponseCompleted (= 12)	Request completed and data received

For example, if we want to determine when a particular document has been downloaded, we place code like this into the Inet1_StateChanged() event handler:

```
        Private Sub Inet1_StateChanged(ByVal State As Integer)

->          If(State = icResponseCompleted) Then ReceivedFlag = True

        End Sub
```

In this way, we're able to determine when a document is fully downloaded when we use the Execute method. (There is no such question when you use the OpenURL method, because that method won't return until the file you have requested has been downloaded.)

Using GetChunk()

When we perform a directory FTP Execute operation such as DIR, LS, or PWD, the data is not returned to us immediately; instead, it is stored in a buffer and we must use the GetChunk() (as in "get a chunk of data") method to read it.

Let's say we performed a DIR operation with the Execute() method. In that case, we use GetChunk() to retrieve the directory data we received. We use GetChunk() like this: Inet1.GetChunk(size, type). Here, size is the number of bytes we want to get from the download buffer, and type can be one of two constants: icString (value = 0, the default) for string data, or icByteArray (value = 1) for binary data. Our goal might be to display the directory data we got in a text box named Text1. We would start in the Internet Transfer control's StateChanged event handler. We wait until the directory data has been downloaded by checking the State variable and making sure it equals icResponseReceived:

```
Private Sub Inet1_StateChanged(ByVal State As Integer)

->        If(State = icResponseReceived) Then   'This constant = 12
                   .
                   .
                   .
->           End If

End Sub
```

If we got the directory data, we can begin by getting, say, 2K of data from the download buffer:

```
Private Sub Inet1_StateChanged(ByVal State As Integer)

        If(State = icResponseReceived) Then   'This constant = 12
->               Dim VariantData As Variant

->               VariantData = Inet1.GetChunk(2048, icString)
                      .
                      .
                      .

            End If

End Sub
```

Note that GetChunk() returns a Variant: an untyped value that can be either a string or numeric data. In this case, we'll keep reading from the download buffer until we exhaust it, in which case GetChunk will return an empty string, "":

```
Private Sub Inet1_StateChanged(ByVal State As Integer)
```

```
               If(State = icResponseReceived) Then   'This constant = 12
                       Dim VariantData As Variant
->                     Dim StringData As String
->                     Dim DoneFlag As Boolean
->                     DoneFlag = False
->                     StringData = ""

                       VariantData = Inet1.GetChunk(2048, icString)

->                 While Not DoneFlag
->                     StringData = Data + VariantData
->                     VariantData = Inet1.GetChunk(2048, icString)
->                     If Len(VariantData) = 0 Then DoneFlag = True
->                 Wend
                           .
                           .
                           .

               End If

       End Sub
```

At this point, the directory data we received is in the string StringData,
and we can display it in our text box Text1 this way:

```
       Private Sub Inet1_StateChanged(ByVal State As Integer)

           If(State = icResponseReceived) Then   'This constant = 12
                   Dim VariantData As Variant
                   Dim StringData As String
                   Dim DoneFlag As Boolean
                   DoneFlag = False
                   StringData = ""

                   VariantData = Inet1.GetChunk(2048, icString)

               While Not DoneFlag
                   StringData = Data + VariantData
                   VariantData = Inet1.GetChunk(2048, icString)
                   If Len(VariantData) = 0 Then DoneFlag = True
```

```
                         Wend

    ->                   Text1.Text = StringData
                 End If

         End Sub
```

Downloading Text FTP Data

Now that we've reviewed FTP methods in Visual Basic, let's put them to work. Our goal in our example program, FTPer, is to download the directory of ftp.microsoft.com, indicate which text files are available, and let the user download the selected one:

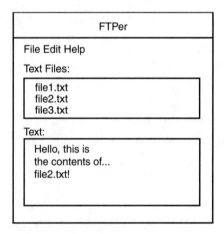

This example is not very fancy, so the Internet Transfer control OpenURL() method will work best here. Using this method, you can fetch files with the HTTP and FTP protocols. That's all it does—if you want to use commands such as DIR or PUT, you must use the Execute method.

Now that we've added an Internet Transfer control to our FTPer project, we can put it to work. When the program starts, we'll have it automatically connect to ftp.microsoft.com and display a directory listing of the text files there (the files with the extension **.txt**). We will use the Form_Load() event handler, which is called when the main form is first displayed; currently it looks like this (where the program positions the form on the screen and sizes it):

```
Private Sub Form_Load()
    Me.Left = GetSetting(App.Title, "Settings", "MainLeft", 1000)
    Me.Top = GetSetting(App.Title, "Settings", "MainTop", 1000)
    Me.Width = GetSetting(App.Title, "Settings", "MainWidth", 6500)
    Me.Height = GetSetting(App.Title, "Settings", "MainHeight", 6500)
End Sub
```

Next, we get the directory of the Microsoft server ftp.microsoft.com. We use the OpenURL() method, loading the directory information into a string named DirectoryText:

```
Private Sub Form_Load()
-> Dim DirectoryText
    Me.Left = GetSetting(App.Title, "Settings", "MainLeft", 1000)
    Me.Top = GetSetting(App.Title, "Settings", "MainTop", 1000)
    Me.Width = GetSetting(App.Title, "Settings", "MainWidth", 6500)
    Me.Height = GetSetting(App.Title, "Settings", "MainHeight", 6500)

-> DirectoryText = Inet1.OpenURL("ftp://ftp.microsoft.com")
        .
        .
        .
```

Because we have not specified a file to download, we will get a listing of ftp.microsoft.com's directory. In general, the OpenURL() method has two arguments: the URL you want to get and a data type setting, which can hold the values icString (= 0, the default) to retrieve the data as a string, or icByteArray (= 1) to retrieve the data as a byte array. Although we skipped the second parameter, we could also have written that line this way:

```
DirectoryText = Inet1.OpenURL("ftp://ftp.microsoft.com", icString)
```

When the program executes this line, it connects to the Internet (assuming that the user has a connection set up for the Internet) if the computer is not already connected and logs in to ftp.microsoft.com. Then it gets the

directory of ftp.microsoft.com and places it into the string
DirectoryString. With the addition of the Inet1 control to our program
and the use of the OpenURL() method, we've connected to the Internet
using the FTP protocol.

We can get the length of the directory data by checking the length of
the string DirectoryString:

```
Private Sub Form_Load()
    Dim DirectoryText
    Me.Left = GetSetting(App.Title, "Settings", "MainLeft", 1000)
    Me.Top = GetSetting(App.Title, "Settings", "MainTop", 1000)
    Me.Width = GetSetting(App.Title, "Settings", "MainWidth", 6500)
    Me.Height = GetSetting(App.Title, "Settings", "MainHeight", 6500)

    DirectoryText = Inet1.OpenURL("ftp://ftp.microsoft.com")
->  DirectoryTextLength = Len(DirectoryText)
        .
        .
        .

End Sub
```

Here's the actual data we would receive for the directory of
ftp.microsoft.com; note that it is set up in HTML to make it easy for Web
browsers:

```
<BODY>
  <H2>FTP root at ftp.microsoft.com</H2>
    <HR>
    <H4><PRE>
    This is FTP.MICROSOFT.COM.  Please see the
    dirmap.txt file for more information.
    </PRE></H4>
    <HR>
    <PRE>
    09/20/96 07:34PM     Directory <A
HREF="/bussys/"><B>bussys</B></A>
    09/23/96 08:46PM     Directory <A
HREF="/deskapps/"><B>deskapps</B></A>
```

```
        08/16/96 05:33PM       Directory <A HREF="/developr/"><B>
developr</B></A>
        09/11/96 01:01AM             8,012 <A
HREF="/dirmap.htm">dirmap.htm</A>
        09/11/96 12:57AM             4,368 <A
HREF="/dirmap.txt">dirmap.txt</A>
        08/25/94 12:00AM                712 <A HREF="/disclaimer.txt">
disclaimer.txt</A>
        11/19/96 01:23AM       Directory <A
HREF="/KBHelp/"><B>KBHelp</B></A>
        12/03/96 11:10AM         8,168,053 <A HREF="/ls-lR.txt">
ls-lR.txt</A>
        12/03/96 11:10AM         1,065,823 <A HREF="/ls-lR.Z">ls-lR.Z</A>
        12/03/96 11:10AM           879,116 <A HREF="/LS-LR.ZIP">
LS-LR.ZIP</A>
        10/20/95 12:00AM       Directory <A
HREF="/MSCorp/"><B>MSCorp</B></A>
        10/27/96 12:24AM       Directory <A
HREF="/msdownload/"><B>msdownload</B></A>
        10/11/95 12:00AM       Directory <A HREF="/peropsys/"><B>
peropsys</B></A>
        11/30/95 12:00AM       Directory <A
HREF="/Products/"><B>Products</B></A>
        10/28/96 11:47PM       Directory <A
HREF="/Services/"><B>Services</B></A>
        05/30/96 01:39AM       Directory <A
HREF="/Softlib/"><B>Softlib</B></A>
        04/08/96 02:21PM       Directory <A HREF="/solutions/"><B>
solutions</B></A>
        </PRE>
        <HR>
</BODY>
</HTML>
```

We want to place the names of the text files into the listbox List1, so we will write our program to search through the listing for **.txt** files; we do that by searching for ".txt," which locates the end of the file name strings that we want. We will place each file name into its own string, so we call the location of the substring ".txt" StringEnd (the end of the file name string):

```
Private Sub Form_Load()
    Dim DirectoryText
    Me.Left = GetSetting(App.Title, "Settings", "MainLeft", 1000)
    Me.Top = GetSetting(App.Title, "Settings", "MainTop", 1000)
    Me.Width = GetSetting(App.Title, "Settings", "MainWidth", 6500)
    Me.Height = GetSetting(App.Title, "Settings", "MainHeight", 6500)

    DirectoryText = Inet1.OpenURL("ftp://ftp.microsoft.com")
    DirectoryTextLength = Len(DirectoryText)
--> StringEnd = InStr(DirectoryText, ".txt""")
        .

        .

        .

End Sub
```

As long as the variable StringEnd is not 0, we have found a match. We should set up a loop, because there will be more than one text file to find:

```
Private Sub Form_Load()
    Dim DirectoryText
    Me.Left = GetSetting(App.Title, "Settings", "MainLeft", 1000)
    Me.Top = GetSetting(App.Title, "Settings", "MainTop", 1000)
    Me.Width = GetSetting(App.Title, "Settings", "MainWidth", 6500)
    Me.Height = GetSetting(App.Title, "Settings", "MainHeight", 6500)

    DirectoryText = Inet1.OpenURL("ftp://ftp.microsoft.com")
    DirectoryTextLength = Len(DirectoryText)
    StringEnd = InStr(DirectoryText, ".txt""")
--> While (StringEnd <> 0)
        .

        .

        .

--> Wend

End Sub
```

Because the directory of ftp.microsoft.com is set up as a Web page (which is quite common), each file name is enclosed in quotation marks:

```
    09/11/96 12:57AM              4,368 <A
HREF="/dirmap.txt">dirmap.txt</A>
```

Now that we've found the ".txt" part of the file name, we can work back to the quotation mark to get the whole file name and the length of the file name (which we place in the variable StringLength):

```
Private Sub Form_Load()
    Dim DirectoryText
    Me.Left = GetSetting(App.Title, "Settings", "MainLeft", 1000)
    Me.Top = GetSetting(App.Title, "Settings", "MainTop", 1000)
    Me.Width = GetSetting(App.Title, "Settings", "MainWidth", 6500)
    Me.Height = GetSetting(App.Title, "Settings", "MainHeight", 6500)

    DirectoryText = Inet1.OpenURL("ftp://ftp.microsoft.com")
    DirectoryTextLength = Len(DirectoryText)
    StringEnd = InStr(DirectoryText, ".txt""")
    While (StringEnd <> 0)
->      StringLength = 0
->      While (InStr(StringEnd - StringLength, Left(DirectoryText,
->      StringEnd),
->          """") = 0)
->          StringLength = StringLength + 1
->      Wend
->      StringLength = StringLength - 1
            .
            .
            .

    Wend

End Sub
```

At this point, we've found a file name in the FTP directory. We know how long it is, so we add it to our listbox List1 this way:

```
Private Sub Form_Load()
    Dim DirectoryText
    Me.Left = GetSetting(App.Title, "Settings", "MainLeft", 1000)
    Me.Top = GetSetting(App.Title, "Settings", "MainTop", 1000)
```

```
    Me.Width = GetSetting(App.Title, "Settings", "MainWidth", 6500)
    Me.Height = GetSetting(App.Title, "Settings", "MainHeight", 6500)

    DirectoryText = Inet1.OpenURL("ftp://ftp.microsoft.com")
    DirectoryTextLength = Len(DirectoryText)
    StringEnd = InStr(DirectoryText, ".txt""")
    While (StringEnd <> 0)
        StringLength = 0
        While (InStr(StringEnd - StringLength, Left(DirectoryText,
        StringEnd),
            """") = 0)
            StringLength = StringLength + 1
        Wend
        StringLength = StringLength - 1
->      List1.AddItem Mid(DirectoryText, StringEnd - StringLength + 1,
            StringLength - 1) + ".txt"
                .
                .
                .

    Wend

End Sub
```

Next, we truncate the directory listing string (we won't need it for
anything else, so we remove the parts we've already searched) to remove
the already-found file name. Then we loop again to find the next
occurrence of ".txt":

```
Private Sub Form_Load()
    Dim DirectoryText
    Me.Left = GetSetting(App.Title, "Settings", "MainLeft", 1000)
    Me.Top = GetSetting(App.Title, "Settings", "MainTop", 1000)
    Me.Width = GetSetting(App.Title, "Settings", "MainWidth", 6500)
    Me.Height = GetSetting(App.Title, "Settings", "MainHeight", 6500)

    DirectoryText = Inet1.OpenURL("ftp://ftp.microsoft.com")
    DirectoryTextLength = Len(DirectoryText)
    StringEnd = InStr(DirectoryText, ".txt""")
    While (StringEnd <> 0)
```

```
        StringLength = 0
        While (InStr(StringEnd - StringLength, Left(DirectoryText,
        StringEnd),
            """") = 0)
            StringLength = StringLength + 1
        Wend
        StringLength = StringLength - 1
        List1.AddItem Mid(DirectoryText, StringEnd - StringLength + 1,
            StringLength - 1) + ".txt"
->      DirectoryText = Right(DirectoryText, DirectoryTextLength -
->      StringEnd)
->      DirectoryTextLength = DirectoryTextLength - StringEnd
->      StringEnd = InStr(DirectoryText, ".txt""")
     Wend

End Sub
```

At this point, our listbox displays the names of the **.txt** files:

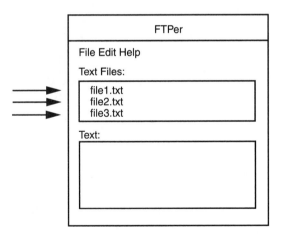

All that remains is to read the files from the FTP server when the user double-clicks its name in the listbox. We use List1_Click(), creating the full name of the file to fetch by adding "ftp://ftp.microsoft.com/" to the name of the file we are supposed to get in List1.Text:

```
Private Sub List1_Click()
    RichTextBox1.Text = Inet1.OpenURL("ftp://ftp.microsoft.com/" +
    List1.Text)
End Sub
```

That's it—the program is now functional. Run it to see the listing of the **.txt** files in the FTP server ftp.microsoft.com, as shown in Figure 3.1. Now click a file, such as **disclaimer.txt**, and it will be downloaded and appear in the rich text box. Our FTP program is a success.

Figure 3.1 Retrieving files from Microsoft via FTP.

That's how to download text. Although we can use the Execute() method, it's usually easier to use OpenURL() if we just want to download a file. We can download binary data, too. Let's look into that now.

Downloading Binary FTP Data

The earlier listing of the ftp.microsoft.com directory shows that one of the files is a binary file named **LS-LR.zip**. Let's download that file now. (Note that when you read this, the contents of the microsoft FTP directory may have changed.) Open the Menu Editor in the Visual Basic Tools menu and add a new item, **Get File**, to FTPer's File menu following the **Close** item, as shown in Figure 3.2. Give this item the name **Getfile**.

Figure 3.2 The FTPer Get File menu item.

Now double-click that item to open its click event:

```
Private Sub Getfile_Click()

End Sub
```

Our task is to download the file **ftp://ftp.microsoft.com/LS-LR.zip**. We can use OpenURL() to get this file, but we can't just assign the output of OpenURL() to a string, because **LS-LR.zip** is not a text file; instead, we set up a binary array:

```
   Private Sub Getfile_Click()
-> Dim binarydata() As Byte

          .

          .

          .


   End Sub
```

Now we are free to get the file we want using OpenURL(), passing it the icByteArray parameter to indicate that we are downloading a binary file:

```
   Private Sub Getfile_Click()

      Dim binarydata() As Byte

-> binarydata() = Inet1.OpenURL("ftp://ftp.microsoft.com/LS-LR.zip",
         icByteArray)
          .

          .

          .

   End Sub
```

Now we store this binary data to disk by opening **LS-LR.zip** and writing the binarydata() array to it:

```
   Private Sub Getfile_Click()

      Dim binarydata() As Byte

      binarydata() = Inet1.OpenURL("ftp://ftp.microsoft.com/LS-LR.zip",
         icByteArray)

-> Open "E:\vb\LS-LR.zip" For Binary Access Write As #1
-> Put #1, , binarydata()
          .

          .

          .

   End Sub
```

Finally, we close the file and pop a message box on the screen to indicate we are finished:

```
Private Sub Getfile_Click()

    Dim binarydata() As Byte

    binarydata() = Inet1.OpenURL("ftp://ftp.microsoft.com/LS-LR.zip",
        icByteArray)

    Open "E:\vb\LS-LR.zip" For Binary Access Write As #1
    Put #1, , binarydata()
-> Close #1
-> MsgBox "Finished."

End Sub
```

And that's it—now we're able to download FTP files, both text and binary, as well as work with the standard FTP commands such as MKDIR, GET, PUT, and CD. The code for our FTPer program appears in Listing 3.1.

Listing 3.1 (FTPer) FrmMain.frm

```
VERSION 5.00
Object = "{F9043C88-F6F2-101A-A3C9-08002B2F49FB}#1.1#0"; "COMDLG32.OCX"
Object = "{6B7E6392-850A-101B-AFC0-4210102A8DA7}#1.1#0"; "COMCTL32.OCX"
Object = "{48E59290-9880-11CF-9754-00AA00C00908}#1.0#0"; "MSINET.OCX"
Object = "{3B7C8863-D78F-101B-B9B5-04021C009402}#1.1#0"; "RICHTX32.OCX"
Begin VB.Form frmMain
    Caption         =   "FTPer"
    ClientHeight    =   4890
    ClientLeft      =   165
    ClientTop       =   735
    ClientWidth     =   4680
    LinkTopic       =   "Form1"
    ScaleHeight     =   4890
    ScaleWidth      =   4680
    StartUpPosition =   3   'Windows Default
    Begin ComctlLib.Toolbar tbToolBar
```

```
Align           =   1  'Align Top
Height          =   420
Left            =   0
TabIndex        =   1
Top             =   0
Width           =   4680
_ExtentX        =   8255
_ExtentY        =   741
ButtonWidth     =   635
ButtonHeight    =   582
Appearance      =   1
ImageList       =   "imlIcons"
BeginProperty Buttons {7791BA41-E020-11CF-8E74-00A0C90F26F8}
   NumButtons    =   17
   BeginProperty Button1 {7791BA43-E020-11CF-8E74-00A0C90F26F8}
      Key              =   "New"
      Object.ToolTipText    =   "New"
      Object.Tag            =   ""
      ImageIndex       =   1
   EndProperty
   BeginProperty Button2 {7791BA43-E020-11CF-8E74-00A0C90F26F8}
      Key              =   "Open"
      Object.ToolTipText    =   "Open"
      Object.Tag            =   ""
      ImageIndex       =   2
   EndProperty
   BeginProperty Button3 {7791BA43-E020-11CF-8E74-00A0C90F26F8}
      Key              =   "Save"
      Object.ToolTipText    =   "Save"
      Object.Tag            =   ""
      ImageIndex       =   3
   EndProperty
   BeginProperty Button4 {7791BA43-E020-11CF-8E74-00A0C90F26F8}
      Object.Tag            =   ""
      Style            =   3
   EndProperty
   BeginProperty Button5 {7791BA43-E020-11CF-8E74-00A0C90F26F8}
      Key              =   "Print"
      Object.ToolTipText    =   "Print"
```

```
      Object.Tag              =      ""
      ImageIndex       =      4
EndProperty
BeginProperty Button6 {7791BA43-E020-11CF-8E74-00A0C90F26F8}
      Object.Tag              =      ""
      Style            =      3
EndProperty
BeginProperty Button7 {7791BA43-E020-11CF-8E74-00A0C90F26F8}
      Key              =      "Cut"
      Object.ToolTipText      =      "Cut"
      Object.Tag              =      ""
      ImageIndex       =      5
EndProperty
BeginProperty Button8 {7791BA43-E020-11CF-8E74-00A0C90F26F8}
      Key              =      "Copy"
      Object.ToolTipText      =      "Copy"
      Object.Tag              =      ""
      ImageIndex       =      6
EndProperty
BeginProperty Button9 {7791BA43-E020-11CF-8E74-00A0C90F26F8}
      Key              =      "Paste"
      Object.ToolTipText      =      "Paste"
      Object.Tag              =      ""
      ImageIndex       =      7
EndProperty
BeginProperty Button10 {7791BA43-E020-11CF-8E74-00A0C90F26F8}
      Object.Tag              =      ""
      Style            =      3
EndProperty
BeginProperty Button11 {7791BA43-E020-11CF-8E74-00A0C90F26F8}
      Key              =      "Bold"
      Object.ToolTipText      =      "Bold"
      Object.Tag              =      ""
      ImageIndex       =      8
EndProperty
BeginProperty Button12 {7791BA43-E020-11CF-8E74-00A0C90F26F8}
      Key              =      "Italic"
      Object.ToolTipText      =      "Italic"
      Object.Tag              =      ""
```

```
                  ImageIndex    =    9
               EndProperty
               BeginProperty Button13 {7791BA43-E020-11CF-8E74-00A0C90F26F8}
                  Key              =    "Underline"
                  Object.ToolTipText    =    "Underline"
                  Object.Tag            =    ""
                  ImageIndex       =    10
               EndProperty
               BeginProperty Button14 {7791BA43-E020-11CF-8E74-00A0C90F26F8}
                  Object.Tag            =    ""
                  Style            =    3
               EndProperty
               BeginProperty Button15 {7791BA43-E020-11CF-8E74-00A0C90F26F8}
                  Key              =    "Left"
                  Object.ToolTipText    =    "Left Justify"
                  Object.Tag            =    ""
                  ImageIndex       =    11
               EndProperty
               BeginProperty Button16 {7791BA43-E020-11CF-8E74-00A0C90F26F8}
                  Key              =    "Center"
                  Object.ToolTipText    =    "Center"
                  Object.Tag            =    ""
                  ImageIndex       =    12
               EndProperty
               BeginProperty Button17 {7791BA43-E020-11CF-8E74-00A0C90F26F8}
                  Key              =    "Right"
                  Object.ToolTipText    =    "Right Justify"
                  Object.Tag            =    ""
                  ImageIndex       =    13
               EndProperty
            EndProperty
         End
         Begin VB.ListBox List1
            Height         =    675
            Left           =    360
            TabIndex       =    3
            Top            =    1320
            Width          =    3975
         End
```

```
Begin MSComDlg.CommonDialog dlgCommonDialog
   Left             =    2880
   Top              =    600
   _ExtentX         =    847
   _ExtentY         =    847
   FontSize         =    1.87198e-37
End
Begin ComctlLib.StatusBar sbStatusBar
   Align            =    2   'Align Bottom
   Height           =    270
   Left             =    0
   TabIndex         =    0
   Top              =    4620
   Width            =    4680
   _ExtentX         =    8255
   _ExtentY         =    476
   SimpleText       =    ""
   BeginProperty Panels {2C787A51-E01C-11CF-8E74-00A0C90F26F8}
      NumPanels     =    3
      BeginProperty Panel1 {2C787A53-E01C-11CF-8E74-00A0C90F26F8}
         AutoSize      =    1
         Object.Width          =    2619
         MinWidth      =    2540
         Text          =    "Status"
         TextSave      =    "Status"
         Object.Tag            =    ""
      EndProperty
      BeginProperty Panel2 {2C787A53-E01C-11CF-8E74-00A0C90F26F8}
         Style         =    6
         AutoSize      =    2
         Object.Width          =    2540
         MinWidth      =    2540
         TextSave      =    "12/4/96"
         Object.Tag            =    ""
      EndProperty
      BeginProperty Panel3 {2C787A53-E01C-11CF-8E74-00A0C90F26F8}
         Style         =    5
         AutoSize      =    2
         Object.Width          =    2540
```

```
                    MinWidth         =    2540
                    TextSave         =    "3:06 PM"
                    Object.Tag              =    ""
                EndProperty
            EndProperty
            BeginProperty Font {0BE35203-8F91-11CE-9DE3-00AA004BB851}
                Name             =    "MS Sans Serif"
                Size             =    8.25
                Charset          =    0
                Weight           =    400
                Underline        =    0    'False
                Italic           =    0    'False
                Strikethrough    =    0    'False
            EndProperty
        End
        Begin InetCtlsObjects.Inet Inet1
            Left             =    1200
            Top              =    480
            _ExtentX         =    1005
            _ExtentY         =    1005
        End
        Begin RichTextLib.RichTextBox RichTextBox1
            Height           =    2175
            Left             =    360
            TabIndex         =    2
            Top              =    2400
            Width            =    3975
            _ExtentX         =    7011
            _ExtentY         =    3836
            ScrollBars       =    3
            TextRTF          =    $"frmMain.frx":0000
        End
        Begin VB.Label Label2
            Caption          =    "Text:"
            Height           =    495
            Left             =    360
            TabIndex         =    5
            Top              =    2160
            Width            =    1215
```

```
End
Begin VB.Label label1
   Caption         =   "Text Files:"
   Height          =   495
   Left            =   360
   TabIndex        =   4
   Top             =   1080
   Width           =   1215
End
Begin ComctlLib.ImageList imlIcons
   Left            =   2040
   Top             =   480
   _ExtentX        =   1005
   _ExtentY        =   1005
   BackColor       =   -2147483643
   ImageWidth      =   16
   ImageHeight     =   16
   MaskColor       =   12632256
   BeginProperty Images {8556BCD1-E01E-11CF-8E74-00A0C90F26F8}
      NumListImages   =   13
      BeginProperty ListImage1 {8556BCD3-E01E-11CF-8E74-00A0C90F26F8}
         Picture         =   "frmMain.frx":00F7
         Key             =   ""
      EndProperty
      BeginProperty ListImage2 {8556BCD3-E01E-11CF-8E74-00A0C90F26F8}
         Picture         =   "frmMain.frx":0449
         Key             =   ""
      EndProperty
      BeginProperty ListImage3 {8556BCD3-E01E-11CF-8E74-00A0C90F26F8}
         Picture         =   "frmMain.frx":079B
         Key             =   ""
      EndProperty
      BeginProperty ListImage4 {8556BCD3-E01E-11CF-8E74-00A0C90F26F8}
         Picture         =   "frmMain.frx":0AED
         Key             =   ""
      EndProperty
      BeginProperty ListImage5 {8556BCD3-E01E-11CF-8E74-00A0C90F26F8}
         Picture         =   "frmMain.frx":0E3F
         Key             =   ""
```

```
            EndProperty
            BeginProperty ListImage6 {8556BCD3-E01E-11CF-8E74-00A0C90F26F8}
                Picture         =       "frmMain.frx":1191
                Key             =       ""
            EndProperty
            BeginProperty ListImage7 {8556BCD3-E01E-11CF-8E74-00A0C90F26F8}
                Picture         =       "frmMain.frx":14E3
                Key             =       ""
            EndProperty
            BeginProperty ListImage8 {8556BCD3-E01E-11CF-8E74-00A0C90F26F8}
                Picture         =       "frmMain.frx":1835
                Key             =       ""
            EndProperty
            BeginProperty ListImage9 {8556BCD3-E01E-11CF-8E74-00A0C90F26F8}
                Picture         =       "frmMain.frx":1B87
                Key             =       ""
            EndProperty
            BeginProperty ListImage10 {8556BCD3-E01E-11CF-8E74-
                                       00A0C90F26F8}
                Picture         =       "frmMain.frx":1ED9
                Key             =       ""
            EndProperty
            BeginProperty ListImage11 {8556BCD3-E01E-11CF-8E74-
                                       00A0C90F26F8}
                Picture         =       "frmMain.frx":222B
                Key             =       ""
            EndProperty
            BeginProperty ListImage12 {8556BCD3-E01E-11CF-8E74-
                                       00A0C90F26F8}
                Picture         =       "frmMain.frx":257D
                Key             =       ""
            EndProperty
            BeginProperty ListImage13 {8556BCD3-E01E-11CF-8E74-
                                       00A0C90F26F8}
                Picture         =       "frmMain.frx":28CF
                Key             =       ""
            EndProperty
        EndProperty
    End
    Begin VB.Menu mnuFile
```

```
Caption        =   "&File"
Begin VB.Menu mnuFileNew
   Caption      =   "&New"
   Shortcut     =   ^N
End
Begin VB.Menu mnuFileOpen
   Caption      =   "&Open"
   Shortcut     =   ^O
End
Begin VB.Menu mnuFileClose
   Caption      =   "&Close"
End
Begin VB.Menu Getfile
   Caption      =   "Get File"
End
Begin VB.Menu mnuFileBar1
   Caption      =   "-"
End
Begin VB.Menu mnuFileSave
   Caption      =   "&Save"
   Shortcut     =   ^S
End
Begin VB.Menu mnuFileSaveAs
   Caption      =   "Save &As..."
End
Begin VB.Menu mnuFileSaveAll
   Caption      =   "Save A&ll"
End
Begin VB.Menu mnuFileBar2
   Caption      =   "-"
End
Begin VB.Menu mnuFileProperties
   Caption      =   "Propert&ies"
End
Begin VB.Menu mnuFileBar3
   Caption      =   "-"
End
Begin VB.Menu mnuFilePageSetup
   Caption      =   "Page Set&up..."
```

```
         End
         Begin VB.Menu mnuFilePrintPreview
            Caption         =   "Print Pre&view"
         End
         Begin VB.Menu mnuFilePrint
            Caption         =   "&Print..."
            Shortcut        =   ^P
         End
         Begin VB.Menu mnuFileBar4
            Caption         =   "-"
         End
         Begin VB.Menu mnuFileSend
            Caption         =   "Sen&d..."
         End
         Begin VB.Menu mnuFileBar5
            Caption         =   "-"
         End
         Begin VB.Menu mnuFileMRU
            Caption         =   ""
            Index           =   0
            Visible         =   0   'False
         End
         Begin VB.Menu mnuFileMRU
            Caption         =   ""
            Index           =   1
            Visible         =   0   'False
         End
         Begin VB.Menu mnuFileMRU
            Caption         =   ""
            Index           =   2
            Visible         =   0   'False
         End
         Begin VB.Menu mnuFileMRU
            Caption         =   ""
            Index           =   3
            Visible         =   0   'False
         End
         Begin VB.Menu mnuFileBar6
            Caption         =   "-"
```

```
        Visible         =   0    'False
    End
    Begin VB.Menu mnuFileExit
        Caption         =   "E&xit"
    End
End
Begin VB.Menu mnuEdit
    Caption         =   "&Edit"
    Begin VB.Menu mnuEditUndo
        Caption         =   "&Undo"
        Shortcut        =   ^Z
    End
    Begin VB.Menu mnuEditBar1
        Caption         =   "-"
    End
    Begin VB.Menu mnuEditCut
        Caption         =   "Cu&t"
        Shortcut        =   ^X
    End
    Begin VB.Menu mnuEditCopy
        Caption         =   "&Copy"
        Shortcut        =   ^C
    End
    Begin VB.Menu mnuEditPaste
        Caption         =   "&Paste"
        Shortcut        =   ^V
    End
    Begin VB.Menu mnuEditPasteSpecial
        Caption         =   "Paste &Special..."
    End
End
Begin VB.Menu mnuHelp
    Caption         =   "&Help"
    Begin VB.Menu mnuHelpContents
        Caption         =   "&Contents"
    End
    Begin VB.Menu mnuHelpSearch
        Caption         =   "&Search For Help On..."
    End
```

```
      Begin VB.Menu mnuHelpBar1
         Caption         =    "-"
      End
      Begin VB.Menu mnuHelpAbout
         Caption         =    "&About FTPer..."
      End
   End
End
Attribute VB_Name = "frmMain"
Attribute VB_GlobalNameSpace = False
Attribute VB_Creatable = False
Attribute VB_PredeclaredId = True
Attribute VB_Exposed = False
Private Declare Function OSWinHelp% Lib "user32" Alias "WinHelpA"
(ByVal hwnd&, ByVal HelpFile$, ByVal wCommand%, dwData As Any)

Private Sub Form_Load()
    Dim DirectoryText
    Me.Left = GetSetting(App.Title, "Settings", "MainLeft", 1000)
    Me.Top = GetSetting(App.Title, "Settings", "MainTop", 1000)
    Me.Width = GetSetting(App.Title, "Settings", "MainWidth", 6500)
    Me.Height = GetSetting(App.Title, "Settings", "MainHeight", 6500)

    DirectoryText = Inet1.OpenURL("ftp://ftp.microsoft.com")
    DirectoryTextLength = Len(DirectoryText)
    StringEnd = InStr(DirectoryText, ".txt""")
    While (StringEnd <> 0)
        StringLength = 0
        While (InStr(StringEnd - StringLength, Left(DirectoryText,
        StringEnd), """") = 0)
            StringLength = StringLength + 1
        Wend
        StringLength = StringLength - 1
        List1.AddItem Mid(DirectoryText, StringEnd - StringLength + 1,
        StringLength - 1) + ".txt"
        DirectoryText = Right(DirectoryText, DirectoryTextLength -
        StringEnd)
        DirectoryTextLength = DirectoryTextLength - StringEnd
        StringEnd = InStr(DirectoryText, ".txt""")
```

```vb
        Wend

End Sub

Private Sub Form_Unload(Cancel As Integer)
    If Me.WindowState <> vbMinimized Then
        SaveSetting App.Title, "Settings", "MainLeft", Me.Left
        SaveSetting App.Title, "Settings", "MainTop", Me.Top
        SaveSetting App.Title, "Settings", "MainWidth", Me.Width
        SaveSetting App.Title, "Settings", "MainHeight", Me.Height
    End If
End Sub

Private Sub Getfile_Click()
    Dim binarydata() As Byte

    binarydata() = Inet1.OpenURL("ftp://ftp.microsoft.com/LS-LR.zip",
    icByteArray)

    Open "E:\vb\LS-LR.zip" For Binary Access Write As #1
    Put #1, , binarydata()
    Close #1
    MsgBox "Finished."

End Sub

Private Sub List1_Click()
    RichTextBox1.Text = Inet1.OpenURL("ftp://ftp.microsoft.com/" + L
    ist1.Text)
End Sub

Private Sub mnuHelpAbout_Click()
    'To Do
    MsgBox "About Box Code goes here!"
End Sub

Private Sub tbToolBar_ButtonClick(ByVal Button As ComctlLib.Button)

    Select Case Button.Key
```

```
        Case "New"
            mnuFileNew_Click
        Case "New"
            mnuFileNew_Click
        Case "Open"
            mnuFileOpen_Click
        Case "Save"
            mnuFileSave_Click
        Case "Print"
            mnuFilePrint_Click
        Case "Cut"
            mnuEditCut_Click
        Case "Copy"
            mnuEditCopy_Click
        Case "Paste"
            mnuEditPaste_Click
        Case "Bold"
            'To Do
            MsgBox "Bold Code goes here!"
        Case "Italic"
            'To Do
            MsgBox "Italic Code goes here!"
        Case "Underline"
            'To Do
            MsgBox "Underline Code goes here!"
        Case "Left"
            'To Do
            MsgBox "Left Code goes here!"
        Case "Center"
            'To Do
            MsgBox "Center Code goes here!"
        Case "Right"
            'To Do
            MsgBox "Right Code goes here!"
    End Select
End Sub

Private Sub mnuHelpContents_Click()
```

```vb
    Dim nRet As Integer

    'if there is no helpfile for this project display a message to t
    'he user you can set the HelpFile for your application in the
    'Project Properties dialog
    If Len(App.HelpFile) = 0 Then
        MsgBox "Unable to display Help Contents. There is no Help
        associated with this project.", vbInformation, Me.Caption
    Else
        On Error Resume Next
        nRet = OSWinHelp(Me.hwnd, App.HelpFile, 3, 0)
        If Err Then
            MsgBox Err.Description
        End If
    End If
End Sub


Private Sub mnuHelpSearch_Click()

    Dim nRet As Integer

    'if there is no helpfile for this project display a message to
    'the user you can set the HelpFile for your application in the
    'Project Properties dialog
    If Len(App.HelpFile) = 0 Then
        MsgBox "Unable to display Help Contents. There is no Help
        associated with this project.", vbInformation, Me.Caption
    Else
        On Error Resume Next
        nRet = OSWinHelp(Me.hwnd, App.HelpFile, 261, 0)
        If Err Then
            MsgBox Err.Description
        End If
    End If
End Sub


Private Sub mnuEditCopy_Click()
    'To Do
    MsgBox "Copy Code goes here!"
End Sub
```

```
Private Sub mnuEditCut_Click()
    'To Do
    MsgBox "Cut Code goes here!"
End Sub


Private Sub mnuEditPaste_Click()
    'To Do
    MsgBox "Paste Code goes here!"
End Sub


Private Sub mnuEditPasteSpecial_Click()
    'To Do
    MsgBox "Paste Special Code goes here!"
End Sub


Private Sub mnuEditUndo_Click()
    'To Do
    MsgBox "Undo Code goes here!"
End Sub


Private Sub mnuFileOpen_Click()
    Dim sFile As String

    With dlgCommonDialog
        'To Do
        'set the flags and attributes of the
        'common dialog control
        .Filter = "All Files (*.*)|*.*"
        .ShowOpen
        If Len(.filename) = 0 Then
            Exit Sub
        End If
        sFile = .filename
    End With
    'To Do
    'process the opened file
End Sub


Private Sub mnuFileClose_Click()
```

```vb
        'To Do
        MsgBox "Close Code goes here!"
End Sub

Private Sub mnuFileSave_Click()
        'To Do
        MsgBox "Save Code goes here!"
End Sub

Private Sub mnuFileSaveAs_Click()
        'To Do
        'Set up the common dialog control
        'prior to calling ShowSave
        dlgCommonDialog.ShowSave
End Sub

Private Sub mnuFileSaveAll_Click()
        'To Do
        MsgBox "Save All Code goes here!"
End Sub

Private Sub mnuFileProperties_Click()
        'To Do
        MsgBox "Properties Code goes here!"
End Sub

Private Sub mnuFilePageSetup_Click()
        dlgCommonDialog.ShowPrinter
End Sub

Private Sub mnuFilePrintPreview_Click()
        'To Do
        MsgBox "Print Preview Code goes here!"
End Sub

Private Sub mnuFilePrint_Click()
        'To Do
        MsgBox "Print Code goes here!"
End Sub
```

```
Private Sub mnuFileSend_Click()
    'To Do
    MsgBox "Send Code goes here!"
End Sub

Private Sub mnuFileMRU_Click(Index As Integer)
    'To Do
    MsgBox "MRU Code goes here!"
End Sub

Private Sub mnuFileExit_Click()
    'unload the form
    Unload Me
End Sub

Private Sub mnuFileNew_Click()
    'To Do
    MsgBox "New File Code goes here!"
End Sub
```

We've explored the FTP protocol, and we've seen how powerful it is. The Internet Transfer control also supports the HTTP protocol, and we'll look into that next.

Using HTTP from Visual Basic

As with the FTP protocol, we can use either the Execute() method or the OpenURL() method with the HTTP protocol. Using the Execute() method, we can use the HTTP GET, HEAD (get header), POST, and PUT commands. These commands appear in Table 3.3. You can also use the secure Web protocol, HTTPS, with the Internet Transfer control; just use that prefix instead of http in the URL of the document you want to establish a secure link to: "https://www.microsoft.com." In this way, you can open a secure Web session (if the user's Web browser supports secure sessions).

Table 3.3 HTTP Commands of the Internet Transfer Control's Execute Method

Command	Does This
GET	Gets the file named in URL (e.g., Execute "http://www.server.com/index.htm", "GET").
HEAD	Gets headers of file given in URL property (e.g., Execute , "HEAD").
POST	Provides additional data to support request to host (e.g., Execute , "POST", strFormData).
PUT	Replaces data at URL (e.g., Execute , "PUT", "new.htm").

Downloading Text HTTP Data

Let's use the HTTP protocol in a program. We'll download the Microsoft Visual Basic Web page itself using the HTTP protocol. This page is named default.htm, and it resides at http://www.microsoft.com/vbasic. Let's name this new program HTTPer. Create that project in Visual Basic, making it an SDI program with the Application Wizard. Then add a rich text box (RichTextbox1) and an Internet Transfer control (Inet1) as we did in the previous example, FTPer:

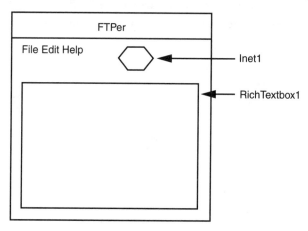

Now we add a new item to the File menu—**Get File**—using the Visual Basic Menu Editor. When the user clicks this item, we'll download the HTML of the Visual Basic Web page. As with FTPer, place this item after the **Close** item in the File menu and give it the name **GetFile**. Now open that item's click event handler:

```
Private Sub GetFile_Click()

End Sub
```

To get the Visual Basic Web page, we use OpenURL() as we have before in this chapter. Because the URL we are opening is prefaced http:, OpenURL() will use the HTTP protocol. We open the Web page and place its text into our rich text box this way:

```
Private Sub GetFile_Click()

-> RichTextBox1.Text =
        Inet1.OpenURL("http://www.microsoft.com/vbasic/default.htm")
        .

        .

        .

End Sub
```

That's all there is to it. Now we can download HTML files using the HTTP protocol. When we run our program, the result appears in Figure 3.3.

Figure 3.3 Downloading the microsoft.com Visual Basic Web page.

We can also download binary data using OpenURL(), and we'll take a look at that now.

Downloading Binary HTTP Data

Let's say that we want to download a file named **image.jpg** at http://www.server.com/museums. We can do that with the Internet Transfer control, as you might expect. We fill a binary array with the data from the binary file and pass the icByteArray parameter to OpenURL() to indicate that we are downloading binary data:

```
Private Sub GetFile_Click()

-> Dim binarydata() As Byte

    RichTextBox1.Text =
        Inet1.OpenURL("http://www.microsoft.com/vbasic/default.htm")

-> binarydata() =
```

```
Inet1.OpenURL("http://www.server.com/museums/image.jpg",
icByteArray)
        .
        .
        .


End Sub
```

Now that the file has been loaded into the binary array, we store the file on disk:

```
Private Sub GetFile_Click()

    Dim binarydata() As Byte

    RichTextBox1.Text =
        Inet1.OpenURL("http://www.microsoft.com/vbasic/default.htm")

    binarydata() =
        Inet1.OpenURL("http://www.server.com/museums/image.jpg",
        icByteArray)

--> Open "E:\vb\image.jpg" For Binary Access Write As #1
--> Put #1, , binarydata()
--> Close #1
        .
        .
        .


End Sub
```

Finally, let's put a message box on the screen indicating that we have finished our downloading operations. (This code would be placed in the Internet Transfer control's StateChanged event handler if you were using the asynchronous Execute method.)

```
Private Sub GetFile_Click()

    Dim binarydata() As Byte
    RichTextBox1.Text =
```

```
        Inet1.OpenURL("http://www.microsoft.com/vbasic/default.htm")
    binarydata() =
        Inet1.OpenURL("http://www.server.com/museums/image.jpg",
        icByteArray)

    Open "E:\vb\image.jpg" For Binary Access Write As #1
    Put #1, , binarydata()
    Close #1

->  MsgBox "Finished."

End Sub
```

Now we can download binary files as well as text files. Using the Internet Transfer control, the process is easy: we just use OpenURL() or the Execute() method, and Visual Basic handles the rest. The code for the HTTPer project appears in Listing 3.2.

Listing 3.2 (HTTPer) FrmMain.frm

```
VERSION 5.00
Object = "{F9043C88-F6F2-101A-A3C9-08002B2F49FB}#1.1#0"; "COMDLG32.OCX"
Object = "{6B7E6392-850A-101B-AFC0-4210102A8DA7}#1.1#0"; "COMCTL32.OCX"
Object = "{48E59290-9880-11CF-9754-00AA00C00908}#1.0#0"; "MSINET.OCX"
Object = "{3B7C8863-D78F-101B-B9B5-04021C009402}#1.1#0"; "RICHTX32.OCX"
Begin VB.Form frmMain
   Caption         =   "HTTPer"
   ClientHeight    =   4050
   ClientLeft      =   165
   ClientTop       =   735
   ClientWidth     =   6315
   LinkTopic       =   "Form1"
   ScaleHeight     =   4050
   ScaleWidth      =   6315
   StartUpPosition =   3  'Windows Default
   Begin ComctlLib.Toolbar tbToolBar
      Align        =   1  'Align Top
      Height       =   420
      Left         =   0
```

```
TabIndex        =   1
Top             =   0
Width           =   6315
_ExtentX        =   11139
_ExtentY        =   741
ButtonWidth     =   635
ButtonHeight    =   582
Appearance      =   1
ImageList       =   "imlIcons"
BeginProperty Buttons {7791BA41-E020-11CF-8E74-00A0C90F26F8}
   NumButtons     =   17
   BeginProperty Button1 {7791BA43-E020-11CF-8E74-00A0C90F26F8}
      Key                  =   "New"
      Object.ToolTipText       =   "New"
      Object.Tag               =   ""
      ImageIndex       =   1
   EndProperty
   BeginProperty Button2 {7791BA43-E020-11CF-8E74-00A0C90F26F8}
      Key                  =   "Open"
      Object.ToolTipText       =   "Open"
      Object.Tag               =   ""
      ImageIndex       =   2
   EndProperty
   BeginProperty Button3 {7791BA43-E020-11CF-8E74-00A0C90F26F8}
      Key                  =   "Save"
      Object.ToolTipText       =   "Save"
      Object.Tag               =   ""
      ImageIndex       =   3
   EndProperty
   BeginProperty Button4 {7791BA43-E020-11CF-8E74-00A0C90F26F8}
      Object.Tag               =   ""
      Style            =   3
   EndProperty
   BeginProperty Button5 {7791BA43-E020-11CF-8E74-00A0C90F26F8}
      Key              =   "Print"
      Object.ToolTipText       =   "Print"
      Object.Tag               =   ""
      ImageIndex       =   4
   EndProperty
```

```
BeginProperty Button6 {7791BA43-E020-11CF-8E74-00A0C90F26F8}
    Object.Tag           =    ""
    Style           =    3
EndProperty
BeginProperty Button7 {7791BA43-E020-11CF-8E74-00A0C90F26F8}
    Key             =    "Cut"
    Object.ToolTipText    =    "Cut"
    Object.Tag           =    ""
    ImageIndex      =    5
EndProperty
BeginProperty Button8 {7791BA43-E020-11CF-8E74-00A0C90F26F8}
    Key             =    "Copy"
    Object.ToolTipText    =    "Copy"
    Object.Tag           =    ""
    ImageIndex      =    6
EndProperty
BeginProperty Button9 {7791BA43-E020-11CF-8E74-00A0C90F26F8}
    Key             =    "Paste"
    Object.ToolTipText    =    "Paste"
    Object.Tag           =    ""
    ImageIndex      =    7
EndProperty
BeginProperty Button10 {7791BA43-E020-11CF-8E74-00A0C90F26F8}
    Object.Tag           =    ""
    Style           =    3
EndProperty
BeginProperty Button11 {7791BA43-E020-11CF-8E74-00A0C90F26F8}
    Key             =    "Bold"
    Object.ToolTipText    =    "Bold"
    Object.Tag           =    ""
    ImageIndex      =    8
EndProperty
BeginProperty Button12 {7791BA43-E020-11CF-8E74-00A0C90F26F8}
    Key             =    "Italic"
    Object.ToolTipText    =    "Italic"
    Object.Tag           =    ""
    ImageIndex      =    9
EndProperty
BeginProperty Button13 {7791BA43-E020-11CF-8E74-00A0C90F26F8}
```

```
                Key              =    "Underline"
                Object.ToolTipText      =    "Underline"
                Object.Tag              =    ""
                ImageIndex       =    10
            EndProperty
            BeginProperty Button14 {7791BA43-E020-11CF-8E74-00A0C90F26F8}
                Object.Tag              =    ""
                Style            =    3
            EndProperty
            BeginProperty Button15 {7791BA43-E020-11CF-8E74-00A0C90F26F8}
                Key              =    "Left"
                Object.ToolTipText      =    "Left Justify"
                Object.Tag              =    ""
                ImageIndex       =    11
            EndProperty
            BeginProperty Button16 {7791BA43-E020-11CF-8E74-00A0C90F26F8}
                Key              =    "Center"
                Object.ToolTipText      =    "Center"
                Object.Tag              =    ""
                ImageIndex       =    12
            EndProperty
            BeginProperty Button17 {7791BA43-E020-11CF-8E74-00A0C90F26F8}
                Key              =    "Right"
                Object.ToolTipText      =    "Right Justify"
                Object.Tag              =    ""
                ImageIndex       =    13
            EndProperty
        EndProperty
    End
    Begin ComctlLib.StatusBar sbStatusBar
        Align            =    2 'Align Bottom
        Height           =    270
        Left             =    0
        TabIndex         =    0
        Top              =    3780
        Width            =    6315
        _ExtentX         =    11139
        _ExtentY         =    476
        SimpleText       =    ""
```

```
BeginProperty Panels {2C787A51-E01C-11CF-8E74-00A0C90F26F8}
    NumPanels       =   3
    BeginProperty Panel1 {2C787A53-E01C-11CF-8E74-00A0C90F26F8}
        AutoSize        =   1
        Object.Width        =   5503
        MinWidth        =   2540
        Text            =   "Status"
        TextSave        =   "Status"
        Object.Tag          =   ""
    EndProperty
    BeginProperty Panel2 {2C787A53-E01C-11CF-8E74-00A0C90F26F8}
        Style           =   6
        AutoSize        =   2
        Object.Width        =   2540
        MinWidth        =   2540
        TextSave        =   "12/4/96"
        Object.Tag          =   ""
    EndProperty
    BeginProperty Panel3 {2C787A53-E01C-11CF-8E74-00A0C90F26F8}
        Style           =   5
        AutoSize        =   2
        Object.Width        =   2540
        MinWidth        =   2540
        TextSave        =   "9:25 PM"
        Object.Tag          =   ""
    EndProperty
EndProperty
BeginProperty Font {0BE35203-8F91-11CE-9DE3-00AA004BB851}
    Name            =   "MS Sans Serif"
    Size            =   8.25
    Charset         =   0
    Weight          =   400
    Underline       =   0   'False
    Italic          =   0   'False
    Strikethrough   =   0   'False
EndProperty
End
Begin MSComDlg.CommonDialog dlgCommonDialog
    Left            =   1740
```

```
      Top              =    1350
      _ExtentX         =    847
      _ExtentY         =    847
      FontSize         =    1.87933e-37
   End
   Begin InetCtlsObjects.Inet Inet1
      Left             =    2040
      Top              =    1320
      _ExtentX         =    1005
      _ExtentY         =    1005
   End
   Begin RichTextLib.RichTextBox RichTextBox1
      Height           =    3135
      Left             =    120
      TabIndex         =    2
      Top              =    600
      Width            =    6015
      _ExtentX         =    10610
      _ExtentY         =    5530
      ScrollBars       =    3
      TextRTF          =    $"frmMain.frx":0000
   End
   Begin ComctlLib.ImageList imlIcons
      Left             =    1740
      Top              =    1350
      _ExtentX         =    1005
      _ExtentY         =    1005
      BackColor        =    -2147483643
      ImageWidth       =    16
      ImageHeight      =    16
      MaskColor        =    12632256
      BeginProperty Images {8556BCD1-E01E-11CF-8E74-00A0C90F26F8}
         NumListImages   =    13
         BeginProperty ListImage1 {8556BCD3-E01E-11CF-8E74-00A0C90F26F8}
            Picture          =    "frmMain.frx":00D2
            Key              =    ""
         EndProperty
         BeginProperty ListImage2 {8556BCD3-E01E-11CF-8E74-00A0C90F26F8}
            Picture          =    "frmMain.frx":0424
```

```
        Key              =    ""
    EndProperty
    BeginProperty ListImage3 {8556BCD3-E01E-11CF-8E74-00A0C90F26F8}
        Picture          =    "frmMain.frx":0776
        Key              =    ""
    EndProperty
    BeginProperty ListImage4 {8556BCD3-E01E-11CF-8E74-00A0C90F26F8}
        Picture          =    "frmMain.frx":0AC8
        Key              =    ""
    EndProperty
    BeginProperty ListImage5 {8556BCD3-E01E-11CF-8E74-00A0C90F26F8}
        Picture          =    "frmMain.frx":0E1A
        Key              =    ""
    EndProperty
    BeginProperty ListImage6 {8556BCD3-E01E-11CF-8E74-00A0C90F26F8}
        Picture          =    "frmMain.frx":116C
        Key              =    ""
    EndProperty
    BeginProperty ListImage7 {8556BCD3-E01E-11CF-8E74-00A0C90F26F8}
        Picture          =    "frmMain.frx":14BE
        Key              =    ""
    EndProperty
    BeginProperty ListImage8 {8556BCD3-E01E-11CF-8E74-00A0C90F26F8}
        Picture          =    "frmMain.frx":1810
        Key              =    ""
    EndProperty
    BeginProperty ListImage9 {8556BCD3-E01E-11CF-8E74-00A0C90F26F8}
        Picture          =    "frmMain.frx":1B62
        Key              =    ""
    EndProperty
    BeginProperty ListImage10 {8556BCD3-E01E-11CF-8E74-
                            00A0C90F26F8}
        Picture          =    "frmMain.frx":1EB4
        Key              =    ""
    EndProperty
    BeginProperty ListImage11 {8556BCD3-E01E-11CF-8E74-
                            00A0C90F26F8}
        Picture          =    "frmMain.frx":2206
        Key              =    ""
```

```
            EndProperty
            BeginProperty ListImage12 {8556BCD3-E01E-11CF-8E74-
                              00A0C90F26F8}
                Picture         =   "frmMain.frx":2558
                Key             =   ""
            EndProperty
            BeginProperty ListImage13 {8556BCD3-E01E-11CF-8E74-
                              00A0C90F26F8}
                Picture         =   "frmMain.frx":28AA
                Key             =   ""
            EndProperty
         EndProperty
      End
      Begin VB.Menu mnuFile
         Caption         =   "&File"
         Begin VB.Menu mnuFileNew
            Caption         =   "&New"
            Shortcut        =   ^N
         End
         Begin VB.Menu mnuFileOpen
            Caption         =   "&Open"
            Shortcut        =   ^O
         End
         Begin VB.Menu mnuFileClose
            Caption         =   "&Close"
         End
         Begin VB.Menu GetFile
            Caption         =   "Get File"
         End
         Begin VB.Menu mnuFileBar1
            Caption         =   "-"
         End
         Begin VB.Menu mnuFileSave
            Caption         =   "&Save"
            Shortcut        =   ^S
         End
         Begin VB.Menu mnuFileSaveAs
            Caption         =   "Save &As..."
         End
```

```
Begin VB.Menu mnuFileSaveAll
   Caption        =   "Save A&ll"
End
Begin VB.Menu mnuFileBar2
   Caption        =   "-"
End
Begin VB.Menu mnuFileProperties
   Caption        =   "Propert&ies"
End
Begin VB.Menu mnuFileBar3
   Caption        =   "-"
End
Begin VB.Menu mnuFilePageSetup
   Caption        =   "Page Set&up..."
End
Begin VB.Menu mnuFilePrintPreview
   Caption        =   "Print Pre&view"
End
Begin VB.Menu mnuFilePrint
   Caption        =   "&Print..."
   Shortcut       =   ^P
End
Begin VB.Menu mnuFileBar4
   Caption        =   "-"
End
Begin VB.Menu mnuFileSend
   Caption        =   "Sen&d..."
End
Begin VB.Menu mnuFileBar5
   Caption        =   "-"
End
Begin VB.Menu mnuFileMRU
   Caption        =   ""
   Index          =   0
   Visible        =   0   'False
End
Begin VB.Menu mnuFileMRU
   Caption        =   ""
   Index          =   1
```

```
            Visible        =   0    'False
         End
         Begin VB.Menu mnuFileMRU
            Caption        =   ""
            Index          =   2
            Visible        =   0    'False
         End
         Begin VB.Menu mnuFileMRU
            Caption        =   ""
            Index          =   3
            Visible        =   0    'False
         End
         Begin VB.Menu mnuFileBar6
            Caption        =   "-"
            Visible        =   0    'False
         End
         Begin VB.Menu mnuFileExit
            Caption        =   "E&xit"
         End
      End
      Begin VB.Menu mnuEdit
         Caption        =   "&Edit"
         Begin VB.Menu mnuEditUndo
            Caption        =   "&Undo"
            Shortcut       =   ^Z
         End
         Begin VB.Menu mnuEditBar1
            Caption        =   "-"
         End
         Begin VB.Menu mnuEditCut
            Caption        =   "Cu&t"
            Shortcut       =   ^X
         End
         Begin VB.Menu mnuEditCopy
            Caption        =   "&Copy"
            Shortcut       =   ^C
         End
         Begin VB.Menu mnuEditPaste
            Caption        =   "&Paste"
```

```
            Shortcut        =    ^V
         End
         Begin VB.Menu mnuEditPasteSpecial
            Caption         =    "Paste &Special..."
         End
      End
      Begin VB.Menu mnuHelp
         Caption          =    "&Help"
         Begin VB.Menu mnuHelpContents
            Caption         =    "&Contents"
         End
         Begin VB.Menu mnuHelpSearch
            Caption         =    "&Search For Help On..."
         End
         Begin VB.Menu mnuHelpBar1
            Caption         =    "-"
         End
         Begin VB.Menu mnuHelpAbout
            Caption         =    "&About HTTPer..."
         End
      End
   End
End
Attribute VB_Name = "frmMain"
Attribute VB_GlobalNameSpace = False
Attribute VB_Creatable = False
Attribute VB_PredeclaredId = True
Attribute VB_Exposed = False
Private Declare Function OSWinHelp% Lib "user32" Alias "WinHelpA"
(ByVal hwnd&, ByVal HelpFile$, ByVal wCommand%, dwData As Any)
Private Sub Form_Load()
    Me.Left = GetSetting(App.Title, "Settings", "MainLeft", 1000)
    Me.Top = GetSetting(App.Title, "Settings", "MainTop", 1000)
    Me.Width = GetSetting(App.Title, "Settings", "MainWidth", 6500)
    Me.Height = GetSetting(App.Title, "Settings", "MainHeight", 6500)
End Sub

Private Sub Form_Unload(Cancel As Integer)
    If Me.WindowState <> vbMinimized Then
        SaveSetting App.Title, "Settings", "MainLeft", Me.Left
```

```
            SaveSetting App.Title, "Settings", "MainTop", Me.Top
            SaveSetting App.Title, "Settings", "MainWidth", Me.Width
            SaveSetting App.Title, "Settings", "MainHeight", Me.Height
        End If
End Sub


Private Sub GetFile_Click()

    Dim binarydata() As Byte
    RichTextBox1.Text =
        Inet1.OpenURL("http://www.microsoft.com/vbasic/default.htm")
    binarydata() =
        Inet1.OpenURL("http://www.server.com/museums/image.jpg",
        icByteArray)

    Open "E:\vb\image.jpg" For Binary Access Write As #1
    Put #1, , binarydata()
    Close #1

    MsgBox "Finished."

End Sub


Private Sub mnuHelpAbout_Click()
    'To Do
    MsgBox "About Box Code goes here!"
End Sub


Private Sub tbToolBar_ButtonClick(ByVal Button As ComctlLib.Button)

    Select Case Button.Key

        Case "New"
            mnuFileNew_Click
        Case "New"
            mnuFileNew_Click
        Case "Open"
            mnuFileOpen_Click
        Case "Save"
            mnuFileSave_Click
```

```
            Case "Print"
                mnuFilePrint_Click
            Case "Cut"
                mnuEditCut_Click
            Case "Copy"
                mnuEditCopy_Click
            Case "Paste"
                mnuEditPaste_Click
            Case "Bold"
                'To Do
                MsgBox "Bold Code goes here!"
            Case "Italic"
                'To Do
                MsgBox "Italic Code goes here!"
            Case "Underline"
                'To Do
                MsgBox "Underline Code goes here!"
            Case "Left"
                'To Do
                MsgBox "Left Code goes here!"
            Case "Center"
                'To Do
                MsgBox "Center Code goes here!"
            Case "Right"
                'To Do
                MsgBox "Right Code goes here!"
        End Select
End Sub


Private Sub mnuHelpContents_Click()

    Dim nRet As Integer

    'if there is no helpfile for this project display a message to
     the user
    'you can set the HelpFile for your application in the
    'Project Properties dialog
    If Len(App.HelpFile) = 0 Then
```

```
            MsgBox "Unable to display Help Contents. There is no Help
            associated with this project.", vbInformation, Me.Caption
        Else
            On Error Resume Next
            nRet = OSWinHelp(Me.hwnd, App.HelpFile, 3, 0)
            If Err Then
                MsgBox Err.Description
            End If
        End If
    End Sub


    Private Sub mnuHelpSearch_Click()

        Dim nRet As Integer

        'if there is no helpfile for this project display a message to
        the user
        'you can set the HelpFile for your application in the
        'Project Properties dialog
        If Len(App.HelpFile) = 0 Then
            MsgBox "Unable to display Help Contents. There is no Help
            associated with this project.", vbInformation, Me.Caption
        Else
            On Error Resume Next
            nRet = OSWinHelp(Me.hwnd, App.HelpFile, 261, 0)
            If Err Then
                MsgBox Err.Description
            End If
        End If
    End Sub


    Private Sub mnuEditCopy_Click()
        'To Do
        MsgBox "Copy Code goes here!"
    End Sub


    Private Sub mnuEditCut_Click()
        'To Do
        MsgBox "Cut Code goes here!"
    End Sub
```

```vb
Private Sub mnuEditPaste_Click()
    'To Do
    MsgBox "Paste Code goes here!"
End Sub

Private Sub mnuEditPasteSpecial_Click()
    'To Do
    MsgBox "Paste Special Code goes here!"
End Sub

Private Sub mnuEditUndo_Click()
    'To Do
    MsgBox "Undo Code goes here!"
End Sub

Private Sub mnuFileOpen_Click()
    Dim sFile As String

    With dlgCommonDialog
        'To Do
        'set the flags and attributes of the
        'common dialog control
        .Filter = "All Files (*.*)|*.*"
        .ShowOpen
        If Len(.filename) = 0 Then
            Exit Sub
        End If
        sFile = .filename
    End With
    'To Do
    'process the opened file
End Sub

Private Sub mnuFileClose_Click()
    'To Do
    MsgBox "Close Code goes here!"
End Sub

Private Sub mnuFileSave_Click()
```

```
        'To Do
        MsgBox "Save Code goes here!"
End Sub

Private Sub mnuFileSaveAs_Click()
        'To Do
        'Set up the common dialog control
        'prior to calling ShowSave
        dlgCommonDialog.ShowSave
End Sub

Private Sub mnuFileSaveAll_Click()
        'To Do
        MsgBox "Save All Code goes here!"
End Sub

Private Sub mnuFileProperties_Click()
        'To Do
        MsgBox "Properties Code goes here!"
End Sub

Private Sub mnuFilePageSetup_Click()
        dlgCommonDialog.ShowPrinter
End Sub

Private Sub mnuFilePrintPreview_Click()
        'To Do
        MsgBox "Print Preview Code goes here!"
End Sub

Private Sub mnuFilePrint_Click()
        'To Do
        MsgBox "Print Code goes here!"
End Sub

Private Sub mnuFileSend_Click()
        'To Do
        MsgBox "Send Code goes here!"
End Sub
```

```
Private Sub mnuFileMRU_Click(Index As Integer)
    'To Do
    MsgBox "MRU Code goes here!"
End Sub

Private Sub mnuFileExit_Click()
    'unload the form
    Unload Me
End Sub

Private Sub mnuFileNew_Click()
    'To Do
    MsgBox "New File Code goes here!"
End Sub
```

That's it for our coverage of the FTP and HTTP protocols for the moment. In this chapter we've worked with powerful methods of interacting with the Internet using these protocols. We've discussed the Execute() method, FTP commands such as CD, MKDIR, GET, PUT, and DIR, and the HTTP commands GET, HEAD, POST, and PUT, as well as the OpenURL() method, which handles a great many of the details. In the next chapter, we'll continue our exploration of Visual Basic on the Internet when we turn to email.

CHAPTER 4

VB ON THE INTERNET: EMAIL

In this chapter, we'll take a look at working with email in Visual Basic programs. Using the email support in Visual Basic, you can read email, send email, compose email messages, save, copy, and delete messages, display an address book, read and send attachments, forward email, and more. These functions are performed by the Messaging Application Program Interface (MAPI) controls that we'll add to our Visual Basic programs.

There are two MAPI controls: MAPISession and MAPIMessages. The MAPISession control establishes an email session, and the MAPIMessages control works with individual email messages in that session. The MAPI controls work with the underlying email system of your computer, and here we'll use the Microsoft Exchange email system, which comes with Windows. (It is reasonable to expect that your users will also have Microsoft Exchange.) We'll begin by making sure that Microsoft Exchange is set up for Internet Mail.

Setting Up Internet Mail

The underlying email system installed on the user's computer does the actual work, as directed by the MAPI controls. For this reason, you should make sure that you have Microsoft Exchange set up for Internet Mail before working with the examples in this chapter. In Windows 95, open the Control Panel and double-click the **Mail and Fax** icon there, opening the MS Exchange Properties Settings dialog box. Then select the **Services** tab. If Internet Mail is one of the services listed in the Services dialog box, you're already set up. If it is not there, click the **Add** button to open the Add Service to Profile dialog box and click the **Internet Mail** entry. This opens the Internet Mail dialog box, as shown in Figure 4.1. Here you fill out the information about your Internet service provider, including your account name and password. Click **OK**.

Figure 4.1 Setting up Internet mail.

For the purposes of this chapter, we will assume that Microsoft Exchange is set up only for Internet mail this way and not for Microsoft mail or any other option. (Otherwise, you must make sure that you are set up to receive Microsoft Mail and any other types you specify; here, we'll look only at Internet mail.)

As before, if you are using a modem, you must also have a connection set up to your ISP so that the connection can be made. To do that in Windows 95, double-click the **My Computer** icon on the desktop and then open the **Dial-up Networking** icon. To add a new connection, double-click the **Make New Connection** icon and follow the directions there.

The MAPI controls are centered around the computer's Inbox; the **Inbox** icon appears on the Windows desktop. The MAPISession control, for example, automatically downloads any new email to the Inbox when it establishes a connection with your ISP. After your email is downloaded to the Inbox, you double-click the **Inbox** icon on the desktop to read it. (You can also fetch email from the Inbox in your Visual Basic program using the MAPIMessages control, as we'll see.)

Now that we know our email system is set up, let's start working with email in our Visual Basic programs.

Our eMailer Application

Our first example will be called eMailer:

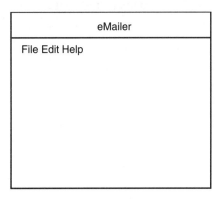

With this program, we can check email and download it as well as compose and send email. We can even perform another function with eMailer:

many programs allow the user to "register" with the click of the mouse, and we'll do that, too. We will set up eMailer to send a prewritten registration message to our email address; to register, all the user must do is to click a **Register Now** item in the Help menu. This action will send the message to us automatically, including the user's name and email address so that we can register him or her.

Using the Visual Basic Application Wizard, create a new SDI application named eMailer. This is the example program that we will add email capabilities to, so add the two MAPI controls that we'll need—MAPISession and MAPIMessages—by selecting the **Components** item of the Visual Basic Project menu. Select the entry marked **Microsoft MAPI Control 5.0** and click **OK**. Next, double-click each icon of these new controls in the toolbox, adding two new controls to our application: MAPISession1 and MAPIMessages1. Now we're ready to go; we will start by checking the user's email from eMailer.

Checking Email

Many applications are becoming Internet-aware even if they have little to do with the Internet. You can browse the Web from many word-processing programs, and we've already seen how to add a Web browser to our programs. In much the same way, we'll add email capabilities to our eMailer example. To start, let's let users check their email.

We'll use the MAPISession control. Add a new item, **Check email**, in eMailer's File menu. Use the Visual Basic Menu Editor and give the new item the name **email**:

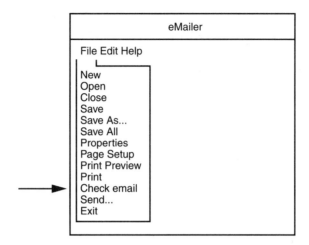

Now click the new menu item to open its click event:

```
Private Sub email_Click()

End Sub
```

Using the MAPISession Control

We begin by setting the MAPISession control's DownLoadMail property to True so that we will download mail when we establish a MAPI session:

```
Private Sub email_Click()
-> MAPISession1.DownLoadMail = True
        .
        .
        .


End Sub
```

The MAPISession control has only two methods: SignOn and SignOff. These are the methods you use to connect to the computer's email system and from there to the Internet. To check the user's email, we need only establish an email session with the MAPISession control. If the user's computer is not currently connected to the Internet, the email system automatically makes the connection. All we have to do is to establish an email session with our MAPISession1 control:

```
Private Sub email_Click()
    MAPISession1.DownLoadMail = True
-> MAPISession1.SignOn
      .
      .
      .


End Sub
```

At this point, the connection is made to the Internet (if necessary) and the user's email (if any) is downloaded into the Inbox. If you want to fetch the messages from the Inbox and display them, you can use the MAPIMessages control, as we'll see later.

There is always the possibility of error when a user signs on to an ISP, so we check for errors using the Err keyword:

```
Private Sub email_Click()
    MAPISession1.DownLoadMail = True
    MAPISession1.SignOn
-> If Err <> 0 Then
->     MsgBox "Logon Failure: " + Error$
-> End If
      .
      .
      .

End Sub
```

If there has been an error, we report that to the user and send the Visual Basic error message that we get from the Error$ function.

Now that the email has been downloaded into the Inbox, we quit the MAPI session using the MAPISession control's SignOff method:

```
Private Sub email_Click()
    MAPISession1.DownLoadMail = True
    MAPISession1.SignOn
    If Err <> 0 Then
        MsgBox "Logon Failure: " + Error$
    End If
-> MAPISession1.SignOff

End Sub
```

It's as simple as that to check the user's email. It's also worth noting that although the MAPISession control has a UserName property and a Password property, the user usually sets them in the Internet Mail dialog box when setting up the email system, so it's not usually necessary to include them here. If the connection is refused, Microsoft Exchange will ask the user to enter the user name and password again in any case, and it stores that information.

Now let's use the MAPIMessages control to send email.

Sending Email

To send email, we'll add a new item to the File menu: **Send email...**. There is already a **Send...** item in the File menu for sending files:

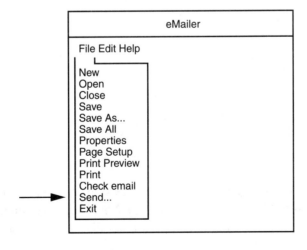

We change that to **Send email...** in the Menu Editor:

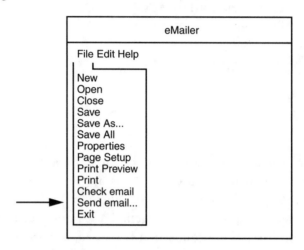

Now let's add the ability to send email to our program. Click the **Send email...** item to open its click event:

```
Private Sub mnuFileSend_Click()

End Sub
```

We start by creating a MAPI session, as we did when we checked email:

```
Private Sub mnuFileSend_Click()
-> MAPISession1.SignOn
-> If Err <> 0 Then
->     MsgBox "Logon Failure: " + Error$
-> End If
         .
         .
         .
End Sub
```

Now we want to compose a new email message and send it. To do that, we will use the MAPIMessage1 control; the MAPISession1 control is used to establish an email session and to automatically download new email, and the MAPIMessages1 control is used to work with individual messages, including examining the text in incoming messages and composing new messages. To connect the MAPIMessages control to our new MAPI session, we load the MAPI session ID into the MAPIMessages SessionID property. We get the session ID from the MAPISession control's SessionID property:

```
Private Sub mnuFileSend_Click()
    MAPISession1.SignOn
    If Err <> 0 Then
        MsgBox "Logon Failure: " + Error$
    End If
-> MAPIMessages1.SessionID = MAPISession1.SessionID
    .
    .
    .

End Sub
```

Now the MAPIMessages1 control is connected to our MAPI session.

The MAPIMessages control is an *indexed* control; its methods appear in Table 4.1, and its important properties appear in Table 4.2.

Table 4.1 MAPIMessages Control Email Operations

Do This	Method	Action Method Constant (Obsolete)
Get email from Inbox	Fetch	MESSAGE_FETCH
Send email with Compose box	Send	MESSAGE_SENDDLG
Send email	Send	MESSAGE_SEND
Save a message	Save	MESSAGE_SAVEMSG
Copy message for reply	Copy	MESSAGE_COPY
Compose email	Compose	MESSAGE_COMPOSE
Reply to a message	Reply	MESSAGE_REPLY

Table 4.1 MAPIMessages Control Email Operations (continued)

Do This	Method	Action Method Constant (Obsolete)
Reply to all messages	ReplyAll	MESSAGE_REPLYALL
Forward a message	Forward	MESSAGE_FORWARD
Delete a message	Delete	MESSAGE_DELETE
Show address book	Show	MESSAGE_SHOWAD-BOOK
Show message details	Show	MESSAGE_SHOWDETAILS
Resolve recipient name	ResolveName	MESSAGE_RESOLVE-NAME
Delete recipient	Delete	RECIPIENT_DELETE
Delete attachment	Delete	ATTACHMENT_DELETE

Table 4.2 MAPIMessages Control Email Properties

Property	Does This
Action Property	Obsolete. Performs actions now performed by methods.
AddressCaption	Sets caption of the address book.
AddressEditFieldCount	Sets which address book edit controls to display.
AddressLabel	Sets appearance of "To" edit control in address book.
AddressModifiable	Sets whether address book can be modified by user.
AttachmentCount	Gets total number of attachments for current message.
AttachmentIndex	Set currently indexed attachment.

Table 4.2 MAPIMessages Control Email Properties (continued)

Property	Does This
AttachmentName	Sets the name of the currently indexed attachment.
AttachmentPathName	Sets full path name of the currently indexed attachment.
AttachmentPosition	Sets position of indexed attachment in the message body.
AttachmentType	Sets type of currently indexed attachment.
FetchSorted Property	Sets message order when creating message set.
MsgConversationID	Sets the conversation thread identification value.
MsgCount	Gets the total number of messages in message set.
MsgDateReceived	Gets date on which current indexed message was received.
MsgID	Gets string identifier of current message.
MsgIndex	Sets index number of current message.
MsgNoteText	Text of current message.
MsgOrigAddress	Gets email address of originator of current message.
MsgOrigDisplayName	Gets originator's name for current message.
MsgRead	True or False depending on whether message has been read.
MsgReceiptRequested	Indicates if return receipt is requested for message.

Table 4.2 MAPIMessages Control Email Properties (continued)

Property	Does This
MsgSent	Indicates if the message has been sent to mail server.
MsgSubject	Message's subject.
MsgType	Sets type of current message.

To get the messages in the Inbox, we use the MAPIMessage method Fetch. This creates a *message set* in the MAPIMessages control, and you can find out how many messages are in this set using the control's MsgCount property. Then you set the MAPIMessages control's MsgIndex property to point to the various messages in the message set. When a message is selected, you can examine it (and display it to the user) by using the various properties of the MAPIMessages control, such as the MsgOrigDisplayName property, which gives the name of the sender, or *originator*, of the message. You can get the email's subject from the MsgSubject property, the text of the message from the MsgNoteText property, and the date it was received from the MsgDateReceived property. In this way, you can work with the email messages in the computer's Inbox.

The MAPIMessages control also has an Action property, and you can perform standard email operations by setting the Action property to pre-defined constants, as in Table 4.1. However, the Action property is now considered obsolete, and Microsoft recommends use of the MAPIMessages methods, such as Fetch, Compose, and so on.

When we compose a new email message to send, that message is clearly not part of a message set, because it doesn't yet exist. For that reason, we set the MAPIMessages1 control's MsgIndex to –1 (this is necessary when you want to compose a new message):

```
Private Sub mnuFileSend_Click()
    MAPISession1.SignOn
    If Err <> 0 Then
        MsgBox "Logon Failure: " + Error$
    End If
```

```
        MAPIMessages1.SessionID = MAPISession1.SessionID
->  MAPIMessages1.MsgIndex = -1
            .

            .

            .

End Sub
```

To compose the new message, we use the MAPIMessages Compose method:

```
Private Sub mnuFileSend_Click()
    MAPISession1.SignOn
    If Err <> 0 Then
        MsgBox "Logon Failure: " + Error$
    End If
    MAPIMessages1.SessionID = MAPISession1.SessionID
    MAPIMessages1.MsgIndex = -1
->  MAPIMessages1.Compose
        .

        .

        .

End Sub
```

To let the user compose and send an email message, we use the Send method. This method takes an optional parameter that we can set to True or False (the default). Setting it to True places the Compose dialog box on the screen; leaving it False hides that box. We'll set the parameter to True:

```
Private Sub mnuFileSend_Click()
    MAPISession1.SignOn
    If Err <> 0 Then
        MsgBox "Logon Failure: " + Error$
    End If
    MAPIMessages1.SessionID = MAPISession1.SessionID
    MAPIMessages1.MsgIndex = -1
    MAPIMessages1.Compose
->  MAPIMessages1.Send True
        .

        .
```

```
End Sub
```

The preceding code will place the Microsoft Exchange Compose dialog box on the screen:

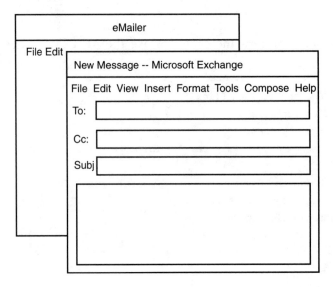

The user then addresses and types the message and clicks the **Send** button, sending the message. All that's left is to sign off from the MAPI session using the MAPISession SignOff method:

```
Private Sub mnuFileSend_Click()
    MAPISession1.SignOn
    If Err <> 0 Then
        MsgBox "Logon Failure: " + Error$
    End If
    MAPIMessages1.SessionID = MAPISession1.SessionID
    MAPIMessages1.MsgIndex = -1
    MAPIMessages1.Compose
    MAPIMessages1.Send True
-> MAPISession1.SignOff
End Sub
```

Run eMailer and select the **Send email...** item in the File menu. The Microsoft Exchange Compose dialog box appears, as shown in Figure 4.2, and you can use it to send email.

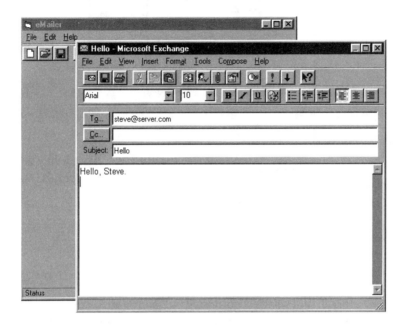

Figure 4.2 Composing and sending email.

At this point, we can send and receive email. Our final goal for eMailer is to let the user register automatically through email with the click of the mouse.

Using Email to Register a User

It's becoming common to let users register their software with the manufacturers online. One way of doing that is through email, where all the details are hidden from users; all they have to do is to click a menu item. Let's add that menu item and give it the caption **Register Now** and the name **Register**; place it in the eMailer Help menu like this:

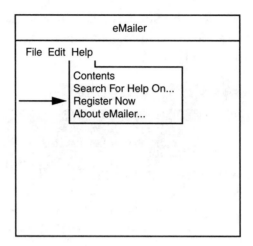

Open the new menu item's click event handler:

```
Private Sub Register_Click()

End Sub
```

In this event handler, we'll compose our own email message and send it without the user's intervention. We begin by starting a new MAPI session as we have done before:

```
Private Sub Register_Click()
-> MAPISession1.SignOn
-> If Err <> 0 Then
->     MsgBox "Logon Failure: " + Error$
-> End If
                .
                .
                .

End Sub
```

Next, we pass the MAPI session ID to the MAPIMessages control:

```
Private Sub Register_Click()
    MAPISession1.SignOn
```

```
    If Err <> 0 Then
        MsgBox "Logon Failure: " + Error$
    End If
->     MAPIMessages1.SessionID = MAPISession1.SessionID
                .
                .
                .

End Sub
```

Now we're ready to compose the new message; we start by setting MAPIMessages1's MsgIndex property to –1, as we did before, and calling the Compose method:

```
Private Sub Register_Click()
    MAPISession1.SignOn
    If Err <> 0 Then
        MsgBox "Logon Failure: " + Error$
    End If
        MAPIMessages1.SessionID = MAPISession1.SessionID
->      MAPIMessages1.MsgIndex = -1
->      MAPIMessages1.Compose
                .
                .
                .

End Sub
```

At this point, we're ready to address our email message. We use the MAPIMessages RecipDisplayName and RecipAddress properties. The RecipAddress property holds the email address where we will send our message. The RecipDisplayName property holds the name of the recipient. We will use the same entry ("VBISoft@server.com") for both properties:

```
Private Sub Register_Click()
    MAPISession1.SignOn
    If Err <> 0 Then
        MsgBox "Logon Failure: " + Error$
    End If
```

```
      MAPIMessages1.SessionID = MAPISession1.SessionID
      MAPIMessages1.MsgIndex = -1
      MAPIMessages1.Compose
->    MAPIMessages1.RecipDisplayName = "VBISoft@server.com"
->    MAPIMessages1.RecipAddress = "VBISoft@server.com"
          .
          .
          .


End Sub
```

If the recipient's name appears in the Microsoft Exchange address book, you can have it converted to an email address using the AddressResolveUI property and the ResolveName method. (You can place entries in the address book by selecting the **Address Book** item of Microsoft Exchange's Tools menu.) We set these properties here (although they are not needed, because we have set the email address) to show how to use them. We set AddressResolveUI to True to have Microsoft Exchange resolve the name from the address book, and we call the ResolveName method:

```
Private Sub Register_Click()
    MAPISession1.SignOn
    If Err <> 0 Then
        MsgBox "Logon Failure: " + Error$
    End If
        MAPIMessages1.SessionID = MAPISession1.SessionID
        MAPIMessages1.MsgIndex = -1
        MAPIMessages1.Compose
        MAPIMessages1.RecipDisplayName = "VBISoft@server.com"
        MAPIMessages1.RecipAddress = "VBISoft@server.com"
->      MAPIMessages1.AddressResolveUI = True
->      MAPIMessages1.ResolveName
            .
            .
            .


End Sub
```

Now we set the subject line of our email to "Registering" by setting the MsgSubject property this way:

```
Private Sub Register_Click()
    MAPISession1.SignOn
    If Err <> 0 Then
        MsgBox "Logon Failure: " + Error$
    End If
        MAPIMessages1.SessionID = MAPISession1.SessionID
        MAPIMessages1.MsgIndex = -1
        MAPIMessages1.Compose
        MAPIMessages1.RecipDisplayName = "VBISoft@server.com"
        MAPIMessages1.RecipAddress = "VBISoft@server.com"
        MAPIMessages1.AddressResolveUI = True
        MAPIMessages1.ResolveName
 ->     MAPIMessages1.MsgSubject = "Registering"
                  .
                  .
                  .


End Sub
```

When we get the email, the Subject line will read "Registering." Next, we set the text of the message using the MsgNoteText property. We set the text to "Normal Registration Message":

```
Private Sub Register_Click()
    MAPISession1.SignOn
    If Err <> 0 Then
        MsgBox "Logon Failure: " + Error$
    End If
        MAPIMessages1.SessionID = MAPISession1.SessionID
        MAPIMessages1.MsgIndex = -1
        MAPIMessages1.Compose
        MAPIMessages1.RecipDisplayName = "VBISoft@server.com"
        MAPIMessages1.RecipAddress = "VBISoft@server.com"
        MAPIMessages1.AddressResolveUI = True
        MAPIMessages1.ResolveName
        MAPIMessages1.MsgSubject = "Registering"
```

```
->    MAPIMessages1.MsgNoteText = "Normal Registration Message"
          .
          .
          .


End Sub
```

The email message is ready to send. We use the Send method, also closing the MAPI session with SignOff:

```
Private Sub Register_Click()
    MAPISession1.SignOn
    If Err <> 0 Then
        MsgBox "Logon Failure: " + Error$
    End If
        MAPIMessages1.SessionID = MAPISession1.SessionID
        MAPIMessages1.MsgIndex = -1
        MAPIMessages1.Compose
        MAPIMessages1.RecipDisplayName = "VBISoft@server.com"
        MAPIMessages1.RecipAddress = "VBISoft@server.com"
        MAPIMessages1.AddressResolveUI = True
        MAPIMessages1.ResolveName
        MAPIMessages1.MsgSubject = "Registering"
        MAPIMessages1.MsgNoteText = "Normal Registration Message"
  ->    MAPIMessages1.Send
  ->    MAPISession1.SignOff


End Sub
```

And that's it—now we can send registration email with the click of the mouse. The code for our eMailer project appears in Listing 4.1.

Listing 4.1 (eMailer) frmMain.frm

```
VERSION 5.00
Object = "{F9043C88-F6F2-101A-A3C9-08002B2F49FB}#1.1#0"; "COMDLG32.OCX"
Object = "{6B7E6392-850A-101B-AFC0-4210102A8DA7}#1.1#0"; "COMCTL32.OCX"
Object = "{48E59290-9880-11CF-9754-00AA00C00908}#1.0#0"; "MSINET.OCX"
Object = "{20C62CAE-15DA-101B-B9A8-444553540000}#1.1#0"; "MSMAPI32.OCX"
```

```
Begin VB.Form frmMain
   Caption         =   "eMailer"
   ClientHeight    =   3195
   ClientLeft      =   165
   ClientTop       =   735
   ClientWidth     =   4680
   LinkTopic       =   "Form1"
   ScaleHeight     =   3195
   ScaleWidth      =   4680
   StartUpPosition =   3  'Windows Default
   Begin ComctlLib.Toolbar tbToolBar
      Align        =   1  'Align Top
      Height       =   1080
      Left         =   0
      TabIndex     =   1
      Top          =   0
      Width        =   4680
      _ExtentX     =   8255
      _ExtentY     =   1905
      Appearance   =   1
      ImageList    =   "imlIcons"
      BeginProperty Buttons {7791BA41-E020-11CF-8E74-00A0C90F26F8}
         NumButtons    =   17
         BeginProperty Button1 {7791BA43-E020-11CF-8E74-00A0C90F26F8}
            Key              =   "New"
            Object.ToolTipText     =   "New"
            Object.Tag             =   ""
            ImageIndex       =   1
         EndProperty
         BeginProperty Button2 {7791BA43-E020-11CF-8E74-00A0C90F26F8}
            Key              =   "Open"
            Object.ToolTipText     =   "Open"
            Object.Tag             =   ""
            ImageIndex       =   2
         EndProperty
         BeginProperty Button3 {7791BA43-E020-11CF-8E74-00A0C90F26F8}
            Key              =   "Save"
            Object.ToolTipText     =   "Save"
            Object.Tag             =   ""
```

```
    ImageIndex      =    3
EndProperty
BeginProperty Button4 {7791BA43-E020-11CF-8E74-00A0C90F26F8}
    Key             =    ""
    Object.Tag            =    ""
    Style           =    3
EndProperty
BeginProperty Button5 {7791BA43-E020-11CF-8E74-00A0C90F26F8}
    Key             =    "Print"
    Object.ToolTipText    =    "Print"
    Object.Tag            =    ""
    ImageIndex      =    4
EndProperty
BeginProperty Button6 {7791BA43-E020-11CF-8E74-00A0C90F26F8}
    Key             =    ""
    Object.Tag            =    ""
    Style           =    3
EndProperty
BeginProperty Button7 {7791BA43-E020-11CF-8E74-00A0C90F26F8}
    Key             =    "Cut"
    Object.ToolTipText    =    "Cut"
    Object.Tag            =    ""
    ImageIndex      =    5
EndProperty
BeginProperty Button8 {7791BA43-E020-11CF-8E74-00A0C90F26F8}
    Key             =    "Copy"
    Object.ToolTipText    =    "Copy"
    Object.Tag            =    ""
    ImageIndex      =    6
EndProperty
BeginProperty Button9 {7791BA43-E020-11CF-8E74-00A0C90F26F8}
    Key             =    "Paste"
    Object.ToolTipText    =    "Paste"
    Object.Tag            =    ""
    ImageIndex      =    7
EndProperty
BeginProperty Button10 {7791BA43-E020-11CF-8E74-00A0C90F26F8}
    Key             =    ""
    Object.Tag            =    ""
```

```
         Style            =    3
   EndProperty
   BeginProperty Button11 {7791BA43-E020-11CF-8E74-00A0C90F26F8}
      Key              =    "Bold"
      Object.ToolTipText     =    "Bold"
      Object.Tag             =    ""
      ImageIndex       =    8
   EndProperty
   BeginProperty Button12 {7791BA43-E020-11CF-8E74-00A0C90F26F8}
      Key              =    "Italic"
      Object.ToolTipText     =    "Italic"
      Object.Tag             =    ""
      ImageIndex       =    9
   EndProperty
   BeginProperty Button13 {7791BA43-E020-11CF-8E74-00A0C90F26F8}
      Key              =    "Underline"
      Object.ToolTipText     =    "Underline"
      Object.Tag             =    ""
      ImageIndex       =    10
   EndProperty
   BeginProperty Button14 {7791BA43-E020-11CF-8E74-00A0C90F26F8}
      Key              =    ""
      Object.Tag             =    ""
      Style            =    3
   EndProperty
   BeginProperty Button15 {7791BA43-E020-11CF-8E74-00A0C90F26F8}
      Key              =    "Left"
      Object.ToolTipText     =    "Left Justify"
      Object.Tag             =    ""
      ImageIndex       =    11
   EndProperty
   BeginProperty Button16 {7791BA43-E020-11CF-8E74-00A0C90F26F8}
      Key              =    "Center"
      Object.ToolTipText     =    "Center"
      Object.Tag             =    ""
      ImageIndex       =    12
   EndProperty
   BeginProperty Button17 {7791BA43-E020-11CF-8E74-00A0C90F26F8}
      Key              =    "Right"
```

```
            Object.ToolTipText    =    "Right Justify"
            Object.Tag            =    ""
            ImageIndex       =    13
         EndProperty
      EndProperty
      MouseIcon        =    "frmMain.frx":0000
   End
   Begin ComctlLib.StatusBar sbStatusBar
      Align            =    2   'Align Bottom
      Height           =    270
      Left             =    0
      TabIndex         =    0
      Top              =    2925
      Width            =    4680
      _ExtentX         =    8255
      _ExtentY         =    476
      SimpleText       =    ""
      BeginProperty Panels {2C787A51-E01C-11CF-8E74-00A0C90F26F8}
         NumPanels       =    3
         BeginProperty Panel1 {2C787A53-E01C-11CF-8E74-00A0C90F26F8}
            AutoSize       =    1
            Object.Width        =    2619
            MinWidth       =    2540
            Text           =    "Status"
            TextSave       =    "Status"
            Key            =    ""
            Object.Tag          =    ""
         EndProperty
         BeginProperty Panel2 {2C787A53-E01C-11CF-8E74-00A0C90F26F8}
            Style          =    6
            AutoSize       =    2
            Object.Width        =    2540
            MinWidth       =    2540
            TextSave       =    "12/4/96"
            Key            =    ""
            Object.Tag          =    ""
         EndProperty
         BeginProperty Panel3 {2C787A53-E01C-11CF-8E74-00A0C90F26F8}
            Style          =    5
```

```
            AutoSize        =    2
            Object.Width            =    2540
            MinWidth        =    2540
            TextSave        =    "2:37 PM"
            Key             =    ""
            Object.Tag              =    ""
        EndProperty
    EndProperty
    BeginProperty Font {0BE35203-8F91-11CE-9DE3-00AA004BB851}
        Name            =    "MS Sans Serif"
        Size            =    8.25
        Charset         =    0
        Weight          =    400
        Underline       =    0    'False
        Italic          =    0    'False
        Strikethrough   =    0    'False
    EndProperty
    MouseIcon       =    "frmMain.frx":001C
End
Begin MSComDlg.CommonDialog dlgCommonDialog
    Left            =    1740
    Top             =    1350
    _ExtentX        =    847
    _ExtentY        =    847
    FontSize        =    1.89257e-37
End
Begin InetCtlsObjects.Inet Inet1
    Left            =    2040
    Top             =    1320
    _ExtentX        =    1005
    _ExtentY        =    1005
End
Begin MSMAPI.MAPISession MAPISession1
    Left            =    2040
    Top             =    1320
    _ExtentX        =    1005
    _ExtentY        =    1005
    DownloadMail    =    -1   'True
    LogonUI         =    -1   'True
```

```
      NewSession      =   0    'False
End
Begin MSMAPI.MAPIMessages MAPIMessages1
   Left              =   2040
   Top               =   1320
   _ExtentX          =   1005
   _ExtentY          =   1005
   AddressEditFieldCount=   1
   AddressModifiable=   0    'False
   AddressResolveUI=   0    'False
   FetchSorted       =   0    'False
   FetchUnreadOnly =   0    'False
End
Begin ComctlLib.ImageList imlIcons
   Left              =   1740
   Top               =   1350
   _ExtentX          =   1005
   _ExtentY          =   1005
   BackColor         =   -2147483643
   ImageWidth        =   16
   ImageHeight       =   16
   MaskColor         =   12632256
   BeginProperty Images {8556BCD1-E01E-11CF-8E74-00A0C90F26F8}
      NumListImages   =   13
      BeginProperty ListImage1 {8556BCD3-E01E-11CF-8E74-
                               00A0C90F26F8}
         Picture          =   "frmMain.frx":0038
         Key              =   ""
      EndProperty
      BeginProperty ListImage2 {8556BCD3-E01E-11CF-8E74-
                               00A0C90F26F8}
         Picture          =   "frmMain.frx":038A
         Key              =   ""
      EndProperty
      BeginProperty ListImage3 {8556BCD3-E01E-11CF-8E74-
                               00A0C90F26F8}
         Picture          =   "frmMain.frx":06DC
         Key              =   ""
      EndProperty
```

```
BeginProperty ListImage4 {8556BCD3-E01E-11CF-8E74-
                          00A0C90F26F8}
   Picture          =    "frmMain.frx":0A2E
   Key              =    ""
EndProperty
BeginProperty ListImage5 {8556BCD3-E01E-11CF-8E74-
                          00A0C90F26F8}
   Picture          =    "frmMain.frx":0D80
   Key              =    ""
EndProperty
BeginProperty ListImage6 {8556BCD3-E01E-11CF-8E74-
                          00A0C90F26F8}
   Picture          =    "frmMain.frx":10D2
   Key              =    ""
EndProperty
BeginProperty ListImage7 {8556BCD3-E01E-11CF-8E74-
                          00A0C90F26F8}
   Picture          =    "frmMain.frx":1424
   Key              =    ""
EndProperty
BeginProperty ListImage8 {8556BCD3-E01E-11CF-8E74-
                          00A0C90F26F8}
   Picture          =    "frmMain.frx":1776
   Key              =    ""
EndProperty
BeginProperty ListImage9 {8556BCD3-E01E-11CF-8E74-
                          00A0C90F26F8}
   Picture          =    "frmMain.frx":1AC8
   Key              =    ""
EndProperty
BeginProperty ListImage10 {8556BCD3-E01E-11CF-8E74-
                          00A0C90F26F8}
   Picture          =    "frmMain.frx":1E1A
   Key              =    ""
EndProperty
BeginProperty ListImage11 {8556BCD3-E01E-11CF-8E74-
                          00A0C90F26F8}
   Picture          =    "frmMain.frx":216C
   Key              =    ""
EndProperty
```

```
        BeginProperty ListImage12 {8556BCD3-E01E-11CF-8E74-
                              00A0C90F26F8}
            Picture           =    "frmMain.frx":24BE
            Key               =    ""
        EndProperty
        BeginProperty ListImage13 {8556BCD3-E01E-11CF-8E74-
                              00A0C90F26F8}
            Picture           =    "frmMain.frx":2810
            Key               =    ""
        EndProperty
    EndProperty
End
Begin VB.Menu mnuFile
    Caption           =    "&File"
    Begin VB.Menu mnuFileNew
        Caption           =    "&New"
        Shortcut          =    ^N
    End
    Begin VB.Menu mnuFileOpen
        Caption           =    "&Open"
        Shortcut          =    ^O
    End
    Begin VB.Menu mnuFileClose
        Caption           =    "&Close"
    End
    Begin VB.Menu mnuFileBar1
        Caption           =    "-"
    End
    Begin VB.Menu mnuFileSave
        Caption           =    "&Save"
        Shortcut          =    ^S
    End
    Begin VB.Menu mnuFileSaveAs
        Caption           =    "Save &As..."
    End
    Begin VB.Menu mnuFileSaveAll
        Caption           =    "Save A&ll"
    End
    Begin VB.Menu mnuFileBar2
```

```
      Caption         =    "-"
End
Begin VB.Menu mnuFileProperties
   Caption         =    "Propert&ies"
End
Begin VB.Menu mnuFileBar3
   Caption         =    "-"
End
Begin VB.Menu mnuFilePageSetup
   Caption         =    "Page Set&up..."
End
Begin VB.Menu mnuFilePrintPreview
   Caption         =    "Print Pre&view"
End
Begin VB.Menu mnuFilePrint
   Caption         =    "&Print..."
   Shortcut        =    ^P
End
Begin VB.Menu mnuFileBar4
   Caption         =    "-"
End
Begin VB.Menu email
   Caption         =    "Check email"
End
Begin VB.Menu mnuFileSend
   Caption         =    "Sen&d email..."
End
Begin VB.Menu mnuFileBar5
   Caption         =    "-"
End
Begin VB.Menu mnuFileMRU
   Caption         =    ""
   Index           =    0
   Visible         =    0    'False
End
Begin VB.Menu mnuFileMRU
   Caption         =    ""
   Index           =    1
   Visible         =    0    'False
```

```
      End
      Begin VB.Menu mnuFileMRU
         Caption         =   ""
         Index           =   2
         Visible         =   0    'False
      End
      Begin VB.Menu mnuFileMRU
         Caption         =   ""
         Index           =   3
         Visible         =   0    'False
      End
      Begin VB.Menu mnuFileBar6
         Caption         =   "-"
         Visible         =   0    'False
      End
      Begin VB.Menu mnuFileExit
         Caption         =   "E&xit"
      End
   End
   Begin VB.Menu mnuEdit
      Caption         =   "&Edit"
      Begin VB.Menu mnuEditUndo
         Caption         =   "&Undo"
         Shortcut        =   ^Z
      End
      Begin VB.Menu mnuEditBar1
         Caption         =   "-"
      End
      Begin VB.Menu mnuEditCut
         Caption         =   "Cu&t"
         Shortcut        =   ^X
      End
      Begin VB.Menu mnuEditCopy
         Caption         =   "&Copy"
         Shortcut        =   ^C
      End
      Begin VB.Menu mnuEditPaste
         Caption         =   "&Paste"
         Shortcut        =   ^V
```

```
            End
        Begin VB.Menu mnuEditPasteSpecial
            Caption        =    "Paste &Special..."
        End
    End
    Begin VB.Menu mnuHelp
        Caption        =    "&Help"
        Begin VB.Menu mnuHelpContents
            Caption        =    "&Contents"
        End
        Begin VB.Menu mnuHelpSearch
            Caption        =    "&Search For Help On..."
        End
        Begin VB.Menu Register
            Caption        =    "Register Now"
        End
        Begin VB.Menu mnuHelpBar1
            Caption        =    "-"
        End
        Begin VB.Menu mnuHelpAbout
            Caption        =    "&About eMailer..."
        End
    End
End
Attribute VB_Name = "frmMain"
Attribute VB_GlobalNameSpace = False
Attribute VB_Creatable = False
Attribute VB_PredeclaredId = True
Attribute VB_Exposed = False
Private Declare Function OSWinHelp% Lib "user32" Alias "WinHelpA"
(ByVal hwnd&, ByVal HelpFile$, ByVal wCommand%, dwData As Any)

Private Sub email_Click()
    MAPISession1.DownLoadMail = True
    MAPISession1.SignOn
    If Err <> 0 Then
        MsgBox "Logon Failure: " + Error$
    End If
        MAPISession1.SignOff
```

```
    End Sub

    Private Sub Form_Load()
        Me.Left = GetSetting(App.Title, "Settings", "MainLeft", 1000)
        Me.Top = GetSetting(App.Title, "Settings", "MainTop", 1000)
        Me.Width = GetSetting(App.Title, "Settings", "MainWidth", 6500)
        Me.Height = GetSetting(App.Title, "Settings", "MainHeight", 6500)
    End Sub

    Private Sub Form_Unload(Cancel As Integer)
        If Me.WindowState <> vbMinimized Then
            SaveSetting App.Title, "Settings", "MainLeft", Me.Left
            SaveSetting App.Title, "Settings", "MainTop", Me.Top
            SaveSetting App.Title, "Settings", "MainWidth", Me.Width
            SaveSetting App.Title, "Settings", "MainHeight", Me.Height
        End If
    End Sub

    Private Sub mnuHelpAbout_Click()
        'To Do
        MsgBox "About Box Code goes here!"
    End Sub

    Private Sub Register_Click()
        MAPISession1.SignOn
        If Err <> 0 Then
            MsgBox "Logon Failure: " + Error$
        End If
        MAPIMessages1.SessionID = MAPISession1.SessionID
        MAPIMessages1.MsgIndex = -1
        MAPIMessages1.Compose
        MAPIMessages1.RecipDisplayName = "VBISoft@server.com"
        MAPIMessages1.RecipAddress = "VBISoft@server.com"
        MAPIMessages1.AddressResolveUI = True
        MAPIMessages1.ResolveName
        MAPIMessages1.MsgSubject = "Registering"
        MAPIMessages1.MsgNoteText = "Normal Registration Message"
        MAPIMessages1.Send
        MAPISession1.SignOff
```

```vb
End Sub

Private Sub tbToolBar_ButtonClick(ByVal Button As ComctlLib.Button)

    Select Case Button.Key

        Case "New"
            mnuFileNew_Click
        Case "New"
            mnuFileNew_Click
        Case "Open"
            mnuFileOpen_Click
        Case "Save"
            mnuFileSave_Click
        Case "Print"
            mnuFilePrint_Click
        Case "Cut"
            mnuEditCut_Click
        Case "Copy"
            mnuEditCopy_Click
        Case "Paste"
            mnuEditPaste_Click
        Case "Bold"
            'To Do
            MsgBox "Bold Code goes here!"
        Case "Italic"
            'To Do
            MsgBox "Italic Code goes here!"
        Case "Underline"
            'To Do
            MsgBox "Underline Code goes here!"
        Case "Left"
            'To Do
            MsgBox "Left Code goes here!"
        Case "Center"
            'To Do
            MsgBox "Center Code goes here!"
        Case "Right"
            'To Do
```

```
            MsgBox "Right Code goes here!"
        End Select
    End Sub


Private Sub mnuHelpContents_Click()

    Dim nRet As Integer

    'if there is no helpfile for this project display a message to the
    'user you can set the HelpFile for your application in the Project
    'Properties dialog
    If Len(App.HelpFile) = 0 Then
        MsgBox "Unable to display Help Contents. There is no Help asso-
        ciated with this project.", vbInformation, Me.Caption
    Else
        On Error Resume Next
        nRet = OSWinHelp(Me.hwnd, App.HelpFile, 3, 0)
        If Err Then
            MsgBox Err.Description
        End If
    End If
End Sub


Private Sub mnuHelpSearch_Click()

    Dim nRet As Integer

    'if there is no helpfile for this project display a message to
    'the user you can set the HelpFile for your application in the
    'Project Properties dialog
    If Len(App.HelpFile) = 0 Then
        MsgBox "Unable to display Help Contents. There is no Help asso-
        ciated with this project.", vbInformation, Me.Caption
    Else
        On Error Resume Next
        nRet = OSWinHelp(Me.hwnd, App.HelpFile, 261, 0)
        If Err Then
            MsgBox Err.Description
        End If
    End If
End Sub
```

```vb
Private Sub mnuEditCopy_Click()
    'To Do
    MsgBox "Copy Code goes here!"
End Sub

Private Sub mnuEditCut_Click()
    'To Do
    MsgBox "Cut Code goes here!"
End Sub

Private Sub mnuEditPaste_Click()
    'To Do
    MsgBox "Paste Code goes here!"
End Sub

Private Sub mnuEditPasteSpecial_Click()
    'To Do
    MsgBox "Paste Special Code goes here!"
End Sub

Private Sub mnuEditUndo_Click()
    'To Do
    MsgBox "Undo Code goes here!"
End Sub

Private Sub mnuFileOpen_Click()
    Dim sFile As String

    With dlgCommonDialog
        'To Do
        'set the flags and attributes of the
        'common dialog control
        .Filter = "All Files (*.*)|*.*"
        .ShowOpen
        If Len(.filename) = 0 Then
            Exit Sub
        End If
        sFile = .filename
    End With
```

```
    'To Do
    'process the opened file
End Sub

Private Sub mnuFileClose_Click()
    'To Do
    MsgBox "Close Code goes here!"
End Sub

Private Sub mnuFileSave_Click()
    'To Do
    MsgBox "Save Code goes here!"
End Sub

Private Sub mnuFileSaveAs_Click()
    'To Do
    'Setup the common dialog control
    'prior to calling ShowSave
    dlgCommonDialog.ShowSave
End Sub

Private Sub mnuFileSaveAll_Click()
    'To Do
    MsgBox "Save All Code goes here!"
End Sub

Private Sub mnuFileProperties_Click()
    'To Do
    MsgBox "Properties Code goes here!"
End Sub

Private Sub mnuFilePageSetup_Click()
    dlgCommonDialog.ShowPrinter
End Sub

Private Sub mnuFilePrintPreview_Click()
    'To Do
    MsgBox "Print Preview Code goes here!"
End Sub
```

```
Private Sub mnuFilePrint_Click()
    'To Do
    MsgBox "Print Code goes here!"
End Sub

Private Sub mnuFileSend_Click()
    MAPISession1.SignOn
    If Err <> 0 Then
        MsgBox "Logon Failure: " + Error$
    End If
    MAPIMessages1.SessionID = MAPISession1.SessionID
    MAPIMessages1.MsgIndex = -1
    MAPIMessages1.Compose
    MAPIMessages1.Send True
    MAPISession1.SignOff
End Sub

Private Sub mnuFileMRU_Click(Index As Integer)
    'To Do
    MsgBox "MRU Code goes here!"
End Sub

Private Sub mnuFileExit_Click()
    'unload the form
    Unload Me
End Sub

Private Sub mnuFileNew_Click()
    'To Do
    MsgBox "New File Code goes here!"
End Sub
```

That's it for our eMailer project. As you can see, the email system that we have access to in Visual Basic is powerful, allowing us to compose, send, receive, and read email. In the next chapter, we'll turn to another powerful part of Visual Basic Internet programming: ActiveX controls.

CHAPTER ·5

CREATING AND USING ACTIVEX CONTROLS

In this chapter, we'll trace the entire process of creating a full ActiveX control complete with properties, events, and built-in methods. We'll also see how to deploy ActiveX controls on the Internet so that users can download them automatically.

What are ActiveX controls? We already have some familiarity with them: for example, the Rich Textbox control we used in Chapter 3 is an ActiveX control. We added the Rich Textbox control to a Visual Basic program by using the **Components** item in the Project menu (you can also right-click the toolbox), which added the Rich Textbox control to the toolbox. (If an ActiveX control is not listed in the Components dialog box, you can install it by clicking the **Browse** button and finding that control's **.ocx** file.) Then we were able to add rich text boxes to our applications with a simple double-click in the toolbox. The ActiveX controls that come with Visual Basic are shown in Table 5.1. You can find more ActiveX controls to download free at http://www.microsoft.com/activex/gallery.

Table 5.1 Visual Basic ActiveX Controls

ActiveX Control	Support File
Animation	ComCt232.ocx
Communications	Mscomm32.ocx
HTML	HTML.ocx
ImageList	Comctl32.ocx
Internet Transfer	MSInet.ocx
ListView	Comctl32.ocx
MAPI	Msmapi32.ocx
Masked edit	Msmask32.ocx
MSFlex Grid	Msflexgrid.ocx
Multimedia MCI	Mci32.ocx
Picture clip	Picclp32.ocx
ProgressBar	Comctl32.ocx
RichTextBox	Richtx32.ocx
Slider	Comctl32.ocx
SSTab	Tabctl32.ocx
StatusBar	Comctl32.ocx
TabStrip	Comctl32.ocx
Toolbar	Comctl32.ocx
TreeView	Comctl32.ocx
UpDown	ComCt232.ocx
Visual Components Chart	VCChart.ocx
Winsock TCP	Winsock.ocx
Winsock UDP	Winsock.ocx

In general, ActiveX controls come in files with the extension **.ocx**.

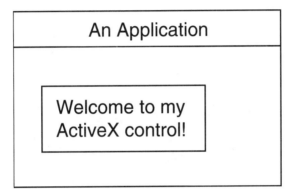

If you have an ActiveX control, you can usually use it in a Visual Basic program:

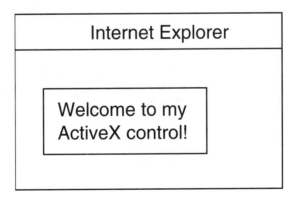

You can also use it in ActiveX-enabled Web browsers such as Internet Explorer:

As you can see, these controls are powerful and versatile. We'll begin by creating our first ActiveX control.

Our First ActiveX Control

For our first ActiveX control, we'll create a small control that displays the text "Hello World!":

> Hello World!

Start Visual Basic and create a new project of type ActiveX control by selecting the **ActiveX Control** icon in the New Project dialog box, as shown in Figure 5.1.

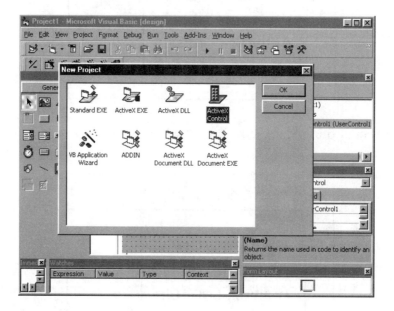

Figure 5.1 Creating our first ActiveX control.

This action opens Visual Basic, as shown in Figure 5.2. As you can see, designing an ActiveX control looks much like designing any other Visual Basic form. The toolbox holds tools that we can add to our control. Controls that we place in an ActiveX control are called *constituent controls*.

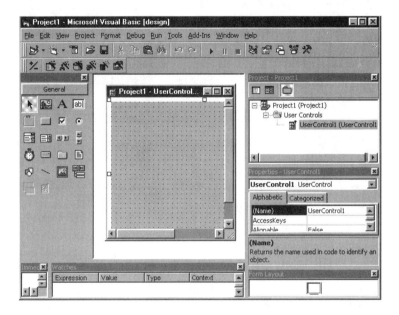

Figure 5.2 Working on our first ActiveX control.

In this first example, we'll place in our ActiveX control a Label control holding the text "Hello World!" Double-click the **Label** control in the toolbox and add the text, as shown in Figure 5.3.

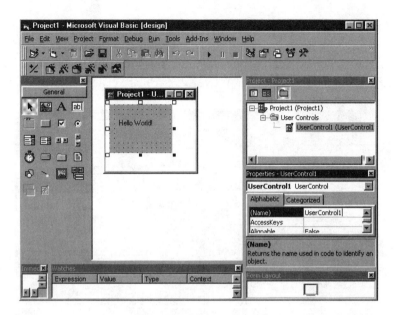

Figure 5.3 Adding a Label control to our ActiveX control.

Visual Basic ActiveX controls are based on the UserControl object. As you can see in the Properties window in Figure 5.3, Visual Basic has named our new ActiveX control UserControl1. This is the name that will be used when the user adds controls of our new ActiveX type to other Visual Basic projects. The first such control will be UserControl1, the second UserControl2, and so on (just as new text box controls are called Text1, Text2, and so on). Because that's a little confusing, let's change the name of our control to FirstX in the properties window. In addition, Visual Basic has named our project Project1; this is the name that will appear in the Components dialog box when the user adds our control. Let's change that to FirstXControl. (The project name is different from the control name, because a project can contain several ActiveX controls.) Double-click the entry marked **Project1** in the project window and set the project's name to **FirstXControl** in the properties window.

Testing Our New ActiveX Control

Visual Basic gives us a convenient way to test the control, as we'll see. First, save your work (you must save an ActiveX project before trying to test or run the control you're creating). After you select the **Save Project As** item in the File menu and select a folder to save the project in, Visual Basic will save the control as **FirstX.ctl** and the project file as **FirstXControl.vbp**. The **.ctl** file is like a **.frm** file for a form; it contains the specification of our new ActiveX control. If there is binary data, such as an image, to be saved in the control, a **.ctx** file will be created, just as an **.frx** file is created along with an **.frm** file.

To test our control, we'll need a Visual Basic project to insert the control into. We'll add a new project to our current ActiveX control project. This new project will be a standard SDI Visual Basic project and, together with the ActiveX project, will form a *project group*.

Let's add the new Visual Basic project now. Select the **Add Project** item in the File menu and select the **VB Application Wizard** icon. In the Application Wizard, create a new SDI application, accepting all the defaults and giving it the name **FirstXTest** in the final Application Wizard box, labeled Finished! This adds the new project, as shown in Figure 5.4. Save all files in the new project group by selecting **Save Project Group As** in the File menu, accepting the default name for all but the group file itself. Call that file **FirstX.vbg**. (The default name is **Group1.vbg**. **.vbg** stands for Visual Basic group.)

Now we're ready to add the FirstX ActiveX control to our new project and see it in action. To do that, close the FirstXControl window that you see in Figure 5.4. The window itself is called a project *designer*, and this is where the control under design appears. By closing this window (temporarily—you can open FirstXControl again by clicking it in the project window), we make the control available to our FirstXTest project.

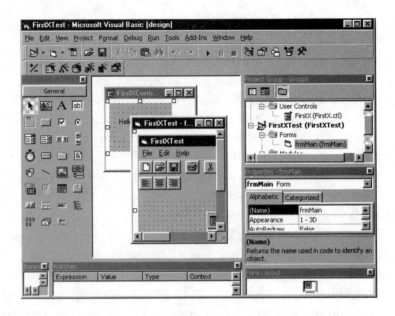

Figure 5.4 Our new application will test our ActiveX control.

Now add the FirstXControl ActiveX control to the FirstXTest project's toolbox. Click the FirstXControl box in the Components dialog box (which you reach by clicking **Components** in the Project menu) and click **OK**. This action adds our new ActiveX control to the FirstXTest toolbox, as shown in Figure 5.5. The icon for our new ActiveX control is indicated with the mouse cursor. (That's the standard default icon for Visual Basic–created ActiveX controls.)

Now double-click the **FirstX** icon in the toolbox to create a new control of that type in FirstXTest's form, as shown in Figure 5.6. As you can see, our "Hello World!" message already appears in our new control, even at design time. You can also see in the properties window that Visual Basic has given this control the name FirstX1.

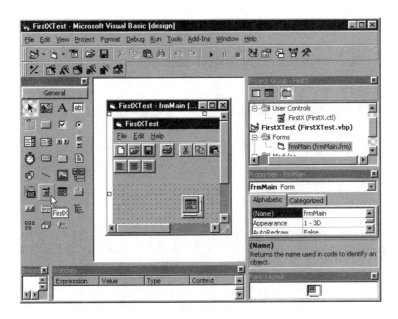

Figure 5.5 Our FirstX ActiveX control in the Visual Basic toolbox.

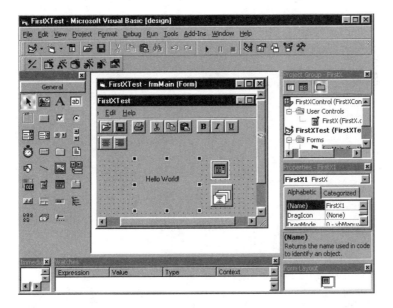

Figure 5.6 Creating a new FirstX control in a Visual Basic project.

Now run the FirstXTest application by selecting the **Start** item in the Run menu. The test project runs, as shown in Figure 5.7, and you can see our first ActiveX control at work. Even though this control is not very exciting, our project is a success.

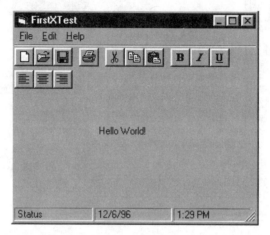

Figure 5.7 Our FirstX ActiveX control at work.

The code for these projects appears in Listing 5.1 (**FirstX.ctl**) and Listing 5.2 (FirstXTest's **FrmMain.frm**).

Listing 5.1 FirstX.ctl

```
VERSION 5.00
Begin VB.UserControl FirstX
    ClientHeight    =    1215
    ClientLeft      =    0
    ClientTop       =    0
    ClientWidth     =    1620
    PropertyPages   =    "FirstX.ctx":0000
    ScaleHeight     =    1215
    ScaleWidth      =    1620
    Begin VB.Label Label1
        Caption     =    "Hello World!"
        Height      =    495
        Left        =    240
```

```
         TabIndex       =    0
         Top            =    360
         Width          =    1215
      End
   End
Attribute VB_Name = "FirstX"
Attribute VB_GlobalNameSpace = False
Attribute VB_Creatable = True
Attribute VB_PredeclaredId = False
Attribute VB_Exposed = True
```

Listing 5.2 (FirstXTest) FrmMain.frm

```
VERSION 5.00
Object = "{F9043C88-F6F2-101A-A3C9-08002B2F49FB}#1.1#0"; "COMDLG32.OCX"
Object = "{6B7E6392-850A-101B-AFC0-4210102A8DA7}#1.1#0"; "COMCTL32.OCX"
Begin VB.Form frmMain
   Caption         =    "FirstXTest"
   ClientHeight    =    3195
   ClientLeft      =    165
   ClientTop       =    735
   ClientWidth     =    4680
   LinkTopic       =    "Form1"
   ScaleHeight     =    3195
   ScaleWidth      =    4680
   StartUpPosition =    3   'Windows Default
   Begin ComctlLib.Toolbar tbToolBar
      Align        =    1   'Align Top
      Height       =    1080
      Left         =    0
      TabIndex     =    1
      Top          =    0
      Width        =    4680
      _ExtentX     =    8255
      _ExtentY     =    1905
      Appearance   =    1
      ImageList    =    "imlIcons"
      BeginProperty Buttons {7791BA41-E020-11CF-8E74-00A0C90F26F8}
```

```
NumButtons      =   17
BeginProperty Button1 {7791BA43-E020-11CF-8E74-00A0C90F26F8}
   Key            =   "New"
   Object.ToolTipText    =   "New"
   Object.Tag        =   ""
   ImageIndex     =   1
EndProperty
BeginProperty Button2 {7791BA43-E020-11CF-8E74-00A0C90F26F8}
   Key            =   "Open"
   Object.ToolTipText    =   "Open"
   Object.Tag        =   ""
   ImageIndex     =   2
EndProperty
BeginProperty Button3 {7791BA43-E020-11CF-8E74-00A0C90F26F8}
   Key            =   "Save"
   Object.ToolTipText    =   "Save"
   Object.Tag        =   ""
   ImageIndex     =   3
EndProperty
BeginProperty Button4 {7791BA43-E020-11CF-8E74-00A0C90F26F8}
   Key            =   ""
   Object.Tag        =   ""
   Style          =   3
EndProperty
BeginProperty Button5 {7791BA43-E020-11CF-8E74-00A0C90F26F8}
   Key            =   "Print"
   Object.ToolTipText    =   "Print"
   Object.Tag        =   ""
   ImageIndex     =   4
EndProperty
BeginProperty Button6 {7791BA43-E020-11CF-8E74-00A0C90F26F8}
   Key            =   ""
   Object.Tag        =   ""
   Style          =   3
EndProperty
BeginProperty Button7 {7791BA43-E020-11CF-8E74-00A0C90F26F8}
   Key            =   "Cut"
   Object.ToolTipText    =   "Cut"
   Object.Tag        =   ""
```

```
         ImageIndex     =   5
EndProperty
BeginProperty Button8 {7791BA43-E020-11CF-8E74-00A0C90F26F8}
   Key            =   "Copy"
   Object.ToolTipText    =     "Copy"
   Object.Tag            =     ""
   ImageIndex     =   6
EndProperty
BeginProperty Button9 {7791BA43-E020-11CF-8E74-00A0C90F26F8}
   Key            =   "Paste"
   Object.ToolTipText    =     "Paste"
   Object.Tag            =     ""
   ImageIndex     =   7
EndProperty
BeginProperty Button10 {7791BA43-E020-11CF-8E74-00A0C90F26F8}
   Key            =   ""
   Object.Tag            =     ""
   Style          =   3
EndProperty
BeginProperty Button11 {7791BA43-E020-11CF-8E74-00A0C90F26F8}
   Key            =   "Bold"
   Object.ToolTipText    =     "Bold"
   Object.Tag            =     ""
   ImageIndex     =   8
EndProperty
BeginProperty Button12 {7791BA43-E020-11CF-8E74-00A0C90F26F8}
   Key            =   "Italic"
   Object.ToolTipText    =     "Italic"
   Object.Tag            =     ""
   ImageIndex     =   9
EndProperty
BeginProperty Button13 {7791BA43-E020-11CF-8E74-00A0C90F26F8}
   Key            =   "Underline"
   Object.ToolTipText    =     "Underline"
   Object.Tag            =     ""
   ImageIndex     =   10
EndProperty
BeginProperty Button14 {7791BA43-E020-11CF-8E74-00A0C90F26F8}
   Key            =   ""
```

```
                    Object.Tag             =     ""
                    Style          =    3
                EndProperty
                BeginProperty Button15 {7791BA43-E020-11CF-8E74-00A0C90F26F8}
                    Key            =     "Left"
                    Object.ToolTipText     =     "Left Justify"
                    Object.Tag             =     ""
                    ImageIndex     =    11
                EndProperty
                BeginProperty Button16 {7791BA43-E020-11CF-8E74-00A0C90F26F8}
                    Key            =     "Center"
                    Object.ToolTipText     =     "Center"
                    Object.Tag             =     ""
                    ImageIndex     =    12
                EndProperty
                BeginProperty Button17 {7791BA43-E020-11CF-8E74-00A0C90F26F8}
                    Key            =     "Right"
                    Object.ToolTipText     =     "Right Justify"
                    Object.Tag             =     ""
                    ImageIndex     =    13
                EndProperty
            EndProperty
        EndProperty
        MouseIcon      =     "frmMain.frx":0000
    End
    Begin MSComDlg.CommonDialog dlgCommonDialog
        Left           =     1740
        Top            =     1350
        _ExtentX       =     847
        _ExtentY       =     847
        FontSize       =     2.54016e-29
    End
    Begin ComctlLib.StatusBar sbStatusBar
        Align          =     2  'Align Bottom
        Height         =     270
        Left           =     0
        TabIndex       =     0
        Top            =     2925
        Width          =     4680
        _ExtentX       =     8255
```

```
_ExtentY        =   476
SimpleText      =   ""
BeginProperty Panels {2C787A51-E01C-11CF-8E74-00A0C90F26F8}
   NumPanels    =   3
   BeginProperty Panel1 {2C787A53-E01C-11CF-8E74-00A0C90F26F8}
      AutoSize      =   1
      Object.Width          =   2619
      MinWidth      =   2540
      Text          =   "Status"
      TextSave      =   "Status"
      Key           =   ""
      Object.Tag            =   ""
   EndProperty
   BeginProperty Panel2 {2C787A53-E01C-11CF-8E74-00A0C90F26F8}
      Style         =   6
      AutoSize      =   2
      Object.Width          =   2540
      MinWidth      =   2540
      TextSave      =   "12/6/96"
      Key           =   ""
      Object.Tag            =   ""
   EndProperty
   BeginProperty Panel3 {2C787A53-E01C-11CF-8E74-00A0C90F26F8}
      Style         =   5
      AutoSize      =   2
      Object.Width          =   2540
      MinWidth      =   2540
      TextSave      =   "12:57 PM"
      Key           =   ""
      Object.Tag            =   ""
   EndProperty
EndProperty
BeginProperty Font {0BE35203-8F91-11CE-9DE3-00AA004BB851}
   Name          =   "MS Sans Serif"
   Size          =   8.25
   Charset       =   0
   Weight        =   400
   Underline     =   0    'False
   Italic        =   0    'False
```

```
       Strikethrough   =   0    'False
    EndProperty
    MouseIcon        =    "frmMain.frx":001C
End
Begin ComctlLib.ImageList imlIcons
    Left             =    1740
    Top              =    1350
    _ExtentX         =    1005
    _ExtentY         =    1005
    BackColor        =    -2147483643
    ImageWidth       =    16
    ImageHeight      =    16
    MaskColor        =    12632256
    BeginProperty Images {8556BCD1-E01E-11CF-8E74-00A0C90F26F8}
       NumListImages  =   13
       BeginProperty ListImage1 {8556BCD3-E01E-11CF-8E74-00A0C90F26F8}
          Picture         =    "frmMain.frx":0038
          Key             =    ""
       EndProperty
       BeginProperty ListImage2 {8556BCD3-E01E-11CF-8E74-00A0C90F26F8}
          Picture         =    "frmMain.frx":038A
          Key             =    ""
       EndProperty
       BeginProperty ListImage3 {8556BCD3-E01E-11CF-8E74-00A0C90F26F8}
          Picture         =    "frmMain.frx":06DC
          Key             =    ""
       EndProperty
       BeginProperty ListImage4 {8556BCD3-E01E-11CF-8E74-00A0C90F26F8}
          Picture         =    "frmMain.frx":0A2E
          Key             =    ""
       EndProperty
       BeginProperty ListImage5 {8556BCD3-E01E-11CF-8E74-00A0C90F26F8}
          Picture         =    "frmMain.frx":0D80
          Key             =    ""
       EndProperty
       BeginProperty ListImage6 {8556BCD3-E01E-11CF-8E74-00A0C90F26F8}
          Picture         =    "frmMain.frx":10D2
          Key             =    ""
       EndProperty
```

```
        BeginProperty ListImage7 {8556BCD3-E01E-11CF-8E74-00A0C90F26F8}
            Picture         =       "frmMain.frx":1424
            Key             =       ""
        EndProperty
        BeginProperty ListImage8 {8556BCD3-E01E-11CF-8E74-00A0C90F26F8}
            Picture         =       "frmMain.frx":1776
            Key             =       ""
        EndProperty
        BeginProperty ListImage9 {8556BCD3-E01E-11CF-8E74-00A0C90F26F8}
            Picture         =       "frmMain.frx":1AC8
            Key             =       ""
        EndProperty
        BeginProperty ListImage10 {8556BCD3-E01E-11CF-8E74-
                            00A0C90F26F8}
            Picture         =       "frmMain.frx":1E1A
            Key             =       ""
        EndProperty
        BeginProperty ListImage11 {8556BCD3-E01E-11CF-8E74-
                            00A0C90F26F8}
            Picture         =       "frmMain.frx":216C
            Key             =       ""
        EndProperty
        BeginProperty ListImage12 {8556BCD3-E01E-11CF-8E74-
                            00A0C90F26F8}
            Picture         =       "frmMain.frx":24BE
            Key             =       ""
        EndProperty
        BeginProperty ListImage13 {8556BCD3-E01E-11CF-8E74-
                            00A0C90F26F8}
            Picture         =       "frmMain.frx":2810
            Key             =       ""
        EndProperty
    EndProperty
End
Begin VB.Menu mnuFile
    Caption         =   "&File"
    Begin VB.Menu mnuFileNew
        Caption         =   "&New"
        Shortcut        =   ^N
    End
```

```
Begin VB.Menu mnuFileOpen
   Caption          =    "&Open"
   Shortcut         =    ^O
End
Begin VB.Menu mnuFileClose
   Caption          =    "&Close"
End
Begin VB.Menu mnuFileBar1
   Caption          =    "-"
End
Begin VB.Menu mnuFileSave
   Caption          =    "&Save"
   Shortcut         =    ^S
End
Begin VB.Menu mnuFileSaveAs
   Caption          =    "Save &As..."
End
Begin VB.Menu mnuFileSaveAll
   Caption          =    "Save A&ll"
End
Begin VB.Menu mnuFileBar2
   Caption          =    "-"
End
Begin VB.Menu mnuFileProperties
   Caption          =    "Propert&ies"
End
Begin VB.Menu mnuFileBar3
   Caption          =    "-"
End
Begin VB.Menu mnuFilePageSetup
   Caption          =    "Page Set&up..."
End
Begin VB.Menu mnuFilePrintPreview
   Caption          =    "Print Pre&view"
End
Begin VB.Menu mnuFilePrint
   Caption          =    "&Print..."
   Shortcut         =    ^P
End
```

```
   Begin VB.Menu mnuFileBar4
      Caption         =   "-"
   End
   Begin VB.Menu mnuFileSend
      Caption         =   "Sen&d..."
   End
   Begin VB.Menu mnuFileBar5
      Caption         =   "-"
   End
   Begin VB.Menu mnuFileMRU
      Caption         =   ""
      Index           =   0
      Visible         =   0   'False
   End
   Begin VB.Menu mnuFileMRU
      Caption         =   ""
      Index           =   1
      Visible         =   0   'False
   End
   Begin VB.Menu mnuFileMRU
      Caption         =   ""
      Index           =   2
      Visible         =   0   'False
   End
   Begin VB.Menu mnuFileMRU
      Caption         =   ""
      Index           =   3
      Visible         =   0   'False
   End
   Begin VB.Menu mnuFileBar6
      Caption         =   "-"
      Visible         =   0   'False
   End
   Begin VB.Menu mnuFileExit
      Caption         =   "E&xit"
   End
End
Begin VB.Menu mnuEdit
   Caption            =   "&Edit"
```

```
         Begin VB.Menu mnuEditUndo
            Caption         =    "&Undo"
            Shortcut        =    ^Z
         End
         Begin VB.Menu mnuEditBar1
            Caption         =    "-"
         End
         Begin VB.Menu mnuEditCut
            Caption         =    "Cu&t"
            Shortcut        =    ^X
         End
         Begin VB.Menu mnuEditCopy
            Caption         =    "&Copy"
            Shortcut        =    ^C
         End
         Begin VB.Menu mnuEditPaste
            Caption         =    "&Paste"
            Shortcut        =    ^V
         End
         Begin VB.Menu mnuEditPasteSpecial
            Caption         =    "Paste &Special..."
         End
      End
      Begin VB.Menu mnuHelp
         Caption         =    "&Help"
         Begin VB.Menu mnuHelpContents
            Caption         =    "&Contents"
         End
         Begin VB.Menu mnuHelpSearch
            Caption         =    "&Search For Help On..."
         End
         Begin VB.Menu mnuHelpBar1
            Caption         =    "-"
         End
         Begin VB.Menu mnuHelpAbout
            Caption         =    "&About FirstXTest..."
         End
      End
   End
End
```

```
Attribute VB_Name = "frmMain"
Attribute VB_GlobalNameSpace = False
Attribute VB_Creatable = False
Attribute VB_PredeclaredId = True
Attribute VB_Exposed = False
Private Declare Function OSWinHelp% Lib "user32" Alias "WinHelpA"
(ByVal hwnd&, ByVal HelpFile$, ByVal wCommand%, dwData As Any)
Private Sub Form_Load()
    Me.Left = GetSetting(App.Title, "Settings", "MainLeft", 1000)
    Me.Top = GetSetting(App.Title, "Settings", "MainTop", 1000)
    Me.Width = GetSetting(App.Title, "Settings", "MainWidth", 6500)
    Me.Height = GetSetting(App.Title, "Settings", "MainHeight", 6500)
End Sub

Private Sub Form_Unload(Cancel As Integer)
    If Me.WindowState <> vbMinimized Then
        SaveSetting App.Title, "Settings", "MainLeft", Me.Left
        SaveSetting App.Title, "Settings", "MainTop", Me.Top
        SaveSetting App.Title, "Settings", "MainWidth", Me.Width
        SaveSetting App.Title, "Settings", "MainHeight", Me.Height
    End If
End Sub

Private Sub mnuHelpAbout_Click()
    'To Do
    MsgBox "About Box Code goes here!"
End Sub

Private Sub tbToolBar_ButtonClick(ByVal Button As ComctlLib.Button)

    Select Case Button.Key

        Case "New"
            mnuFileNew_Click
        Case "New"
            mnuFileNew_Click
        Case "Open"
            mnuFileOpen_Click
        Case "Save"
```

```
                    mnuFileSave_Click
            Case "Print"
                    mnuFilePrint_Click
            Case "Cut"
                    mnuEditCut_Click
            Case "Copy"
                    mnuEditCopy_Click
            Case "Paste"
                    mnuEditPaste_Click
            Case "Bold"
                    'To Do
                    MsgBox "Bold Code goes here!"
            Case "Italic"
                    'To Do
                    MsgBox "Italic Code goes here!"
            Case "Underline"
                    'To Do
                    MsgBox "Underline Code goes here!"
            Case "Left"
                    'To Do
                    MsgBox "Left Code goes here!"
            Case "Center"
                    'To Do
                    MsgBox "Center Code goes here!"
            Case "Right"
                    'To Do
                    MsgBox "Right Code goes here!"
        End Select
    End Sub


Private Sub mnuHelpContents_Click()

    Dim nRet As Integer

    'if there is no helpfile for this project display a message to the
    'user you can set the HelpFile for your application in the
    'Project Properties dialog
    If Len(App.HelpFile) = 0 Then
        MsgBox "Unable to display Help Contents. There is no Help
        associated with this project.", vbInformation, Me.Caption
```

```
    Else
        On Error Resume Next
        nRet = OSWinHelp(Me.hwnd, App.HelpFile, 3, 0)
        If Err Then
            MsgBox Err.Description
        End If
    End If
End Sub


Private Sub mnuHelpSearch_Click()

    Dim nRet As Integer

    'if there is no helpfile for this project display a message to the
    'user you can set the HelpFile for your application in the
    'Project Properties dialog
    If Len(App.HelpFile) = 0 Then
        MsgBox "Unable to display Help Contents. There is no Help
        associated with this project.", vbInformation, Me.Caption
    Else
        On Error Resume Next
        nRet = OSWinHelp(Me.hwnd, App.HelpFile, 261, 0)
        If Err Then
            MsgBox Err.Description
        End If
    End If
End Sub


Private Sub mnuEditCopy_Click()
    'To Do
    MsgBox "Copy Code goes here!"
End Sub


Private Sub mnuEditCut_Click()
    'To Do
    MsgBox "Cut Code goes here!"
End Sub


Private Sub mnuEditPaste_Click()
    'To Do
```

```
        MsgBox "Paste Code goes here!"
    End Sub

    Private Sub mnuEditPasteSpecial_Click()
        'To Do
        MsgBox "Paste Special Code goes here!"
    End Sub

    Private Sub mnuEditUndo_Click()
        'To Do
        MsgBox "Undo Code goes here!"
    End Sub

    Private Sub mnuFileOpen_Click()
        Dim sFile As String

        With dlgCommonDialog
            'To Do
            'set the flags and attributes of the
            'common dialog control
            .Filter = "All Files (*.*)|*.*"
            .ShowOpen
            If Len(.filename) = 0 Then
                Exit Sub
            End If
            sFile = .filename
        End With
        'To Do
        'process the opened file
    End Sub

    Private Sub mnuFileClose_Click()
        'To Do
        MsgBox "Close Code goes here!"
    End Sub

    Private Sub mnuFileSave_Click()
        'To Do
        MsgBox "Save Code goes here!"
```

```
End Sub

Private Sub mnuFileSaveAs_Click()
    'To Do
    'Set up the common dialog control
    'prior to calling ShowSave
    dlgCommonDialog.ShowSave
End Sub

Private Sub mnuFileSaveAll_Click()
    'To Do
    MsgBox "Save All Code goes here!"
End Sub

Private Sub mnuFileProperties_Click()
    'To Do
    MsgBox "Properties Code goes here!"
End Sub

Private Sub mnuFilePageSetup_Click()
    dlgCommonDialog.ShowPrinter
End Sub

Private Sub mnuFilePrintPreview_Click()
    'To Do
    MsgBox "Print Preview Code goes here!"
End Sub

Private Sub mnuFilePrint_Click()
    'To Do
    MsgBox "Print Code goes here!"
End Sub

Private Sub mnuFileSend_Click()
    'To Do
    MsgBox "Send Code goes here!"
End Sub

Private Sub mnuFileMRU_Click(Index As Integer)
```

```
    'To Do
    MsgBox "MRU Code goes here!"
End Sub

Private Sub mnuFileExit_Click()
    'unload the form
    Unload Me
End Sub

Private Sub mnuFileNew_Click()
    'To Do
    MsgBox "New File Code goes here!"
End Sub
```

That's it for our first ActiveX control. However, that's just the beginning. We have yet to explore how to add properties, events, and methods to our ActiveX controls, as well as how to deploy controls on the Internet, not to mention taking a look at Internet security issues. Let's continue by creating a new and more powerful ActiveX control: an alarm clock.

The Clock ActiveX Control

The next ActiveX control we'll create is an alarm clock. We'll display the time like this in our control:

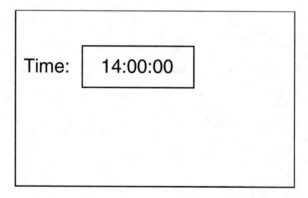

We'll allow the user to set the alarm in a text box:

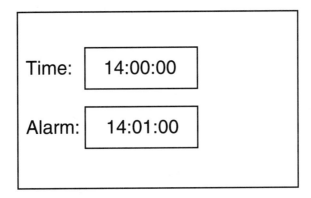

In addition, we'll implement a way to let the user turn the alarm on and off. We'll add two option buttons marked **Alarm On** and **Alarm Off**:

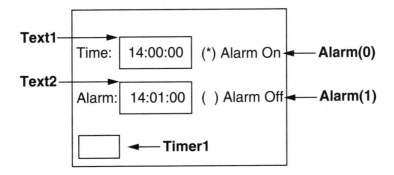

Create this new project by clicking the **ActiveX Control** icon in the New Project dialog box, and give this new project the name **Clock**. Now we add the controls we need: two text boxes (Text1 and Text2), a Timer control (Timer1, the icon in the toolbox that looks like a watch), and two option buttons. When you create the first option button, give it the name **Alarm** and the caption **Alarm On**. When you create the next option button, also give it the name **Alarm**. Visual Basic will ask whether you want to create a control array; answer **yes**. This means that the two option buttons will become Alarm(0) and Alarm(1). When one is clicked, the other one is automatically unclicked. This arrangement will be handier for us, too, because both buttons will share the same event handling subroutine. Also add the labels **Time:** and **Alarm:** as shown previously. Here's what the controls look like when we add them to our ActiveX control project:

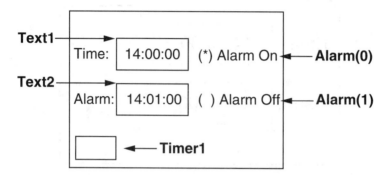

In Visual Basic, our ActiveX control-under-design appears in Figure 5.8.

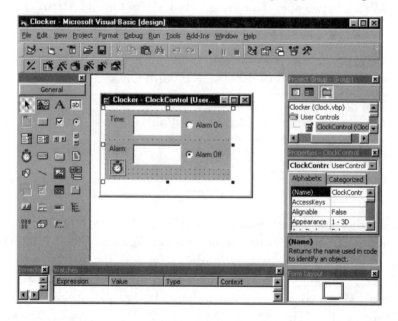

Figure 5.8 Designing our Alarm Clock ActiveX control.

In addition, change the name of the project from Project1 to **Clocker** in the properties window, and change the name of the control itself from UserControl1 to **ClockControl**.

Now let's add the code we'll need. First, we'll make the timer, Timer1, active; do that by setting its Interval property to **1000**. This property indicates how often the event handler Timer1_Timer() is called, in milliseconds. Here, we set that interval to 1000 milliseconds, so Timer1_Timer() is called once per second. Next, double-click the **Font** property of the two text boxes, opening the Font dialog box and setting the font size in those text boxes to **18**.

At this point, our project is ready for some code. To display the time in the time text box, all we have to do is to add the following line to Timer1_Timer(). We use the Visual Basic Time$ function. (Double-click the Timer control Timer1 to open the Timer1_Timer() subroutine.)

```
Private Sub Timer1_Timer()
-> Text1.Text = Time$
End Sub
```

That's all we need to display the time. Next, we make the alarm active. We add a Boolean flag named AlarmFlag to indicate whether the alarm is active (this flag will be set by the option buttons). To add the AlarmFlag flag, open the Clock project's code window and select the **(General)** object in the left-hand drop-down listbox. Here is where we store global variables; add this text to the general object:

```
Dim AlarmFlag As Boolean
```

In addition, we initialize this variable to False, indicating that the alarm is off, in the UserControl_Initialize() subroutine. In the code window, select **UserControl** as the object and **Initialize** as the subroutine, opening that subroutine:

```
Private Sub UserControl_Initialize()

End Sub
```

Here is where we do general initialization for our ActiveX controls. We set AlarmFlag to False:

```
Private Sub UserControl_Initialize()
-> AlarmFlag = False
End Sub
```

Next, we connect the AlarmFlag variable to the option buttons. Clicking the **Alarm(0)** option button turns the alarm on, and clicking **Alarm(1)** turns it off. Open the Alarm_Click() subroutine:

```
Private Sub Alarm_Click(Index As Integer)

End Sub
```

Note the Integer, named Index, passed to us. This is the index of the control that was clicked in our control array: 0 (alarm on) or 1 (alarm off). We use that value to set the AlarmFlag variable to match what the user wants:

```
Private Sub Alarm_Click(Index As Integer)
-> If (Index = 0) Then AlarmFlag = True
-> If (Index = 1) Then AlarmFlag = False
End Sub
```

Now the AlarmFlag variable is ready, and it indicates whether the alarm is supposed to be on or off. We activate the alarm itself by comparing the current time, returned as a string from the Time\$ function, with the setting for the alarm that the user has placed in the text box Text2 like this: If Time\$ > Text2.Text Then.... Visual Basic is smart enough to make the comparison correctly. We must also make sure that the alarm is set before making the program beep, and we do that by checking the AlarmFlag Boolean flag:

```
Private Sub Timer1_Timer()
-> If Time$ > Text2.Text And AlarmFlag Then Beep
   Text1.Text = Time$
End Sub
```

Here it looks as though we are making the alarm beep only once. But don't forget that Timer1_Timer() is called once per second, so the alarm will beep once per second as soon as the alarm is supposed to go off. To turn it off, the user clicks the **Alarm Off** option button.

Our alarm clock ActiveX control is ready to go. We can test it by adding a new project and inserting the Clock control there. Do that with the **Add Project** item in the Visual Basic File menu, using Application Wizard to create an SDI project and accepting all the defaults. Now close the clock control's window—its designer window—so that we can test it.

Add the Clock ActiveX control to the test project by clicking the **Clocker** item in the Components window (which you reach by selecting **Components** in the Project window). Then add a new ClockControl control, which Visual Basic will call ClockControl1, to the test project's main form. The result appears in Figure 5.9. As you can see, our clock is already working.

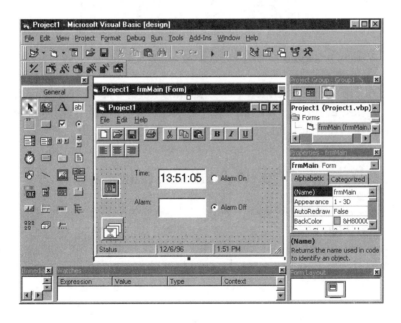

Figure 5.9 Adding our Clock ActiveX control to a project.

Run the test project by clicking **Start** in the Run menu, as shown in Figure 5.10. As you can see, we indicate the time that the alarm should go off, and we set the alarm by clicking the **Alarm On** option button. When we reach that time, the alarm beeps once per second until we turn it off. Our Clock ActiveX control is a success so far.

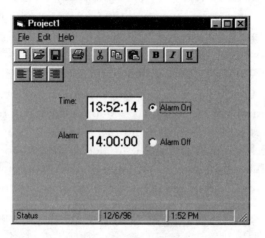

Figure 5.10 Our Clock ActiveX control at work.

Of course, there is much more to add here. We have yet to add any properties, events, or methods to our ActiveX control. We'll begin with a new property that holds the time the alarm should go off.

Adding a Property to an ActiveX Control

The property we add to our Clock ActiveX control will be called AlarmSetting, and we'll use it to set the time the alarm should go off. If someone has one of our clock controls in a Visual Basic control and has named it, say, Clock1, he or she could set the alarm to go off at 2 PM this way:

```
Clock1.AlarmSetting = "14:00:00"  'Set alarm to 2 PM
```

To add this property, open the code window for the clock control and select **Add Procedure** in the Visual Basic Tools menu. This action opens the Add Procedure dialog box, as shown in Figure 5.11. Click the option button marked **Property**, making this a new property, and give it the name **AlarmSetting**, as shown in Figure 5.11. Then click **OK** to create the new property.

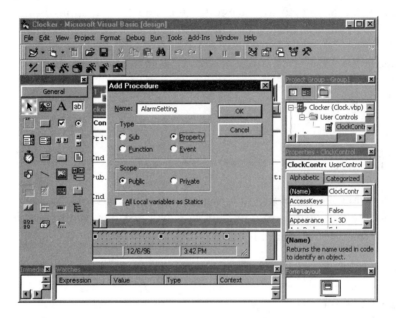

Figure 5.11 Creating the AlarmSetting property in our Clock ActiveX control.

This process creates two new functions—a Get and a Let function—for the AlarmSetting property. We can find these new functions in the code window:

```
Public Property Get AlarmSetting() As Variant

End Property

Public Property Let AlarmSetting(ByVal vNewValue As Variant)

End Property
```

When a project places a new value in the AlarmSetting property, the Let function is called; when a project reads the value in the AlarmSetting property, the Get function is called.

These functions work with Variants, but we know that the setting is saved as a String, so we change the Get and Let functions from working with Variants to working with Strings:

```
Public Property Get AlarmSetting() As String      <-

End Property


Public Property Let AlarmSetting(ByVal vNewValue As String)   <-

End Property
```

Let's add code to the Get and Let functions. In the Clock control, we keep the time the alarm is to go off in the Text2 text box. We return that value from the Get function this way:

```
Public Property Get AlarmSetting() As String
-> AlarmSetting = Text2.Text
End Property
```

On the other hand, in the Let function, the project that contains our control wants to change the alarm time. It passes a new string in the variable vNewValue, which we place in Text2:

```
Public Property Let AlarmSetting(ByVal vNewValue As String)
-> Text2.Text = vNewValue
End Property
```

That's all it takes—now other projects can reach our AlarmSetting property (just as you would use any property of an object) and set the time in our alarm clock from code. We can also reach this new property at design time, as we see in Figure 5.12.

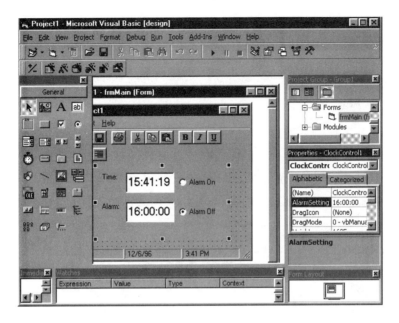

Figure 5.12 Setting our new AlarmSetting property.

We have added a new property to our Clock ActiveX control. We can also add events—and what is more appropriate to an alarm clock than adding a Tick event?

Adding an Event to an ActiveX Control

The Tick event will be just like any other Visual Basic event, such as Click or KeyPress. To add this event, select the Clock control's code window and select **Add Procedure** in the Tools menu again, opening the Add Procedure dialog box as shown in Figure 5.13.

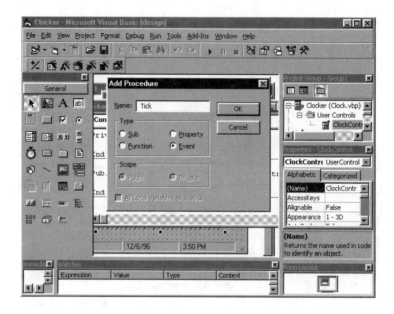

Figure 5.13 Adding the Tick event to our Clock ActiveX control.

Give this new event the name **Tick** and click the option button marked **Event**, as shown in Figure 5.13; then click **OK**. This creates the new event named Tick, and it appears in the (general) object. (As with any new procedure, you can add parameters to the declaration so that the Tick event passes values to its event handler.)

```
Public Event Tick()            <-
Dim AlarmFlag As Boolean
```

To make this event occur—called *raising* an event—once per second, we call the Visual Basic procedure RaiseEvent in Timer1_Timer(), which is called once per second:

```
Private Sub Timer1_Timer()
    If Time$ > Text2.Text And AlarmFlag Then Beep
    Text1.Text = Time$
-> RaiseEvent Tick
End Sub
```

Now our clock's Tick event occurs once per second. To observe that, run the Clock ActiveX control by closing its designer window; find the Tick event handler in the test project's code window. Add this code to ClockControl1_Tick() in the test project, making the test project beep once per second:

```
Private Sub ClockControl1_Tick()
-> Beep
End Sub
```

Now when the test project runs, you'll hear it beep once per second. Our new event, Tick, is a success. Now that we've added a property and an event to our ActiveX control, let's find out how to work with methods.

Adding a Method to an ActiveX Control

We can also add a method to our Clock control. Let's set up a method named AlarmOn. When we pass a value of True to the AlarmOn method, it will turn the alarm on. If we pass False, it will turn the alarm off. For example, we can turn the alarm on this way in the test project:

```
Private Sub Form_Click()
    ClockControl1.AlarmOn True  <-
End Sub
```

To add this method to our clock project, all we have to do is to add a public procedure (subroutine or function) to our Clock control. Open the Add Procedure dialog box and create the new AlarmOn() method. Click **Public**, **Sub**, and give the new procedure the name **AlarmOn()**, as shown in Figure 5.14.

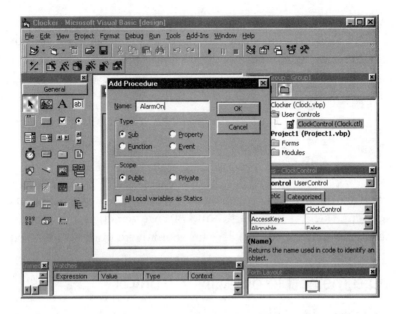

Figure 5.14 Adding the AlarmOn method to our Clock ActiveX control.

Now open the new method:

```
Public Sub AlarmOn()

End Sub
```

We are passed a Boolean variable in this method, so add that to the parameter list as the variable named Setting:

```
Public Sub AlarmOn(Setting As Boolean)   <-

End Sub
```

Next, make the internal AlarmFlag variable match the new setting:

```
Public Sub AlarmOn(Setting As Boolean)
-> AlarmFlag = Setting
        .
        .
```

```
End Sub
```

In addition, we'll set the option buttons to indicate whether the alarm is on or off:

```
Public Sub AlarmOn(Setting As Boolean)
    AlarmFlag = Setting
-> Alarm(0).Value = Setting
-> Alarm(1).Value = Not Setting
End Sub
```

And that's it—now we've added the AlarmOn method. To test it, we add this code to the form click event handler in the test project:

```
Private Sub Form_Click()
    ClockControl1.AlarmOn True  <-
End Sub
```

Now when you run the test project and click the form, the alarm is turned on. Our alarm clock is a success.

Note that one method you should add to your ActiveX controls is the Refresh() method, which is called when the control needs to be redrawn:

```
Public Sub Refresh()

End Sub
```

In this method, you call the underlying object's Refresh method. That object is the UserControl object, and we call its Refresh method like this:

```
Public Sub Refresh()
    UserControl.Refresh
End Sub
```

This takes care of redrawing our control along with any constituent controls we may have used.

The code for our alarm clock, **Clock.ctl**, appears in Listing 5.3, and the code for the test project, **frmMain.frm**, appears in Listing 5.4.

Listing 5.3 Clock.ctl

```
VERSION 5.00
Begin VB.UserControl ClockControl
    ClientHeight    =   1710
    ClientLeft      =   0
    ClientTop       =   0
    ClientWidth     =   3195
    PropertyPages   =   "Clock.ctx":0000
    ScaleHeight     =   1710
    ScaleWidth      =   3195
    Begin VB.OptionButton Alarm
        Caption         =   "Alarm Off"
        Height          =   495
        Index           =   1
        Left            =   2040
        TabIndex        =   5
        Top             =   840
        Value           =   -1  'True
        Width           =   1095
    End
    Begin VB.OptionButton Alarm
        Caption         =   "Alarm On"
        Height          =   495
        Index           =   0
        Left            =   2040
        TabIndex        =   4
        Top             =   120
        Width           =   1095
    End
    Begin VB.TextBox Text2
        BeginProperty Font
            Name            =   "MS Sans Serif"
            Size            =   13.5
            Charset         =   0
            Weight          =   400
```

```
            Underline       =   0    'False
            Italic          =   0    'False
            Strikethrough   =   0    'False
         EndProperty
         Height          =    495
         Left            =    720
         TabIndex        =    1
         Top             =    840
         Width           =    1215
      End
      Begin VB.Timer Timer1
         Interval        =    1000
         Left            =    120
         Top             =    1200
      End
      Begin VB.TextBox Text1
         BeginProperty Font
            Name            =    "MS Sans Serif"
            Size            =    13.5
            Charset         =    0
            Weight          =    400
            Underline       =    0    'False
            Italic          =    0    'False
            Strikethrough   =    0    'False
         EndProperty
         Height          =    495
         Left            =    720
         TabIndex        =    0
         Top             =    120
         Width           =    1215
      End
      Begin VB.Label Label2
         Caption         =    "Alarm:"
         Height          =    495
         Left            =    120
         TabIndex        =    3
         Top             =    840
         Width           =    495
      End
```

```
    Begin VB.Label Label1
        Caption         =    "Time:"
        Height          =    495
        Left            =    120
        TabIndex        =    2
        Top             =    120
        Width           =    495
    End
End
Attribute VB_Name = "ClockControl"
Attribute VB_GlobalNameSpace = False
Attribute VB_Creatable = True
Attribute VB_PredeclaredId = False
Attribute VB_Exposed = True
Option Explicit
Public Event Tick()
Dim AlarmFlag As Boolean

Private Sub Alarm_Click(Index As Integer)
    If (Index = 0) Then AlarmFlag = True
    If (Index = 1) Then AlarmFlag = False
End Sub

Private Sub Timer1_Timer()
    If Time$ > Text2.Text And AlarmFlag Then Beep
    Text1.Text = Time$
    RaiseEvent Tick
End Sub

Private Sub UserControl_Initialize()
    AlarmFlag = False
End Sub

Public Property Get AlarmSetting() As String
    AlarmSetting = Text2.Text
End Property

Public Property Let AlarmSetting(ByVal vNewValue As String)
    Text2.Text = vNewValue
```

```
End Property

Public Sub AlarmOn(Setting As Boolean)
    AlarmFlag = Setting
    Alarm(0).Value = Setting
    Alarm(1).Value = Not Setting
End Sub

Public Sub Refresh()
    UserControl.Refresh
End Sub
```

Listing 5.4 (Clock) frmmain.frm

```
VERSION 5.00
Object = "{F9043C88-F6F2-101A-A3C9-08002B2F49FB}#1.1#0"; "COMDLG32.OCX"
Object = "{6B7E6392-850A-101B-AFC0-4210102A8DA7}#1.1#0"; "COMCTL32.OCX"
Object = "*\AClock.vbp"
Begin VB.Form frmMain
    Caption        =   "Project1"
    ClientHeight   =   3195
    ClientLeft     =   165
    ClientTop      =   735
    ClientWidth    =   4680
    LinkTopic      =   "Form1"
    ScaleHeight    =   3195
    ScaleWidth     =   4680
    StartUpPosition =  3   'Windows Default
    Begin ComctlLib.Toolbar tbToolBar
        Align          =   1   'Align Top
        Height         =   1080
        Left           =   0
        TabIndex       =   1
        Top            =   0
        Width          =   4680
        _ExtentX       =   8255
        _ExtentY       =   1905
        ButtonWidth    =   635
```

```
ButtonHeight     =    582
Appearance       =    1
ImageList        =    "imlIcons"
BeginProperty Buttons {7791BA41-E020-11CF-8E74-00A0C90F26F8}
   NumButtons    =    17
   BeginProperty Button1 {7791BA43-E020-11CF-8E74-00A0C90F26F8}
      Key             =    "New"
      Object.ToolTipText    =    "New"
      Object.Tag      =    ""
      ImageIndex      =    1
   EndProperty
   BeginProperty Button2 {7791BA43-E020-11CF-8E74-00A0C90F26F8}
      Key             =    "Open"
      Object.ToolTipText    =    "Open"
      Object.Tag      =    ""
      ImageIndex      =    2
   EndProperty
   BeginProperty Button3 {7791BA43-E020-11CF-8E74-00A0C90F26F8}
      Key             =    "Save"
      Object.ToolTipText    =    "Save"
      Object.Tag      =    ""
      ImageIndex      =    3
   EndProperty
   BeginProperty Button4 {7791BA43-E020-11CF-8E74-00A0C90F26F8}
      Key             =    ""
      Object.Tag      =    ""
      Style           =    3
   EndProperty
   BeginProperty Button5 {7791BA43-E020-11CF-8E74-00A0C90F26F8}
      Key             =    "Print"
      Object.ToolTipText    =    "Print"
      Object.Tag      =    ""
      ImageIndex      =    4
   EndProperty
   BeginProperty Button6 {7791BA43-E020-11CF-8E74-00A0C90F26F8}
      Key             =    ""
      Object.Tag      =    ""
      Style           =    3
   EndProperty
```

```
BeginProperty Button7 {7791BA43-E020-11CF-8E74-00A0C90F26F8}
   Key              =   "Cut"
   Object.ToolTipText    =   "Cut"
   Object.Tag            =   ""
   ImageIndex       =   5
EndProperty
BeginProperty Button8 {7791BA43-E020-11CF-8E74-00A0C90F26F8}
   Key              =   "Copy"
   Object.ToolTipText    =   "Copy"
   Object.Tag            =   ""
   ImageIndex       =   6
EndProperty
BeginProperty Button9 {7791BA43-E020-11CF-8E74-00A0C90F26F8}
   Key              =   "Paste"
   Object.ToolTipText    =   "Paste"
   Object.Tag            =   ""
   ImageIndex       =   7
EndProperty
BeginProperty Button10 {7791BA43-E020-11CF-8E74-00A0C90F26F8}
   Key              =   ""
   Object.Tag            =   ""
   Style            =   3
EndProperty
BeginProperty Button11 {7791BA43-E020-11CF-8E74-00A0C90F26F8}
   Key              =   "Bold"
   Object.ToolTipText    =   "Bold"
   Object.Tag            =   ""
   ImageIndex       =   8
EndProperty
BeginProperty Button12 {7791BA43-E020-11CF-8E74-00A0C90F26F8}
   Key              =   "Italic"
   Object.ToolTipText    =   "Italic"
   Object.Tag            =   ""
   ImageIndex       =   9
EndProperty
BeginProperty Button13 {7791BA43-E020-11CF-8E74-00A0C90F26F8}
   Key              =   "Underline"
   Object.ToolTipText    =   "Underline"
   Object.Tag            =   ""
```

```
            ImageIndex        =    10
         EndProperty
         BeginProperty Button14 {7791BA43-E020-11CF-8E74-00A0C90F26F8}
            Key               =    ""
            Object.Tag             =    ""
            Style             =    3
         EndProperty
         BeginProperty Button15 {7791BA43-E020-11CF-8E74-00A0C90F26F8}
            Key               =    "Left"
            Object.ToolTipText     =    "Left Justify"
            Object.Tag             =    ""
            ImageIndex        =    11
         EndProperty
         BeginProperty Button16 {7791BA43-E020-11CF-8E74-00A0C90F26F8}
            Key               =    "Center"
            Object.ToolTipText     =    "Center"
            Object.Tag             =    ""
            ImageIndex        =    12
         EndProperty
         BeginProperty Button17 {7791BA43-E020-11CF-8E74-00A0C90F26F8}
            Key               =    "Right"
            Object.ToolTipText     =    "Right Justify"
            Object.Tag             =    ""
            ImageIndex        =    13
         EndProperty
      EndProperty
      MouseIcon       =    "frmMain.frx":0000
   End
   Begin ComctlLib.StatusBar sbStatusBar
      Align           =    2  'Align Bottom
      Height          =    270
      Left            =    0
      TabIndex        =    0
      Top             =    2925
      Width           =    4680
      _ExtentX        =    8255
      _ExtentY        =    476
      SimpleText      =    ""
      BeginProperty Panels {2C787A51-E01C-11CF-8E74-00A0C90F26F8}
```

```
NumPanels          =    3
BeginProperty Panel1 {2C787A53-E01C-11CF-8E74-00A0C90F26F8}
   AutoSize        =    1
   Object.Width          =    2619
   MinWidth        =    2540
   Text            =    "Status"
   TextSave        =    "Status"
   Key             =    ""
   Object.Tag            =    ""
EndProperty
BeginProperty Panel2 {2C787A53-E01C-11CF-8E74-00A0C90F26F8}
   Style           =    6
   AutoSize        =    2
   Object.Width          =    2540
   MinWidth        =    2540
   TextSave        =    "12/6/96"
   Key             =    ""
   Object.Tag            =    ""
EndProperty
BeginProperty Panel3 {2C787A53-E01C-11CF-8E74-00A0C90F26F8}
   Style           =    5
   AutoSize        =    2
   Object.Width          =    2540
   MinWidth        =    2540
   TextSave        =    "4:30 PM"
   Key             =    ""
   Object.Tag            =    ""
EndProperty
EndProperty
BeginProperty Font {0BE35203-8F91-11CE-9DE3-00AA004BB851}
   Name            =    "MS Sans Serif"
   Size            =    8.25
   Charset         =    0
   Weight          =    400
   Underline       =    0    'False
   Italic          =    0    'False
   Strikethrough   =    0    'False
EndProperty
MouseIcon        =    "frmMain.frx":001C
```

```
End
Begin MSComDlg.CommonDialog dlgCommonDialog
    Left            =    120
    Top             =    1320
    _ExtentX        =    847
    _ExtentY        =    847
    FontSize        =    2.89174e-37
End
Begin Clocker.ClockControl ClockControl1
    Height          =    1695
    Left            =    840
    TabIndex        =    2
    Top             =    960
    Width           =    3255
    _ExtentX        =    5741
    _ExtentY        =    2990
End
Begin ComctlLib.ImageList imlIcons
    Left            =    120
    Top             =    2280
    _ExtentX        =    1005
    _ExtentY        =    1005
    BackColor       =    -2147483643
    ImageWidth      =    16
    ImageHeight     =    16
    MaskColor       =    12632256
    BeginProperty Images {8556BCD1-E01E-11CF-8E74-00A0C90F26F8}
        NumListImages   =    13
        BeginProperty ListImage1 {8556BCD3-E01E-11CF-8E74-00A0C90F26F8}
            Picture         =    "frmMain.frx":0038
            Key             =    ""
        EndProperty
        BeginProperty ListImage2 {8556BCD3-E01E-11CF-8E74-00A0C90F26F8}
            Picture         =    "frmMain.frx":038A
            Key             =    ""
        EndProperty
        BeginProperty ListImage3 {8556BCD3-E01E-11CF-8E74-00A0C90F26F8}
            Picture         =    "frmMain.frx":06DC
            Key             =    ""
```

```
EndProperty
BeginProperty ListImage4 {8556BCD3-E01E-11CF-8E74-00A0C90F26F8}
   Picture         =    "frmMain.frx":0A2E
   Key             =    ""
EndProperty
BeginProperty ListImage5 {8556BCD3-E01E-11CF-8E74-00A0C90F26F8}
   Picture         =    "frmMain.frx":0D80
   Key             =    ""
EndProperty
BeginProperty ListImage6 {8556BCD3-E01E-11CF-8E74-00A0C90F26F8}
   Picture         =    "frmMain.frx":10D2
   Key             =    ""
EndProperty
BeginProperty ListImage7 {8556BCD3-E01E-11CF-8E74-00A0C90F26F8}
   Picture         =    "frmMain.frx":1424
   Key             =    ""
EndProperty
BeginProperty ListImage8 {8556BCD3-E01E-11CF-8E74-00A0C90F26F8}
   Picture         =    "frmMain.frx":1776
   Key             =    ""
EndProperty
BeginProperty ListImage9 {8556BCD3-E01E-11CF-8E74-00A0C90F26F8}
   Picture         =    "frmMain.frx":1AC8
   Key             =    ""
EndProperty
BeginProperty ListImage10 {8556BCD3-E01E-11CF-8E74-
                  00A0C90F26F8}
   Picture         =    "frmMain.frx":1E1A
   Key             =    ""
EndProperty
BeginProperty ListImage11 {8556BCD3-E01E-11CF-8E74-
                  00A0C90F26F8}
   Picture         =    "frmMain.frx":216C
   Key             =    ""
EndProperty
BeginProperty ListImage12 {8556BCD3-E01E-11CF-8E74-
                  00A0C90F26F8}
   Picture         =    "frmMain.frx":24BE
   Key             =    ""
```

```
      EndProperty
      BeginProperty ListImage13 {8556BCD3-E01E-11CF-8E74-
                               00A0C90F26F8}
         Picture         =   "frmMain.frx":2810
         Key             =   ""
      EndProperty
   EndProperty
End
Begin VB.Menu mnuFile
   Caption         =   "&File"
   Begin VB.Menu mnuFileNew
      Caption         =   "&New"
      Shortcut        =   ^N
   End
   Begin VB.Menu mnuFileOpen
      Caption         =   "&Open"
      Shortcut        =   ^O
   End
   Begin VB.Menu mnuFileClose
      Caption         =   "&Close"
   End
   Begin VB.Menu mnuFileBar1
      Caption         =   "-"
   End
   Begin VB.Menu mnuFileSave
      Caption         =   "&Save"
      Shortcut        =   ^S
   End
   Begin VB.Menu mnuFileSaveAs
      Caption         =   "Save &As..."
   End
   Begin VB.Menu mnuFileSaveAll
      Caption         =   "Save A&ll"
   End
   Begin VB.Menu mnuFileBar2
      Caption         =   "-"
   End
   Begin VB.Menu mnuFileProperties
      Caption         =   "Propert&ies"
```

```
      End
      Begin VB.Menu mnuFileBar3
         Caption         =    "-"
      End
      Begin VB.Menu mnuFilePageSetup
         Caption         =    "Page Set&up..."
      End
      Begin VB.Menu mnuFilePrintPreview
         Caption         =    "Print Pre&view"
      End
      Begin VB.Menu mnuFilePrint
         Caption         =    "&Print..."
         Shortcut        =    ^P
      End
      Begin VB.Menu mnuFileBar4
         Caption         =    "-"
      End
      Begin VB.Menu mnuFileSend
         Caption         =    "Sen&d..."
      End
      Begin VB.Menu mnuFileBar5
         Caption         =    "-"
      End
      Begin VB.Menu mnuFileMRU
         Caption         =    ""
         Index           =    0
         Visible         =    0    'False
      End
      Begin VB.Menu mnuFileMRU
         Caption         =    ""
         Index           =    1
         Visible         =    0    'False
      End
      Begin VB.Menu mnuFileMRU
         Caption         =    ""
         Index           =    2
         Visible         =    0    'False
      End
      Begin VB.Menu mnuFileMRU
```

```
            Caption         =    " "
            Index           =    3
            Visible         =    0     'False
         End
         Begin VB.Menu mnuFileBar6
            Caption         =    "-"
            Visible         =    0     'False
         End
         Begin VB.Menu mnuFileExit
            Caption         =    "E&xit"
         End
      End
      Begin VB.Menu mnuEdit
         Caption         =    "&Edit"
         Begin VB.Menu mnuEditUndo
            Caption         =    "&Undo"
            Shortcut        =    ^Z
         End
         Begin VB.Menu mnuEditBar1
            Caption         =    "-"
         End
         Begin VB.Menu mnuEditCut
            Caption         =    "Cu&t"
            Shortcut        =    ^X
         End
         Begin VB.Menu mnuEditCopy
            Caption         =    "&Copy"
            Shortcut        =    ^C
         End
         Begin VB.Menu mnuEditPaste
            Caption         =    "&Paste"
            Shortcut        =    ^V
         End
         Begin VB.Menu mnuEditPasteSpecial
            Caption         =    "Paste &Special..."
         End
      End
      Begin VB.Menu mnuHelp
         Caption         =    "&Help"
```

```
        Begin VB.Menu mnuHelpContents
            Caption         =   "&Contents"
        End
        Begin VB.Menu mnuHelpSearch
            Caption         =   "&Search For Help On..."
        End
        Begin VB.Menu mnuHelpBar1
            Caption         =   "-"
        End
        Begin VB.Menu mnuHelpAbout
            Caption         =   "&About Project1..."
        End
    End
End
Attribute VB_Name = "frmMain"
Attribute VB_GlobalNameSpace = False
Attribute VB_Creatable = False
Attribute VB_PredeclaredId = True
Attribute VB_Exposed = False
Private Declare Function OSWinHelp% Lib "user32" Alias "WinHelpA"
(ByVal hwnd&, ByVal HelpFile$, ByVal wCommand%, dwData As Any)

Private Sub ClockControl1_Tick()
    'Beep
End Sub

Private Sub Form_Click()
    ClockControl1.AlarmOn True
End Sub

Private Sub Form_Load()
    Me.Left = GetSetting(App.Title, "Settings", "MainLeft", 1000)
    Me.Top = GetSetting(App.Title, "Settings", "MainTop", 1000)
    Me.Width = GetSetting(App.Title, "Settings", "MainWidth", 6500)
    Me.Height = GetSetting(App.Title, "Settings", "MainHeight", 6500)
End Sub

Private Sub Form_Unload(Cancel As Integer)
    If Me.WindowState <> vbMinimized Then
```

```
        SaveSetting App.Title, "Settings", "MainLeft", Me.Left
        SaveSetting App.Title, "Settings", "MainTop", Me.Top
        SaveSetting App.Title, "Settings", "MainWidth", Me.Width
        SaveSetting App.Title, "Settings", "MainHeight", Me.Height
    End If
End Sub

Private Sub mnuHelpAbout_Click()
    'To Do
    MsgBox "About Box Code goes here!"
End Sub

Private Sub tbToolBar_ButtonClick(ByVal Button As ComctlLib.Button)

    Select Case Button.Key

        Case "New"
            mnuFileNew_Click
        Case "New"
            mnuFileNew_Click
        Case "Open"
            mnuFileOpen_Click
        Case "Save"
            mnuFileSave_Click
        Case "Print"
            mnuFilePrint_Click
        Case "Cut"
            mnuEditCut_Click
        Case "Copy"
            mnuEditCopy_Click
        Case "Paste"
            mnuEditPaste_Click
        Case "Bold"
            'To Do
            MsgBox "Bold Code goes here!"
        Case "Italic"
            'To Do
            MsgBox "Italic Code goes here!"
        Case "Underline"
```

```
            'To Do
            MsgBox "Underline Code goes here!"
        Case "Left"
            'To Do
            MsgBox "Left Code goes here!"
        Case "Center"
            'To Do
            MsgBox "Center Code goes here!"
        Case "Right"
            'To Do
            MsgBox "Right Code goes here!"
    End Select
End Sub


Private Sub mnuHelpContents_Click()

    Dim nRet As Integer

    'if there is no helpfile for this project display a message to the
    'user you can set the HelpFile for your application in the
    'Project Properties dialog
    If Len(App.HelpFile) = 0 Then
        MsgBox "Unable to display Help Contents. There is no Help
        associated with this project.", vbInformation, Me.Caption
    Else
        On Error Resume Next
        nRet = OSWinHelp(Me.hwnd, App.HelpFile, 3, 0)
        If Err Then
            MsgBox Err.Description
        End If
    End If
End Sub


Private Sub mnuHelpSearch_Click()

    Dim nRet As Integer

    'if there is no helpfile for this project display a message to the
    'user you can set the HelpFile for your application in the
    'Project Properties dialog
```

```vb
        If Len(App.HelpFile) = 0 Then
            MsgBox "Unable to display Help Contents. There is no Help
            associated with this project.", vbInformation, Me.Caption
        Else
            On Error Resume Next
            nRet = OSWinHelp(Me.hwnd, App.HelpFile, 261, 0)
            If Err Then
                MsgBox Err.Description
            End If
        End If
End Sub


Private Sub mnuEditCopy_Click()
    'To Do
    MsgBox "Copy Code goes here!"
End Sub

Private Sub mnuEditCut_Click()
    'To Do
    MsgBox "Cut Code goes here!"
End Sub

Private Sub mnuEditPaste_Click()
    'To Do
    MsgBox "Paste Code goes here!"
End Sub

Private Sub mnuEditPasteSpecial_Click()
    'To Do
    MsgBox "Paste Special Code goes here!"
End Sub

Private Sub mnuEditUndo_Click()
    'To Do
    MsgBox "Undo Code goes here!"
End Sub


Private Sub mnuFileOpen_Click()
    Dim sFile As String
```

```
    With dlgCommonDialog
        'To Do
        'set the flags and attributes of the
        'common dialog control
        .Filter = "All Files (*.*)|*.*"
        .ShowOpen
        If Len(.filename) = 0 Then
            Exit Sub
        End If
        sFile = .filename
    End With
    'To Do
    'process the opened file
End Sub

Private Sub mnuFileClose_Click()
    'To Do
    MsgBox "Close Code goes here!"
End Sub

Private Sub mnuFileSave_Click()
    'To Do
    MsgBox "Save Code goes here!"
End Sub

Private Sub mnuFileSaveAs_Click()
    'To Do
    'Set up the common dialog control
    'prior to calling ShowSave
    dlgCommonDialog.ShowSave
End Sub

Private Sub mnuFileSaveAll_Click()
    'To Do
    MsgBox "Save All Code goes here!"
End Sub

Private Sub mnuFileProperties_Click()
    'To Do
```

```vb
    MsgBox "Properties Code goes here!"
End Sub

Private Sub mnuFilePageSetup_Click()
    dlgCommonDialog.ShowPrinter
End Sub

Private Sub mnuFilePrintPreview_Click()
    'To Do
    MsgBox "Print Preview Code goes here!"
End Sub

Private Sub mnuFilePrint_Click()
    'To Do
    MsgBox "Print Code goes here!"
End Sub

Private Sub mnuFileSend_Click()
    'To Do
    MsgBox "Send Code goes here!"
End Sub

Private Sub mnuFileMRU_Click(Index As Integer)
    'To Do
    MsgBox "MRU Code goes here!"
End Sub

Private Sub mnuFileExit_Click()
    'unload the form
    Unload Me
End Sub

Private Sub mnuFileNew_Click()
    'To Do
    MsgBox "New File Code goes here!"
End Sub
```

There are many methods and events that a full ActiveX control should have: Click, DoubleClick, and so on. Visual Basic includes a tool to help make sure you handle them all: the ActiveX Control Interface Wizard. To run this wizard, select it in the Add-Ins menu, as shown in Figure 5.15.

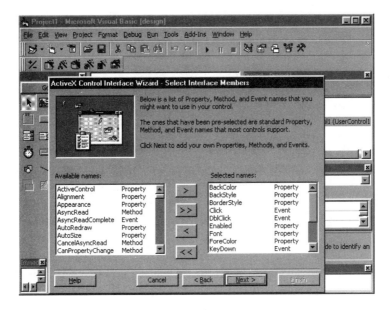

Figure 5.15 The ActiveX Control Interface Wizard.

This wizard helps provide default events and methods that your control should have if you want to release it commercially, and that's a useful thing. Try the wizard on your controls; it usually picks up something that you've forgotten.

Now that we've created some working ActiveX controls, let's find out how to set up our controls on the Internet.

Distributing ActiveX Controls on the Internet

We can include ActiveX controls in Web pages if we use an ActiveX-aware browser such as Internet Explorer. We include an ActiveX control by using the <Object> HTML tag. For example, one of the ActiveX controls Microsoft distributes from its Web site is the Stock Ticker control,

iestock.ocx. Here's what the <Object> tag looks like from the Stock Ticker's example Web page:

```
<OBJECT
ID=iexr2
        TYPE="application/x-oleobject"
        CLASSID="clsid:0CA4A620-8E3D-11CF-A3A9-00A0C9034920"
        CODEBASE="http://activex.microsoft.com/controls/
        iexplorer/iestock.ocx#Version=4,70,0,1161"
        WIDTH=300
        HEIGHT=50>
        <PARAM NAME="DataObjectActive" VALUE="1">
        <PARAM NAME="scrollwidth" VALUE="5">
        <PARAM NAME="forecolor" VALUE="#ff0000">
        <PARAM NAME="backcolor" VALUE="#0000ff">
        <PARAM NAME="ReloadInterval" VALUE="5000">
</OBJECT>
```

Here, the Stock Ticker is given an ID of "iexr2," which is how it can be referred to in scripting languages such as VBScript. Note also the CODEBASE keyword, which indicates where the Web browser will find the **.ocx** file for download. The WIDTH and HEIGHT values give the control some space on the Web page. Also note that you can fill the properties of the ActiveX control by passing values using the PARAM tag.

Also notice the class ID number shown in the <Object> tag. Each ActiveX control gets a class ID when it is created, as our Clock ActiveX control will. Let's create **Clock.ocx** now. Open the clock group in Visual Basic and select **Make Clock.ocx** in the File menu. When the **Clock.ocx** file is made, we are ready to go.

All that was needed for the Stock Ticker ActiveX control was the **.ocx** file, but the Clock ActiveX control needs more. Like any Visual Basic ActiveX control, it needs the file **vbrun500.dll** to work, and possibly other files (depending on any constituent controls you may have added). How do we know which files the control needs? And how do we download them automatically from our Web site? We do that with the Setup Wizard.

Using the Setup Wizard

The Visual Basic Setup Wizard packages our control and the files it needs—or references to the files it needs—into a file with the extension **.cab**. This file is what is downloaded by the Web browser. You'll find the Setup Wizard in **VB\setupkit\kitfil32\Setupwiz.exe**. Close Visual Basic and run the Setup Wizard, as shown in Figure 5.16.

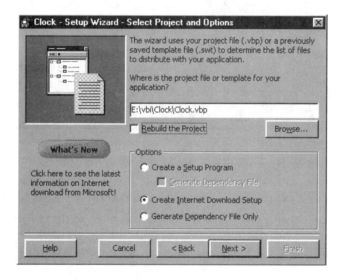

Figure 5.16 The Visual Basic Setup Wizard.

Type in the path and name of the project for the ActiveX control you have created, as shown in Figure 5.16, and click **Create Internet Download Setup**; then click **Next>**. In the next window, specify where you want to store the **.cab** file on your disk when the file is built, and click **Next>** again. As the following window indicates, the various runtime components needed for your ActiveX control can be downloaded from the Microsoft site (except for your **.ocx** file, of course), so leave that option clicked, as shown in Figure 5.17. This means that you won't have to place those components on your ISP for download.

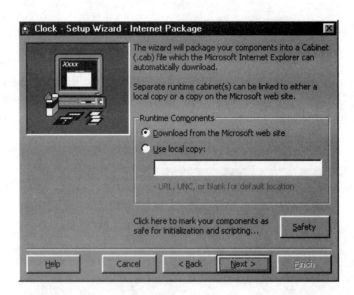

Figure 5.17 Setup Wizard download options.

Keep clicking **Next>** as the Setup Wizard determines what files should go into your **.cab** file, and then click **Finish**. The Setup Wizard constructs not only your **.cab** file but also a sample **.html** file for you:

```
<HTML>
<!—If any of the controls on this page require licensing, you must
create a license package file.
    Run LPK_TOOL.EXE in the tools directory to create the required LPK
file.

<OBJECT
CLASSID="clsid:5220cb21-c88d-11cf-b347-00aa00a28331">
    <PARAM NAME="LPKPath" VALUE="LPKfilename.LPK">
</OBJECT>
classid="clsid:3B9913F6-4ED6-11D0-885E-444553540000"

—>

<OBJECT
classid="clsid:81651E50-4ED6-11D0-885E-444553540000"
```

```
id=Clock
codebase="Clock.CAB#version=1,0,0,0">
</OBJECT>
</HTML>
```

Here's where we see our Clock ActiveX's class ID: 81651E50-4ED6-11D0-885E-444553540000. (This value is created whenever the **clock.ocx** file is built, so the value you get will be different.) You can customize this Web page by specifying the width and height you want for your control:

```
<HTML>
<!—If any of the controls on this page require licensing, you must
create a license package file.
    Run LPK_TOOL.EXE in the tools directory to create the required LPK
file.

<OBJECT
CLASSID="clsid:5220cb21-c88d-11cf-b347-00aa00a28331">
    <PARAM NAME="LPKPath" VALUE="LPKfilename.LPK">
</OBJECT>
classid="clsid:3B9913F6-4ED6-11D0-885E-444553540000"

<OBJECT
WIDTH=200        <—
HEIGHT=200       <—
classid="clsid:81651E50-4ED6-11D0-885E-444553540000"
id=Clock
codebase="Clock.CAB#version=1,0,0,0">
</OBJECT>
</HTML>
```

This, then, is how the <Object> tag should look for your control. That's all there is to it. Now you can use ActiveX controls on the Web.

If you have problems, make sure that the class ID in the <Object> tag for your control is the same one listed in the Windows registry for that control. Because Setup Wizard rebuilds your control by default, the class ID of your control in the <Object> tag may end up being different from the class ID of the **.ocx** file Visual Basic may have already placed in the Windows registry.

Security

Before we end the chapter, there is another area of interest to discuss: security. As it stands, Web browsers such as Internet Explorer will refuse to display your control (although they will download it) for security reasons. You need to get a digital certificate before the browser will display your control using the browser's default settings.

One way to fix this is to have your user turn off the browser's security checks. In Internet Explorer, select the **Options** item in the View menu and select the **Security** tab in the Options dialog box that opens. Next, click **Safety Level** to open the Safety Level dialog box; click the option button marked **None**, followed by **OK**. This action turns security checks off so that the user can download your control. Obviously, the user should turn security on again when the control is downloaded. You should also note that before distributing any licensed matter of any kind, including the **.ocx** controls of others, you must get permission from the manufacturers.

Another way to deal with the security issue when downloading ActiveX controls is through the use of digital signatures.

Digital Signatures

A *digital signature* provides a way of creating a path from your user to you in case anything should go wrong. When you create an **.ocx** file, you work with a third party, called a Certificate Authority (CA), to get a digital certificate. The CA also authenticates your identity and handles liability issues for the code you digitally sign and distribute. To get a digital signature, you run your code through a one-way hash function, which produces a *digest*. This digest is encrypted with a private key that you create and put into a signature block with the name of your hash algorithm and your digital certificate. The certificate holds your name, your public key, and the CA's name. Setup Wizard will insert the signature block into your **.cab** file.

After the **.cab** file is downloaded, Internet Explorer calls functions in the WinVerifyTrust API (Application Programming Interface), extracting the digital signature, determining the CA, and obtaining your public key. The public key is then used to decrypt the digest from the hash function. The browser then runs the same hash function on your code, creating a new digest. If the code does not match, the control is rejected.

As you can see, creating digital signatures is not an easy task. If you want to make your **.ocx** control available freely on the Internet, however, it's the way you have to go. Because security on the Internet is becoming an ever more serious issue, using digital signatures will become more popular in time.

That's it for this chapter: we've come far, from creating ActiveX controls to using the in Visual Basic, from adding properties, events, and methods to our controls to seeing how to download ActiveX controls from the Internet. In the next chapter, we'll continue this process as we take a look at ActiveX documents and how they work on the Internet.

CHAPTER •6

CREATING AND USING ACTIVEX DOCUMENTS

One of the most powerful aspects of Visual Basic Internet programming is the ability it gives you to create ActiveX *documents*, which are nothing less than full Visual Basic programs that you can download and run in a Web browser. You create a working Visual Basic program as usual—including controls such as buttons, list boxes, text boxes, and so on—and run it in a Web browser. Visual Basic includes the ActiveX Document Migration Wizard, which translates standard forms into ActiveX document forms.

In this chapter, we will look at the process of creating and using ActiveX documents. We'll see how to integrate them seamlessly into Visual Basic programs. We'll create a real estate program that downloads the latest listings into a list box in an ActiveX document. To get more information on a particular listing, the agent simply clicks it in the list box. But let's start at once with a simpler ActiveX document.

Our First ActiveX Document

Our first ActiveX document will hold a single label with the text **Hello World!** (we'll add more active controls soon):

Hello World!

Using Visual Basic, we will create this document and call it **FirstDocument.vbd**. (The **.vbd** extension is standard for Visual Basic ActiveX documents; it stands for Visual Basic document.) We'll be able to open **FirstDocument.vbd** in Internet Explorer:

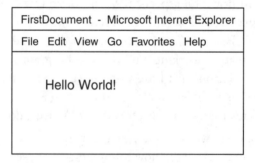

Start Visual Basic and create a new project, selecting the **ActiveX Document EXE** icon in the New Project dialog box. This action opens our new project, as shown in Figure 6.1.

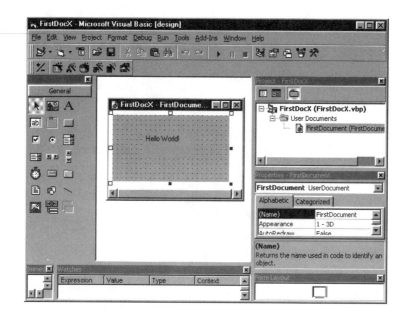

Figure 6.1 Creating our first ActiveX document.

Next, add a label with the text **Hello World!** in the middle of the new document. In the properties window, change the name of the project to **FirstDocX** and change the name of the document under design to **FirstDocument**. Then save the project; the document itself is saved as **FirstDocument.dob**.

That completes the design of our first ActiveX document. Now select the **Make FirstDocX.exe** item in the Visual Basic File menu. This action creates **FirstDocument.vbd**, and that's the document we examine in Internet Explorer. Start Internet Explorer and open the **FirstDocument.vbd** file, as shown in Figure 6.2.

Figure 6.2 Our first ActiveX document at work.

Now you can see our ActiveX document in Internet Explorer. Our first ActiveX document is a success; the code for this document, **FirstDocument.dob**, appears in Listing 6.1. You can upload **FirstDocument.vbp** to an ISP and download it as needed. (You may have to inform your ISP that the format of **.vbd** files is binary. Otherwise, you may find your Web browser downloading **.vbd** files as text, which is the default for unknown file formats.) These documents require **vbrun500.dll** (as well as other files if you include ActiveX controls in your document). If the target computer doesn't have the required support files, you can create a **.cab** file using the Visual Basic Setup Wizard, just as we did with ActiveX controls. The Setup Wizard will also create a sample **.htm** file.

Listing 6.1 FirstDocument.dob

```
VERSION 5.00
Begin VB.UserDocument FirstDocument
    ClientHeight    =    1650
    ClientLeft      =    0
    ClientTop       =    0
```

```
ClientWidth     =   2970
HScrollSmallChange=   225
ScaleHeight     =   1650
ScaleWidth      =   2970
VScrollSmallChange=   225
Begin VB.Label Label1
   Caption      =   "Hello World!"
   Height       =   495
   Left         =   840
   TabIndex     =   0
   Top          =   480
   Width        =   1215
End
End
Attribute VB_Name = "FirstDocument"
Attribute VB_GlobalNameSpace = False
Attribute VB_Creatable = True
Attribute VB_PredeclaredId = False
Attribute VB_Exposed = True
Option Explicit
```

FirstDocument isn't very impressive—all we did was to place a label in it. Let's see something more powerful.

The Calculator Example

In one attractive method that uses ActiveX documents, you place entire applications on an Internet server and download them as needed. With this technique, bank loan officers could download the newest rate calculators, which have been loaded with up-to-date rate schedules. Let's take a look at an example. Our calculator application is an ActiveX document that comprises three text boxes and a command button marked with an **=** sign:

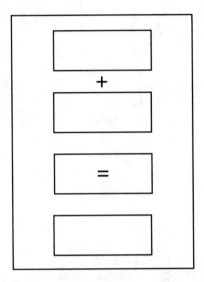

After downloading this document in a Web browser, the user can use it for calculations. To add two integers, users enter the numbers in the top two text boxes and click the button marked **=**. The sum appears in the bottom text box:

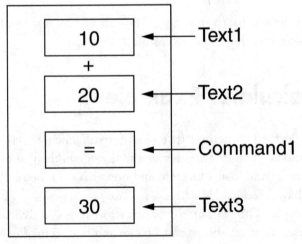

Let's put this example to work. Our Visual Basic application will load the calculator document either from disk or from the Internet. We'll use the Visual Basic Application Wizard and build a Web browser right into the application. The Web browser is invoked with the **Web Browser** menu item:

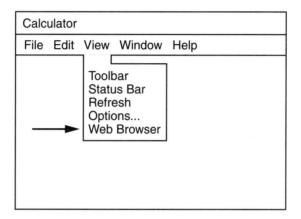

We'll change this menu item to **Calculator**:

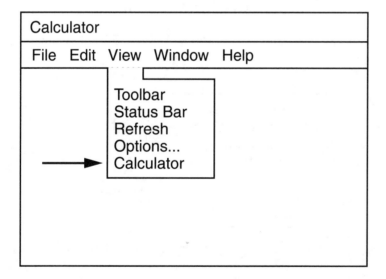

This menu item displays our calculator document (loading it either locally or from the Internet—it's transparent to the user), which can be complete with the latest rate schedules and so on:

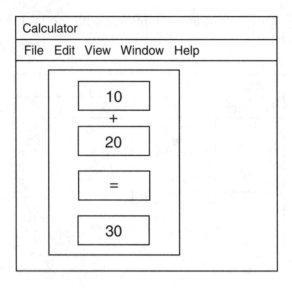

Creating the Calculator ActiveX Document

Open Visual Basic and create a new ActiveX EXE Document project, calling it **calcdoc**. Now add the controls:

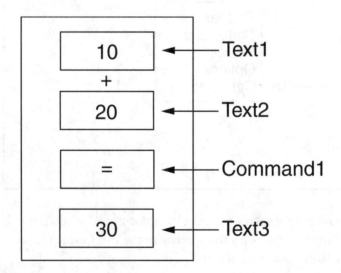

The result appears in Figure 6.3. In the Project window, click the new document's entry and give it the name **Calculator** in the properties window.

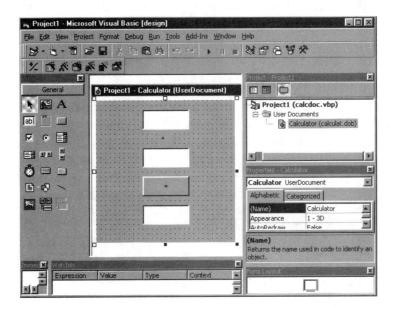

Figure 6.3 Designing our calculator ActiveX document.

Now we can make the calculator active. When the user places integers into the top two text boxes and then clicks the = button, we want to add the two integers and display the sum in the bottom text box, Text3. All we have to do is to add this line to the = button's click event handler, Command1_Click():

```
Private Sub Command1_Click()
-> Text3 = Str(Val(Text1.Text) + Val(Text2.Text))
End Sub
```

That's it—our ActiveX document is complete. Create **Calculator.vbd** by clicking **Make calcdoc.exe** in the File menu.

Creating the Calculator ActiveX Application

The next step is to create the application that will load and use this ActiveX document. Create a new project in Visual Basic. Using the Application Wizard, make it an MDI application and add Web browser support. Give this application the name **Calculator**.

Loading the ActiveX Document

Next, use the Menu Editor to change the new application's **Web Browser** item in the View menu to **Calculator** by changing its caption, as shown in Figure 6.4.

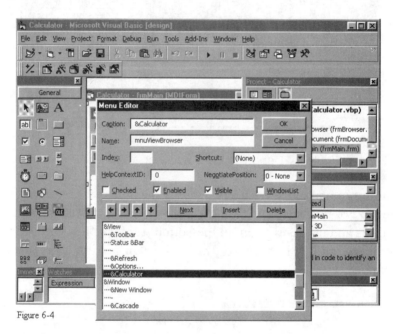

Figure 6-4

Figure 6.4 Setting up our application with the Menu Editor.

Now double-click that item to open its click handler:

```
Private Sub mnuViewBrowser_Click()
    Dim frmB As New frmBrowser
```

```
    frmB.StartingAddress = "http://www.microsoft.com"
    frmB.Show
End Sub
```

Here is where we will load our new ActiveX document, so add its address (either local or as an URL) here as the Web browser's starting address:

```
Private Sub mnuViewBrowser_Click()
    Dim frmB As New frmBrowser
->  frmB.StartingAddress = "c:\vbi\calculator.vbd"
    frmB.Show
End Sub
```

When the browser is invoked, it will load and display our ActiveX calculator document, **calculator.vbd**.

Customizing Our Web Browser

There are some changes we can make to the Web browser form. For example, the current caption of the Web browser form shows the current URL of the browser:

```
Private Sub timTimer_Timer()
    If brwWebBrowser.Busy = False Then
        timTimer.Enabled = False
->      Me.Caption = brwWebBrowser.LocationName
    Else
        Me.Caption = "Working..."
    End If
End Sub
```

Let's replace that with the simple caption **Calculator**:

```
Private Sub timTimer_Timer()
    If brwWebBrowser.Busy = False Then
        timTimer.Enabled = False
->      Me.Caption = "Calculator"
    Else
```

```
        Me.Caption = "Working..."
    End If
End Sub
```

In addition, we'll remove both Web browser buttons—they are not required—and remove the combo box in which the URL is displayed (see Figure 6.5). (Click the buttons and the combo box, pressing the **Del** key to remove each control.)

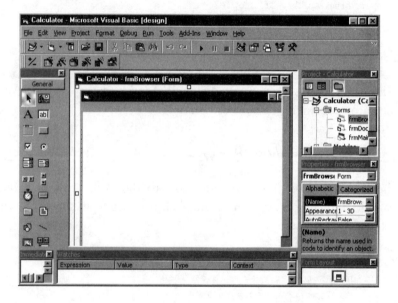

Figure 6.5 Redesigning our Web browser.

We must comment out all code, such as the combo box click event, that makes reference to these controls:

```
'Private Sub cboAddress_Click()
'    If mbDontNavigateNow Then Exit Sub
'    timTimer.Enabled = True
'    brwWebBrowser.Navigate cboAddress.Text
'End Sub
```

Run the Calculator application, as shown in Figure 6.6, and select the **Calculator** item in the View menu to open the Calculator ActiveX document. As far as users are concerned, this document is ready to use, whether it came from their disk or the Internet. As you can see, this is an exceptionally powerful technique. Our Calculator ActiveX document is a success. The code for **calculator.dob** appears in Listing 6.2, **frmBrowser.frm** in Listing 6.3, and **frmMain.frm** in Listing 6.4.

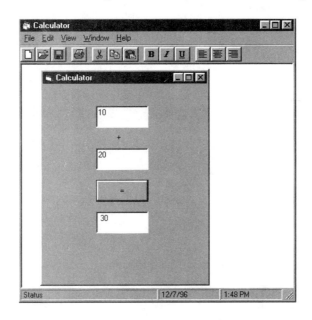

Figure 6.6 Our Calculator ActiveX document at work.

Listing 6.2 calculat.dob

```
VERSION 5.00
Begin VB.UserDocument UserDocument1
   ClientHeight    =   3585
   ClientLeft      =   0
   ClientTop       =   0
   ClientWidth     =   3585
   HScrollSmallChange=   225
   ScaleHeight     =   3585
```

```
ScaleWidth      =   3585
VScrollSmallChange=   225
Begin VB.CommandButton Command1
   Caption          =    "="
   Height           =    495
   Left             =    1200
   TabIndex         =    3
   Top              =    1920
   Width            =    1215
End
Begin VB.TextBox Text3
   Height           =    495
   Left             =    1200
   TabIndex         =    2
   Top              =    2640
   Width            =    1215
End
Begin VB.TextBox Text2
   Height           =    495
   Left             =    1200
   TabIndex         =    1
   Top              =    1200
   Width            =    1215
End
Begin VB.TextBox Text1
   Height           =    495
   Left             =    1200
   TabIndex         =    0
   Top              =    240
   Width            =    1215
End
Begin VB.Label Label1
   Caption          =    "+"
   Height           =    255
   Left             =    1680
   TabIndex         =    4
   Top              =    840
   Width            =    255
End
```

```
End
Attribute VB_Name = "UserDocument1"
Attribute VB_GlobalNameSpace = False
Attribute VB_Creatable = True
Attribute VB_PredeclaredId = False
Attribute VB_Exposed = True
Option Explicit

Private Sub Command1_Click()
    Text3 = Str(Val(Text1.Text) + Val(Text2.Text))
End Sub
```

Listing 6.3 frmBrowser.frm

```
VERSION 5.00
Object = "{6B7E6392-850A-101B-AFC0-4210102A8DA7}#1.1#0"; "COMCTL32.OCX"
Object = "{EAB22AC0-30C1-11CF-A7EB-0000C05BAE0B}#1.0#0"; "SHDOCVW.DLL"
Begin VB.Form frmBrowser
   ClientHeight    =     5055
   ClientLeft      =     3060
   ClientTop       =     3345
   ClientWidth     =     5775
   LinkTopic       =     "Form1"
   MDIChild        =     -1   'True
   ScaleHeight     =     5055
   ScaleWidth      =     5775
   ShowInTaskbar   =     0    'False
   Begin SHDocVwCtl.WebBrowser brwWebBrowser
      Height           =     4800
      Left             =     45
      TabIndex         =     0
      Top              =     255
      Width            =     5400
      Object.Height        =     320
      Object.Width         =     360
      AutoSize         =     0
      ViewMode         =     1
      AutoSizePercentage=     0
```

```
         AutoArrange     =   -1  'True
         NoClientEdge    =   -1  'True
         AlignLeft       =   0   'False
      End
      Begin VB.Timer timTimer
         Enabled         =   0   'False
         Interval        =   5
         Left            =   4920
         Top             =   1500
      End
      Begin VB.PictureBox picAddress
         Align           =   1   'Align Top
         BorderStyle     =   0   'None
         Height          =   675
         Left            =   0
         ScaleHeight     =   675
         ScaleWidth      =   5775
         TabIndex        =   1
         TabStop         =   0   'False
         Top             =   0
         Width           =   5775
      End
      Begin ComctlLib.ImageList imlIcons
         Left            =   2670
         Top             =   2325
         _ExtentX        =   1005
         _ExtentY        =   1005
         BackColor       =   -2147483643
         ImageWidth      =   24
         ImageHeight     =   24
         MaskColor       =   12632256
         BeginProperty Images {8556BCD1-E01E-11CF-8E74-00A0C90F26F8}
            NumListImages   =   6
            BeginProperty ListImage1 {8556BCD3-E01E-11CF-8E74-00A0C90F26F8}
               Picture         =   "frmBrowser.frx":0000
               Key             =   ""
            EndProperty
            BeginProperty ListImage2 {8556BCD3-E01E-11CF-8E74-00A0C90F26F8}
               Picture         =   "frmBrowser.frx":0712
```

```
                    Key              =    ""
              EndProperty
              BeginProperty ListImage3 {8556BCD3-E01E-11CF-8E74-
                                        00A0C90F26F8}
                    Picture          =    "frmBrowser.frx":0E24
                    Key              =    ""
              EndProperty
              BeginProperty ListImage4 {8556BCD3-E01E-11CF-8E74-
                                        00A0C90F26F8}
                    Picture          =    "frmBrowser.frx":1536
                    Key              =    ""
              EndProperty
              BeginProperty ListImage5 {8556BCD3-E01E-11CF-8E74-
                                        00A0C90F26F8}
                    Picture          =    "frmBrowser.frx":1C48
                    Key              =    ""
              EndProperty
              BeginProperty ListImage6 {8556BCD3-E01E-11CF-8E74-
                                        00A0C90F26F8}
                    Picture          =    "frmBrowser.frx":235A
                    Key              =    ""
              EndProperty
          EndProperty
      End
End
Attribute VB_Name = "frmBrowser"
Attribute VB_GlobalNameSpace = False
Attribute VB_Creatable = False
Attribute VB_PredeclaredId = True
Attribute VB_Exposed = False
Public StartingAddress As String
Dim mbDontNavigateNow As Boolean
Private Sub Form_Load()
    On Error Resume Next
    Me.Show
    'tbToolBar.Refresh
    Form_Resize

    'cboAddress.Move 50, lblAddress.Top + lblAddress.Height + 15
```

```
    If Len(StartingAddress) > 0 Then
        'cboAddress.Text = StartingAddress
        'cboAddress.AddItem cboAddress.Text
        'try to navigate to the starting address
        timTimer.Enabled = True
        brwWebBrowser.Navigate StartingAddress
    End If

End Sub

'Private Sub brwWebBrowser_DownloadComplete()
'    On Error Resume Next
'    Me.Caption = brwWebBrowser.LocationName
'End Sub

'Private Sub brwWebBrowser_NavigateComplete(ByVal URL As String)
'    Dim i As Integer
'    Dim bFound As Boolean
'    Me.Caption = brwWebBrowser.LocationName
'    For i = 0 To cboAddress.ListCount - 1
'        If cboAddress.List(i) = brwWebBrowser.LocationURL Then
'            bFound = True
'            Exit For
'        End If
'    Next i
'    mbDontNavigateNow = True
'    If bFound Then
'        cboAddress.RemoveItem i
'    End If
'    cboAddress.AddItem brwWebBrowser.LocationURL, 0
'    cboAddress.ListIndex = 0
'    mbDontNavigateNow = False
'End Sub

'Private Sub cboAddress_Click()
'    If mbDontNavigateNow Then Exit Sub
'    timTimer.Enabled = True
'    brwWebBrowser.Navigate cboAddress.Text
'End Sub
```

```
'Private Sub cboAddress_KeyPress(KeyAscii As Integer)
'    On Error Resume Next
'    If KeyAscii = vbKeyReturn Then
'        cboAddress_Click
'    End If
'End Sub

Private Sub Form_Resize()
    'cboAddress.Width = Me.ScaleWidth - 100
    brwWebBrowser.Width = Me.ScaleWidth - 100
    brwWebBrowser.Height = Me.ScaleHeight - (picAddress.Top +
picAddress.Height) - 100
End Sub

Private Sub timTimer_Timer()
    If brwWebBrowser.Busy = False Then
        timTimer.Enabled = False
        'Me.Caption = brwWebBrowser.LocationName
        Me.Caption = "Calculator"
    Else
        Me.Caption = "Working..."
    End If
End Sub

'Private Sub tbToolBar_ButtonClick(ByVal Button As Button)
'    On Error Resume Next

'    timTimer.Enabled = True

'    Select Case Button.Key
'        Case "Back"
'            brwWebBrowser.GoBack
'        Case "Forward"
'            brwWebBrowser.GoForward
'        Case "Refresh"
'            brwWebBrowser.Refresh
'        Case "Home"
'            brwWebBrowser.GoHome
'        Case "Search"
```

```
'                    brwWebBrowser.GoSearch
'            Case "Stop"
'                timTimer.Enabled = False
'                brwWebBrowser.Stop
'                Me.Caption = brwWebBrowser.LocationName
'        End Select

'End Sub
```

Listing 6.4 frmMain.frm

```
VERSION 5.00
Object = "{F9043C88-F6F2-101A-A3C9-08002B2F49FB}#1.1#0"; "COMDLG32.OCX"
Object = "{6B7E6392-850A-101B-AFC0-4210102A8DA7}#1.1#0"; "COMCTL32.OCX"
Begin VB.MDIForm frmMain
    BackColor       =   &H8000000C&
    Caption         =   "Calculator"
    ClientHeight    =   3195
    ClientLeft      =   165
    ClientTop       =   735
    ClientWidth     =   4680
    LinkTopic       =   "MDIForm1"
    StartUpPosition =   3  'Windows Default
    Begin ComctlLib.Toolbar tbToolBar
        Align           =   1  'Align Top
        Height          =   420
        Left            =   0
        TabIndex        =   1
        Top             =   0
        Width           =   4680
        _ExtentX        =   8255
        _ExtentY        =   741
        ButtonWidth     =   635
        ButtonHeight    =   582
        Appearance      =   1
        ImageList       =   "imlIcons"
        BeginProperty Buttons {7791BA41-E020-11CF-8E74-00A0C90F26F8}
            NumButtons      =   17
```

```
BeginProperty Button1 {7791BA43-E020-11CF-8E74-00A0C90F26F8}
    Key             =   "New"
    Object.ToolTipText      =   "New"
    Object.Tag              =   ""
    ImageIndex      =   1
EndProperty
BeginProperty Button2 {7791BA43-E020-11CF-8E74-00A0C90F26F8}
    Key             =   "Open"
    Object.ToolTipText      =   "Open"
    Object.Tag              =   ""
    ImageIndex      =   2
EndProperty
BeginProperty Button3 {7791BA43-E020-11CF-8E74-00A0C90F26F8}
    Key             =   "Save"
    Object.ToolTipText      =   "Save"
    Object.Tag              =   ""
    ImageIndex      =   3
EndProperty
BeginProperty Button4 {7791BA43-E020-11CF-8E74-00A0C90F26F8}
    Key             =   ""
    Object.Tag              =   ""
    Style           =   3
EndProperty
BeginProperty Button5 {7791BA43-E020-11CF-8E74-00A0C90F26F8}
    Key             =   "Print"
    Object.ToolTipText      =   "Print"
    Object.Tag              =   ""
    ImageIndex      =   4
EndProperty
BeginProperty Button6 {7791BA43-E020-11CF-8E74-00A0C90F26F8}
    Key             =   ""
    Object.Tag              =   ""
    Style           =   3
EndProperty
BeginProperty Button7 {7791BA43-E020-11CF-8E74-00A0C90F26F8}
    Key             =   "Cut"
    Object.ToolTipText      =   "Cut"
    Object.Tag              =   ""
    ImageIndex      =   5
```

```
            EndProperty
            BeginProperty Button8 {7791BA43-E020-11CF-8E74-00A0C90F26F8}
                Key             =       "Copy"
                Object.ToolTipText      =       "Copy"
                Object.Tag              =       ""
                ImageIndex      =       6
            EndProperty
            BeginProperty Button9 {7791BA43-E020-11CF-8E74-00A0C90F26F8}
                Key             =       "Paste"
                Object.ToolTipText      =       "Paste"
                Object.Tag              =       ""
                ImageIndex      =       7
            EndProperty
            BeginProperty Button10 {7791BA43-E020-11CF-8E74-00A0C90F26F8}
                Key             =       ""
                Object.Tag              =       ""
                Style           =       3
            EndProperty
            BeginProperty Button11 {7791BA43-E020-11CF-8E74-00A0C90F26F8}
                Key             =       "Bold"
                Object.ToolTipText      =       "Bold"
                Object.Tag              =       ""
                ImageIndex      =       8
            EndProperty
            BeginProperty Button12 {7791BA43-E020-11CF-8E74-00A0C90F26F8}
                Key             =       "Italic"
                Object.ToolTipText      =       "Italic"
                Object.Tag              =       ""
                ImageIndex      =       9
            EndProperty
            BeginProperty Button13 {7791BA43-E020-11CF-8E74-00A0C90F26F8}
                Key             =       "Underline"
                Object.ToolTipText      =       "Underline"
                Object.Tag              =       ""
                ImageIndex      =       10
            EndProperty
            BeginProperty Button14 {7791BA43-E020-11CF-8E74-00A0C90F26F8}
                Key             =       ""
                Object.Tag              =       ""
```

```
            Style            =   3
        EndProperty
        BeginProperty Button15 {7791BA43-E020-11CF-8E74-00A0C90F26F8}
            Key              =   "Left"
            Object.ToolTipText    =   "Left Justify"
            Object.Tag            =   ""
            ImageIndex       =   11
        EndProperty
        BeginProperty Button16 {7791BA43-E020-11CF-8E74-00A0C90F26F8}
            Key              =   "Center"
            Object.ToolTipText    =   "Center"
            Object.Tag            =   ""
            ImageIndex       =   12
        EndProperty
        BeginProperty Button17 {7791BA43-E020-11CF-8E74-00A0C90F26F8}
            Key              =   "Right"
            Object.ToolTipText    =   "Right Justify"
            Object.Tag            =   ""
            ImageIndex       =   13
        EndProperty
    EndProperty
    MouseIcon        =   "frmMain.frx":0000
End
Begin MSComDlg.CommonDialog dlgCommonDialog
    Left             =   1740
    Top              =   1350
    _ExtentX         =   847
    _ExtentY         =   847
    FontSize         =   2.89174e-37
End
Begin ComctlLib.StatusBar sbStatusBar
    Align            =   2   'Align Bottom
    Height           =   270
    Left             =   0
    TabIndex         =   0
    Top              =   2925
    Width            =   4680
    _ExtentX         =   8255
    _ExtentY         =   476
```

```
SimpleText     =    ""
BeginProperty Panels {2C787A51-E01C-11CF-8E74-00A0C90F26F8}
   NumPanels    =   3
   BeginProperty Panel1 {2C787A53-E01C-11CF-8E74-00A0C90F26F8}
      AutoSize       =   1
      Object.Width        =    2619
      MinWidth       =   2540
      Text           =   "Status"
      TextSave       =   "Status"
      Key            =   ""
      Object.Tag              =    ""
   EndProperty
   BeginProperty Panel2 {2C787A53-E01C-11CF-8E74-00A0C90F26F8}
      Style          =   6
      AutoSize       =   2
      Object.Width        =    2540
      MinWidth       =   2540
      TextSave       =   "12/7/96"
      Key            =   ""
      Object.Tag              =    ""
   EndProperty
   BeginProperty Panel3 {2C787A53-E01C-11CF-8E74-00A0C90F26F8}
      Style          =   5
      AutoSize       =   2
      Object.Width        =    2540
      MinWidth       =   2540
      TextSave       =   "2:01 PM"
      Key            =   ""
      Object.Tag              =    ""
   EndProperty
EndProperty
BeginProperty Font {0BE35203-8F91-11CE-9DE3-00AA004BB851}
   Name           =   "MS Sans Serif"
   Size           =   8.25
   Charset        =   0
   Weight         =   400
   Underline      =   0    'False
   Italic         =   0    'False
   Strikethrough  =   0    'False
```

```
      EndProperty
      MouseIcon        =    "frmMain.frx":001C
End
Begin ComctlLib.ImageList imlIcons
      Left             =    1740
      Top              =    1350
      _ExtentX         =    1005
      _ExtentY         =    1005
      BackColor        =    -2147483643
      ImageWidth       =    16
      ImageHeight      =    16
      MaskColor        =    12632256
      BeginProperty Images {8556BCD1-E01E-11CF-8E74-00A0C90F26F8}
         NumListImages   =    13
         BeginProperty ListImage1 {8556BCD3-E01E-11CF-8E74-00A0C90F26F8}
            Picture          =    "frmMain.frx":0038
            Key              =    ""
         EndProperty
         BeginProperty ListImage2 {8556BCD3-E01E-11CF-8E74-00A0C90F26F8}
            Picture          =    "frmMain.frx":038A
            Key              =    ""
         EndProperty
         BeginProperty ListImage3 {8556BCD3-E01E-11CF-8E74-00A0C90F26F8}
            Picture          =    "frmMain.frx":06DC
            Key              =    ""
         EndProperty
         BeginProperty ListImage4 {8556BCD3-E01E-11CF-8E74-00A0C90F26F8}
            Picture          =    "frmMain.frx":0A2E
            Key              =    ""
         EndProperty
         BeginProperty ListImage5 {8556BCD3-E01E-11CF-8E74-00A0C90F26F8}
            Picture          =    "frmMain.frx":0D80
            Key              =    ""
         EndProperty
         BeginProperty ListImage6 {8556BCD3-E01E-11CF-8E74-00A0C90F26F8}
            Picture          =    "frmMain.frx":10D2
            Key              =    ""
         EndProperty
         BeginProperty ListImage7 {8556BCD3-E01E-11CF-8E74-00A0C90F26F8}
```

```
                 Picture         =    "frmMain.frx":1424
                 Key             =    ""
              EndProperty
              BeginProperty ListImage8 {8556BCD3-E01E-11CF-8E74-00A0C90F26F8}
                 Picture         =    "frmMain.frx":1776
                 Key             =    ""
              EndProperty
              BeginProperty ListImage9 {8556BCD3-E01E-11CF-8E74-00A0C90F26F8}
                 Picture         =    "frmMain.frx":1AC8
                 Key             =    ""
              EndProperty
              BeginProperty ListImage10 {8556BCD3-E01E-11CF-8E74-
                                  00A0C90F26F8}
                 Picture         =    "frmMain.frx":1E1A
                 Key             =    ""
              EndProperty
              BeginProperty ListImage11 {8556BCD3-E01E-11CF-8E74-
                                  00A0C90F26F8}
                 Picture         =    "frmMain.frx":216C
                 Key             =    ""
              EndProperty
              BeginProperty ListImage12 {8556BCD3-E01E-11CF-8E74-
                                  00A0C90F26F8}
                 Picture         =    "frmMain.frx":24BE
                 Key             =    ""
              EndProperty
              BeginProperty ListImage13 {8556BCD3-E01E-11CF-8E74-
                                  00A0C90F26F8}
                 Picture         =    "frmMain.frx":2810
                 Key             =    ""
              EndProperty
           EndProperty
        End
        Begin VB.Menu mnuFile
           Caption         =    "&File"
           Begin VB.Menu mnuFileNew
              Caption         =    "&New"
              Shortcut        =    ^N
           End
           Begin VB.Menu mnuFileOpen
```

```
      Caption         =   "&Open"
      Shortcut        =   ^O
End
Begin VB.Menu mnuFileClose
      Caption         =   "&Close"
End
Begin VB.Menu mnuFileBar1
      Caption         =   "-"
End
Begin VB.Menu mnuFileSave
      Caption         =   "&Save"
      Shortcut        =   ^S
End
Begin VB.Menu mnuFileSaveAs
      Caption         =   "Save &As..."
End
Begin VB.Menu mnuFileSaveAll
      Caption         =   "Save A&ll"
End
Begin VB.Menu mnuFileBar2
      Caption         =   "-"
End
Begin VB.Menu mnuFileProperties
      Caption         =   "Propert&ies"
End
Begin VB.Menu mnuFileBar3
      Caption         =   "-"
End
Begin VB.Menu mnuFilePageSetup
      Caption         =   "Page Set&up..."
End
Begin VB.Menu mnuFilePrintPreview
      Caption         =   "Print Pre&view"
End
Begin VB.Menu mnuFilePrint
      Caption         =   "&Print..."
      Shortcut        =   ^P
End
Begin VB.Menu mnuFileBar4
```

```
            Caption       =    "-"
         End
         Begin VB.Menu mnuFileSend
            Caption       =    "Sen&d..."
         End
         Begin VB.Menu mnuFileBar5
            Caption       =    "-"
         End
         Begin VB.Menu mnuFileMRU
            Caption       =    ""
            Index         =    0
            Visible       =    0    'False
         End
         Begin VB.Menu mnuFileMRU
            Caption       =    ""
            Index         =    1
            Visible       =    0    'False
         End
         Begin VB.Menu mnuFileMRU
            Caption       =    ""
            Index         =    2
            Visible       =    0    'False
         End
         Begin VB.Menu mnuFileMRU
            Caption       =    ""
            Index         =    3
            Visible       =    0    'False
         End
         Begin VB.Menu mnuFileBar6
            Caption       =    "-"
            Visible       =    0    'False
         End
         Begin VB.Menu mnuFileExit
            Caption       =    "E&xit"
         End
      End
      Begin VB.Menu mnuEdit
         Caption       =    "&Edit"
         Begin VB.Menu mnuEditUndo
```

```
            Caption         =    "&Undo"
            Shortcut        =    ^Z
         End
         Begin VB.Menu mnuEditBar1
            Caption         =    "-"
         End
         Begin VB.Menu mnuEditCut
            Caption         =    "Cu&t"
            Shortcut        =    ^X
         End
         Begin VB.Menu mnuEditCopy
            Caption         =    "&Copy"
            Shortcut        =    ^C
         End
         Begin VB.Menu mnuEditPaste
            Caption         =    "&Paste"
            Shortcut        =    ^V
         End
         Begin VB.Menu mnuEditPasteSpecial
            Caption         =    "Paste &Special..."
         End
      End
      Begin VB.Menu mnuView
         Caption         =    "&View"
         Begin VB.Menu mnuViewToolbar
            Caption         =    "&Toolbar"
            Checked         =    -1  'True
         End
         Begin VB.Menu mnuViewStatusBar
            Caption         =    "Status &Bar"
            Checked         =    -1  'True
         End
         Begin VB.Menu mnuViewBar2
            Caption         =    "-"
         End
         Begin VB.Menu mnuViewRefresh
            Caption         =    "&Refresh"
         End
         Begin VB.Menu mnuViewOptions
```

```
            Caption         =    "&Options..."
         End
         Begin VB.Menu mnuViewBrowser
            Caption         =    "&Calculator"
         End
      End
      Begin VB.Menu mnuWindow
         Caption         =    "&Window"
         WindowList      =    -1  'True
         Begin VB.Menu mnuWindowNewWindow
            Caption         =    "&New Window"
         End
         Begin VB.Menu mnuWindowBar1
            Caption         =    "-"
         End
         Begin VB.Menu mnuWindowCascade
            Caption         =    "&Cascade"
         End
         Begin VB.Menu mnuWindowTileHorizontal
            Caption         =    "Tile &Horizontal"
         End
         Begin VB.Menu mnuWindowTileVertical
            Caption         =    "Tile &Vertical"
         End
         Begin VB.Menu mnuWindowArrangeIcons
            Caption         =    "&Arrange Icons"
         End
      End
      Begin VB.Menu mnuHelp
         Caption         =    "&Help"
         Begin VB.Menu mnuHelpContents
            Caption         =    "&Contents"
         End
         Begin VB.Menu mnuHelpSearch
            Caption         =    "&Search For Help On..."
         End
         Begin VB.Menu mnuHelpBar1
            Caption         =    "-"
         End
```

```vb
        Begin VB.Menu mnuHelpAbout
            Caption         =   "&About Calculator..."
        End
    End
End
Attribute VB_Name = "frmMain"
Attribute VB_GlobalNameSpace = False
Attribute VB_Creatable = False
Attribute VB_PredeclaredId = True
Attribute VB_Exposed = False
Private Declare Function OSWinHelp% Lib "user32" Alias "WinHelpA"
(ByVal hwnd&, ByVal HelpFile$, ByVal wCommand%, dwData As Any)
Private Sub MDIForm_Load()
    Me.Left = GetSetting(App.Title, "Settings", "MainLeft", 1000)
    Me.Top = GetSetting(App.Title, "Settings", "MainTop", 1000)
    Me.Width = GetSetting(App.Title, "Settings", "MainWidth", 6500)
    Me.Height = GetSetting(App.Title, "Settings", "MainHeight", 6500)
    LoadNewDoc
End Sub

Private Sub LoadNewDoc()
    Static lDocumentCount As Long
    Dim frmD As frmDocument

    lDocumentCount = lDocumentCount + 1
    Set frmD = New frmDocument
    frmD.Caption = "Document " & lDocumentCount
    frmD.Show
End Sub

Private Sub MDIForm_Unload(Cancel As Integer)
    If Me.WindowState <> vbMinimized Then
        SaveSetting App.Title, "Settings", "MainLeft", Me.Left
        SaveSetting App.Title, "Settings", "MainTop", Me.Top
        SaveSetting App.Title, "Settings", "MainWidth", Me.Width
        SaveSetting App.Title, "Settings", "MainHeight", Me.Height
    End If
End Sub
```

```
Private Sub mnuViewBrowser_Click()
    Dim frmB As New frmBrowser
    frmB.StartingAddress = "c:\vbi\calculator\calculator.vbd"
    frmB.Show
End Sub

Private Sub mnuHelpAbout_Click()
    'To Do
    MsgBox "About Box Code goes here!"
End Sub

Private Sub mnuViewOptions_Click()
    'To Do
    MsgBox "Options Dialog Code goes here!"
End Sub

Private Sub mnuViewStatusBar_Click()
    If mnuViewStatusBar.Checked Then
        sbStatusBar.Visible = False
        mnuViewStatusBar.Checked = False
    Else
        sbStatusBar.Visible = True
        mnuViewStatusBar.Checked = True
    End If
End Sub

Private Sub mnuViewToolbar_Click()
    If mnuViewToolbar.Checked Then
        tbToolBar.Visible = False
        mnuViewToolbar.Checked = False
    Else
        tbToolBar.Visible = True
        mnuViewToolbar.Checked = True
    End If
End Sub

Private Sub tbToolBar_ButtonClick(ByVal Button As ComctlLib.Button)

    Select Case Button.Key
```

```
        Case "New"
            LoadNewDoc
        Case "New"
            mnuFileNew_Click
        Case "Open"
            mnuFileOpen_Click
        Case "Save"
            mnuFileSave_Click
        Case "Print"
            mnuFilePrint_Click
        Case "Cut"
            mnuEditCut_Click
        Case "Copy"
            mnuEditCopy_Click
        Case "Paste"
            mnuEditPaste_Click
        Case "Bold"
            'To Do
            MsgBox "Bold Code goes here!"
        Case "Italic"
            'To Do
            MsgBox "Italic Code goes here!"
        Case "Underline"
            'To Do
            MsgBox "Underline Code goes here!"
        Case "Left"
            'To Do
            MsgBox "Left Code goes here!"
        Case "Center"
            'To Do
            MsgBox "Center Code goes here!"
        Case "Right"
            'To Do
            MsgBox "Right Code goes here!"
    End Select
End Sub

Private Sub mnuHelpContents_Click()
```

```
    Dim nRet As Integer

    'if there is no helpfile for this project display a message to
    'the user you can set the HelpFile for your application in the
    'Project Properties dialog
    If Len(App.HelpFile) = 0 Then
        MsgBox "Unable to display Help Contents. There is no Help
        associated with this project.", vbInformation, Me.Caption
    Else
        On Error Resume Next
        nRet = OSWinHelp(Me.hwnd, App.HelpFile, 3, 0)
        If Err Then
            MsgBox Err.Description
        End If
    End If
End Sub


Private Sub mnuHelpSearch_Click()

    Dim nRet As Integer

    'if there is no helpfile for this project display a message to
    'the user you can set the HelpFile for your application in the
    'Project Properties dialog
    If Len(App.HelpFile) = 0 Then
        MsgBox "Unable to display Help Contents. There is no Help
        associated with this project.", vbInformation, Me.Caption
    Else
        On Error Resume Next
        nRet = OSWinHelp(Me.hwnd, App.HelpFile, 261, 0)
        If Err Then
            MsgBox Err.Description
        End If
    End If
End Sub


Private Sub mnuWindowArrangeIcons_Click()
    Me.Arrange vbArrangeIcons
End Sub
```

```vb
Private Sub mnuWindowCascade_Click()
    Me.Arrange vbCascade
End Sub


Private Sub mnuWindowNewWindow_Click()
    'To Do
    MsgBox "New Window Code goes here!"
End Sub


Private Sub mnuWindowTileHorizontal_Click()
    Me.Arrange vbTileHorizontal
End Sub


Private Sub mnuWindowTileVertical_Click()
    Me.Arrange vbTileVertical
End Sub


Private Sub mnuViewRefresh_Click()
    'To Do
    MsgBox "Refresh Code goes here!"
End Sub


Private Sub mnuEditCopy_Click()
    'To Do
    MsgBox "Copy Code goes here!"
End Sub


Private Sub mnuEditCut_Click()
    'To Do
    MsgBox "Cut Code goes here!"
End Sub


Private Sub mnuEditPaste_Click()
    'To Do
    MsgBox "Paste Code goes here!"
End Sub


Private Sub mnuEditPasteSpecial_Click()
    'To Do
```

```
        MsgBox "Paste Special Code goes here!"
End Sub

Private Sub mnuEditUndo_Click()
        'To Do
        MsgBox "Undo Code goes here!"
End Sub

Private Sub mnuFileOpen_Click()
        Dim sFile As String

        With dlgCommonDialog
            'To Do
            'set the flags and attributes of the
            'common dialog control
            .Filter = "All Files (*.*)|*.*"
            .ShowOpen
            If Len(.filename) = 0 Then
                Exit Sub
            End If
            sFile = .filename
        End With
        'To Do
        'process the opened file
End Sub

Private Sub mnuFileClose_Click()
        'To Do
        MsgBox "Close Code goes here!"
End Sub

Private Sub mnuFileSave_Click()
        'To Do
        MsgBox "Save Code goes here!"
End Sub

Private Sub mnuFileSaveAs_Click()
        'To Do
        'Set up the common dialog control
```

```vb
    'prior to calling ShowSave
    dlgCommonDialog.ShowSave
End Sub

Private Sub mnuFileSaveAll_Click()
    'To Do
    MsgBox "Save All Code goes here!"
End Sub

Private Sub mnuFileProperties_Click()
    'To Do
    MsgBox "Properties Code goes here!"
End Sub

Private Sub mnuFilePageSetup_Click()
    dlgCommonDialog.ShowPrinter
End Sub

Private Sub mnuFilePrintPreview_Click()
    'To Do
    MsgBox "Print Preview Code goes here!"
End Sub

Private Sub mnuFilePrint_Click()
    'To Do
    MsgBox "Print Code goes here!"
End Sub

Private Sub mnuFileSend_Click()
    'To Do
    MsgBox "Send Code goes here!"
End Sub

Private Sub mnuFileMRU_Click(Index As Integer)
    'To Do
    MsgBox "MRU Code goes here!"
End Sub

Private Sub mnuFileExit_Click()
```

```
    'unload the form
    Unload Me
End Sub

Private Sub mnuFileNew_Click()
    LoadNewDoc
End Sub
```

That's it for our Calculator ActiveX document example. As you can see, using ActiveX documents provides a powerful method of *distributed* programming in which programs are downloaded as needed. Let's press on now to a new example that is a little more involved, allowing us to navigate from document to document.

The House Example

Our next example might be designed for real estate agents operating in the field. Real estate listings must be kept up-to-date, so let's download them from the Internet. Our new application, House, includes a menu item labeled **Check Listings**:

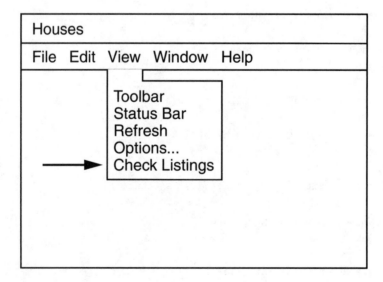

When the agent clicks this item, a new ActiveX document is loaded (either locally or from the Internet), complete with a listbox displaying the current house listings:

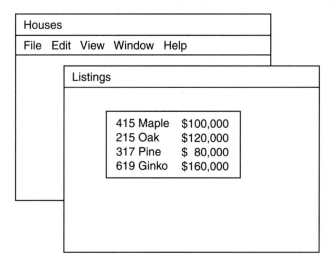

To get more information about any listing, agents click the matching entry in the listbox. We navigate to a Web page that shows more information about that particular house:

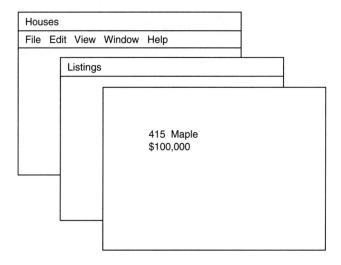

Creating the RealEstate ActiveX Document

First, we will create the ActiveX document that will be loaded to show the real estate listings. Let's call this document **RealEstate**:

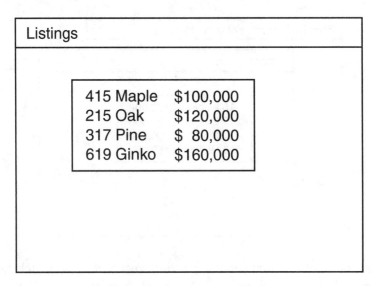

Open Visual Basic and create a new ActiveX Document EXE project, giving it the name **HousesDocument**. Open the new ActiveX document and give it the name **RealEstate**, as shown in Figure 6.7. Next, add a listbox, List1, to this document.

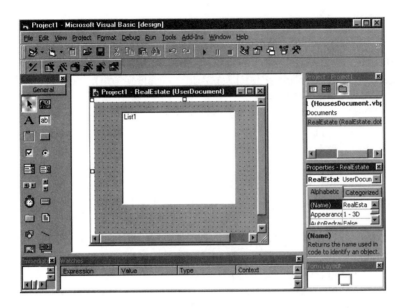

Figure 6.7 Adding a listbox to our RealEstate ActiveX document.

Now we place the entries for each house into the listbox. We use the UserDocument_Initialize() event handler, which is called when the ActiveX document is first loaded. Double-click the document to open that event handler:

```
Private Sub UserDocument_Initialize()

End Sub
```

First, we fill the listbox with information about the available houses:

```
Private Sub UserDocument_Initialize()
        List1.AddItem "415 Maple $100,000"
        List1.AddItem "215 Oak   $120,000"
        List1.AddItem "317 Pine  $80,000"
        List1.AddItem "619 Ginko $160,000"
        .
        .
        .

End Sub
```

When the user clicks one of these entries, we want to navigate to a new page showing more information about the selection. This means that we should store an URL for each entry in the house list, and we do that by creating an array named URLs(). Add that array to the (general) object in the code window:

```
Option Explicit
Dim URLs(4) As String          <-
```

We fill that array in the UserDocument_Initialize() event handler—called when the document is opened—with the URLs of the appropriate Web pages:

```
Private Sub UserDocument_Initialize()
        List1.AddItem "415 Maple $100,000"
        List1.AddItem "215 Oak   $120,000"
        List1.AddItem "317 Pine  $80,000"
        List1.AddItem "619 Ginko $160,000"

  ->    URLs(1) = "c:\vbi\house\a.htm"
  ->    URLs(2) = "c:\vbi\house\b.htm"
  ->    URLs(3) = "c:\vbi\house\c.htm"
  ->    URLs(4) = "c:\vbi\house\d.htm"

End Sub
```

In our example, each Web page will contain only a minimum entry—the address and price of the house:

```
415 Maple
$100,000
```

To navigate to the corresponding URL in the URLs() array, open the listbox's click event handler:

```
Private Sub List1_Click()

End Sub
```

The new URL is stored in URLs(List1.ListIndex + 1), and we get there using the UserDocument object's Hyperlink member object. (UserDocument is the base object of our ActiveX document.) The hyperlink object has a member subroutine named NavigateTo:

```
Private Sub List1_Click()
 ->     Hyperlink.NavigateTo URLs(List1.ListIndex + 1)
End Sub
```

This subroutine navigates us to the new URL, displaying additional information about the house. Now create the **realestate.vbd** document by selecting the **MakeHousesDocument.exe** item in Visual Basic's File menu.

Creating the Houses ActiveX Application

The next step is to create the application that uses our RealEstate document. This is the application that the user can use to load our ActiveX document by clicking the **Check Listings** item:

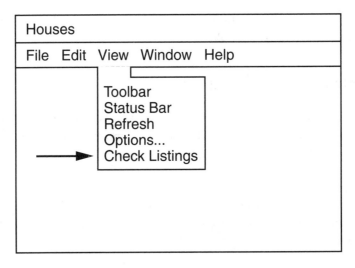

Create a new SDI Visual Basic application using the Application Wizard, naming the application **Houses**, and open this new application.

Loading the ActiveX Document

Using the Menu Editor, change the caption of the **Web Browser** item in the main form to **Check Listings**. In addition, open that menu item's click event and change this line:

```
Private Sub mnuViewBrowser_Click()
    Dim frmB As New frmBrowser
-> frmB.StartingAddress = "http://www.microsoft.com"
    frmB.Show
End Sub
```

Now the starting address of the browser form is our **RealEstate.vbd** ActiveX document:

```
Private Sub mnuViewBrowser_Click()
    Dim frmB As New frmBrowser
    frmB.StartingAddress = "c:\vbi\house\realestate.vbd"
    frmB.Show
End Sub
```

That's it for the main form of our Houses application. The next step is to customize the frmBrowser Web browser.

Customizing Our Web Browser

Open the browser form now. Remove the combo box that displays URLs; just click it and press **Del**. In addition, we remove the code that references that combo box, such as the combo box's click event:

```
'Private Sub cboAddress_Click()
'    If mbDontNavigateNow Then Exit Sub
'    timTimer.Enabled = True
'    brwWebBrowser.Navigate cboAddress.Text
'End Sub
```

We also change the caption from displaying the current URL, which it does now:

```
Private Sub timTimer_Timer()
    If brwWebBrowser.Busy = False Then
        timTimer.Enabled = False
  ->    Me.Caption = brwWebBrowser.LocationName
    Else
        Me.Caption = "Working..."
    End If
End Sub
```

to displaying the title **Listings** this way:

```
Private Sub timTimer_Timer()
    If brwWebBrowser.Busy = False Then
        timTimer.Enabled = False
  ->    Me.Caption = "Listings"
    Else
        Me.Caption = "Working..."
    End If
End Sub
```

Run the Houses application and click **Check Listings** in the View menu, as shown in Figure 6.8, opening our RealEstate ActiveX document. Here all the current houses are listed—whether locally or from the Internet makes no difference to the user. We can keep an updated list of houses on our ISP ready for download.

Next, click one of the house entries in the house list. This action opens Internet Explorer, and you'll see additional information on the selected house (see Figure 6.9). Our Houses application is a success. The code for **RealEstate.dob** appears in Listing 6.5, **frmBrowser.frm** in Listing 6.6, and **frmMain.frm** in Listing 6.7.

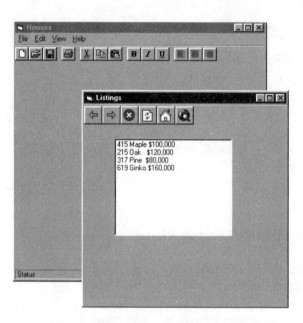

Figure 6.8 Our Houses application loads a new ActiveX document.

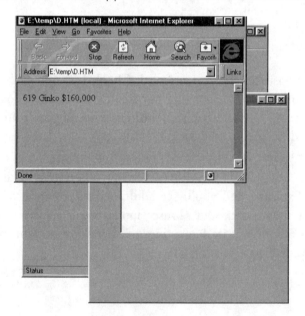

Figure 6.9 Navigating to a new URL from an ActiveX document.

Listing 6.5 RealEstate.dob

```
VERSION 5.00
Begin VB.UserDocument RealEstate
   ClientHeight    =   3600
   ClientLeft      =   0
   ClientTop       =   0
   ClientWidth     =   4800
   HScrollSmallChange=   225
   ScaleHeight     =   3600
   ScaleWidth      =   4800
   VScrollSmallChange=   225
   Begin VB.ListBox List1
      Height          =    2430
      Left            =    720
      TabIndex        =    0
      Top             =    240
      Width           =    3015
   End
End
Attribute VB_Name = "RealEstate"
Attribute VB_GlobalNameSpace = False
Attribute VB_Creatable = True
Attribute VB_PredeclaredId = False
Attribute VB_Exposed = True
Option Explicit
Dim URLs(4) As String

Private Sub List1_Click()
      Hyperlink.NavigateTo URLs(List1.ListIndex + 1)
End Sub

Private Sub UserDocument_Initialize()
      List1.AddItem "415 Maple $100,000"
      List1.AddItem "215 Oak   $120,000"
      List1.AddItem "317 Pine  $80,000"
      List1.AddItem "619 Ginko $160,000"

      URLs(1) = "c:\vbi\house\a.htm"
```

```
                    URLs(2) = "c:\vbi\house\b.htm"
                    URLs(3) = "c:\vbi\house\c.htm"
                    URLs(4) = "c:\vbi\house\d.htm"

            End Sub
```

Listing 6.6 frmBrowser.frm

```
VERSION 5.00
Object = "{6B7E6392-850A-101B-AFC0-4210102A8DA7}#1.1#0"; "COMCTL32.OCX"
Object = "{EAB22AC0-30C1-11CF-A7EB-0000C05BAE0B}#1.0#0"; "SHDOCVW.DLL"
Begin VB.Form frmBrowser
   ClientHeight    =   4605
   ClientLeft      =   3060
   ClientTop       =   3345
   ClientWidth     =   4815
   LinkTopic       =   "Form1"
   ScaleHeight     =   4605
   ScaleWidth      =   4815
   ShowInTaskbar   =   0    'False
   Begin ComctlLib.Toolbar tbToolBar
      Align        =   1    'Align Top
      Height       =   540
      Left         =   0
      TabIndex     =   1
      Top          =   0
      Width        =   4815
      _ExtentX     =   8493
      _ExtentY     =   953
      ButtonWidth  =   635
      ButtonHeight =   582
      Appearance   =   1
      ImageList    =   "imlIcons"
      BeginProperty Buttons {7791BA41-E020-11CF-8E74-00A0C90F26F8}
         NumButtons    =   6
         BeginProperty Button1 {7791BA43-E020-11CF-8E74-00A0C90F26F8}
            Key             =   "Back"
            Object.ToolTipText     =   "Back"
```

```
                 Object.Tag            =     ""
                 ImageIndex      =   1
             EndProperty
             BeginProperty Button2 {7791BA43-E020-11CF-8E74-00A0C90F26F8}
                 Key             =     "Forward"
                 Object.ToolTipText    =     "Forward"
                 Object.Tag            =     ""
                 ImageIndex      =   2
             EndProperty
             BeginProperty Button3 {7791BA43-E020-11CF-8E74-00A0C90F26F8}
                 Key             =     "Stop"
                 Object.ToolTipText    =     "Stop"
                 Object.Tag            =     ""
                 ImageIndex      =   3
             EndProperty
             BeginProperty Button4 {7791BA43-E020-11CF-8E74-00A0C90F26F8}
                 Key             =     "Refresh"
                 Object.ToolTipText    =     "Refresh"
                 Object.Tag            =     ""
                 ImageIndex      =   4
             EndProperty
             BeginProperty Button5 {7791BA43-E020-11CF-8E74-00A0C90F26F8}
                 Key             =     "Home"
                 Object.ToolTipText    =     "Home"
                 Object.Tag            =     ""
                 ImageIndex      =   5
             EndProperty
             BeginProperty Button6 {7791BA43-E020-11CF-8E74-00A0C90F26F8}
                 Key             =     "Search"
                 Object.ToolTipText    =     "Search"
                 Object.Tag            =     ""
                 ImageIndex      =   6
             EndProperty
         EndProperty
      MouseIcon      =    "frmBrowser.frx":0000
End
Begin SHDocVwCtl.WebBrowser brwWebBrowser
   Height         =     4335
   Left           =     45
```

```
      TabIndex        =    0
      Top             =    615
      Width           =    5400
      Object.Height         =    289
      Object.Width          =    360
      AutoSize        =    0
      ViewMode        =    1
      AutoSizePercentage=   0
      AutoArrange     =    -1   'True
      NoClientEdge    =    -1   'True
      AlignLeft       =    0    'False
   End
   Begin VB.Timer timTimer
      Enabled         =    0    'False
      Interval        =    5
      Left            =    6180
      Top             =    1500
   End
   Begin VB.PictureBox picAddress
      Align           =    1    'Align Top
      BorderStyle     =    0    'None
      Height          =    675
      Left            =    0
      ScaleHeight     =    675
      ScaleWidth      =    4815
      TabIndex        =    2
      TabStop         =    0    'False
      Top             =    540
      Width           =    4815
   End
   Begin ComctlLib.ImageList imlIcons
      Left            =    2670
      Top             =    2325
      _ExtentX        =    1005
      _ExtentY        =    1005
      BackColor       =    -2147483643
      ImageWidth      =    24
      ImageHeight     =    24
      MaskColor       =    12632256
```

```
         BeginProperty Images {8556BCD1-E01E-11CF-8E74-00A0C90F26F8}
            NumListImages    =    6
            BeginProperty ListImage1 {8556BCD3-E01E-11CF-8E74-00A0C90F26F8}
               Picture           =    "frmBrowser.frx":001C
               Key               =    ""
            EndProperty
            BeginProperty ListImage2 {8556BCD3-E01E-11CF-8E74-00A0C90F26F8}
               Picture           =    "frmBrowser.frx":072E
               Key               =    ""
            EndProperty
            BeginProperty ListImage3 {8556BCD3-E01E-11CF-8E74-00A0C90F26F8}
               Picture           =    "frmBrowser.frx":0E40
               Key               =    ""
            EndProperty
            BeginProperty ListImage4 {8556BCD3-E01E-11CF-8E74-00A0C90F26F8}
               Picture           =    "frmBrowser.frx":1552
               Key               =    ""
            EndProperty
            BeginProperty ListImage5 {8556BCD3-E01E-11CF-8E74-00A0C90F26F8}
               Picture           =    "frmBrowser.frx":1C64
               Key               =    ""
            EndProperty
            BeginProperty ListImage6 {8556BCD3-E01E-11CF-8E74-00A0C90F26F8}
               Picture           =    "frmBrowser.frx":2376
               Key               =    ""
            EndProperty
         EndProperty
      End
End
Attribute VB_Name = "frmBrowser"
Attribute VB_GlobalNameSpace = False
Attribute VB_Creatable = False
Attribute VB_PredeclaredId = True
Attribute VB_Exposed = False
Public StartingAddress As String
Dim mbDontNavigateNow As Boolean
Private Sub Form_Load()
    On Error Resume Next
    Me.Show
```

```
    tbToolBar.Refresh
    Form_Resize

    'cboAddress.Move 50, lblAddress.Top + lblAddress.Height + 15

    If Len(StartingAddress) > 0 Then
        'cboAddress.Text = StartingAddress
        'cboAddress.AddItem cboAddress.Text
        'try to navigate to the starting address
        timTimer.Enabled = True
        brwWebBrowser.Navigate StartingAddress
    End If

End Sub


Private Sub brwWebBrowser_DownloadComplete()
    On Error Resume Next
    Me.Caption = brwWebBrowser.LocationName
End Sub

'Private Sub brwWebBrowser_NavigateComplete(ByVal URL As String)
'    Dim i As Integer
'    Dim bFound As Boolean
'    Me.Caption = brwWebBrowser.LocationName
'    For i = 0 To cboAddress.ListCount - 1
'        If cboAddress.List(i) = brwWebBrowser.LocationURL Then
'            bFound = True
'            Exit For
'        End If
'    Next i
'    mbDontNavigateNow = True
'    If bFound Then
'        cboAddress.RemoveItem i
'    End If
'    cboAddress.AddItem brwWebBrowser.LocationURL, 0
'    cboAddress.ListIndex = 0
'    mbDontNavigateNow = False
'End Sub
```

```
'Private Sub cboAddress_Click()
'    If mbDontNavigateNow Then Exit Sub
'    timTimer.Enabled = True
'    brwWebBrowser.Navigate cboAddress.Text
'End Sub

'Private Sub cboAddress_KeyPress(KeyAscii As Integer)
'    On Error Resume Next
'    If KeyAscii = vbKeyReturn Then
'        cboAddress_Click
'    End If
'End Sub

Private Sub Form_Resize()
    'cboAddress.Width = Me.ScaleWidth - 100
    brwWebBrowser.Width = Me.ScaleWidth - 100
    brwWebBrowser.Height = Me.ScaleHeight - (picAddress.Top +
    picAddress.Height) - 100
End Sub

Private Sub timTimer_Timer()
    If brwWebBrowser.Busy = False Then
        timTimer.Enabled = False
        Me.Caption = "Listings"
        'Me.Caption = brwWebBrowser.LocationName
    Else
        Me.Caption = "Working..."
    End If
End Sub

Private Sub tbToolBar_ButtonClick(ByVal Button As Button)
    On Error Resume Next

    timTimer.Enabled = True

    Select Case Button.Key
        Case "Back"
            brwWebBrowser.GoBack
        Case "Forward"
```

```
                brwWebBrowser.GoForward
        Case "Refresh"
                brwWebBrowser.Refresh
        Case "Home"
                brwWebBrowser.GoHome
        Case "Search"
                brwWebBrowser.GoSearch
        Case "Stop"
                timTimer.Enabled = False
                brwWebBrowser.Stop
                Me.Caption = brwWebBrowser.LocationName
    End Select

End Sub
```

Listing 6.7 frmMain.frm

```
VERSION 5.00
Object = "{F9043C88-F6F2-101A-A3C9-08002B2F49FB}#1.1#0"; "COMDLG32.OCX"
Object = "{6B7E6392-850A-101B-AFC0-4210102A8DA7}#1.1#0"; "COMCTL32.OCX"
Begin VB.Form frmMain
    Caption         =    "Houses"
    ClientHeight    =    3195
    ClientLeft      =    165
    ClientTop       =    735
    ClientWidth     =    4680
    LinkTopic       =    "Form1"
    ScaleHeight     =    3195
    ScaleWidth      =    4680
    StartUpPosition =    3  'Windows Default
    Begin ComctlLib.Toolbar tbToolBar
        Align       =    1  'Align Top
        Height      =    1080
        Left        =    0
        TabIndex    =    1
        Top         =    0
        Width       =    4680
        _ExtentX    =    8255
```

```
_ExtentY        =     1905
ButtonWidth     =     635
ButtonHeight    =     582
Appearance      =     1
ImageList       =     "imlIcons"
BeginProperty Buttons {7791BA41-E020-11CF-8E74-00A0C90F26F8}
   NumButtons       =     17
   BeginProperty Button1 {7791BA43-E020-11CF-8E74-00A0C90F26F8}
      Key             =     "New"
      Object.ToolTipText      =     "New"
      Object.Tag              =     ""
      ImageIndex      =     1
   EndProperty
   BeginProperty Button2 {7791BA43-E020-11CF-8E74-00A0C90F26F8}
      Key             =     "Open"
      Object.ToolTipText      =     "Open"
      Object.Tag              =     ""
      ImageIndex      =     2
   EndProperty
   BeginProperty Button3 {7791BA43-E020-11CF-8E74-00A0C90F26F8}
      Key             =     "Save"
      Object.ToolTipText      =     "Save"
      Object.Tag              =     ""
      ImageIndex      =     3
   EndProperty
   BeginProperty Button4 {7791BA43-E020-11CF-8E74-00A0C90F26F8}
      Object.Tag              =     ""
      Style           =     3
   EndProperty
   BeginProperty Button5 {7791BA43-E020-11CF-8E74-00A0C90F26F8}
      Key             =     "Print"
      Object.ToolTipText      =     "Print"
      Object.Tag              =     ""
      ImageIndex      =     4
   EndProperty
   BeginProperty Button6 {7791BA43-E020-11CF-8E74-00A0C90F26F8}
      Object.Tag              =     ""
      Style           =     3
   EndProperty
```

```
BeginProperty Button7 {7791BA43-E020-11CF-8E74-00A0C90F26F8}
    Key              =    "Cut"
    Object.ToolTipText    =    "Cut"
    Object.Tag            =    ""
    ImageIndex    =    5
EndProperty
BeginProperty Button8 {7791BA43-E020-11CF-8E74-00A0C90F26F8}
    Key              =    "Copy"
    Object.ToolTipText    =    "Copy"
    Object.Tag            =    ""
    ImageIndex    =    6
EndProperty
BeginProperty Button9 {7791BA43-E020-11CF-8E74-00A0C90F26F8}
    Key              =    "Paste"
    Object.ToolTipText    =    "Paste"
    Object.Tag            =    ""
    ImageIndex    =    7
EndProperty
BeginProperty Button10 {7791BA43-E020-11CF-8E74-00A0C90F26F8}
    Object.Tag            =    ""
    Style            =    3
EndProperty
BeginProperty Button11 {7791BA43-E020-11CF-8E74-00A0C90F26F8}
    Key              =    "Bold"
    Object.ToolTipText    =    "Bold"
    Object.Tag            =    ""
    ImageIndex    =    8
EndProperty
BeginProperty Button12 {7791BA43-E020-11CF-8E74-00A0C90F26F8}
    Key              =    "Italic"
    Object.ToolTipText    =    "Italic"
    Object.Tag            =    ""
    ImageIndex    =    9
EndProperty
BeginProperty Button13 {7791BA43-E020-11CF-8E74-00A0C90F26F8}
    Key              =    "Underline"
    Object.ToolTipText    =    "Underline"
    Object.Tag            =    ""
    ImageIndex    =    10
```

```
            EndProperty
            BeginProperty Button14 {7791BA43-E020-11CF-8E74-00A0C90F26F8}
                Object.Tag               =    ""
                Style          =    3
            EndProperty
            BeginProperty Button15 {7791BA43-E020-11CF-8E74-00A0C90F26F8}
                Key            =    "Left"
                Object.ToolTipText    =    "Left Justify"
                Object.Tag            =    ""
                ImageIndex     =    11
            EndProperty
            BeginProperty Button16 {7791BA43-E020-11CF-8E74-00A0C90F26F8}
                Key            =    "Center"
                Object.ToolTipText    =    "Center"
                Object.Tag            =    ""
                ImageIndex     =    12
            EndProperty
            BeginProperty Button17 {7791BA43-E020-11CF-8E74-00A0C90F26F8}
                Key            =    "Right"
                Object.ToolTipText    =    "Right Justify"
                Object.Tag            =    ""
                ImageIndex     =    13
            EndProperty
        EndProperty
     EndProperty
End
Begin ComctlLib.StatusBar sbStatusBar
    Align           =    2    'Align Bottom
    Height          =    270
    Left            =    0
    TabIndex        =    0
    Top             =    2925
    Width           =    4680
    _ExtentX        =    8255
    _ExtentY        =    476
    SimpleText      =    ""
    BeginProperty Panels {2C787A51-E01C-11CF-8E74-00A0C90F26F8}
        NumPanels      =    3
        BeginProperty Panel1 {2C787A53-E01C-11CF-8E74-00A0C90F26F8}
            AutoSize       =    1
```

```
                Object.Width           =    2619
                MinWidth          =   2540
                Text              =   "Status"
                TextSave          =   "Status"
                Object.Tag             =    ""
             EndProperty
             BeginProperty Panel2 {2C787A53-E01C-11CF-8E74-00A0C90F26F8}
                Style             =   6
                AutoSize          =   2
                Object.Width           =    2540
                MinWidth          =   2540
                TextSave          =   "12/7/96"
                Object.Tag             =    ""
             EndProperty
             BeginProperty Panel3 {2C787A53-E01C-11CF-8E74-00A0C90F26F8}
                Style             =   5
                AutoSize          =   2
                Object.Width           =    2540
                MinWidth          =   2540
                TextSave          =   "2:04 PM"
                Object.Tag             =    ""
             EndProperty
          EndProperty
          BeginProperty Font {0BE35203-8F91-11CE-9DE3-00AA004BB851}
             Name              =   "MS Sans Serif"
             Size              =   8.25
             Charset           =   0
             Weight            =   400
             Underline         =   0    'False
             Italic            =   0    'False
             Strikethrough     =   0    'False
          EndProperty
       End
       Begin MSComDlg.CommonDialog dlgCommonDialog
          Left           =   1740
          Top            =   1350
          _ExtentX       =   847
          _ExtentY       =   847
          FontSize       =   2.67133e-37
```

```
End
Begin ComctlLib.ImageList imlIcons
    Left            =    1740
    Top             =    1350
    _ExtentX        =    1005
    _ExtentY        =    1005
    BackColor       =    -2147483643
    ImageWidth      =    16
    ImageHeight     =    16
    MaskColor       =    12632256
    BeginProperty Images {8556BCD1-E01E-11CF-8E74-00A0C90F26F8}
        NumListImages   =   13
        BeginProperty ListImage1 {8556BCD3-E01E-11CF-8E74-00A0C90F26F8}
            Picture         =    "frmMain.frx":0000
            Key             =    ""
        EndProperty
        BeginProperty ListImage2 {8556BCD3-E01E-11CF-8E74-00A0C90F26F8}
            Picture         =    "frmMain.frx":0352
            Key             =    ""
        EndProperty
        BeginProperty ListImage3 {8556BCD3-E01E-11CF-8E74-00A0C90F26F8}
            Picture         =    "frmMain.frx":06A4
            Key             =    ""
        EndProperty
        BeginProperty ListImage4 {8556BCD3-E01E-11CF-8E74-00A0C90F26F8}
            Picture         =    "frmMain.frx":09F6
            Key             =    ""
        EndProperty
        BeginProperty ListImage5 {8556BCD3-E01E-11CF-8E74-00A0C90F26F8}
            Picture         =    "frmMain.frx":0D48
            Key             =    ""
        EndProperty
        BeginProperty ListImage6 {8556BCD3-E01E-11CF-8E74-00A0C90F26F8}
            Picture         =    "frmMain.frx":109A
            Key             =    ""
        EndProperty
        BeginProperty ListImage7 {8556BCD3-E01E-11CF-8E74-00A0C90F26F8}
            Picture         =    "frmMain.frx":13EC
            Key             =    ""
```

```
        EndProperty
        BeginProperty ListImage8 {8556BCD3-E01E-11CF-8E74-00A0C90F26F8}
            Picture         =   "frmMain.frx":173E
            Key             =   ""
        EndProperty
        BeginProperty ListImage9 {8556BCD3-E01E-11CF-8E74-00A0C90F26F8}
            Picture         =   "frmMain.frx":1A90
            Key             =   ""
        EndProperty
        BeginProperty ListImage10 {8556BCD3-E01E-11CF-8E74-
                        00A0C90F26F8}
            Picture         =   "frmMain.frx":1DE2
            Key             =   ""
        EndProperty
        BeginProperty ListImage11 {8556BCD3-E01E-11CF-8E74-
                        00A0C90F26F8}
            Picture         =   "frmMain.frx":2134
            Key             =   ""
        EndProperty
        BeginProperty ListImage12 {8556BCD3-E01E-11CF-8E74-
                        00A0C90F26F8}
            Picture         =   "frmMain.frx":2486
            Key             =   ""
        EndProperty
        BeginProperty ListImage13 {8556BCD3-E01E-11CF-8E74-
                        00A0C90F26F8}
            Picture         =   "frmMain.frx":27D8
            Key             =   ""
        EndProperty
    EndProperty
End
Begin VB.Menu mnuFile
    Caption         =   "&File"
    Begin VB.Menu mnuFileNew
        Caption         =   "&New"
        Shortcut        =   ^N
    End
    Begin VB.Menu mnuFileOpen
        Caption         =   "&Open"
        Shortcut        =   ^O
```

```
End
Begin VB.Menu mnuFileClose
   Caption          =   "&Close"
End
Begin VB.Menu mnuFileBar1
   Caption          =   "-"
End
Begin VB.Menu mnuFileSave
   Caption          =   "&Save"
   Shortcut         =   ^S
End
Begin VB.Menu mnuFileSaveAs
   Caption          =   "Save &As..."
End
Begin VB.Menu mnuFileSaveAll
   Caption          =   "Save A&ll"
End
Begin VB.Menu mnuFileBar2
   Caption          =   "-"
End
Begin VB.Menu mnuFileProperties
   Caption          =   "Propert&ies"
End
Begin VB.Menu mnuFileBar3
   Caption          =   "-"
End
Begin VB.Menu mnuFilePageSetup
   Caption          =   "Page Set&up..."
End
Begin VB.Menu mnuFilePrintPreview
   Caption          =   "Print Pre&view"
End
Begin VB.Menu mnuFilePrint
   Caption          =   "&Print..."
   Shortcut         =   ^P
End
Begin VB.Menu mnuFileBar4
   Caption          =   "-"
End
```

```
Begin VB.Menu mnuFileSend
   Caption         =   "Sen&d..."
End
Begin VB.Menu mnuFileBar5
   Caption         =   "-"
End
Begin VB.Menu mnuFileMRU
   Caption         =   ""
   Index           =   0
   Visible         =   0   'False
End
Begin VB.Menu mnuFileMRU
   Caption         =   ""
   Index           =   1
   Visible         =   0   'False
End
Begin VB.Menu mnuFileMRU
   Caption         =   ""
   Index           =   2
   Visible         =   0   'False
End
Begin VB.Menu mnuFileMRU
   Caption         =   ""
   Index           =   3
   Visible         =   0   'False
End
Begin VB.Menu mnuFileBar6
   Caption         =   "-"
   Visible         =   0   'False
End
Begin VB.Menu mnuFileExit
   Caption         =   "E&xit"
End
End
Begin VB.Menu mnuEdit
   Caption       =   "&Edit"
   Begin VB.Menu mnuEditUndo
      Caption         =   "&Undo"
      Shortcut        =   ^Z
```

```
        End
        Begin VB.Menu mnuEditBar1
            Caption         =   "-"
        End
        Begin VB.Menu mnuEditCut
            Caption         =   "Cu&t"
            Shortcut        =   ^X
        End
        Begin VB.Menu mnuEditCopy
            Caption         =   "&Copy"
            Shortcut        =   ^C
        End
        Begin VB.Menu mnuEditPaste
            Caption         =   "&Paste"
            Shortcut        =   ^V
        End
        Begin VB.Menu mnuEditPasteSpecial
            Caption         =   "Paste &Special..."
        End
    End
    Begin VB.Menu mnuView
        Caption         =   "&View"
        Begin VB.Menu mnuViewToolbar
            Caption         =   "&Toolbar"
            Checked         =   -1  'True
        End
        Begin VB.Menu mnuViewStatusBar
            Caption         =   "Status &Bar"
            Checked         =   -1  'True
        End
        Begin VB.Menu mnuViewBar2
            Caption         =   "-"
        End
        Begin VB.Menu mnuViewRefresh
            Caption         =   "&Refresh"
        End
        Begin VB.Menu mnuViewOptions
            Caption         =   "&Options..."
        End
```

```
        Begin VB.Menu mnuViewBrowser
            Caption          =   "&Check Listings"
        End
    End
    Begin VB.Menu mnuHelp
        Caption          =   "&Help"
        Begin VB.Menu mnuHelpContents
            Caption          =   "&Contents"
        End
        Begin VB.Menu mnuHelpSearch
            Caption          =   "&Search For Help On..."
        End
        Begin VB.Menu mnuHelpBar1
            Caption          =   "-"
        End
        Begin VB.Menu mnuHelpAbout
            Caption          =   "&About Houses..."
        End
    End
End
Attribute VB_Name = "frmMain"
Attribute VB_GlobalNameSpace = False
Attribute VB_Creatable = False
Attribute VB_PredeclaredId = True
Attribute VB_Exposed = False
Private Declare Function OSWinHelp% Lib "user32" Alias "WinHelpA"
(ByVal hwnd&, ByVal HelpFile$, ByVal wCommand%, dwData As Any)
Private Sub Form_Load()
    Me.Left = GetSetting(App.Title, "Settings", "MainLeft", 1000)
    Me.Top = GetSetting(App.Title, "Settings", "MainTop", 1000)
    Me.Width = GetSetting(App.Title, "Settings", "MainWidth", 6500)
    Me.Height = GetSetting(App.Title, "Settings", "MainHeight", 6500)
End Sub

Private Sub Form_Unload(Cancel As Integer)
    If Me.WindowState <> vbMinimized Then
        SaveSetting App.Title, "Settings", "MainLeft", Me.Left
        SaveSetting App.Title, "Settings", "MainTop", Me.Top
        SaveSetting App.Title, "Settings", "MainWidth", Me.Width
```

```
        SaveSetting App.Title, "Settings", "MainHeight", Me.Height
    End If
End Sub

Private Sub mnuViewBrowser_Click()
    Dim frmB As New frmBrowser
    frmB.StartingAddress = "c:\vbi\house\realestate.vbd"
    frmB.Show
End Sub

Private Sub mnuHelpAbout_Click()
    'To Do
    MsgBox "About Box Code goes here!"
End Sub

Private Sub mnuViewOptions_Click()
    'To Do
    MsgBox "Options Dialog Code goes here!"
End Sub

Private Sub mnuViewStatusBar_Click()
    If mnuViewStatusBar.Checked Then
        sbStatusBar.Visible = False
        mnuViewStatusBar.Checked = False
    Else
        sbStatusBar.Visible = True
        mnuViewStatusBar.Checked = True
    End If
End Sub

Private Sub mnuViewToolbar_Click()
    If mnuViewToolbar.Checked Then
        tbToolBar.Visible = False
        mnuViewToolbar.Checked = False
    Else
        tbToolBar.Visible = True
        mnuViewToolbar.Checked = True
    End If
End Sub
```

```vb
Private Sub tbToolBar_ButtonClick(ByVal Button As ComctlLib.Button)

    Select Case Button.Key

        Case "New"
            mnuFileNew_Click
        Case "New"
            mnuFileNew_Click
        Case "Open"
            mnuFileOpen_Click
        Case "Save"
            mnuFileSave_Click
        Case "Print"
            mnuFilePrint_Click
        Case "Cut"
            mnuEditCut_Click
        Case "Copy"
            mnuEditCopy_Click
        Case "Paste"
            mnuEditPaste_Click
        Case "Bold"
            'To Do
            MsgBox "Bold Code goes here!"
        Case "Italic"
            'To Do
            MsgBox "Italic Code goes here!"
        Case "Underline"
            'To Do
            MsgBox "Underline Code goes here!"
        Case "Left"
            'To Do
            MsgBox "Left Code goes here!"
        Case "Center"
            'To Do
            MsgBox "Center Code goes here!"
        Case "Right"
            'To Do
            MsgBox "Right Code goes here!"
    End Select
```

```vb
End Sub

Private Sub mnuHelpContents_Click()

    Dim nRet As Integer

    'if there is no helpfile for this project display a message to
    'the user you can set the HelpFile for your application in the
    'Project Properties dialog
    If Len(App.HelpFile) = 0 Then
        MsgBox "Unable to display Help Contents. There is no Help
        associated with this project.", vbInformation, Me.Caption
    Else
        On Error Resume Next
        nRet = OSWinHelp(Me.hwnd, App.HelpFile, 3, 0)
        If Err Then
            MsgBox Err.Description
        End If
    End If
End Sub

Private Sub mnuHelpSearch_Click()

    Dim nRet As Integer

    'if there is no helpfile for this project display a message to
    'the user you can set the HelpFile for your application in the
    'Project Properties dialog
    If Len(App.HelpFile) = 0 Then
        MsgBox "Unable to display Help Contents. There is no Help
        associated with this project.", vbInformation, Me.Caption
    Else
        On Error Resume Next
        nRet = OSWinHelp(Me.hwnd, App.HelpFile, 261, 0)
        If Err Then
            MsgBox Err.Description
        End If
    End If
End Sub
```

```
Private Sub mnuViewRefresh_Click()
    'To Do
    MsgBox "Refresh Code goes here!"
End Sub

Private Sub mnuEditCopy_Click()
    'To Do
    MsgBox "Copy Code goes here!"
End Sub

Private Sub mnuEditCut_Click()
    'To Do
    MsgBox "Cut Code goes here!"
End Sub

Private Sub mnuEditPaste_Click()
    'To Do
    MsgBox "Paste Code goes here!"
End Sub

Private Sub mnuEditPasteSpecial_Click()
    'To Do
    MsgBox "Paste Special Code goes here!"
End Sub

Private Sub mnuEditUndo_Click()
    'To Do
    MsgBox "Undo Code goes here!"
End Sub

Private Sub mnuFileOpen_Click()
    Dim sFile As String

    With dlgCommonDialog
        'To Do
        'set the flags and attributes of the
        'common dialog control
        .Filter = "All Files (*.*)|*.*"
        .ShowOpen
```

```
            If Len(.filename) = 0 Then
                Exit Sub
            End If
            sFile = .filename
        End With
        'To Do
        'process the opened file
End Sub

Private Sub mnuFileClose_Click()
        'To Do
        MsgBox "Close Code goes here!"
End Sub

Private Sub mnuFileSave_Click()
        'To Do
        MsgBox "Save Code goes here!"
End Sub

Private Sub mnuFileSaveAs_Click()
        'To Do
        'Setup the common dialog control
        'prior to calling ShowSave
        dlgCommonDialog.ShowSave
End Sub

Private Sub mnuFileSaveAll_Click()
        'To Do
        MsgBox "Save All Code goes here!"
End Sub

Private Sub mnuFileProperties_Click()
        'To Do
        MsgBox "Properties Code goes here!"
End Sub

Private Sub mnuFilePageSetup_Click()
        dlgCommonDialog.ShowPrinter
End Sub
```

```
Private Sub mnuFilePrintPreview_Click()
    'To Do
    MsgBox "Print Preview Code goes here!"
End Sub

Private Sub mnuFilePrint_Click()
    'To Do
    MsgBox "Print Code goes here!"
End Sub

Private Sub mnuFileSend_Click()
    'To Do
    MsgBox "Send Code goes here!"
End Sub

Private Sub mnuFileMRU_Click(Index As Integer)
    'To Do
    MsgBox "MRU Code goes here!"
End Sub

Private Sub mnuFileExit_Click()
    'unload the form
    Unload Me
End Sub

Private Sub mnuFileNew_Click()
    'To Do
    MsgBox "New File Code goes here!"
End Sub
```

That's it for our coverage of ActiveX documents for the moment. In Chapter 7, we will look at another powerful part of Visual Basic Internet programming: VBScript.

CHAPTER • 7

VBSCRIPT: BUTTONS AND TEXT BOXES

We mentioned in Chapter 1 that Microsoft's espousal of the Internet is manifested in the Internet capabilities it has built in to Visual Basic. Nowhere is this enthusiasm more pronounced than in VBScript. VBScript is popular among Web programmers for many reasons, not least of which is that you don't have to buy a compiler to run it. You need only Internet Explorer to run our VBScript programs.

In this chapter, we begin our exploration of VBScript by putting it to work at once. Before this book is finished with VBScript, we'll make our Web pages VBScript-aware by adding text boxes, buttons, check boxes, and more. In this chapter, we'll focus on two of the most important HTML controls: buttons and text boxes. As we work with them, we'll see how to use VBScript.

Our First VBScript Example: Hello World!

In our first VBScript example, we'll have VBScript say hello to us in a Web page:

We'll do that with the aid of an HTML text box; in this type of control, we can display text placed there from our program or typed by the user. To begin, we'll place a text box in the middle of our Web page:

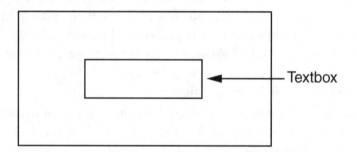

Inserting Text Boxes into Web Pages

What does all this look like in our Web page's HTML file? Let's write that page now. First, we start with an empty Web page:

```
<HTML>

<TITLE>Hello world example</TITLE>
```

```
<BODY>
   .
   .
   .
</BODY>

</HTML>
```

We've done nothing but set up the outlines of a Web page here, but that provides us with the framework we'll need to display our text box. Internet Explorer comes with the built-in ability to display certain HTML controls, including text boxes, buttons, radio buttons, combo boxes, and check boxes. These controls, called *input* controls, are placed in our Web page with the <INPUT> tag:

```
<INPUT>
```

First, we specify the type of control using the TYPE keyword; in this case, we want a text box, so we select that as follows. (The default type is actually a text box, so if we didn't specify the control type, we'd get a text box anyway.)

```
<INPUT TYPE = TEXT>
```

Now we give the text box a size, in characters; we'll give it a size of 20, using the SIZE keyword:

```
<INPUT TYPE = TEXT SIZE = 20>
```

Now we place our new control in the Web page, making it look like this:

```
<HTML>

<TITLE>Hello world example</TITLE>

<BODY>

<CENTER>
```

```
<INPUT TYPE = TEXT SIZE = 20>              <--
</CENTER>

</BODY>

</HTML>
```

The result appears in Figure 7.1. We've placed a text box in our Web page. The text box is active; there is a cursor in it, and you can type text directly into the text box. In addition, you can use the browser's **Copy**, **Cut**, and **Paste** items from the Edit menu to manipulate the text.

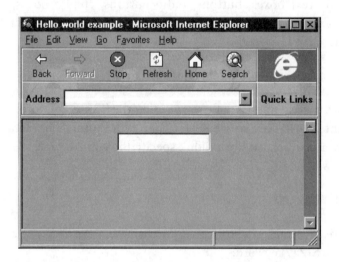

Figure 7.1 Our first Web page control is a text box.

However, the only way we can get the text box to display the "Hello World!" message is to type it there ourselves, as shown in Figure 7.2. This is a far cry from getting VBScript to say hello to us by itself, so let's press on.

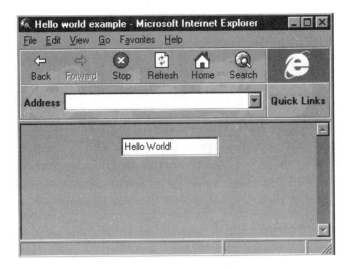

Figure 7.2 Displaying typed text in a text box.

Inserting Buttons into Web Pages

Let's insert a button into our Web page and label it **Click Me**:

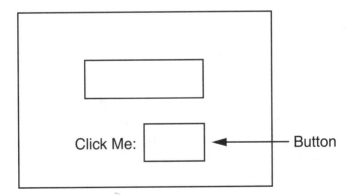

Now, when the user clicks the button, we'll have VBScript display the message in the text box:

Properties

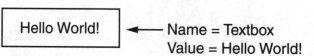

Name = Textbox
Value = Hello World!

Let's see how this works. First, we add a button control with the caption **Click Me:**. As you might expect, we use the <INPUT> tag, setting the TYPE keyword to BUTTON. (Note that we add a few line breaks, <BR>, to space apart the text box and button controls vertically.)

```
<HTML>

<TITLE>Hello world example</TITLE>

<BODY>

<CENTER>
<INPUT TYPE = TEXT SIZE = 20>
<BR>
<BR>
Click me: <INPUT TYPE = BUTTON>            <--
</CENTER>

</BODY>

</HTML>
```

The result appears in Figure 7.3. As you can see, there is now a button with the label **Click Me:** beneath the text box. But if you click this button, nothing much happens. It appears pressed and then reverts to its normal state, but that's all. How do we make it display our "Hello World!" message in the text box?

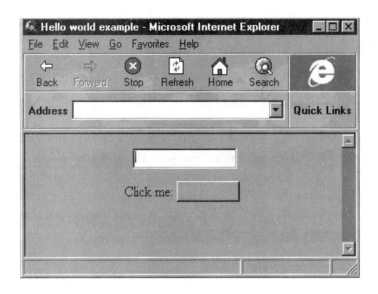

Figure 7.3 We add a button to our Web page.

The first step is to give our button a name so that we can refer to it in VBScript and make things happen when it is clicked. We'll give our button the name HelloButton; from now on, we'll be able to refer to it that way in our program. We use the NAME keyword in the <INPUT> tag. Note that we also give the text box the name Textbox at the same time:

```
<HTML>

<TITLE>Hello world example</TITLE>

<BODY>

<CENTER>
<INPUT TYPE = TEXT NAME = Textbox SIZE = 20>           <-
<BR>
<BR>
Click me: <INPUT TYPE = BUTTON NAME = "HelloButton">   <-
</CENTER>

</BODY>

</HTML>
```

Now our button is named, and we can set up the actions we want when it is clicked. We will do that with VBScript.

Welcome to VBScript

VBScript is the programming language that we insert into our Web page using the <SCRIPT> tag. VBScript is a subset of true Visual Basic. The built-in VBScript commands appear in Table 7.1, and the additional commands that come in the dynamic link libraries that accompany VBScript appear in Table 7.2. These tables are for reference only—there is no need to read them carefully at this point.

Table 7.1 VBScript Language

Category	Feature
Arrays	Declaration (Dim, Static, etc.), LBound, UBound, ReDim, Erase
Assignment	=, Let, Set
Comments	Using REM and `
Control flow	Do...Loop, For...Next, For Each...Next, While...Wend, If...Then...Else
Error trapping	On Error Resume Next, Err object
Literals	Empty, Nothing, Null, True, False User-defined literals: 123.456; "Foo", etc.
Miscellaneous	Line continuation character (_), line separation character (:)
Nonconforming identifiers	o.(My long method name)
Operators	Arithmetic: +, -, *, /, \, ^, Mod, Negation (-), String concatenation (&) Comparison: =, <>, <, >, <=, >=, Is Logical: Not, And, Or, Xor, Eqv, Imp

Table 7.1 VBScript Language (continued)

Category	Feature
Options	Option Explicit
Procedures	Declaring procedures: Function, Sub Calling procedures: CallExiting procedures: Exit Function, Exit Sub Parameters for procedures: ByVal, ByRef
Variables	Procedure-level: Dim, Static Module-level: Private, Dim

Table 7.2 VBScript Runtime Features

Category	Feature
Arrays	Array function
Conversion	Abs, Asc, Chr, CBool, CByte, CDate, CDbl, CInt, CLng, CSng, CStr, CVErr, DateSerial, DateValue, Fix, Int, Sgn, Hex, Oct
Dates	Date function, Time function, Day, Month, Weekday, Year, Hour, Minute, Second, Now, TimeSerial, TimeValue
Math	Atn, Cos, Sin, Tan, Exp, Log, Sqr, Randomize, Rnd
Object	CreateObject
Strings	Asc, AscB, AscW, Chr, ChrB, ChrW, Instr, InStrB, Len, LenB, LCase, UCase, Left, Right, LeftB, MidB, RightB, Mid function, Space(number), StrComp, String(number, character), Trim, LTrim, RTrim

Table 7.2 VBScript Language (continued)

Category	Feature
UI	InputBox
	MsgBox
Variant support	IsArray
	IsDate
	IsEmpty
	IsError
	IsNull
	IsNumeric
	IsObject
	VarType

We'll set up the VBScript program needed to place our text into the text box, and we'll connect that program to our button. We'll use the <SCRIPT> tag, indicating that this is the VBScript program for the button named HelloButton: <SCRIPT FOR = "HelloButton">. In our Web page's HTML, note that this <SCRIPT> tag comes after the </BODY> tag; we can place a VBScript anywhere in a Web page, even in the header.

```
<HTML>

<TITLE>Hello world example</TITLE>

<BODY>

<CENTER>
<INPUT TYPE = TEXT NAME = Textbox SIZE = 20>
<BR>
<BR>
Click me: <INPUT TYPE = BUTTON NAME = "HelloButton">
</CENTER>

</BODY>

<SCRIPT FOR = "HelloButton">                    <--
```

```
          .
          .
          .

</SCRIPT>

</HTML>
```

VBScript Events

The Web browser knows that the ensuing code (up to the </SCRIPT> tag) is the script we'll use with the button we've added to our page. We want this script to be executed when the button is clicked; in VBScript, we create a click event. VBScript click events are a little different from standard Visual Basic click events. When the user clicks a button, it's called an onClick event; entering text into a text box causes an onChange event; selecting text in a text box causes an onSelect event. Here, we indicate that the following script is for the HelloButton's onClick event:

```
<HTML>

<TITLE>Hello world example</TITLE>

<BODY>

<CENTER>
<INPUT TYPE = TEXT NAME = Textbox SIZE = 20>
<BR>
<BR>
Click me: <INPUT TYPE = BUTTON NAME = "HelloButton">
</CENTER>

</BODY>

<SCRIPT FOR = "HelloButton" EVENT = "onClick">          <--
          .
          .
          .
```

```
</SCRIPT>

</HTML>
```

There may be other scripts supported (such as JavaScript), so the final step here is to indicate to the Web browser what type of script this is. What follows is a VBScript, so we set the LANGUAGE keyword to VBScript:

```
<HTML>

<TITLE>Hello world example</TITLE>

<BODY>

<CENTER>
<INPUT TYPE = TEXT NAME = Textbox SIZE = 20>
<BR>
<BR>
Click me: <INPUT TYPE = BUTTON NAME = "HelloButton">
</CENTER>

</BODY>

<SCRIPT FOR = "HelloButton" EVENT = "onClick" LANGUAGE = VBScript>   <-
    .
    .
    .
</SCRIPT>

</HTML>
```

Now the Web browser knows that what follows is the VBScript it should execute when the button is clicked.

VBScript Properties

Our next task is to place the text **Hello World!** into the text box when the button is clicked. To do that, we use the HTML text box property Value. As in standard Visual Basic, in addition to events, controls also have properties, and we use them to get and set data in the control. A control's Name property holds the name we reference in our programs—we've given the text box the name Textbox—and the Value property usually holds the control's significant data. For a text box, that data is the text being displayed:

Properties

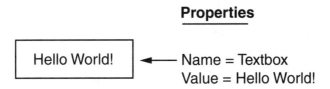

To reach the text box's Value property, we refer to it this way: Textbox.Value. In this way, we can reach the text inside the text box directly. To place **Hello World!** into the text box, we set the text box's Value property to that text string in our script (recall that this script is executed when the button is clicked):

```
<HTML>

<TITLE>Hello world example</TITLE>

<BODY>

<CENTER>
<INPUT TYPE = TEXT NAME = Textbox SIZE = 20>
<BR>
<BR>
Click me: <INPUT TYPE = BUTTON NAME = "HelloButton">
</CENTER>

</BODY>
```

```
<SCRIPT FOR = "HelloButton" EVENT = "onClick" LANGUAGE = VBScript>
        Textbox.Value = "Hello World!"              <-
</SCRIPT>

</HTML>
```

And that's all there is to it—the result appears in Figure 7.4. When we click the button marked **Click Me:**, we see the **Hello World!** message in the text box.

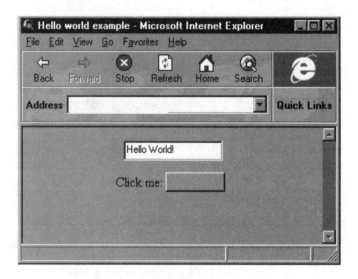

Figure 7.4 Clicking the button displays the message.

Handling Web Browsers That Don't Handle VBScript

Now that we've started inserting VBScript into our Web pages, it's worth mentioning that many browsers don't yet support VBScript. Although they will ignore the <SCRIPT> and </SCRIPT> tags, such browsers will display the VBScript line itself (Textbox.Value = "Hello World!"). To fix that, you can place the VBScript inside a comment. Non-VBScript Web browsers will ignore it, and browsers that support VBScript will ignore the comment tag:

```
<SCRIPT FOR = "HelloButton" EVENT = "onClick" LANGUAGE = VBScript>
<!-----------------            <-
        Textbox.Value = "Hello World!"
------------------->           <-
</SCRIPT>
```

As in standard Visual Basic, VBScript comments begin with an apostrophe ('). VBScript ignores everything on a line after the apostrophe. If you wanted to let people with pre-VBScript browsers know that your Web page uses VBScript (and therefore that they are missing a great deal), you could print a message that would appear only in pre-VBScript browsers:

```
<SCRIPT LANGUAGE = VBScript>
        'Note: This page uses VBScript!
</SCRIPT>
```

VBScript Subroutines

Our VBScript program is a success. However, it is more common to use a VBScript subroutine to handle events such as button clicks instead of a specialized script like the one we wrote for the onClick event:

```
<SCRIPT FOR = "HelloButton" EVENT = "onClick" LANGUAGE = VBScript>    <-
        Textbox.Value = "Hello World!"
</SCRIPT>
```

As in standard Visual Basic, a VBScript subroutine is a series of VBScript statements that we can execute, as we'll see in a minute. In fact, our HelloButton is already set up by VBScript so that when that button is clicked, the series of statements in a subroutine we'll write (HelloButton_OnClick) will be executed:

```
<HTML>

<TITLE>Hello world example</TITLE>

<BODY>

<CENTER>
<INPUT TYPE = TEXT NAME = Textbox SIZE = 20>
<BR>
<BR>
Click me: <INPUT TYPE = BUTTON NAME = "HelloButton">     <--
</CENTER>

</BODY>
      .
      .
      .
```

Next, we set up a section of our Web page to hold VBScript:

```
<HTML>

<TITLE>Hello world example</TITLE>

<BODY>

<CENTER>
<INPUT TYPE = TEXT NAME = Textbox SIZE = 20>
<BR>
<BR>
Click me: <INPUT TYPE = BUTTON NAME = "HelloButton">
</CENTER>

</BODY>

<SCRIPT LANGUAGE = VBScript>              <--
      .
      .
      .
```

```
</SCRIPT>                      <-

</HTML>
```

This is where the HelloButton_OnClick subroutine will go. To set up that subroutine, we use the keyword Sub; to show that we are finished with the subroutine, we add End Sub. The body of the subroutine is made up of the lines of VBScript we want to execute. In this case, we set the text box's Value property to "Hello World!":

```
<HTML>

<TITLE>Hello world example</TITLE>

<BODY>

<CENTER>
<INPUT TYPE = TEXT NAME = Textbox SIZE = 20>
<BR>
<BR>
Click me: <INPUT TYPE = BUTTON NAME = "HelloButton">
</CENTER>

</BODY>

<SCRIPT LANGUAGE = VBScript>
  ->    Sub HelloButton_OnClick
  ->            Textbox.Value = "Hello World!"
  ->    End Sub
</SCRIPT>

</HTML>
```

When the button is clicked, the VBScript in our subroutine will be executed by the Web browser, and the result will be the same as in Figure 7.4.

In this case, our subroutine contains only a single line (Textbox.Value = "Hello World!"), but usually there will be several such lines.

There are further refinements we could make to our page. As things stand, we must label our button **Click Me:**, although the button itself stays blank:

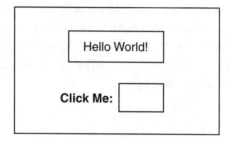

It would be better if the button itself had some fitting caption, such as **Say Hello**:

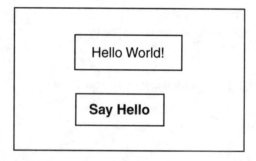

We'll put this together in VBScript.

Giving Buttons Captions

The primary data connected to a control is stored in its Value property. For a text box, that's the text in the text box; for a button, it's the button's caption. We'll give our button the caption **Say Hello** by setting its Value property in its <INPUT> tag:

```
<HTML>

<TITLE>Hello world example</TITLE>
```

```
<BODY>

<CENTER>
<INPUT TYPE = TEXT NAME = Textbox SIZE = 20>
<BR>
<BR>
<INPUT TYPE = BUTTON VALUE = "Say Hello" NAME = "HelloButton">   <-
</CENTER>

</BODY>

<SCRIPT LANGUAGE = VBScript>
        Sub HelloButton_OnClick
                Textbox.Value = "Hello World!"
        End Sub
</SCRIPT>

</HTML>
```

This technique lets you set the control's caption or text when it is first displayed. The result appears in Figure 7.5. As you can see, our button displays the caption **Say Hello**. When you click it, the **Hello World!** message appears in the text box, as shown in Figure 7.5. Our new caption is a success.

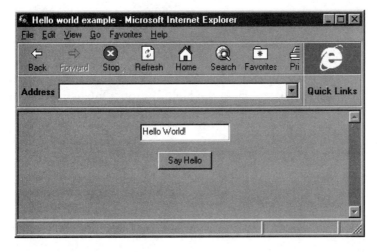

Figure 7.5 We give our button a caption.

There are still other ways of displaying our message with VBScript. For example, we can display text in a message box:

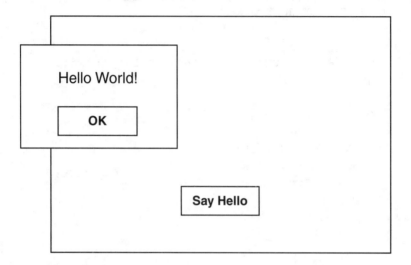

When the user clicks the **Say Hello** button, we pop this message box on the screen, and it displays our message until the user clicks **OK**. Let's look into this process.

Using a Message Box

It turns out to be easy to use message boxes in VBScript. All we have to do is to use the VBScript MsgBox statement when the user clicks the button. We place the following line in the HelloButton_OnClick subroutine; when the MsgBox statement is executed, it will display a message box with the text **Hello World!**:

```
<HTML>

<TITLE>Hello' world example</TITLE>

<BODY>

<INPUT TYPE = BUTTON VALUE="Say Hello" NAME="HelloButton">
```

```
</BODY>

<SCRIPT LANGUAGE=VBScript>
        Sub HelloButton_OnClick
                MsgBox "Hello World!"    <—
        End Sub
</SCRIPT>

</HTML>
```

And that's all there is to it; the result appears in Figure 7.6. Now when the user clicks the **Say Hello** button, a message box will appear with the text **Hello World!**, staying on the screen until the user clicks **OK**. As you can see, using message boxes is a good way to communicate with the user.

Figure 7.6 We display a message box from VBScript.

Although we have been using a button to display our text, it's also possible to place the text into our text box automatically when we first display the page in the browser:

As we know, we can do this by using the VALUE keyword in the <INPUT> tag:

```
<INPUT TYPE = TEXT VALUE = "Hello World!" NAME = Textbox SIZE = 20>
```

But there is another way to fill the text box with text when the page first appears. We can initialize our Web page, setting control properties in an initialization subroutine that is run when the page first appears. Let's see how this works.

Initializing Web Pages

It is possible to initialize a VBScript Web page by having a subroutine run when the page is first loaded. We do that by using the onLoad event, which occurs when the page is first displayed in the Web browser. We'll connect that event to a subroutine named Page_Initialize by setting that up in the <BODY> tag:

```
<HTML>

<TITLE>Hello world example</TITLE>

<BODY LANGUAGE = VBScript onLoad = "Page_Initialize">        <—
                .
                .
                .
```

When the Web page is first displayed, the subroutine Page_Initialize will be run. The next step is to write that subroutine, so we add this code to the script section of our Web page:

```
<HTML>

<TITLE>Hello world example</TITLE>

<BODY LANGUAGE = VBScript onLoad = "Page_Initialize">

<CENTER>
<INPUT TYPE = TEXT NAME = Textbox SIZE = 20>
</CENTER>

</BODY>

<SCRIPT LANGUAGE = VBScript>
   ->  Sub Page_Initialize

           .

           .

           .

   ->   End Sub
</SCRIPT>

</HTML>
```

The VBScript inside this subroutine will be run when the Web page first appears, so we place the correct text in the text box here:

```
<HTML>

<TITLE>Hello world example</TITLE>

<BODY LANGUAGE = VBScript onLoad = "Page_Initialize">

<CENTER>
<INPUT TYPE = TEXT NAME = Textbox SIZE = 20>
</CENTER>
```

```
</BODY>

<SCRIPT LANGUAGE = VBScript>
        Sub Page_Initialize
  ->            Textbox.Value = "Hello World!"
        End Sub
</SCRIPT>

</HTML>
```

It is useful to be able to specify how controls are initialized (making check boxes appear checked, for example, depending on the time of day the Web page is loaded), and we can do that in the Page_Initialize subroutine.

We can also add scroll bars to our text boxes and make them into multirow text boxes. Let's see how that works.

Using Larger Text Boxes

So far our HTML text boxes have been rather small and confined to a single line of text. Now let's use a larger text box that can enclose multiple lines of text:

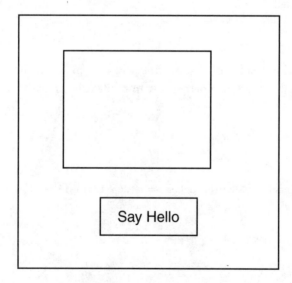

We'll also make our message appear in two lines:

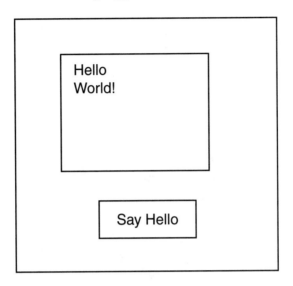

A larger text box like this is called a *textarea*, and we create it with a
<TEXTAREA> tag. We'll give the textarea control the name Textarea:

```
<HTML>

<TITLE>Hello world example</TITLE>

<BODY>

<CENTER>
<TEXTAREA NAME = Textarea>              <—
    .
    .
    .
```

We specify the number of text rows and columns in our textarea using the
ROWS and COLS keywords. Let's give our textarea five rows and 60 text
columns:

```
<HTML>
```

```
<TITLE>Hello world example</TITLE>

<BODY>

<CENTER>
<TEXTAREA ROWS=5 COLS=60 NAME = Textarea>          <-
    .
    .
    .
```

Next, we add the **Say Hello** button as before so that when the user clicks it we display our message in the textarea:

```
<HTML>

<TITLE>Hello world example</TITLE>

<BODY>

<CENTER>
<TEXTAREA ROWS=5 COLS=60 NAME = Textarea>
<BR>
<BR>
<INPUT TYPE = BUTTON VALUE = "Say Hello" NAME = "HelloButton">    <-
</CENTER>

</BODY>
    .
    .
    .
```

Finally, we place our message in the textarea with a subroutine tied to the **Say Hello** button:

```
<HTML>

<TITLE>Hello world example</TITLE>

<BODY>
```

```
<CENTER>
<TEXTAREA ROWS=5 COLS=60 NAME = Textarea>
<BR>
<BR>
<INPUT TYPE = BUTTON VALUE = "Say Hello" NAME = "HelloButton">
</CENTER>

</BODY>

<SCRIPT LANGUAGE = VBScript>                            <-
       Sub HelloButton_OnClick                         <-
              TextArea.Value = "Hello World!"          <-
       End Sub                                         <-
</SCRIPT>                                               <-

</HTML>
```

This technique works, but it this places our text on one line:

We wanted to display it on two lines:

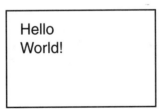

To do that, we insert a carriage return into the text. Like standard Visual Basic, VBScript has a built-in function, Chr(), that translates ASCII codes into the matching characters. We create our new text string, complete with included carriage return–linefeed pair, this way:

```
                    TextArea.Value = "Hello" + Chr(13) + Chr(10) + "World!"
```

And we place that into our Web page:

```
<HTML>

<TITLE>Hello world example</TITLE>

<BODY>

<CENTER>
<TEXTAREA ROWS=5 COLS=60 NAME = Textarea>
<BR>
<BR>
<INPUT TYPE = BUTTON VALUE = "Say Hello" NAME = "HelloButton">
</CENTER>

</BODY>

<SCRIPT LANGUAGE = VBScript>
        Sub HelloButton_OnClick
   ->            TextArea.Value = "Hello" + Chr(13) + Chr(10) + "World!"
        End Sub
</SCRIPT>

</HTML>
```

And that's it—now our message appears on two lines of our multiline text box, as shown in Figure 7.7.

Because using carriage returns in lines of text is a common thing to do, VBScript defines a special keyword, vbCrLf, which stands for Chr(13) + Chr(10). We could also use it this way:

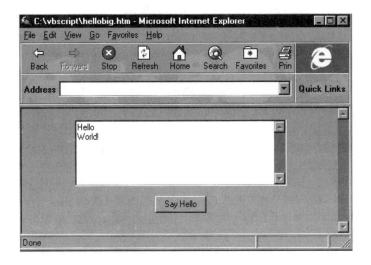

Figure 7.7 Breaking our text into two lines.

```
<HTML>

<TITLE>Hello world example</TITLE>

<BODY>

<CENTER>
<TEXTAREA ROWS=5 COLS=60 NAME = Textarea>
<BR>
<BR>
<INPUT TYPE = BUTTON VALUE = "Say Hello" NAME = "HelloButton">
</CENTER>

</BODY>

<SCRIPT LANGUAGE = VBScript>
        Sub HelloButton_OnClick
  —>            TextArea.Value = "Hello" + vbCrLf + Chr(10) + "World!"
        End Sub
</SCRIPT>

</HTML>
```

Our multiline text box example is a success. To this point, we've been using text boxes for output: to display a text string. Now let's let the user type into a text box, where we can read it as input for our programs.

Using Text Boxes for Input

Let's create two text boxes—Textbox1 and Textbox2—and have the user type in one text box:

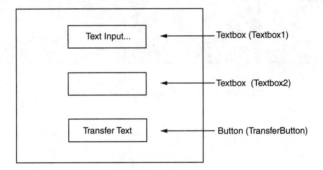

When the button labeled **Transfer Text** is clicked, we'll transfer the text from Textbox1 to Textbox2:

Let's see how this works. All we need to do is to set up the two text boxes:

```
<HTML>

<TITLE>Hello world example</TITLE>

<BODY>

<CENTER>
<INPUT TYPE = Text NAME = Textbox1 SIZE = 20>
<BR>
<BR>
<INPUT TYPE = TEXT NAME = Textbox2 SIZE = 20>
        .
        .
        .
```

Next, we set up the button labeled **Transfer Text**:

```
<HTML>

<TITLE>Hello world example</TITLE>

<BODY>

<CENTER>
<INPUT TYPE = Text NAME = Textbox1 SIZE = 20>
<BR>
<BR>
<INPUT TYPE = TEXT NAME = Textbox2 SIZE = 20>
<BR>
<BR>
<INPUT TYPE = BUTTON Value = "Transfer text" NAME = "TransferButton">
<-
</CENTER>
        .
        .
        .
```

Then, we connect a subroutine, Transfer_OnClick, to the **Transfer Text** button and transfer the text from Textbox1 to Textbox2:

```
<HTML>

<TITLE>Hello world example</TITLE>

<BODY>

<CENTER>
<INPUT TYPE = Text NAME = Textbox1 SIZE = 20>
<BR>
<BR>
<INPUT TYPE = TEXT NAME = Textbox2 SIZE = 20>
<BR>
<BR>
<INPUT TYPE = BUTTON Value = "Transfer text" NAME = "TransferButton">
</CENTER>

</BODY>

<SCRIPT LANGUAGE = VBScript>
        Sub TransferButton_OnClick
                Textbox2.Value = Textbox1.Value          <-
        End Sub
</SCRIPT>

</HTML>
```

Now we can use text boxes for both input and output. The result appears in Figure 7.8; after typing in the top text box, we transfer the text to the bottom text box with the click of a button.

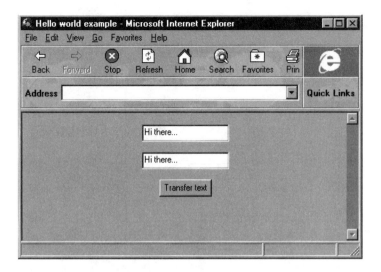

Figure 7.8 Transferring text from one text box to another.

Although we have read data from a text box, we haven't yet done anything with it. Let's change that as we read numbers from text boxes and create our own Web page calculator.

A Web Page with a Built-in Calculator

In our next example, we'll add a calculator to a Web page just as we did in Chapter 6, but this time we'll use VBScript. Again, this simple calculator will simply add two numbers and display the result, but you can modify it to create a full-function calculator if you wish.

In this case, the user types in the two numbers to add in two text boxes (Textbox1 and Textbox2):

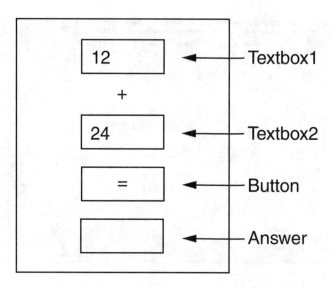

Then, when the user clicks the button marked **=**, we add the two numbers and place the result in the third text box, which we'll call Answer:

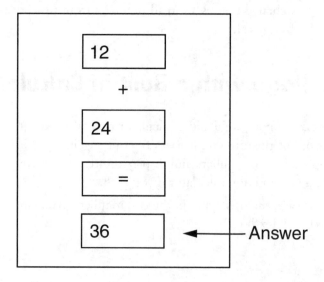

We start the calculator Web page with the top text box, Textbox1:

```
<HTML>
```

```
<TITLE>Calculator example</TITLE>

<BODY>

<CENTER>
<INPUT TYPE = TEXT NAME = Textbox1 SIZE = 20>        <—
<BR>
    .
    .
    .
```

Next, we add the + sign that goes between the two text boxes. Because this is HTML, we place the plus sign in the Web page this way, without a Label control:

```
<HTML>

<TITLE>Calculator example</TITLE>

<BODY>

<CENTER>
<INPUT TYPE = TEXT NAME = Textbox1 SIZE = 20>
<BR>
+          <—
```

Now we add Textbox2 and the button with the = sign as its caption:

```
<HTML>

<TITLE>Calculator example</TITLE>

<BODY>

<CENTER>
<INPUT TYPE = TEXT NAME = Textbox1 SIZE = 20>
<BR>
+
<BR>
```

```
<INPUT TYPE = TEXT NAME = Textbox2 SIZE = 20>                    <-
<BR>
<BR>
<INPUT TYPE = BUTTON Value = "=" NAME = "ShowButton">           <-
      .
      .
      .
```

The last step in setting up our user interface is to add the Answer text box, where the sum will appear:

```
<HTML>

<TITLE>Calculator example</TITLE>

<BODY>

<CENTER>
<INPUT TYPE = TEXT NAME = Textbox1 SIZE = 20>
<BR>
+
<BR>
<INPUT TYPE = TEXT NAME = Textbox2 SIZE = 20>
<BR>
<BR>
<INPUT TYPE = BUTTON Value = "=" NAME = "ShowButton">
<BR>
<BR>
<INPUT TYPE = TEXT NAME = Answer SIZE = 20>        <-
</CENTER>

</BODY>
      .
      .
      .
```

Now we write the subroutine in which we'll add the two numbers supplied by the user:

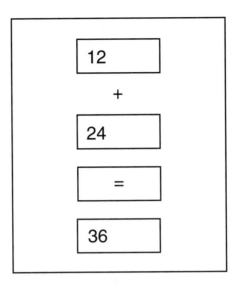

But how do we get a numerical value from a text box? To do that, we must treat the entries in the text boxes as numbers and not as text. We'll use the built-in VBScript function Int(). This function takes a string, such as Textbox1.Value, and converts it to the corresponding numerical value. We will add Int(Textbox1) and Int(Textbox2) this way (the resulting numerical sum is converted to a string automatically when we display it):

```
<HTML>

<TITLE>Calculator example</TITLE>

<BODY>

<CENTER>
<INPUT TYPE = TEXT NAME = Textbox1 SIZE = 20>
<BR>
+
<BR>
<INPUT TYPE = TEXT NAME = Textbox2 SIZE = 20>
<BR>
<BR>
<INPUT TYPE = BUTTON Value = "=" NAME = "ShowButton">
```

```
<BR>
<BR>
.<INPUT TYPE = TEXT NAME = Answer SIZE = 20>
</CENTER>

</BODY>

<SCRIPT LANGUAGE = VBScript>
        Sub ShowButton_OnClick
  ->             Answer.Value = Int(Textbox1.Value) + Int(Textbox2.Value)
        End Sub
</SCRIPT>

</HTML>
```

And that's it—when the user enters numbers in Textbox1 and Textbox2 and clicks the **=** button, the result of the addition appears in the bottom text box, as shown in Figure 7.9.

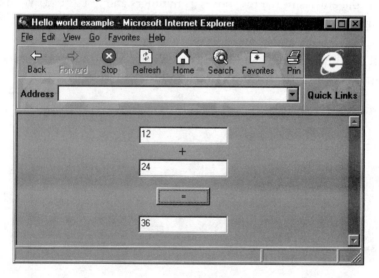

Figure 7.9 Our Web page calculator at work.

Our calculator is a success so far. This is the first time we've worked with values supplied by the user, however, and that introduces a new set of questions. How, for example, can we be sure that the data we are to add is really numeric? For example, what if the user types **Hello** in one text box and tries to add that to 24? Let's look into this now.

Checking User Input

Suppose the user tries to add a non-numeric value to a number:

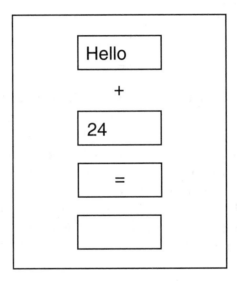

Ideally, we should display a message box with an error message, where we explain to the user what went wrong:

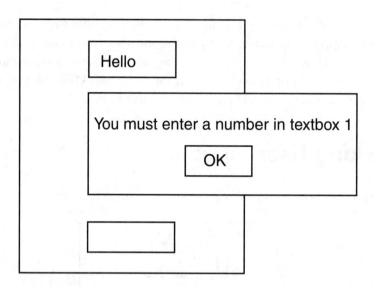

Currently, we assume that the entries in Textbox1 and Textbox2 are both numbers, and we add them. However, we should first check to make sure that the user actually typed numbers in the text boxes before trying to add them (and possibly generating an error). We'll check those values using the VBScript IsNumeric() function, which takes a text string argument and returns a Boolean result. We check this return result with the VBScript If statement, which is just like the standard Visual Basic If statement. To make sure that a text box holds a text string that we can interpret as a number, we use this code:

```
If (IsNumeric(Textbox1.Value)) Then
        NumberPlus1.Value = Int(Textbox1.Value) + 1
    End If
```

This gets us closer to a solution; we want to place a message box on the screen if the text in Textbox1 does not represent a number, so we start this way:

```
<SCRIPT LANGUAGE = VBScript>
    Sub ShowButton_OnClick
        If (Not IsNumeric(Textbox1.Value)) Then        <-
            .
```

.
.

If Textbox1 does not contain a text string that can be interpreted as a number, we place a message box on the screen and inform the user of the problem:

```
<SCRIPT LANGUAGE = VBScript>
        Sub ShowButton_OnClick
                If (Not IsNumeric(Textbox1.Value)) Then
    ->              MsgBox "You must enter a number in textbox 1"
                            .
                            .
                            .
```

After users click **OK** in the message box, we continue with our program. We clear the text in Textbox1 by setting it to the empty string, "", this way:

```
<SCRIPT LANGUAGE = VBScript>
        Sub ShowButton_OnClick
                If (Not IsNumeric(Textbox1.Value)) Then
                        MsgBox "You must enter a number in textbox 1"
    ->              Textbox1.Value = ""
                            .
                            .
                            .
```

Now we have to let the user re-enter the numbers, so we exit the subroutine. We use the Exit Sub statement (there is also an Exit Function statement for functions):

```
<SCRIPT LANGUAGE = VBScript>
        Sub ShowButton_OnClick
                If (Not IsNumeric(Textbox1.Value)) Then
                        MsgBox "You must enter a number in textbox 1"
                        Textbox1.Value = ""
    ->              Exit Sub
                End If
                    .
```

.
.
.

The next step is to repeat the process for Textbox2:

```
<SCRIPT LANGUAGE = VBScript>
        Sub ShowButton_OnClick
                If (Not IsNumeric(Textbox1.Value)) Then
                        MsgBox "You must enter a number in textbox 1"
                        Textbox1.Value = ""
                        Exit Sub
                End If
 ->             If (Not IsNumeric(Textbox2.Value)) Then
 ->                     MsgBox "You must enter a number in textbox 2"
 ->                     Textbox2.Value = ""
 ->                     Exit Sub
 ->             End If
```

.
.
.

At this point, we've tested the contents of both text boxes and found them safe, so we add their contents and place the result in the Answer text box:

```
<SCRIPT LANGUAGE = VBScript>
        Sub ShowButton_OnClick
                If (Not IsNumeric(Textbox1.Value)) Then
                        MsgBox "You must enter a number in textbox 1"
                        Textbox1.Value = ""
                        Exit Sub
                End If
                If (Not IsNumeric(Textbox2.Value)) Then
                        MsgBox "You must enter a number in textbox 2"
                        Textbox2.Value = ""
                        Exit Sub
                End If
 ->             Answer.Value = Int(Textbox1.Value) + Int(Textbox2.Value)
        End Sub
</SCRIPT>
```

And that's it. If the user places non-numeric text in a text box, we display a message, as shown in Figure 7.10.

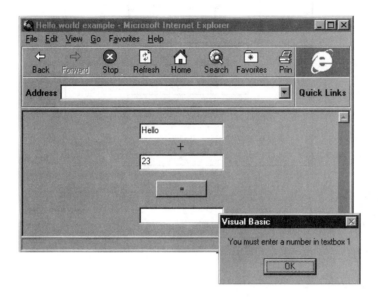

Figure 7.10 We test user input.

Our programs are a success so far. The final topic we'll cover in this chapter is password controls.

Reading Passwords

A password control is like any other text box, except that whenever the user types in a password control, asterisks (*) appear instead of text. When the user enters a password, it is not visible to others but can be read in your VBScript program. The Value property of a password control holds the text that was typed. We'll convert the top text box in our text-transferring example into a password control. When you click the button to transfer the text to the bottom text box, you'll see the actual typed text:

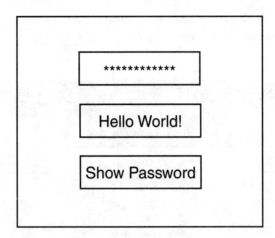

Doing this is easy. We replace the TEXT type of the first text box with
PASSWORD:

```
<HTML>

<TITLE>Hello world example</TITLE>

<BODY>

<CENTER>
<INPUT TYPE = PASSWORD NAME = Password SIZE = 20>          <--
<BR>
<BR>
<INPUT TYPE = TEXT NAME = Textbox SIZE = 20>
<BR>
<BR>
<INPUT TYPE = BUTTON Value = "Show Password" NAME = "ShowButton">
</CENTER>

</BODY>

<SCRIPT LANGUAGE = VBScript>
        Sub ShowButton_OnClick
                Textbox.Value = Password.Value
        End Sub
```

```
</SCRIPT>

</HTML>
```

And that's it. When the user types in the top password text box, we see only asterisks, but when our program wants to read the text, it simply checks the Value property.

And that completes this chapter. We've introduced VBScript and two important controls: buttons and text boxes. We've learned how to use buttons' onClick events in VBScript, how to give buttons captions, how to get or set the text in a text box, how to use multiple lines in a text box, how to check user input from text boxes, and more. In Chapter 8, we'll continue our exploration of VBScript as we turn to a new HTML control—option buttons—which are like the ones we know in Visual Basic. We'll also introduce the idea of forms. Like those in standard Visual Basic, VBScript forms are used to manage collections of controls.

VBScript: Radio Buttons and Forms

In this chapter, we continue our exploration of VBScript by taking a look at ways of handling multiple controls as well as new controls, such as radio buttons (called *option* buttons in standard Visual Basic), that act in a group. We'll also see how some of VBScript's built-in objects, such as the form and document objects, give us control over what goes on in the Web page. Let's get started by looking at the ways of handling multiple controls—in this case, buttons—with the Flippit game.

The Flippit Game: Handling Many Buttons

Our first example in this chapter is the two-player Flippit game, which demonstrates how to work with VBScript controls when we have many controls to handle. First, we'll put Flippit together the brute force way. Later in this chapter, we'll see how to save a great deal of programming using VBScript forms.

Flippit works like this: the user sees 16 buttons in four rows of four. As with tic-tac-toe, half of the buttons have the caption **x** and the others have the caption **o**:

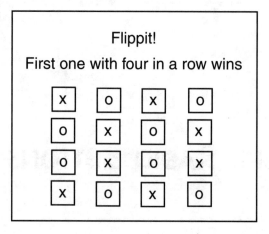

The idea is that each of two players clicks buttons in turn, flipping the captions—**x** becomes **o** and **o** becomes **x**—until one player gets four in a row. The game ends, for example, like this, where the **x** player has gotten four vertically in the first column:

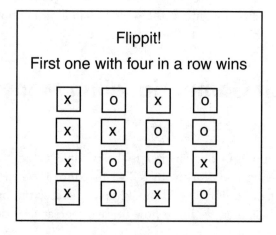

To write this program in VBScript, we start by setting up four rows of four buttons. Each button has its own name (Button1 to Button16) so that we can refer to it in VBScript, and each has its own default caption, **x** or **o**:

```
<HTML>

<TITLE>Flippit example</TITLE>

<BODY>

<CENTER>
<BR>
<H1>Flippit! </H1>
<H3>First one with four in a row wins</H3>
<INPUT TYPE = BUTTON VALUE = "x" NAME = "Button1">
<INPUT TYPE = BUTTON VALUE = "o" NAME = "Button2">
<INPUT TYPE = BUTTON VALUE = "x" NAME = "Button3">
<INPUT TYPE = BUTTON VALUE = "o" NAME = "Button4">
<BR>
<INPUT TYPE = BUTTON VALUE = "o" NAME = "Button5">
<INPUT TYPE = BUTTON VALUE = "x" NAME = "Button6">
<INPUT TYPE = BUTTON VALUE = "o" NAME = "Button7">
<INPUT TYPE = BUTTON VALUE = "x" NAME = "Button8">
<BR>
<INPUT TYPE = BUTTON VALUE = "o" NAME = "Button9">
<INPUT TYPE = BUTTON VALUE = "x" NAME = "Button10">
<INPUT TYPE = BUTTON VALUE = "o" NAME = "Button11">
<INPUT TYPE = BUTTON VALUE = "x" NAME = "Button12">
<BR>
<INPUT TYPE = BUTTON VALUE = "x" NAME = "Button13">
<INPUT TYPE = BUTTON VALUE = "o" NAME = "Button14">
<INPUT TYPE = BUTTON VALUE = "x" NAME = "Button15">
<INPUT TYPE = BUTTON VALUE = "o" NAME = "Button16">
<BR>
</CENTER>
        .
        .
        .
```

At this point, the buttons have appeared in our Web page, and it's time to make them active. Using the skills we developed in Chapter 7, we'll write a subroutine for each of the 16 buttons. To save space, we'll write an additional function, NewCaption(), to change the captions. When we pass the NewCaption() function an "x," it returns an "o," and vice versa. (Remember that functions can both take values and return them.) Here are the subroutines that handle the button clicks for the 16 buttons:

```
<HTML>

<TITLE>Flippit example</TITLE>
      .
      .
      .
<INPUT TYPE = BUTTON VALUE = "o" NAME = "Button16">
<BR>
</CENTER>

</BODY>

<SCRIPT LANGUAGE = VBScript>
  ->    Sub Button1_OnClick
      .             Button1.Value = NewCaption(Button1.Value)
      .       End Sub
      .       Sub Button2_OnClick
      .             Button2.Value = NewCaption(Button2.Value)
      .       End Sub
      .       Sub Button3_OnClick
      .             Button3.Value = NewCaption(Button3.Value)
      .       End Sub
      .       Sub Button4_OnClick
      .             Button4.Value = NewCaption(Button4.Value)
      .       End Sub
      .       Sub Button5_OnClick
      .             Button5.Value = NewCaption(Button5.Value)
      .       End Sub
      .       Sub Button6_OnClick
      .             Button6.Value = NewCaption(Button6.Value)
```

```
.      End Sub
.      Sub Button7_OnClick
.              Button7.Value = NewCaption(Button7.Value)
.      End Sub
.      Sub Button8_OnClick
.              Button8.Value = NewCaption(Button8.Value)
.      End Sub
.      Sub Button9_OnClick
.              Button9.Value = NewCaption(Button9.Value)
.      End Sub
.      Sub Button10_OnClick
.              Button10.Value = NewCaption(Button10.Value)
.      End Sub
.      Sub Button11_OnClick
.              Button11.Value = NewCaption(Button11.Value)
.      End Sub
.      Sub Button12_OnClick
.              Button12.Value = NewCaption(Button12.Value)
.      End Sub
.      Sub Button13_OnClick
.              Button13.Value = NewCaption(Button13.Value)
.      End Sub
.      Sub Button14_OnClick
.              Button14.Value = NewCaption(Button14.Value)
.      End Sub
.      Sub Button15_OnClick
.              Button15.Value = NewCaption(Button15.Value)
.      End Sub
.      Sub Button16_OnClick
.              Button16.Value = NewCaption(Button16.Value)
-->    End Sub
.
.
.

</SCRIPT>

</HTML>
```

We call the NewCaption() function each time a button is pressed, and that means we'll have 16 subroutines. That's a lot of code for a Web page to have, because it all must be downloaded. In a few pages, we'll see a better solution, one that is much like setting up a control array in standard Visual Basic.

The last step is to write the NewCaption() function. We start by checking whether the caption we are supposed to flip is an **x**:

```
<SCRIPT LANGUAGE = VBScript>
    Sub Button1_OnClick
            Button1.Value = NewCaption(Button1.Value)
    End Sub
         .

         .

         .
    Sub Button16_OnClick
            Button16.Value = NewCaption(Button16.Value)
    End Sub

  ->   Function NewCaption(OldCaption)
  ->           If OldCaption = "x" Then
           .

           .

           .
```

If the old caption is **x**, we return an **o** from the function:

```
<SCRIPT LANGUAGE = VBScript>
    Sub Button1_OnClick
            Button1.Value = NewCaption(Button1.Value)
    End Sub
         .

         .

         .
    Sub Button16_OnClick
            Button16.Value = NewCaption(Button16.Value)
    End Sub
```

```
    Function NewCaption(OldCaption)
          If OldCaption = "x" Then
->            NewCaption = "o"
                    .
                    .
                    .
```

And that's it; if we pass NewCaption() a value of "x," it will pass us back an "o." What if we pass an "o" to NewCaption()? Let's handle that case next:

```
<SCRIPT LANGUAGE = VBScript>
     Sub Button1_OnClick
            Button1.Value = NewCaption(Button1.Value)
     End Sub
        .
        .
        .
     Sub Button16_OnClick
            Button16.Value = NewCaption(Button16.Value)
     End Sub

     Function NewCaption(OldCaption)
            If OldCaption = "x" Then
                NewCaption = "o"
->          Else
->              NewCaption = "x"
->          End If
->  End Function
</SCRIPT>
```

That completes our first, long version of the Flippit game. It works, as shown in Figure 8.1.

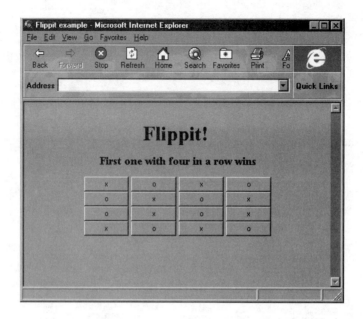

Figure 8.1 The Flippit game, original version.

The complete HTML and VBScript file for this Web page appears in Listing 8.1.

Listing 8.1 Flippit.htm

```
<HTML>

<TITLE>Flippit example</TITLE>

<BODY>

<CENTER>
<BR>
<H1>Flippit! </H1>
<H3>First one with four in a row wins</H3>
<INPUT TYPE = BUTTON VALUE = "x" NAME = "Button1">
<INPUT TYPE = BUTTON VALUE = "o" NAME = "Button2">
<INPUT TYPE = BUTTON VALUE = "x" NAME = "Button3">
<INPUT TYPE = BUTTON VALUE = "o" NAME = "Button4">
```

```
<BR>
<INPUT TYPE = BUTTON VALUE = "o" NAME = "Button5">
<INPUT TYPE = BUTTON VALUE = "x" NAME = "Button6">
<INPUT TYPE = BUTTON VALUE = "o" NAME = "Button7">
<INPUT TYPE = BUTTON VALUE = "x" NAME = "Button8">
<BR>
<INPUT TYPE = BUTTON VALUE = "o" NAME = "Button9">
<INPUT TYPE = BUTTON VALUE = "x" NAME = "Button10">
<INPUT TYPE = BUTTON VALUE = "o" NAME = "Button11">
<INPUT TYPE = BUTTON VALUE = "x" NAME = "Button12">
<BR>
<INPUT TYPE = BUTTON VALUE = "x" NAME = "Button13">
<INPUT TYPE = BUTTON VALUE = "o" NAME = "Button14">
<INPUT TYPE = BUTTON VALUE = "x" NAME = "Button15">
<INPUT TYPE = BUTTON VALUE = "o" NAME = "Button16">
<BR>
</CENTER>

</BODY>

<SCRIPT LANGUAGE = VBScript>
        Sub Button1_OnClick
                Button1.Value = NewCaption(Button1.Value)
        End Sub
        Sub Button2_OnClick
                Button2.Value = NewCaption(Button2.Value)
        End Sub
        Sub Button3_OnClick
                Button3.Value = NewCaption(Button3.Value)
        End Sub
        Sub Button4_OnClick
                Button4.Value = NewCaption(Button4.Value)
        End Sub
        Sub Button5_OnClick
                Button5.Value = NewCaption(Button5.Value)
        End Sub
        Sub Button6_OnClick
                Button6.Value = NewCaption(Button6.Value)
        End Sub
```

```
Sub Button7_OnClick
      Button7.Value = NewCaption(Button7.Value)
End Sub
Sub Button8_OnClick
      Button8.Value = NewCaption(Button8.Value)
End Sub
Sub Button9_OnClick
      Button9.Value = NewCaption(Button9.Value)
End Sub
Sub Button10_OnClick
      Button10.Value = NewCaption(Button10.Value)
End Sub
Sub Button11_OnClick
      Button11.Value = NewCaption(Button11.Value)
End Sub
Sub Button12_OnClick
      Button12.Value = NewCaption(Button12.Value)
End Sub
Sub Button13_OnClick
      Button13.Value = NewCaption(Button13.Value)
End Sub
Sub Button14_OnClick
      Button14.Value = NewCaption(Button14.Value)
End Sub
Sub Button15_OnClick
      Button15.Value = NewCaption(Button15.Value)
End Sub
Sub Button16_OnClick
      Button16.Value = NewCaption(Button16.Value)
End Sub
Function NewCaption(OldCaption)
      If OldCaption = "x" Then
          NewCaption = "o"
      Else
          NewCaption = "x"
      End If
End Function
</SCRIPT>

</HTML>
```

Now that we've seen how to write Flippit the brute force way, let's look at ways to make this process easier and our VBScript code shorter. The next section introduces the idea of VBScript forms, and we'll start by using the VBScript controls that were designed to be used in forms: radio buttons.

Weekday Example: Using Radio Buttons and Forms

Our next example, Weekday, is a Web page with seven radio (or option) buttons, one for each day of the week. Here, we ask the user to tell us what day of the week it is:

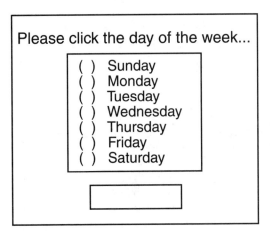

When the user clicks one of the radio buttons, we display a message indicating that we've understood the input:

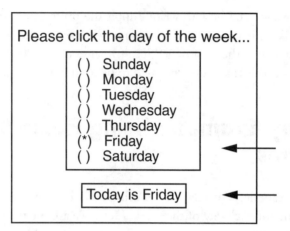

Note that it can only be one day of the week at a time, so if the user clicks another of the radio buttons, we must make sure that the previously clicked button is cleared before setting the new one. For example, if the user now clicks **Saturday**, we clear **Friday** and set the **Saturday** radio button:

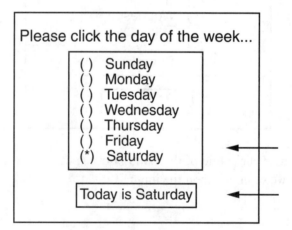

This is what radio buttons excel at: letting the user select from a number of options (that's why they are also called option buttons) but allowing only one selection at a time. How do we make sure that only one option may be selected? That happens automatically when you install option buttons as a group in a form.

VBScript Forms

A *form* is a group of controls that act together in some way. For example, we know that when we collect radio buttons in a group, usually only one should be selected at a time. But in the following case, we have two columns of radio buttons—one for the day of the week and the other for the month:

Please click the day of the week and the month:

```
() Sunday          () January
() Monday          () February
() Tuesday         () March
() Wednesday       () April
() Thursday        () May
() Friday          () June
() Saturday        () July
                   () August
                   () September
                   () October
                   () November
                   () December
```

Now the day and month radio buttons can be set at once. In this case, it's good to divide the whole Web page, called the *document*, into forms (not to be confused with standard Visual Basic's forms):

Please click the day of the week and the month:

( ) Sunday	( ) January
( ) Monday	( ) February
( ) Tuesday	( ) March
( ) Wednesday	( ) April
( ) Thursday	( ) May
( ) Friday	( ) June
(*) Saturday	(*) July
	( ) August
	( ) September
	( ) October
	( ) November
	( ) December

Now there is no confusion. When the user clicks a radio button, all the other radio buttons in the same form (but not those in the other form) should be cleared. One of the built-in objects of forms is the *elements* array, which holds all the controls in a particular form. As we'll see soon, an element array allows us to work with groups of controls easily, provided we place them in their own form.

Forms are also used in HTML to allow you to send data to an Internet server. For example, suppose you have a guestbook in your Web page. All these controls are in a form:

Please add something to the guestbook!

Name: Steve

Email: steve@server.com

Your comments:

Great Web page!

Submit   Clear

Notice the **Submit** button at the bottom of the form. After users have filled in the text boxes, they press the **Submit** button. Using the form's Submit method, we send the data in the form to the server, where it will be handled by a server program or script such as a Perl script. If we have given the name TheForm to a form, we submit it this way: TheForm.Submit. In addition, forms have an OnSubmit event, which is activated when the **Submit** button is clicked so that you can check what's being submitted.

At this point, we are ready to set up our own forms. We will put together the day of the week example, because radio buttons are a perfect way to illustrate the operation of forms. When the user selects one of the radio buttons, all the others will be cleared automatically (by the Web browser). We'll put our radio buttons into a form named DayForm:

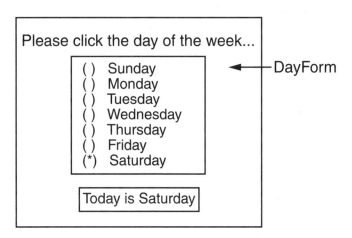

We start by setting up our form, DayForm, using the <Form> tag:

```
<HTML>
<HEAD>
<TITLE>Day of the Week</TITLE>
</HEAD>

<BODY LANGUAGE = VBScript onLoad = Page_Initialize>
```

```
<CENTER>
<H1>Day of the Week</H1>
<H3>Please click the day of the week...</H3>

<BR>
<FORM NAME = "DayForm">              <—
    .
    .
    .
```

Let's put the radio buttons in a table and give that table a background color of yellow to emphasize that the buttons make up a group of controls:

```
<HTML>
<HEAD>
<TITLE>Day of the Week</TITLE>
</HEAD>

<BODY LANGUAGE = VBScript onLoad = Page_Initialize>

<CENTER>
<H1>Day of the Week</H1>
<H3>Please click the day of the week...</H3>

<BR>
<FORM NAME = "DayForm">
<TABLE BORDER BGCOLOR = "#ffff00" WIDTH = 150>  <—
    .
    .
    .
```

Next, we'll add the seven radio buttons. To indicate that they are all connected (so that when we click one, all the others in the form should be deselected), we will give them all the same name. In addition, we give each radio button its own onClick subroutine, which is called when the radio button is clicked so that we can display a message ("This is Friday"). In the following HTML, we name the **Sunday** button's onClick subroutine SetSunday, the **Monday** button's onClick subroutine SetMonday, and so on:

```
<HTML>
<HEAD>
<TITLE>Day of the Week</TITLE>
</HEAD>

<BODY LANGUAGE = VBScript onLoad = Page_Initialize>

<CENTER>
<H1>Day of the Week</H1>
<H3>Please click the day of the week...</H3>

<BR>
<FORM NAME = "DayForm">
<TABLE BORDER BGCOLOR = "#ffff00" WIDTH = 150>
 <TR><TD><INPUT TYPE = RADIO VALUE = CHECKED NAME = RadioDays onClick =
       "SetSunday">Sunday</TD></TR>                            <-
 <TR><TD><INPUT TYPE = RADIO NAME = RadioDays onClick =        .
       "SetMonday">Monday</TD></TR>                            .
 <TR><TD><INPUT TYPE = RADIO NAME = RadioDays onClick =        .
       "SetTuesday">Tuesday</TD></TR>
 <TR><TD><INPUT TYPE = RADIO NAME = RadioDays onClick =
       "SetWednesday">Wednesday</TD></TR>
 <TR><TD><INPUT TYPE = RADIO NAME = RadioDays onClick =
       "SetThursday">Thursday</TD></TR>
 <TR><TD><INPUT TYPE = RADIO NAME = RadioDays onClick =
       "SetFriday">Friday</TD></TR>
 <TR><TD><INPUT TYPE = RADIO NAME = RadioDays onClick =
       "SetSaturday">Saturday</TD></TR>
          .
          .
          .
```

Now we finish the table with </TABLE> and finish the form with </FORM>. Next, we add the text box for our "This is Friday" message, calling that text box Daybox:

```
<HTML>
<HEAD>
<TITLE>Day of the Week</TITLE>
```

```
</HEAD>

<BODY LANGUAGE = VBScript onLoad = Page_Initialize>

<CENTER>
<H1>Day of the Week</H1>
<H3>Please click the day of the week...</H3>

<BR>
<FORM NAME = "DayForm">
<TABLE BORDER BGCOLOR = "#ffff00" WIDTH = 150>
 <TR><TD><INPUT TYPE = RADIO VALUE = CHECKED NAME = RadioDays onClick =
          "SetSunday">Sunday</TD></TR>
 <TR><TD><INPUT TYPE = RADIO NAME = RadioDays onClick =
          "SetMonday">Monday</TD></TR>
 <TR><TD><INPUT TYPE = RADIO NAME = RadioDays onClick =
          "SetTuesday">Tuesday</TD></TR>
 <TR><TD><INPUT TYPE = RADIO NAME = RadioDays onClick =
          "SetWednesday">Wednesday</TD></TR>
 <TR><TD><INPUT TYPE = RADIO NAME = RadioDays onClick =
          "SetThursday">Thursday</TD></TR>
 <TR><TD><INPUT TYPE = RADIO NAME = RadioDays onClick =
          "SetFriday">Friday</TD></TR>
 <TR><TD><INPUT TYPE = RADIO NAME = RadioDays onClick =
          "SetSaturday">Saturday</TD></TR>
</TABLE>
</FORM>
<BR>
<INPUT TYPE = TEXT NAME = Daybox SIZE = 30>                <--
</CENTER>
    .
    .
    .
```

Now our radio buttons form a group; when we click one, all the others will be cleared automatically by the Web browser.

The last step is to write the onClick subroutines, one for each radio button, so that when a radio button is clicked, the matching text is put into the text box:

```
        .
        .
        .
 <TR><TD><INPUT TYPE = RADIO NAME = RadioDays onClick =
        "SetSaturday">Saturday</TD></TR>
</TABLE>
</FORM>
<BR>
<INPUT TYPE = TEXT NAME = Daybox SIZE = 30>
</CENTER>

<SCRIPT LANGUAGE = VBScript>
-> Sub page_Initialize
   .  End Sub
   .  Sub SetSunday
   .      Daybox.Value = "Today is Sunday"
   .  End Sub
   .  Sub SetMonday
   .      Daybox.Value = "Today is Monday"
   .  End Sub
   .  Sub SetTuesday
   .      Daybox.Value = "Today is Tuesday"
   .  End Sub
   .  Sub SetWednesday
   .      Daybox.Value = "Today is Wednesday"
   .  End Sub
   .  Sub SetThursday
   .      Daybox.Value = "Today is Thursday"
   .  End Sub
   .  Sub SetFriday
   .      Daybox.Value = "Today is Friday"
   .  End Sub
   .  Sub SetSaturday
   .      Daybox.Value = "Today is Saturday"
-> End Sub
```

```
</SCRIPT>

</BODY>
</HTML>
```

And that's it—we've set up our first radio button example as well as our first form example. The result appears in Figure 8.2; when you click one of the radio buttons, it gets selected, the matching message appears in the text box, and the previously clicked radio button is cleared.

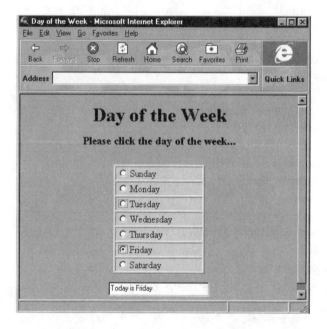

Figure 8.2 Our Weekday example uses forms and radio buttons.

The HTML and VBScript file for this Web page appears in Listing 8.2.

Listing 8.2 Weekday.htm

```
<HTML>
<HEAD>
<TITLE>Day of the Week</TITLE>
</HEAD>
```

```
<BODY LANGUAGE = VBScript onLoad = Page_Initialize>

<CENTER>
<H1>Day of the Week</H1>
<H3>Please click the day of the week...</H3>

<BR>
<FORM NAME = "DayForm">
<TABLE BORDER BGCOLOR = "#ffff00" WIDTH = 150>
 <TR><TD><INPUT TYPE = RADIO VALUE = CHECKED NAME = RadioDays onClick =
        "SetSunday">Sunday</TD></TR>
 <TR><TD><INPUT TYPE = RADIO NAME = RadioDays onClick =
        "SetMonday">Monday</TD></TR>
 <TR><TD><INPUT TYPE = RADIO NAME = RadioDays onClick =
        "SetTuesday">Tuesday</TD></TR>
 <TR><TD><INPUT TYPE = RADIO NAME = RadioDays onClick =
        "SetWednesday">Wednesday</TD></TR>
 <TR><TD><INPUT TYPE = RADIO NAME = RadioDays onClick =
        "SetThursday">Thursday</TD></TR>
 <TR><TD><INPUT TYPE = RADIO NAME = RadioDays onClick =
        "SetFriday">Friday</TD></TR>
 <TR><TD><INPUT TYPE = RADIO NAME = RadioDays onClick =
        "SetSaturday">Saturday</TD></TR>
</TABLE>
</FORM>
<BR>
<INPUT TYPE = TEXT NAME = Daybox SIZE = 30>
</CENTER>

<SCRIPT LANGUAGE = VBScript>
    Sub page_Initialize
    End Sub
    Sub SetSunday
        Daybox.Value = "Today is Sunday"
    End Sub
    Sub SetMonday
        Daybox.Value = "Today is Monday"
    End Sub
    Sub SetTuesday
```

```
        Daybox.Value = "Today is Tuesday"
    End Sub
    Sub SetWednesday
        Daybox.Value = "Today is Wednesday"
    End Sub
    Sub SetThursday
        Daybox.Value = "Today is Thursday"
    End Sub
    Sub SetFriday
        Daybox.Value = "Today is Friday"
    End Sub
    Sub SetSaturday
        Daybox.Value = "Today is Saturday"
    End Sub
</SCRIPT>

</BODY>
</HTML>
```

Our Weekday example works. Now that we have introduced forms, we can make this program even easier and shorter. Let's take a look at that next.

Handling Web Page Controls: The elements() Array

In the program we just wrote, we had one onClick event-handling subroutine for each radio button, generating many subroutines and a lot of text. But there is an easier way. Instead of treating each radio control as entirely separate, we can reach it as part of our form's elements() array.

An *array* is simply an indexed way of holding data or other information. We usually set up an array using the Dim statement in VBScript, just as in standard Visual Basic. For example, let's set up an array to hold the seven text strings in our program:

"Today is Sunday"

"Today is Monday"

"Today is Tuesday"

"Today is Wednesday"

"Today is Thursday"

"Today is Friday"

"Today is Saturday"

For easy access, we store these text strings in an array named Days. We start by setting up the array with the Dim keyword:

```
Dim Days(7)
     .
     .
     .
```

Now we have an array with seven elements, and each one is accessed by setting an array *index*. To fill the array with our text strings, we fill array elements 0 to 6 this way:

```
        Dim Days(7)
 ->     Days(0) = "Today is Sunday"
 ->     Days(1) = "Today is Monday"
 ->     Days(2) = "Today is Tuesday"
 ->     Days(3) = "Today is Wednesday"
 ->     Days(4) = "Today is Thursday"
 ->     Days(5) = "Today is Friday"
 ->     Days(6) = "Today is Saturday"
```

Now we can refer to element 3 in the array as Days(3). For example, the following VBScript line would set the text in the Daybox text box to "Today is Wednesday":

```
DayBox.Value = Days(3)
```

In addition to data (such as strings or numbers), we can place controls in an array. Each control in a form is stored in the form's elements() array like this for our Weekday example:

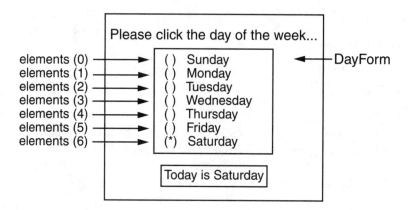

This means that we can simplify our Weekdays program. Instead of having one onClick subroutine for each radio button, we can use just one subroutine and then check which (if any) of the radio buttons in the elements() array is clicked and set the text string in the text box to match.

Let's see this at work. First, we set up all the radio buttons as before except that this time we set the onClick event subroutine to a new subroutine named RadioDays:

```
<HTML>
<HEAD>
<TITLE>Day of the Week</TITLE>
</HEAD>

<BODY LANGUAGE = VBScript onLoad = Page_Initialize>

<CENTER>
<H1>Day of the Week</H1>
<H3>Please click the day of the week...</H3>

<BR>
<FORM Name = "DayForm">
<TABLE BORDER BGCOLOR = "#ffff00" WIDTH = 150>
 <TR><TD><INPUT TYPE = RADIO VALUE = CHECKED NAME = RadioDays onClick =
        SetDay>Sunday</TD></TR>
 <TR><TD><INPUT TYPE = RADIO NAME = RadioDays onClick =
        SetDay>Monday</TD></TR>                                    <--
```

```
    <TR><TD><INPUT TYPE = RADIO NAME = RadioDays onClick =          .
          Setday>Tuesday</TD></TR>                                  .
    <TR><TD><INPUT TYPE = RADIO NAME = RadioDays onClick =          .
          Setday>Wednesday</TD></TR>
    <TR><TD><INPUT TYPE = RADIO NAME = RadioDays onClick =
          Setday>Thursday</TD></TR>
    <TR><TD><INPUT TYPE = RADIO NAME = RadioDays onClick =
          Setday>Friday</TD></TR>
    <TR><TD><INPUT TYPE = RADIO NAME = RadioDays onClick =
          Setday>Saturday</TD></TR>
</TABLE>
<BR>
<INPUT TYPE = TEXT NAME = DayBox SIZE = 30>
</FORM>
</CENTER>
    .
    .
    .
```

Now we write the RadioDays subroutine. In this subroutine, we determine which of the radio buttons is checked and set the text to match. We start by placing the text strings into an array for easy handling:

```
<HTML>
<HEAD>
<TITLE>Day of the Week</TITLE>
        .
        .
        .
<SCRIPT LANGUAGE = VBScript>
    Sub Page_Initialize
    End Sub
-> Sub SetDay
->      Dim Days(7)
->      Days(0) = "Today is Sunday"
->      Days(1) = "Today is Monday"
->      Days(2) = "Today is Tuesday"
->      Days(3) = "Today is Wednesday"
->      Days(4) = "Today is Thursday"
```

```
-->      Days(5) = "Today is Friday"
-->      Days(6) = "Today is Saturday"
           .
           .
           .
```

Now we work with the radio buttons in the elements() array of our form DayForm to see which radio button has been checked:

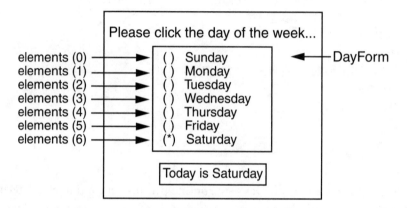

To do that, we will set up a form variable. We use the Dim statement to set up the variable, which we'll name DForm (short for DayForm):

```
<SCRIPT LANGUAGE = VBScript>
    Sub Page_Initialize
    End Sub
    Sub SetDay
        Dim Days(7)
        Days(0) = "Today is Sunday"
        Days(1) = "Today is Monday"
        Days(2) = "Today is Tuesday"
        Days(3) = "Today is Wednesday"
        Days(4) = "Today is Thursday"
        Days(5) = "Today is Friday"
        Days(6) = "Today is Saturday"
-->     Dim DForm
           .
           .
```

Now we load DayForm into the form variable DForm. We can't do it like this: DForm = DayForm; that's because forms are not standard VBScript variables. Instead, forms are VBScript objects, so, just as in standard Visual Basic, we to use a Set statement:

```
Set DForm = Dayform
```

Actually, even that is not quite enough, because DayForm is itself part of the larger document object. In VBScript, the whole Web page is called the document:

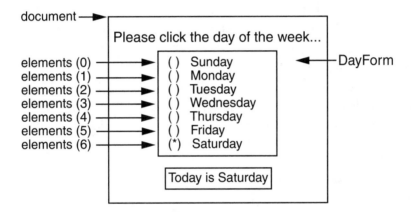

This means that we should refer to our DayForm form as document.DayForm. So we fill our DForm form variable this way:

```
<SCRIPT LANGUAGE = VBScript>
    Sub Page_Initialize
    End Sub
    Sub SetDay
        Dim Days(7)
        Days(0) = "Today is Sunday"
        Days(1) = "Today is Monday"
        Days(2) = "Today is Tuesday"
        Days(3) = "Today is Wednesday"
        Days(4) = "Today is Thursday"
        Days(5) = "Today is Friday"
        Days(6) = "Today is Saturday"
```

```
->    Dim DForm
->    Set DForm = document.DayForm
          .
          .
          .
```

Now we're ready to look at the radio buttons in our form by accessing the form's elements() array. For example, we can now refer to the first radio button in the DayForm as DForm.elements(0). That makes it easier, because now we can use a variable to reference the radio buttons: DForm.elements(my_index). In this case, we can keep changing my_index, scanning over all the radio buttons, until we find the one that the user checked; we'll do that by checking the radio button's Checked property, which returns True or False. We can now refer to it as DForm.elements(my_index).Checked.

To determine which of the radio buttons was checked, we'll use a loop. Because there are seven radio buttons, numbered 0 to 6, in the elements() array, we loop over all of them using the new variable loop_index:

```
<SCRIPT LANGUAGE = VBScript>
    Sub Page_Initialize
    End Sub
    Sub SetDay
        Dim Days(7)
        Days(0) = "Today is Sunday"
        Days(1) = "Today is Monday"
        Days(2) = "Today is Tuesday"
        Days(3) = "Today is Wednesday"
        Days(4) = "Today is Thursday"
        Days(5) = "Today is Friday"
        Days(6) = "Today is Saturday"
        Dim DForm, loop_index              <-
        Set DForm = document.DayForm
->      For loop_index = 0 to 6
          .
          .
          .
->      Next
    End Sub
```

The first time through the loop, loop_index is set to 0, the next time to 1, and so on. That means we can now use an If statement to examine all the radio buttons to see which one is checked:

```
<SCRIPT LANGUAGE = VBScript>
    Sub Page_Initialize
    End Sub
    Sub SetDay
        Dim Days(7)
        Days(0) = "Today is Sunday"
        Days(1) = "Today is Monday"
        Days(2) = "Today is Tuesday"
        Days(3) = "Today is Wednesday"
        Days(4) = "Today is Thursday"
        Days(5) = "Today is Friday"
        Days(6) = "Today is Saturday"
        Dim DForm, loop_index
        Set DForm = document.DayForm
        For loop_index = 0 to 6
->          If(DForm.elements(loop_index).Checked) Then
                        .

                        .

                        .
->          End If
        Next
    End Sub
```

If the If statement's condition—DForm.elements(loop_index).Checked—is true, this radio button is checked. In that case, we find the corresponding text string (such as "This is Friday") in the array we have named Days() and place it directly in the text box:

```
<SCRIPT LANGUAGE = VBScript>
    Sub Page_Initialize
    End Sub
    Sub SetDay
        Dim Days(7)
        Days(0) = "Today is Sunday"
```

```
        Days(1) = "Today is Monday"
        Days(2) = "Today is Tuesday"
        Days(3) = "Today is Wednesday"
        Days(4) = "Today is Thursday"
        Days(5) = "Today is Friday"
        Days(6) = "Today is Saturday"
        Dim DForm, loop_index
        Set DForm = document.DayForm
        For loop_index = 0 to 6
            If(DForm.elements(loop_index).Checked) Then
  ->            DForm.DayBox.Value = Days(loop_index)
            End If
        Next
    End Sub
</SCRIPT>

</BODY>
</HTML>
```

And that's it—we have made the Weekday VBScript even shorter. But note that the only reason we had to place so much code there was that we didn't know which radio button was clicked. It turns out that we can determine that in another way: by passing arguments to our onClick function.

Improving Weekday: Passing Parameters to Event Handlers

The problem with handling multiple radio buttons was in determining which radio button was clicked. Until now, we've been calling our subroutine SetDay only when a radio button was clicked, and it was up to that subroutine to determine which button was clicked. If we pass the number (0 to 6) of the radio button that was clicked to SetDay, we'll save a lot of work. We use the following code when we set up our radio buttons. Note that instead of lines such as onClick = "SetDay," we now have onClick = "SetDay 0," indicating, in this case, that the number of the clicked button is 0:

```
<FORM Name = "DayForm">
<TABLE BORDER BGCOLOR = "#ffff00" WIDTH = 150>
 <TR><TD><INPUT TYPE = RADIO VALUE = CHECKED NAME = RadioDays onClick =
        "SetDay 0">Sunday</TD></TR>                              <-
 <TR><TD><INPUT TYPE = RADIO NAME = RadioDays onClick =          .
        "SetDay 1">Monday</TD></TR>                              .
 <TR><TD><INPUT TYPE = RADIO NAME = RadioDays onClick =          .
        "Setday 2">Tuesday</TD></TR>
 <TR><TD><INPUT TYPE = RADIO NAME = RadioDays onClick =
        "Setday 3">Wednesday</TD></TR>
 <TR><TD><INPUT TYPE = RADIO NAME = RadioDays onClick =
        "Setday 4">Thursday</TD></TR>
 <TR><TD><INPUT TYPE = RADIO NAME = RadioDays onClick =
        "Setday 5">Friday</TD></TR>
 <TR><TD><INPUT TYPE = RADIO NAME = RadioDays onClick =
        "Setday 6">Saturday</TD></TR>
</TABLE>
</FORM>
```

Now we modify the SetDays subroutine to take an argument (the number of the radio button that was pressed). It's easy. We just name the argument passed to us Day:

```
<SCRIPT LANGUAGE = VBScript>
    Sub Page_Initialize
    End Sub
-> Sub Setday(Day)
        .
        .
        .
```

Now that we have the number of the clicked radio button, it takes only one easy line to set the text in the text box to match:

```
<SCRIPT LANGUAGE = VBScript>
    Sub Page_Initialize
    End Sub
    Sub Setday(Day)
        Dim Days(7)
```

```
          Days(0) = "Today is Sunday"
          Days(1) = "Today is Monday"
          Days(2) = "Today is Tuesday"
          Days(3) = "Today is Wednesday"
          Days(4) = "Today is Thursday"
          Days(5) = "Today is Friday"
          Days(6) = "Today is Saturday"
    ->    DayBox.Value = Days(Day)
       End Sub
   </SCRIPT>
```

And that's it—that's all we need. When the user clicks a radio button, it calls SetDay(), passing its number to that subroutine, and we use that to set the text in the text box correctly. The final version of **Weekday.htm** appears in Listing 8.3.

Listing 8.3 Weekday.htm, Final Version

```
<HTML>
<HEAD>
<TITLE>Day of the Week</TITLE>
</HEAD>

<BODY LANGUAGE = VBScript onLoad = Page_Initialize>

<CENTER>
<H1>Day of the Week</H1>
<H3>Please click the day of the week...</H3>

<BR>
<FORM Name = "DayForm">
<TABLE BORDER BGCOLOR = "#ffff00" WIDTH = 150>
 <TR><TD><INPUT TYPE = RADIO VALUE = CHECKED NAME = RadioDays onClick =
        "SetDay 0">Sunday</TD></TR>
 <TR><TD><INPUT TYPE = RADIO NAME = RadioDays onClick =
        "SetDay 1">Monday</TD></TR>
 <TR><TD><INPUT TYPE = RADIO NAME = RadioDays onClick =
        "Setday 2">Tuesday</TD></TR>
```

```
<TR><TD><INPUT TYPE = RADIO NAME = RadioDays onClick =
       "Setday 3">Wednesday</TD></TR>
<TR><TD><INPUT TYPE = RADIO NAME = RadioDays onClick =
       "Setday 4">Thursday</TD></TR>
<TR><TD><INPUT TYPE = RADIO NAME = RadioDays onClick =
       "Setday 5">Friday</TD></TR>
<TR><TD><INPUT TYPE = RADIO NAME = RadioDays onClick =
       "Setday 6">Saturday</TD></TR>
</TABLE>
</FORM>
<BR>
<INPUT TYPE = TEXT NAME = DayBox SIZE = 30>
</CENTER>

<SCRIPT LANGUAGE = VBScript>
    Sub Page_Initialize
    End Sub
    Sub Setday(Day)
        Dim Days(7)
        Days(0) = "Today is Sunday"
        Days(1) = "Today is Monday"
        Days(2) = "Today is Tuesday"
        Days(3) = "Today is Wednesday"
        Days(4) = "Today is Thursday"
        Days(5) = "Today is Friday"
        Days(6) = "Today is Saturday"
        DayBox.Value = Days(Day)
    End Sub
</SCRIPT>

</BODY>
</HTML>
```

Now that we've upgraded the Weekday program, let's see if we can't do something similar for the Flippit game—that is, shorten the VBScript code we used in the beginning of this chapter (where we had one subroutine for each radio button) by introducing a form into the program.

Improving the Flippit Game

Let's place the 16 buttons of the Flippit game into a form named FlippitForm:

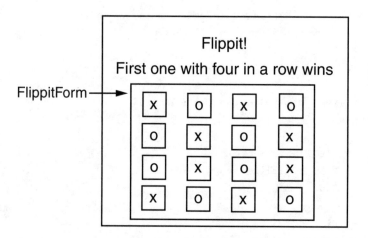

We set that up in our Flippit Web page this way:

```
<FORM NAME = "FlippitForm">                              <-
<INPUT TYPE = BUTTON VALUE = "x" NAME = "Button1">
<INPUT TYPE = BUTTON VALUE = "o" NAME = "Button2">
<INPUT TYPE = BUTTON VALUE = "x" NAME = "Button3">
<INPUT TYPE = BUTTON VALUE = "o" NAME = "Button4">
<BR>
<INPUT TYPE = BUTTON VALUE = "o" NAME = "Button5">
<INPUT TYPE = BUTTON VALUE = "x" NAME = "Button6">
<INPUT TYPE = BUTTON VALUE = "o" NAME = "Button7">
<INPUT TYPE = BUTTON VALUE = "x" NAME = "Button8">
<BR>
<INPUT TYPE = BUTTON VALUE = "o" NAME = "Button9">
<INPUT TYPE = BUTTON VALUE = "x" NAME = "Button10">
<INPUT TYPE = BUTTON VALUE = "o" NAME = "Button11">
<INPUT TYPE = BUTTON VALUE = "x" NAME = "Button12">
<BR>
```

```
<INPUT TYPE = BUTTON VALUE = "x" NAME = "Button13">
<INPUT TYPE = BUTTON VALUE = "o" NAME = "Button14">
<INPUT TYPE = BUTTON VALUE = "x" NAME = "Button15">
<INPUT TYPE = BUTTON VALUE = "o" NAME = "Button16">
</FORM>                                                    <-
```

In addition, we convert the calls to the subroutines Button0–Button15 into one subroutine, SetText, to which we pass an argument indicating which radio button was pressed:

```
<FORM NAME = "FlippitForm">
<INPUT TYPE = BUTTON VALUE = "x" onClick = "SetText 0">      <-
<INPUT TYPE = BUTTON VALUE = "o" onClick = "SetText 1">       .
<INPUT TYPE = BUTTON VALUE = "x" onClick = "SetText 2">       .
<INPUT TYPE = BUTTON VALUE = "o" onClick = "SetText 3">       .
<BR>                                                         .
<INPUT TYPE = BUTTON VALUE = "o" onClick = "SetText 4">       .
<INPUT TYPE = BUTTON VALUE = "x" onClick = "SetText 5">       .
<INPUT TYPE = BUTTON VALUE = "o" onClick = "SetText 6">       .
<INPUT TYPE = BUTTON VALUE = "x" onClick = "SetText 7">       .
<BR>                                                         .
<INPUT TYPE = BUTTON VALUE = "o" onClick = "SetText 8">       .
<INPUT TYPE = BUTTON VALUE = "x" onClick = "SetText 9">       .
<INPUT TYPE = BUTTON VALUE = "o" onClick = "SetText 10">      .
<INPUT TYPE = BUTTON VALUE = "x" onClick = "SetText 11">      .
<BR>                                                         .
<INPUT TYPE = BUTTON VALUE = "x" onClick = "SetText 12">      .
<INPUT TYPE = BUTTON VALUE = "o" onClick = "SetText 13">      .
<INPUT TYPE = BUTTON VALUE = "x" onClick = "SetText 14">      .
<INPUT TYPE = BUTTON VALUE = "o" onClick = "SetText 15">     <-
</FORM>
```

All that remains is to write the SetText() subroutine. Let's name the argument passed to SetText()—which represents the button number—BNumber. We'll also set up a form variable for our FlippitForm named FForm:

```
<SCRIPT LANGUAGE = VBScript>
```

```
        Sub Page_Initialize
        End Sub
->      Sub SetText(BNumber)
->              Dim FForm
->              Set FForm = document.FlippitForm
                    .
                    .
                    .
```

Now we flip the caption of the current radio button. We first check whether the caption is **x**, in which case we turn it to **o** like this:

```
<SCRIPT LANGUAGE = VBScript>
        Sub Page_Initialize
        End Sub
        Sub SetText(BNumber)
                Dim FForm
                Set FForm = document.FlippitForm
->              If FForm.elements(BNumber).Value = "x" Then
->                  FForm.elements(BNumber).Value = "o"
                    .
                    .
                    .
```

Otherwise, the caption must have been **o**, so we turn it to **x**:

```
<SCRIPT LANGUAGE = VBScript>
        Sub Page_Initialize
        End Sub
        Sub SetText(BNumber)
                Dim FForm
                Set FForm = document.FlippitForm
                If FForm.elements(BNumber).Value = "x" Then
                    FForm.elements(BNumber).Value = "o"
->              Else
->                  FForm.elements(BNumber).Value = "x"
->              End If
        End Sub
</SCRIPT>
```

And that's it—the VBScript for our **Flippit.htm** Web page has gone from 53 lines to just 1, all because of the new techniques introduced in this chapter. That's a good reduction, because each line of VBScript must be downloaded along with your Web page. The final version of **Flippit.htm** appears in Listing 8.4.

Listing 8.4 Flippit.htm, Final Version

```
<HTML>

<TITLE>Flippit example</TITLE>

<BODY LANGUAGE = VBScript onLoad = Page_Initialize>

<CENTER>
<BR>
<H1>Flippit! </H1>
<H3>First one with four in a row wins</H3>
<FORM NAME = "FlippitForm">
<INPUT TYPE = BUTTON VALUE = "x" onClick = "SetText 0">
<INPUT TYPE = BUTTON VALUE = "o" onClick = "SetText 1">
<INPUT TYPE = BUTTON VALUE = "x" onClick = "SetText 2">
<INPUT TYPE = BUTTON VALUE = "o" onClick = "SetText 3">
<BR>
<INPUT TYPE = BUTTON VALUE = "o" onClick = "SetText 4">
<INPUT TYPE = BUTTON VALUE = "x" onClick = "SetText 5">
<INPUT TYPE = BUTTON VALUE = "o" onClick = "SetText 6">
<INPUT TYPE = BUTTON VALUE = "x" onClick = "SetText 7">
<BR>
<INPUT TYPE = BUTTON VALUE = "o" onClick = "SetText 8">
<INPUT TYPE = BUTTON VALUE = "x" onClick = "SetText 9">
<INPUT TYPE = BUTTON VALUE = "o" onClick = "SetText 10">
<INPUT TYPE = BUTTON VALUE = "x" onClick = "SetText 11">
<BR>
<INPUT TYPE = BUTTON VALUE = "x" onClick = "SetText 12">
<INPUT TYPE = BUTTON VALUE = "o" onClick = "SetText 13">
<INPUT TYPE = BUTTON VALUE = "x" onClick = "SetText 14">
<INPUT TYPE = BUTTON VALUE = "o" onClick = "SetText 15">
</FORM>
```

```
<BR>
</CENTER>

</BODY>

<SCRIPT LANGUAGE = VBScript>
        Sub Page_Initialize
        End Sub
        Sub SetText(BNumber)
                Dim FForm
                Set FForm = document.FlippitForm
                If FForm.elements(BNumber).Value = "x" Then
                    FForm.elements(BNumber).Value = "o"
                Else
                    FForm.elements(BNumber).Value = "x"
                End If
        End Sub
</SCRIPT>

</HTML>
```

That's it for forms and radio buttons. Here, we've seen how to group controls, how to work with radio buttons, and how to save a great deal of code length using a few new VBScript techniques. In Chapter 9, we'll investigate a new HTML control—check boxes—and we'll dig deeper into VBScript as we examine the document object and other VBScript objects.

CHAPTER •9

VBScript: Check Boxes and Documents

In this chapter, we'll start working with a new HTML control: check boxes. We'll also begin exploring a new VBScript object: the document object. In Chapter 8, we started exploring forms—another VBScript object—and here, we'll work with documents, which enclose forms.

Check Boxes: The Fly-By-Night Travel Co Inc Example

In Chapter 8, we used radio buttons to select one option among several—but only one option was possible. If we want to let the user select several options at the same time, we should use check boxes. We'll let the user select from several tourist packages:

```
┌─────────────────────────────────────────────────────────┐
│                  Fly-By-Night Travel Co Inc              │
│                     Customize your tour                  │
│                                                          │
│   ┌──────────────────────┐   ┌──────────────────────┐   │
│   │ Pick a Package...    │   │ Destinations         │   │
│   ├──────────────────────┤   ├──────────────────────┤   │
│   │ ( ) Asia Major       │   │ ( ) Hong Kong        │   │
│   │ ( ) Gambler's Paradise│  │ ( ) Tokyo            │   │
│   │ ( ) European Capitals│   │ ( ) Las Vegas        │   │
│   │ ( ) Budget Package   │   │ ( ) Atlantic City    │   │
│   │ ( ) All of Them      │   │ ( ) Rome             │   │
│   │                      │   │ ( ) Paris            │   │
│   │                      │   │ ( ) Trenton          │   │
│   └──────────────────────┘   └──────────────────────┘   │
│                                                          │
│              Your Price:   ┌──────────┐                  │
│                            │ $2000    │                  │
│                            └──────────┘                  │
└─────────────────────────────────────────────────────────┘
```

Here, the user can select a tour package, such as European Capitals, by clicking a radio button in the Pick a Package form. Because that form holds radio buttons, it's possible to select only one tour package at once. When the user selects the tour package, we'll use check boxes to indicate which cities the tour involves. Here, the cities are Rome and Paris:

```
┌─────────────────────────────────────────────────────────┐
│                  Fly-By-Night Travel Co Inc              │
│                     Customize your tour                  │
│                                                          │
│   ┌──────────────────────┐   ┌──────────────────────┐   │
│   │ Pick a Package...    │   │ Destinations         │   │
│   ├──────────────────────┤   ├──────────────────────┤   │
│   │ ( ) Asia Major       │   │ ( ) Hong Kong        │   │
│   │ ( ) Gambler's Paradise│  │ ( ) Tokyo            │   │
│   │ (*) European Capitals│   │ ( ) Las Vegas        │   │
│   │ ( ) Budget Package   │   │ ( ) Atlantic City    │   │
│   │ ( ) All of Them      │   │ (v) Rome             │   │
│   │                      │   │ (v) Paris            │   │
│   │                      │   │ ( ) Trenton          │   │
│   └──────────────────────┘   └──────────────────────┘   │
│                                                          │
│              Your Price:   ┌──────────┐                  │
│                            │ $2000    │                  │
│                            └──────────┘                  │
└─────────────────────────────────────────────────────────┘
```

In addition, we'll allow the user to customize a tour by adding other cities at an increased price. The user simply checks the appropriate check boxes, and our program updates the tour price in the lower text box. (For this simple example, we'll charge $1000 per city.) Here, the user has added Hong Kong and Tokyo by clicking the correct check boxes:

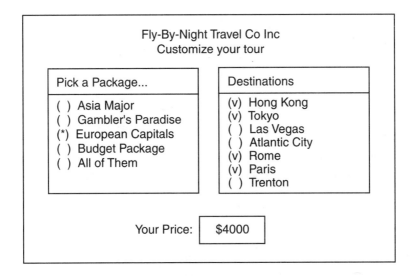

We begin the HTML with a title and the appropriate headers:

```
<HTML>
<HEAD>
<TITLE>Fly-by-Night Travel Co Inc</TITLE>
</HEAD>

<BODY LANGUAGE = VBScript onLoad = Page_Initialize>

<CENTER>
<H1>Fly-by-Night Travel Co Inc</H1>
<H3>Customize your tour</H3>
</CENTER>
     .
     .
     .
```

Next, we add the form with the radio buttons. Each radio button will have the same name—RadioGroup—so that they act in concert. We call this form PackageForm, because we will allow the user to select a tour package here. We set up these radio buttons in a table and connect a matching onClick subroutine to each button:

```
<HTML>
<HEAD>
<TITLE>Fly-by-Night Travel Co Inc</TITLE>
</HEAD>

<BODY LANGUAGE = VBScript onLoad = Page_Initialize>

<CENTER>
<H1>Fly-by-Night Travel Co Inc</H1>
<H3>Customize your tour</H3>
</CENTER>

<BR>
<FORM NAME = "PackageForm">
<TABLE XBORDER = 1 BGCOLOR = "#ffffcc" WIDTH = 200 ALIGN = LEFT>
    <TR><TD BGCOLOR = NAVY ALIGN = CENTER><FONT COLOR
        = FFFFCC>Pick A Package...</TD></TR>
    <TR><TD><INPUT TYPE = RADIO NAME = RadioGroup onClick
        = "AsiaMajor">Asia Major  </TD></TR>
    <TR><TD><INPUT TYPE = RADIO NAME = RadioGroup onClick
        = "GamblersParadise">Gambler's Paradise </TD></TR>
    <TR><TD><INPUT TYPE = RADIO NAME = RadioGroup onClick
        = "EuropeCapitals">European Capitals</TD></TR>
    <TR><TD><INPUT TYPE = RADIO NAME = RadioGroup onClick
        = "BudgetPackage">Budget Package </TD></TR>
    <TR><TD><INPUT TYPE = RADIO NAME = RadioGroup onClick
        = "AllOfThem">All of Them</TD></TR>
</TABLE>
</FORM>
    .
    .
    .
```

Note that we set this table's ALIGN property to LEFT so that the table will appear on the left of the page, leaving room for the City check box table on the right. Now when the user clicks, say, the **Gambler's Paradise** tour package, we call the subroutine GamblersParadise. In that subroutine, we'll select the check boxes corresponding to the cities in that tour: Las Vegas and Atlantic City. Let's set up the check boxes in a new form named CityForm; we set the type of this new control to CHECKBOX and give each one a name corresponding to the city its caption represents (such as HongKong for Hong Kong):

```
<FORM NAME = "CityForm">
<TABLE XBORDER = 1 BGCOLOR = "#FFFFCC" WIDTH = 200 ALIGN = RIGHT>
   <TR><TD BGCOLOR = NAVY ALIGN = CENTER><FONT COLOR
        = FFFFCC>Destinations</TD></TR>
   <TR><TD><INPUT TYPE = CHECKBOX NAME = HongKong>Hong
Kong</TD></TR>
   <TR><TD><INPUT TYPE = CHECKBOX NAME = Tokyo>Tokyo </TD></TR>
   <TR><TD><INPUT TYPE = CHECKBOX NAME = LasVegas>Las
Vegas</TD></TR>
   <TR><TD><INPUT TYPE = CHECKBOX NAME = AtlanticCity>Atlantic
City</TD></TR>
   <TR><TD><INPUT TYPE = CHECKBOX NAME = Rome>Rome</TD></TR>
   <TR><TD><INPUT TYPE = CHECKBOX NAME = Paris>Paris </TD></TR>
   <TR><TD><INPUT TYPE = CHECKBOX NAME = Trenton>Trenton</TD></TR>
</TABLE>
</FORM>
<BR CLEAR  =  ALL>
<BR>
<BR>
<CENTER>
Your price: <INPUT TYPE  =  TEXT NAME  =  PriceBox VALUE = " $ 0"
SIZE  =  30>
</CENTER>
```

Note that we set this new table's ALIGN setting to RIGHT so that it will appear on the right side of our Web page. We also added a text box, named PriceBox, to display the total price of the customized tour.

Our two forms—PackageForm (with radio buttons) and CityForm (with check boxes)—are set up. Now we connect our buttons. When the user clicks the **Asia Major** radio button to select that tour, the AsiaMajor subroutine is called and we select the two check boxes for that tour: **Hong Kong** and **Tokyo**. Let's write the AsiaMajor subroutine. Because we'll set check boxes in the form we've named CityForm, we set up a form variable for that form:

```
     Sub AsiaMajor
 ->      Dim CForm
 ->      Set CForm = document.CityForm
           .
           .
           .

     End Sub
```

Next, we select the HongKong and Tokyo check boxes in CityForm, making them contain a check mark by setting their Checked property to True:

```
     Sub AsiaMajor
         Dim CForm
         Set CForm = document.CityForm
 ->      CForm.HongKong.Checked = True
 ->      CForm.Tokyo.Checked = True
           .
           .
           .

     End Sub
```

However, there is a problem here: what if the user has selected other tours before this one? The cities corresponding to the earlier tour will still be checked, and we need to clear them. Because we'll have to clear the checked cities each time the user clicks a radio button, we add a new subroutine, ClearCities, to clear all check boxes. We call the new subroutine before setting the check boxes we want in AsiaMajor:

```
     Sub AsiaMajor
         Dim CForm
```

```
          Set CForm = document.CityForm
    ->    ClearCities
          CForm.HongKong.Checked = True
          CForm.Tokyo.Checked = True

                  .

                  .

                  .

    End Sub
```

The ClearCities subroutine is easy to write. We loop over all the check boxes in CityForm (using the form's elements() array) and set each check box's Checked property to False, clearing it:

```
    Sub ClearCities
    ->    Dim CForm
    ->    Set CForm = document.CityForm
    ->    For loop_index = 0 to 6
    ->            CForm.elements(loop_index).Checked = False
    ->    Next
    End Sub
```

In addition, when the user selects a new tour such as Asia Major, we should update the listed price in the text box we have named PriceBox:

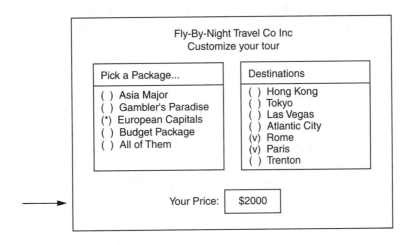

Because we display a new price each time the user clicks a radio button or check box, we add a new subroutine, DisplayPrice, to take care of that task named. DisplayPrice is easy to write. All we do is to loop over the check boxes in CityForm and count how many are checked. We place that number in a variable named NumberCities by first setting the variable to 0 and then looping over all check boxes, adding 1 to NumberCities for each check box that is checked:

```
     Sub DisplayPrice
         Dim NumberCities
         NumberCities = 0
         Dim CForm
         Set CForm = document.CityForm
  ->     For loop_index = 0 to 6
  ->             If CForm.elements(loop_index).Checked Then
  ->                     NumberCities = NumberCities + 1
  ->             End If
  ->     Next
             .
             .
             .
```

At this point, the number of cities that have been checked is in our variable NumberCities. But how do we display this number as text? It turns out that we can convert numbers into text using the CStr() function, which allows us to display the tour package price in PriceBox:

```
     Sub DisplayPrice
         Dim NumberCities
         NumberCities = 0
         Dim CForm
         Set CForm = document.CityForm
         For loop_index = 0 to 6
                 If CForm.elements(loop_index).Checked Then
                         NumberCities = NumberCities + 1
                 End If
         Next
  ->     PriceBox.Value = " $ " + CStr(NumberCities) + "000.00"
     End Sub
```

Now we set the correct price in the text box by calling the DisplayPrice subroutine. We do that in the AsiaMajor subroutine:

```
   Sub AsiaMajor
        Dim CForm
        Set CForm = document.CityForm
        ClearCities
        CForm.HongKong.Checked = True
        CForm.Tokyo.Checked = True
->      DisplayPrice
   End Sub
```

We do the same for the other tour packages, adding subroutines for each of the radio button–controlled tour packages. (Each subroutine is called by a radio button.)

```
   Sub GamblersParadise
        Dim CForm
        Set CForm = document.CityForm
        ClearCities
        CForm.LasVegas.Checked = True
        CForm.AtlanticCity.Checked = True
        DisplayPrice
   End Sub

   Sub EuropeCapitals
        Dim CForm
        Set CForm = document.CityForm
        ClearCities
        CForm.Rome.Checked = True
        CForm.Paris.Checked = True
        DisplayPrice
   End Sub

   Sub BudgetPackage
        Dim CForm
        Set CForm = document.CityForm
        ClearCities
        CForm.AtlanticCity.Checked = True
        CForm.Trenton.Checked = True
```

```
        DisplayPrice
End Sub

Sub AllOfThem
        Dim CForm
        Set CForm = document.CityForm
        ClearCities
        CForm.HongKong.Checked = True
        CForm.Tokyo.Checked = True
        CForm.LasVegas.Checked = True
        CForm.AtlanticCity.Checked = True
        CForm.Rome.Checked = True
        CForm.Paris.Checked = True
        CForm.Trenton.Checked = True
        DisplayPrice
End Sub
```

At this point, when the user selects a tour package, we display the cities in that tour and their total price, as shown in Figure 9.1. Our new program is a success so far.

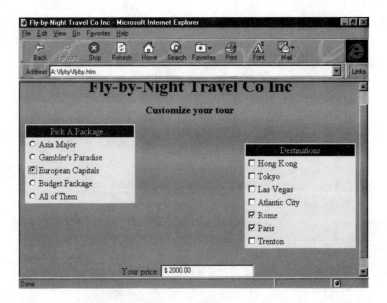

Figure 9.1 We let the user select tour packages.

In addition, customers may want to customize their tours, selecting other cities' check boxes. We call the DisplayPrice subroutine when the user clicks a check box, adding an onClick event handler to each check box (with the text "onClick = "DisplayPrice"") this way:

```
<FORM NAME = "CityForm">
<TABLE XBORDER = 1 BGCOLOR = "#FFFFCC" WIDTH = 200 ALIGN = RIGHT>
   <TR><TD BGCOLOR = NAVY ALIGN = CENTER><FONT COLOR
        = FFFFCC>Destinations</TD></TR>
   <TR><TD><INPUT TYPE = CHECKBOX NAME = HongKong onClick
->      = "DisplayPrice">Hong Kong</TD></TR>
   <TR><TD><INPUT TYPE = CHECKBOX NAME = Tokyo onClick
->      = "DisplayPrice">Tokyo </TD></TR>
   <TR><TD><INPUT TYPE = CHECKBOX NAME = LasVegas onClick
->      = "DisplayPrice">Las Vegas</TD></TR>
   <TR><TD><INPUT TYPE = CHECKBOX NAME = AtlanticCity onClick
->      = "DisplayPrice">Atlantic City  </TD></TR>
   <TR><TD><INPUT TYPE = CHECKBOX NAME = Rome onClick
->      = "DisplayPrice">Rome</TD></TR>
   <TR><TD><INPUT TYPE = CHECKBOX NAME = Paris onClick
->      = "DisplayPrice">Paris </TD></TR>
   <TR><TD><INPUT TYPE = CHECKBOX NAME = Trenton onClick
->      = "DisplayPrice">Trenton</TD></TR>
</TABLE>
</FORM>
```

Now the user can click on various cities, adding them to the tour and customizing the tour package, as shown in Figure 9.2. That's it—our tour package example is a success. The HTML and VBScript for this page appear in Listing 9.1.

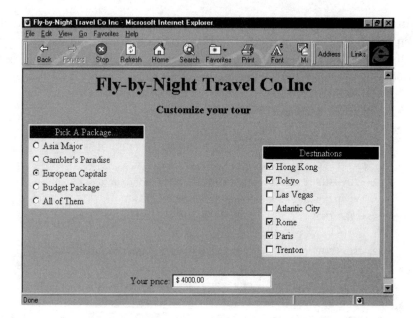

Figure 9.2 The user can customize the tour.

Listing 9.1 Flyby.htm

```
<HTML>
<HEAD>
<TITLE>Fly-by-Night Travel Co Inc</TITLE>
</HEAD>

<BODY LANGUAGE = VBScript onLoad = Page_Initialize>

<CENTER>
<H1>Fly-by-Night Travel Co Inc</H1>
<H3>Customize your tour</H3>
</CENTER>

<BR>
<FORM NAME = "PackageForm">
<TABLE XBORDER = 1 BGCOLOR = "#ffffcc" WIDTH = 200 ALIGN = LEFT>
   <TR><TD BGCOLOR = NAVY ALIGN = CENTER><FONT COLOR = FFFFCC>Pick A
```

```
              Package...</TD></TR>
     <TR><TD><INPUT TYPE = RADIO NAME = RadioGroup onClick
           = "AsiaMajor">Asia Major  </TD></TR>
     <TR><TD><INPUT TYPE = RADIO NAME = RadioGroup onClick
           = "GamblersParadise">Gambler's Paradise </TD></TR>
     <TR><TD><INPUT TYPE = RADIO NAME = RadioGroup onClick
           = "EuropeCapitals">European Capitals</TD></TR>
     <TR><TD><INPUT TYPE = RADIO NAME = RadioGroup onClick
           = "BudgetPackage">Budget Package </TD></TR>
     <TR><TD><INPUT TYPE = RADIO NAME = RadioGroup onClick
           = "AllOfThem">All of Them</TD></TR>
</TABLE>
</FORM>

<FORM NAME = "CityForm">
<TABLE XBORDER = 1 BGCOLOR = "#FFFFCC" WIDTH = 200 ALIGN = RIGHT>
     <TR><TD BGCOLOR = NAVY ALIGN = CENTER><FONT COLOR
           = FFFFCC>Destinations</TD></TR>
     <TR><TD><INPUT TYPE = CHECKBOX NAME = HongKong onClick
           = "DisplayPrice">Hong Kong</TD></TR>
     <TR><TD><INPUT TYPE = CHECKBOX NAME = Tokyo onClick
           = "DisplayPrice">Tokyo </TD></TR>
     <TR><TD><INPUT TYPE = CHECKBOX NAME = LasVegas onClick
           = "DisplayPrice">Las Vegas</TD></TR>
     <TR><TD><INPUT TYPE = CHECKBOX NAME = AtlanticCity onClick
           = "DisplayPrice">Atlantic City  </TD></TR>
     <TR><TD><INPUT TYPE = CHECKBOX NAME = Rome onClick
           = "DisplayPrice">Rome</TD></TR>
     <TR><TD><INPUT TYPE = CHECKBOX NAME = Paris onClick
           = "DisplayPrice">Paris </TD></TR>
     <TR><TD><INPUT TYPE = CHECKBOX NAME = Trenton onClick
           = "DisplayPrice">Trenton</TD></TR>
</TABLE>
</FORM>
<BR CLEAR  =  ALL>
<BR>
<BR>
<CENTER>
```

```
Your price: <INPUT TYPE  =  TEXT NAME  =  PriceBox VALUE = " $ 0"
SIZE = 30>
</CENTER>

<SCRIPT LANGUAGE = VBScript>
    Sub Page_Initialize
    End Sub

    Sub AsiaMajor
        Dim CForm
        Set CForm = document.CityForm
        ClearCities
        CForm.HongKong.Checked = True
        CForm.Tokyo.Checked = True
        DisplayPrice
    End Sub

    Sub GamblersParadise
        Dim CForm
        Set CForm = document.CityForm
        ClearCities
        CForm.LasVegas.Checked = True
        CForm.AtlanticCity.Checked = True
        DisplayPrice
    End Sub

    Sub EuropeCapitals
        Dim CForm
        Set CForm = document.CityForm
        ClearCities
        CForm.Rome.Checked = True
        CForm.Paris.Checked = True
        DisplayPrice
    End Sub

    Sub BudgetPackage
        Dim CForm
        Set CForm = document.CityForm
        ClearCities
```

```
        CForm.AtlanticCity.Checked = True
        CForm.Trenton.Checked = True
        DisplayPrice
End Sub

Sub AllOfThem
        Dim CForm
        Set CForm = document.CityForm
        ClearCities
        CForm.HongKong.Checked = True
        CForm.Tokyo.Checked = True
        CForm.LasVegas.Checked = True
        CForm.AtlanticCity.Checked = True
        CForm.Rome.Checked = True
        CForm.Paris.Checked = True
        CForm.Trenton.Checked = True
        DisplayPrice
End Sub

Sub ClearCities
        Dim CForm
        Set CForm = document.CityForm
        For loop_index = 0 to 6
                CForm.elements(loop_index).Checked = False
        Next
End Sub

Sub DisplayPrice
        Dim NumberCities
        NumberCities = 0
        Dim CForm
        Set CForm = document.CityForm
        For loop_index = 0 to 6
                If CForm.elements(loop_index).Checked Then
                        NumberCities = NumberCities + 1
                End If
        Next
        PriceBox.Value = " $ " + CStr(NumberCities) + "000.00"
End Sub
```

```
</SCRIPT>

</BODY>
</HTML>
```

This completes our first multiform example. A Web page's document can enclose multiple forms like this; we've seen a little about a Web page document in Chapter 8, and we'll make a deeper investigation here.

Documents

A VBScript document corresponds to the current Web page. Such documents can contain forms, which in turn can contain elements such as controls:

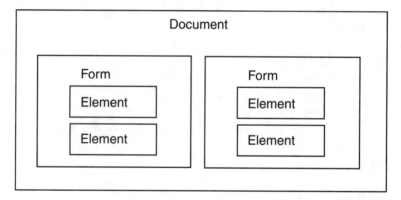

Just as the elements in a form are contained in the elements() array, so the forms in a document are contained in the forms() array. For example, if we have two forms, the first form can be referred to as document.forms(0) and the second as document.forms(1):

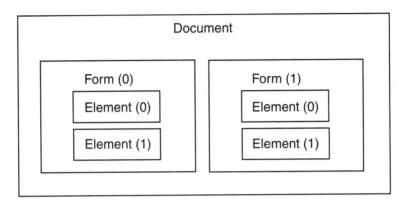

In this way, we can, if we wish, replace references to forms with the corresponding entry in the forms() array. For example, in our AsiaMajor subroutine, we refer to CityForm this way:

```
Sub AsiaMajor
      Dim CForm
->    Set CForm = document.CityForm
      ClearCities
      CForm.HongKong.Checked = True
      CForm.Tokyo.Checked = True
      DisplayPrice
End Sub
```

Instead, we could reference forms(0) this way:

```
Sub AsiaMajor
      Dim CForm
->    Set CForm = document.forms(0)
      ClearCities
      CForm.HongKong.Checked = True
      CForm.Tokyo.Checked = True
      DisplayPrice
End Sub
```

The properties of documents appear in Table 9.1, and the methods of documents appear in Table 9.2.

Table 9.1 Document Properties

Property	Meaning
alinkColor	Sets document's link color
anchors	Returns the anchors array
bgColor	Sets document's background color cookie
fgColor	Sets document's foreground color
linkColor	Sets document's links color
links	Returns the links array
forms	Returns the forms array
lastModified	Returns date document was last modified
title	Returns the title of the document
vlinkColor	Sets document's visited link color
location	Returns read-only copy of the location object

Table 9.2 Document Methods

Methods	Meaning
Clear	
Close	
Open	
Write	Write to the document's HTML
Writeln	Write to the document's HTML with at end

Let's put the document to work now as we explore how to embed active objects in addition to forms in documents.

Image Maps and Mouse Movements

We'll see how to embed an *image map* into a document. An image map is an image with active sections that the user can click to jump to a new

URL. We'll create an image map with an active section labeled **News Link**:

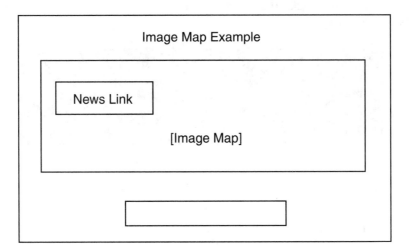

Then the user can jump to the News page by clicking **News Link**. Let's embed the image map into our document. Not only will we activate sections of the map as hyperlinks, but we will also update a text box in our page showing what various links do in the image map as the user moves the mouse over them. For example, as the user moves the mouse over our **News Link**, we explain that link's purpose in a text box:

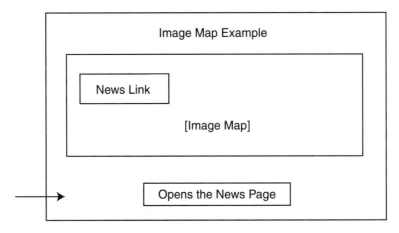

We'll use the image **mainmap.gif** (shown in Figure 9.3) as our image map. In this map, we have various graphical "buttons" that we will make active; when the user clicks the **News** button, for example, we will jump to a News Web page.

Figure 9.3 Our image map.

To make this an active element in our document, we embed it using an anchor (<A>) tag and give it the name MapAnchor:

```
<HTML>

<TITLE>Image Map Example</TITLE>

</BODY>
<H1>Image Map Example</H1>
<HR>
<CENTER>

<A ID = "MapAnchor" HREF = "">              <—
<IMG SRC = "mainmap.gif" ALT="Clickable Map Image" WIDTH = 528
HEIGHT
        = 137 BORDER = 0>
</A>
    .
    .
    .
```

The MouseMove Event

Now that we've embedded our image map and called the associated anchor MapAnchor, we start the VBScript code by connecting a MouseMove event to that anchor:

```
<SCRIPT LANGUAGE = VBScript>

SUB MapAnchor_MouseMove(Shift, Button, X, Y)    <—
    .
    .
    .
```

This event subroutine is called when the mouse moves over our image map. The Shift argument passed to us indicates the status of the **Shift** and **Ctrl** keys, as shown in Table 9.3, and the Button argument indicates which button was pressed, as shown in Table 9.4. In addition, the X and Y parameters indicate the location of the mouse in the image map using this coordinate system in pixels:

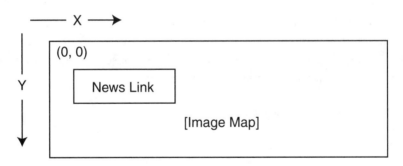

Table 9.3 Values for the Shift Argument (MouseMove)

Shift Value	Binary	Meaning
0	0000000000000000	Neither **Shift** nor **Ctrl** was down
1	0000000000000001	**Shift** key was down
2	0000000000000010	**Ctrl** key was down

Table 9.4 Values for the Button Argument (MouseMove)

Button Value	Binary	Meaning
0	0000000000000000	No button is pressed
1	0000000000000001	Only **Left** button is pressed
2	0000000000000010	Only **Right** button is pressed
3	0000000000000011	**Right** and **Left** buttons are pressed
4	0000000000000100	Only **Middle** button is pressed
5	0000000000000101	**Middle** and **Left** buttons are pressed
6	0000000000000110	**Middle** and **Right** buttons are pressed
7	0000000000000111	All three buttons are pressed

The MapAnchor_MouseMove() subroutine is called when the user moves the mouse over our image map. We update our text box, indicating which hyperlinks the mouse is over (if any). To do that, we check the (X, Y) location of the mouse, and to do that, we write a function called IsInRectangle(), passing it the location of the mouse and the coordinates of a particular graphical button in our image map:

```
<SCRIPT LANGUAGE = VBScript>

SUB MapAnchor_MouseMove(Shift, Button, X, Y)
If IsInRectangle(X, Y,  16, 39, 127, 61) Then
DescriptionTextbox.Value
        = "Reuters news service"
        .
        .
        .
```

In this way, we update the hyperlink description text box as the user moves the mouse over the image map. Let's write the IsInRectangle() function. We will use the < and > VBScript operators to check whether the (X, Y) point is in the rectangle. We specify the rectangle by giving the coordinates of its upper-left corner and its lower-right corner:

(TopLeftX, TopLeftY)

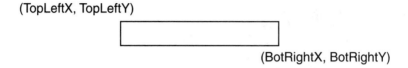

(BotRightX, BotRightY)

We pass those coordinates to IsInRectangle() along with the coordinates of the point we are checking:

```
FUNCTION IsInRectangle(X, Y, TopLeftX, TopLeftY, BotRightX,
BotRightY) <-

END FUNCTION
```

Note that here we have several conditions to check. Is X between TopLeftX and BotRightX? Is Y between TopLeftY and BotRightY? We do that this way:

```
FUNCTION IsInRectangle(X, Y, TopLeftX, TopLeftY, BotRightX,
BotRightY)
        IsInRectangle = X > TopLeftX AND X < BotRightX AND Y >
            TopLeftY AND Y < BotRightY
END FUNCTION
```

That completes the IsInRectangle() function, which we put to work in the MapAnchor_MouseMove() subroutine. We update the hyperlink description text box as the user moves the mouse over the image map:

```
<SCRIPT LANGUAGE = VBScript>

SUB MapAnchor_MouseMove(Shift, Button, X, Y)

If IsInRectangle(X, Y,  16, 39, 127, 61) Then
DescriptionTextbox.Value
        = "Reuters news service"
If IsInRectangle(X, Y,  62, 71, 173, 93) Then
DescriptionTextbox.Value
```

```
          = "Web search page"
If IsInRectangle(X, Y,  98, 104, 209, 126) Then
DescriptionTextbox.Value
          = "Government weather predictions"
If IsInRectangle(X, Y,  411, 35, 522, 57) Then
DescriptionTextbox.Value
          = "The guestbook"
If IsInRectangle(X, Y,  360, 67, 471, 89) Then
DescriptionTextbox.Value
          = "HTML design from Yahoo"
If IsInRectangle(X, Y,  328, 98, 439, 120) Then
DescriptionTextbox.Value
          = "Hot 100 Links of the week"
END SUB
```

Now we indicate which hyperlink the mouse is over. The next step is to activate those hyperlinks when the user clicks them.

Enabling the Image Map

We connect the onClick event to our image map this way:

```
<HTML>

<TITLE>Image Map Example</TITLE>

</BODY>
<H1>Image Map Example</H1>
<HR>
<CENTER>

<A ID = "MapAnchor" HREF = "">
<IMG SRC = "mainmap.gif" ALT="Clickable Map Image" WIDTH = 528
HEIGHT
          = 137 BORDER = 0>
</A>
<BR>
<BR>
<INPUT TYPE = TEXT VALUE = "" NAME = DescriptionTextbox size = 30>
</CENTER>
```

```
<SCRIPT FOR = "MapAnchor" EVENT = "OnClick" LANGUAGE =
VBScript></SCRIPT> <-
    .
    .
    .
```

Now we write the subroutine MapAnchor_OnClick, which will be called when the map is clicked:

```
SUB MapAnchor_OnClick   <-
    .
    .
    .
```

When users click the image map, we check to see whether they clicked a hypertext link. Unfortunately, click event subroutines do not receive the (X, Y) location of the click, and we'll need that information to see which hyperlink the user clicked. On the other hand, the (X, Y) information *is* passed to the MouseMove() subroutine. We can use that same information in the MapAnchor_OnClick() subroutine if we save the most recent mouse position from the MouseMove() subroutine. To do that, in our VBScript section we set up two global variables—XPos and YPos—to hold the mouse location:

```
<SCRIPT LANGUAGE = VBScript>
DIM XPos        <-
DIM YPos        <-
    .
    .
    .
```

Next, we set XPos and YPos to 0 initially:

```
<SCRIPT LANGUAGE = VBScript>
DIM XPos
DIM YPos
XPos  =  0      <-
YPos  =  0      <-
```

.

.

.

When a MouseMove() event occurs, we update XPos and YPos to hold the current mouse location:

```
<SCRIPT LANGUAGE = VBScript>
DIM XPos
DIM YPos
XPos  =  0
YPos  =  0

SUB MapAnchor_MouseMove(Shift, Button, X, Y)
XPos = X          <-
YPos = Y          <-

If IsInRectangle(X, Y,  16, 39, 127, 61) Then
DescriptionTextbox.Value
        = "Reuters news service"
If IsInRectangle(X, Y,  62, 71, 173, 93) Then
DescriptionTextbox.Value
        = "Web search page"
If IsInRectangle(X, Y,  98, 104, 209, 126) Then
DescriptionTextbox.Value
        = "Government weather predictions"
If IsInRectangle(X, Y,  411, 35, 522, 57) Then
DescriptionTextbox.Value
        = "The guestbook"
If IsInRectangle(X, Y,  360, 67, 471, 89) Then
DescriptionTextbox.Value
        = "HTML design from Yahoo"
If IsInRectangle(X, Y,  328, 98, 439, 120) Then
DescriptionTextbox.Value
        = "Hot 100 Links of the week"

END SUB
```

Now the current mouse location is available to us in MapAnchor_OnClick() as XPos and YPos. We check to see whether the mouse is on a particular hyperlink using the IsInRectangle() function:

```
SUB MapAnchor_OnClick
If IsInRectangle(XPos, YPos,  16, 39, 127, 61) Then...
        .
        .
        .
```

Here, we check whether the mouse was clicked in the News hyperlink. If it was, we might jump to, say, the Reuters news page at http://www.reuters.com. To do that, we use the VBScript location object, setting its HREF property to the new URL:

```
SUB MapAnchor_OnClick
If IsInRectangle(XPos, YPos,  16, 39, 127, 61) Then Location.HREF
        = "http://www.reuters.com"
        .
        .
        .
```

We will discuss the location object further in Chapter 10; for now, we put it to work this way in MapAnchor_OnClick:

```
SUB MapAnchor_OnClick
If IsInRectangle(XPos, YPos,  16, 39, 127, 61) Then Location.HREF
        = "http://www.reuters.com"
If IsInRectangle(XPos, YPos,  62, 71, 173, 93) Then Location.HREF
        = "http://www.server.com/search.htm"
If IsInRectangle(XPos, YPos,  98, 104, 209, 126) Then Location.HREF
        = "http://www.nnic.noaa.gov"
If IsInRectangle(XPos, YPos,  411, 35, 522, 57) Then Location.HREF
        = "http://www.server.com/gbook.htm"
If IsInRectangle(XPos, YPos,  360, 67, 471, 89) Then Location.HREF
        = "http://www.yahoo.com/Computers_and_Internet/
        Software/Data_Formats/HTML/Guides_and_Tutorials/"
If IsInRectangle(XPos, YPos,  328, 98, 439, 120) Then Location.HREF
        = "http://www.web21.com/services/hot100/index.html"
END SUB
```

And that's it—now our image map is active, as shown in Figure 9.4. Our new program is a success. When the user clicks a hyperlink in the image map, we jump to the new URL. The HTML and VBScript file for this page appears in Listing 9.2.

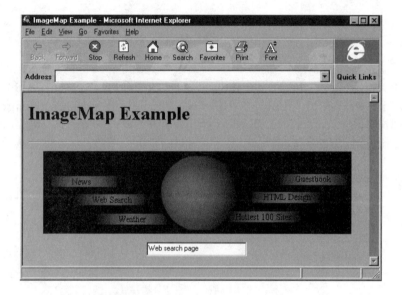

Figure 9.4 Our image map is now active.

Listing 9.2 Map.htm

```
<HTML>

<TITLE>Image Map Example</TITLE>

</BODY>
<H1>Image Map Example</H1>
<HR>
<CENTER>

<A ID = "MapAnchor" HREF = "">
```

```
<IMG SRC = "mainmap.gif" ALT="Clickable Map Image" WIDTH = 528
HEIGHT
       = 137 BORDER = 0>
</A>
<BR>
<BR>
<INPUT TYPE = TEXT VALUE = "" NAME = DescriptionTextbox size = 30>
</CENTER>

<SCRIPT FOR = "MapAnchor" EVENT = "OnClick" LANGUAGE =
VBScript></SCRIPT>

<SCRIPT LANGUAGE = VBScript>
DIM XPos
DIM YPos
XPos  =  0
YPos  =  0

SUB MapAnchor_MouseMove(Shift, Button, X, Y)
XPos = X
YPos = Y

If IsInRectangle(X, Y,  16, 39, 127, 61) Then
DescriptionTextbox.Value
       = "Reuters news service"
If IsInRectangle(X, Y,  62, 71, 173, 93) Then
DescriptionTextbox.Value
       = "Web search page"
If IsInRectangle(X, Y,  98, 104, 209, 126) Then
DescriptionTextbox.Value
       = "Government weather predictions"
If IsInRectangle(X, Y,  411, 35, 522, 57) Then
DescriptionTextbox.Value
       = "The guestbook"
If IsInRectangle(X, Y,  360, 67, 471, 89) Then
DescriptionTextbox.Value
       = "HTML design from Yahoo"
If IsInRectangle(X, Y,  328, 98, 439, 120) Then
DescriptionTextbox.Value
       = "Hot 100 Links of the week"
```

```
END SUB

SUB MapAnchor_OnClick
If IsInRectangle(XPos, YPos,  16, 39, 127, 61) Then Location.HREF
        = "http://www.reuters.com"
If IsInRectangle(XPos, YPos,  62, 71, 173, 93) Then Location.HREF
        = "http://www.server.com/search.htm"
If IsInRectangle(XPos, YPos,  98, 104, 209, 126) Then Location.HREF
        = "http://www.nnic.noaa.gov"
If IsInRectangle(XPos, YPos,  411, 35, 522, 57) Then Location.HREF
        = "http://www.server.com/gbook.htm"
If IsInRectangle(XPos, YPos,  360, 67, 471, 89) Then Location.HREF
        = "http://www.yahoo.com/Computers_and_Internet/
        Software/Data_Formats/HTML/Guides_and_Tutorials/"
If IsInRectangle(XPos, YPos,  328, 98, 439, 120) Then Location.HREF
        = "http://www.web21.com/services/hot100/index.html"
END SUB

FUNCTION IsInRectangle(X, Y, TopLeftX, TopLeftY, BotRightX,
BotRightY)
        IsInRectangle =  X > TopLeftX AND X < BotRightX AND Y >
            TopLeftY AND Y < BotRightY
END FUNCTION

</SCRIPT>
</BODY>
</HTML>
```

In addition to embedding an image map, there is more we can do with documents. For example, it turns out that we can modify the HTML in a document as it loads, allowing a Web page to be self-modifying.

Using the Document Object: Self-Modifying Web Pages

In the following example of a self-modifying Web page, we'll place a message box on the screen asking users whether they want to load the graphics in our page. (Not loading graphics can save a great deal of time.)

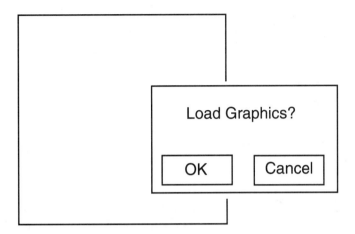

If the user decides to load the graphics, we will use the document Write method to write this HTML to the Web page as it loads:

```
<BR>
<BR>
<IMG WIDTH=236 HEIGHT=118 SRC="gif/yourgif.gif">
</IMG>
```

Otherwise, we will simply not place this HTML into the Web page. We begin by setting up our script in the Web page; when the page is loaded, the VBScript in our <SCRIPT> section is run (unless it is in subroutines or functions, which must be called). To check whether the user wants to load the graphics, we use the VBScript function Confirm:

```
<HTML>

<TITLE>Hello world example</TITLE>

<BODY>

<CENTER>
<INPUT TYPE = TEXT NAME = Textbox SIZE=20>
<BR>
<BR>
Click me: <INPUT TYPE = BUTTON NAME = "HelloButton">
```

```
<SCRIPT LANGUAGE = VBScript>
->    If (confirm("Load graphics?")) Then
            .

            .

            .
        End If
</SCRIPT>
        .

        .

        .
```

That places the Confirm box on the screen, as shown in Figure 9.5. If the user clicks **OK**, we will put the image-loading HTML into the Web page.

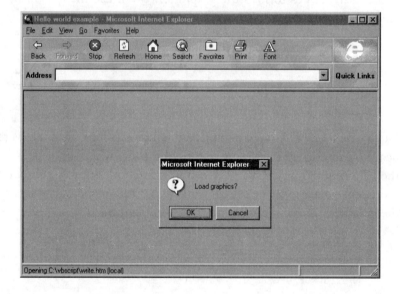

Figure 9.5 Our Web page checks whether it should load graphics.

We use the document.write method:

```
<HTML>

<TITLE>Hello world example</TITLE>
```

```
<BODY>

<CENTER>
<INPUT TYPE = TEXT NAME = Textbox SIZE=20>
<BR>
<BR>
Click me: <INPUT TYPE = BUTTON NAME = "HelloButton">

<SCRIPT LANGUAGE = VBScript>
        If (confirm("Load graphics?")) Then
 ->            document.write "<BR><BR><IMG WIDTH=236 HEIGHT=118
 ->                SRC=""gif/yourgif.gif""></IMG>"
        End If
</SCRIPT>
    .

    .

    .
```

Notice that we enclose in quotation marks the HTML we want to place in the Web page:

```
<SCRIPT LANGUAGE = VBScript>
        If (confirm("Load graphics?")) Then
 ->            document.write "<BR><BR><IMG WIDTH=236 HEIGHT=118
 ->                SRC=""gif/yourgif.gif""></IMG>"
        End If
</SCRIPT>
```

Note that we often enclose items in HTML in quotation marks:

```
                <IMG WIDTH=236 HEIGHT=118 SRC="gif/yourgif.gif">
                </IMG>
```

To pass these quotation marks through to the HTML, we must use double quotation marks:

```
<SCRIPT LANGUAGE = VBScript>
        If (confirm("Load graphics?")) Then
                document.write "<BR><BR><IMG WIDTH=236 HEIGHT=118
```

```
   ->                    SRC=""gif/yourgif.gif""></IMG>"
        End If
</SCRIPT>
```

And that's it—if the user clicks **OK**, we load the graphics file, as shown in Figure 9.6. Our first self-modifying page is a success; the code for this page appears in Listing 9.3.

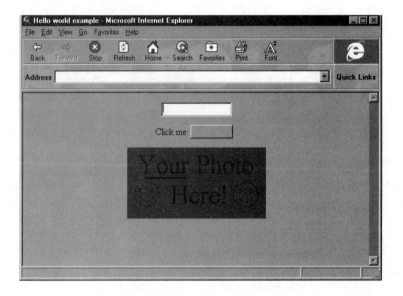

Figure 9.6 Our Web page is self-modifying.

Listing 9.3

```
<HTML>

<TITLE>Hello world example</TITLE>

<BODY>

<CENTER>
<INPUT TYPE = TEXT NAME = Textbox SIZE=20>
<BR>
```

```
<BR>
Click me: <INPUT TYPE = BUTTON NAME = "HelloButton">

<SCRIPT LANGUAGE = VBScript>
        If (confirm("Load graphics?")) Then
                document.write "<BR><BR><IMG WIDTH=236 HEIGHT=118
        SRC=""gif/yourgif.gif""></IMG>"
        End If
</SCRIPT>

</CENTER>

</BODY>

<SCRIPT LANGUAGE = VBScript>
        Sub HelloButton_OnClick
                TextBox.Value = "Hello World!"
        End Sub
</SCRIPT>

</HTML>
```

Our next self-modifying Web page checks the time of day to determine which screen to display to the user.

The VBScript Cafe Self-Modifying Menu

Let's create the menu Web page for the VBScript Cafe. Our page should present the user with a different menu—breakfast, lunch, or dinner—depending on the time of day. Our breakfast menu might look like this:

```
┌──────────────────────────────────────────────┐
│           Welcome to the VBScript Cafe!        │
│                                                │
│         1:00 PM,        12/25/96               │
│     ┌──────────────────────────────────┬────┐ │
│     │            Breakfast              │    │ │
│     ├────────────────────────┬─────────┼────┤ │
│     │ Two fried eggs         │  $2.95  │ [ ]│ │
│     ├────────────────────────┼─────────┼────┤ │
│     │ Two scrambled eggs     │  $2.95  │ [ ]│ │
│     ├────────────────────────┼─────────┼────┤ │
│     │ French Toast           │  $2.95  │ [ ]│ │
│     ├────────────────────────┼─────────┼────┤ │
│     │ Oatmeal                │  $1.95  │ [ ]│ │
│     ├────────────────────────┼─────────┼────┤ │
│     │ Bacon                  │  $1.95  │ [ ]│ │
│     ├────────────────────────┼─────────┼────┤ │
│     │ Coffee                 │  $ .95  │ [ ]│ │
│     ├────────────────────────┼─────────┼────┤ │
│     │ Orange juice           │  $1.50  │ [ ]│ │
│     └────────────────────────┴─────────┴────┘ │
│                                                │
│           ┌──────────────────────────┐         │
│           │  Your bill:    $xxxx     │         │
│           └──────────────────────────┘         │
└──────────────────────────────────────────────┘
```

Later in the day, we automatically present the user with our lunch menu:

```
┌──────────────────────────────────────────────┐
│           Welcome to the VBScript Cafe!        │
│                                                │
│         7:30 AM,        12/25/96               │
│     ┌──────────────────────────────────┬────┐ │
│     │              Lunch               │    │ │
│     ├────────────────────────┬─────────┼────┤ │
│     │ Turkey sandwich        │  $3.95  │ [ ]│ │
│     ├────────────────────────┼─────────┼────┤ │
│     │ Roast beef sandwich    │  $3.95  │ [ ]│ │
│     ├────────────────────────┼─────────┼────┤ │
│     │ Ham sandwich           │  $3.95  │ [ ]│ │
│     ├────────────────────────┼─────────┼────┤ │
│     │ French fries           │  $1.95  │ [ ]│ │
│     ├────────────────────────┼─────────┼────┤ │
│     │ Soup                   │  $1.95  │ [ ]│ │
│     ├────────────────────────┼─────────┼────┤ │
│     │ Coffee          $ .95            │ [ ]│ │
│     ├────────────────────────┼─────────┼────┤ │
│     │ Soda                   │  $1.25  │ [ ]│ │
│     └────────────────────────┴─────────┴────┘ │
│                                                │
│           ┌──────────────────────────┐         │
│           │  Your bill:    $xxxx     │         │
│           └──────────────────────────┘         │
└──────────────────────────────────────────────┘
```

We begin our new Web page by writing a welcome message to the user. Here, we use the built-in VBScript functions Time and Date—which return text strings holding the time and date, respectively—to place that information in our Web page:

```
<HTML>

<BODY>
<SCRIPT LANGUAGE = VBScript>
document.write "<CENTER>"
document.write "<H1>"
document.write "Welcome to the VBScript Cafe!"
document.write "</H1>"
document.write "<H2>"
document.write Time              <-
document.write ", "
document.write Date              <-
document.write "</H2>"
document.write "</CENTER>"
      .
      .
      .
```

Suppose these are the VBScript Cafe's hours:

```
6 AM to 11 AM: Breakfast
11 AM to 4 PM: Lunch
4 PM to 11 PM: Dinner
11 PM to 6 AM: Closed
```

We'll display the correct menu to match. We check the current hour using the VBScript function Now, which returns the current date; to find the current hour, we use the Hour function, passing it the result from Now: Hour(Now). Let's start with the time between 11 PM and 6 AM, when the cafe is closed. If our Web page is loaded at that time, we just put up the closed message using document.write:

```
<HTML>

<BODY>
<SCRIPT LANGUAGE = VBScript>
document.write "<CENTER>"
document.write "<H1>"
document.write "Welcome to the VBScript Cafe!"
```

```
document.write "</H1>"
document.write "<H2>"
document.write Time
document.write ", "
document.write Date
document.write "</H2>"
document.write "</CENTER>"

If Hour(Now) < 6 OR Hour(Now) > 22 Then            <-
        document.write "<CENTER>"                  <-
        document.write "<H1>"                      <-
        document.write "Sorry, we open at 6 AM"    <-
        document.write "</H1>"                     <-
        document.write "</CENTER>"                 <-
End If
    .
    .
    .
```

Next, we handle the breakfast menu, which is a table with check boxes where we list the items and prices:

Welcome to the VB Script Cafe!		
7:30 AM, 12/25/96		
Breakfast		
Two fried eggs	$2.95	[ ]
Two scrambled eggs	$2.95	[ ]
French toast	$2.95	[ ]
Oatmeal	$1.95	[ ]
Bacon	$1.95	[ ]
Coffee	$.95	[ ]
Orange juice	$1.50	[ ]

When the user clicks menu items, we total the price of the items and place the result in a text box named Total. In HTML, that table looks like this:

```
<TABLE BORDER BGCOLOR = "#ffff00">
<TR><TH COLSPAN = 2>Breakfast</TH></TR>
<TR><TD>Two fried eggs $2.95</TD><TD><INPUT TYPE
     = CHECKBOX NAME = BButton onClick = "SetPrice
2.95"></TD></TR>
<TR><TD>Two scrambled eggs $2.95</TD><TD><INPUT TYPE
     = CHECKBOX NAME = BButton onClick = "SetPrice
2.95"></TD></TR>
<TR><TD>French toast $2.95</TD><TD><INPUT TYPE
     = CHECKBOX NAME = BButton onClick = "SetPrice
2.95"></TD></TR>
<TR><TD>Oatmeal $1.95</TD><TD><INPUT TYPE
     = CHECKBOX NAME = BButton onClick = "SetPrice
1.95"></TD></TR>
<TR><TD>Bacon $1.95</TD><TD><INPUT TYPE
     = CHECKBOX NAME = BButton onClick = "SetPrice
1.95"></TD></TR>
<TR><TD>Coffee $.95</TD><TD><INPUT TYPE
     = CHECKBOX NAME = BButton onClick = "SetPrice
.95"></TD></TR>
<TR><TD>Orange juice $1.50</TD><TD><INPUT TYPE
     = CHECKBOX NAME = BButton onClick = "SetPrice
1.50"></TD></TR>
     </TABLE>
```

Note that we call a subroutine named SetPrice, passing it the value of the clicked menu item (for example, "SetPrice 1.50" for orange juice). In the SetPrice subroutine, we receive the price of the item as an argument and add it to a running total that we name TotalCost. We place the running total into the text box named Total:

```
<SCRIPT LANGUAGE = VBScript>
Dim TotalCost
TotalCost = 0

SUB SetPrice(Cost)
     TotalCost = TotalCost + Cost
```

```
        document.MenuForm.Total.Value = " Your bill: $ " +
CStr(TotalCost)
END SUB


</SCRIPT>
```

That's all there is to it. To write the breakfast menu to the Web page we use document.write:

```
If Hour(Now) > 5 AND Hour(Now) < 10 Then
        document.write "<FORM NAME = ""MenuForm"">"
        document.write "<CENTER>"
        document.write "<TABLE BORDER BGCOLOR = ""#ffff00"">"
        document.write "<TR><TH COLSPAN = 2>Breakfast</TH></TR>"
        document.write "<TR><TD>Two fried eggs $2.95</TD><TD><INPUT TYPE
            = CHECKBOX NAME = BButton onClick = ""SetPrice
            2.95""></TD></TR>"
        document.write "<TR><TD>Two scrambled eggs
        $2.95</TD><TD><INPUT TYPE
            = CHECKBOX NAME = BButton onClick = ""SetPrice
            2.95""></TD></TR>"
        document.write "<TR><TD>French toast $2.95</TD><TD><INPUT TYPE
            = CHECKBOX NAME = BButton onClick = ""SetPrice
            2.95""></TD></TR>"
        document.write "<TR><TD>Oatmeal $1.95</TD><TD><INPUT TYPE
            = CHECKBOX NAME = BButton onClick = ""SetPrice
            1.95""></TD></TR>"
        document.write "<TR><TD>Bacon $1.95</TD><TD><INPUT TYPE
            = CHECKBOX NAME = BButton onClick = ""SetPrice
            1.95""></TD></TR>"
        document.write "<TR><TD>Coffee $.95</TD><TD><INPUT TYPE
            = CHECKBOX NAME = BButton onClick = ""SetPrice
            .95""></TD></TR>"
        document.write "<TR><TD>Orange juice $1.50</TD><TD><INPUT TYPE
            = CHECKBOX NAME = BButton onClick = ""SetPrice
            1.50""></TD></TR>"
        document.write "</TABLE>"
        document.write "<INPUT TYPE = TEXT VALUE = """" NAME = Total
        Size = 20>"
        document.write "</CENTER>"
        document.write "</FORM>"
End If
```

For lunch, we include the lunch menu, first checking the hour of the day to make sure we display this menu only during lunch:

```
If Hour(Now) > 10 AND Hour(Now) < 15 Then
        document.write "<FORM NAME = ""MenuForm"">"
        document.write "<CENTER>"
        document.write "<TABLE BORDER BGCOLOR = ""#ffff00"">"
        document.write "<TR><TH COLSPAN = 2>Lunch</TH></TR>"
        document.write "<TR><TD>Turkey sandwich $3.95</TD><TD><INPUT
        TYPE
            = CHECKBOX NAME = BButton onClick = ""SetPrice
            3.95""></TD></TR>"
        document.write "<TR><TD>Roast beef sandwich
        $3.95</TD><TD><INPUT TYPE
            = CHECKBOX NAME = BButton onClick = ""SetPrice
            3.95""></TD></TR>"
        document.write "<TR><TD>Ham sandwich $3.95</TD><TD><INPUT TYPE
            = CHECKBOX NAME = BButton onClick = ""SetPrice
            3.95""></TD></TR>"
        document.write "<TR><TD>French fries $1.95</TD><TD><INPUT TYPE
            = CHECKBOX NAME = BButton onClick = ""SetPrice
            1.95""></TD></TR>"
        document.write "<TR><TD>Soup $1.95</TD><TD><INPUT TYPE
            = CHECKBOX NAME = BButton onClick = ""SetPrice
            1.95""></TD></TR>"
        document.write "<TR><TD>Coffee $.95</TD><TD><INPUT TYPE
            = CHECKBOX NAME = BButton onClick = ""SetPrice
            .95""></TD></TR>"
        document.write "<TR><TD>Soda $1.25</TD><TD><INPUT TYPE
            = CHECKBOX NAME = BButton onClick = ""SetPrice
            1.25""></TD></TR>"
        document.write "</TABLE>"
        document.write "<INPUT TYPE = TEXT VALUE = """" NAME = Total
            Size = 20>"
        document.write "</CENTER>"
        document.write "</FORM>"
End If
```

Finally, we add the dinner menu, also checking the time of day to make sure we display it only during dinner hours:

```
If Hour(Now) > 15 AND Hour(Now) < 22 Then
        document.write "<FORM NAME = ""MenuForm"">"
        document.write "<CENTER>"
        document.write "<TABLE BORDER BGCOLOR = ""#ffff00"">"
        document.write "<TR><TH COLSPAN = 2>Dinner</TH></TR>"
        document.write "<TR><TD>Turkey dinner $7.95</TD><TD><INPUT TYPE
            = CHECKBOX NAME = BButton onClick = ""SetPrice
            7.95""></TD></TR>"
        document.write "<TR><TD>Roast beef dinner
        $7.95</TD><TD><INPUT TYPE
            = CHECKBOX NAME = BButton onClick = ""SetPrice
            7.95""></TD></TR>"
        document.write "<TR><TD>Ham souffle $7.95</TD><TD><INPUT TYPE
            = CHECKBOX NAME = BButton onClick = ""SetPrice
            7.95""></TD></TR>"
        document.write "<TR><TD>Soup $3.95</TD><TD><INPUT TYPE
            = CHECKBOX NAME = BButton onClick = ""SetPrice
            3.95""></TD></TR>"
        document.write "<TR><TD>Baked potato $1.95</TD><TD><INPUT TYPE
            = CHECKBOX NAME = BButton onClick = ""SetPrice
            1.95""></TD></TR>"
        document.write "<TR><TD>Coffee $.95</TD><TD><INPUT TYPE
            = CHECKBOX NAME = BButton onClick = ""SetPrice
            .95""></TD></TR>"
        document.write "<TR><TD>Tea $.80</TD><TD><INPUT TYPE
            = CHECKBOX NAME = BButton onClick = ""SetPrice
            .80""></TD></TR>"
        document.write "</TABLE>"
        document.write "<INPUT TYPE = TEXT VALUE = """" NAME = Total
            Size = 20>"
        document.write "</CENTER>"
        document.write "</FORM>"
End If
```

That's it. When the user downloads our Web page, it will display the correct menu depending on the time of day—breakfast, lunch, or dinner—as shown in Figure 9.7, where we have loaded the dinner menu. Our program is a success. The HTML and VBScript file can be found in Listing 9.4.

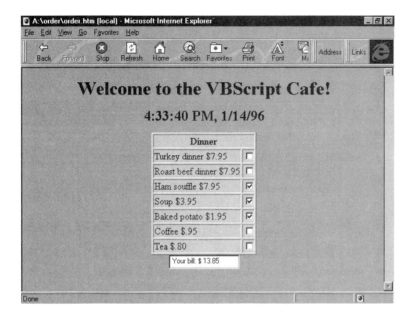

Figure 9.7 Our Cafe menu is self-modifying.

Listing 9.4 Order.htm

```
<HTML>

<BODY>
<SCRIPT LANGUAGE = VBScript>
document.write "<CENTER>"
document.write "<H1>"
document.write "Welcome to the VBScript Cafe!"
document.write "</H1>"
document.write "<H2>"
document.write Time
document.write ", "
document.write Date
document.write "</H2>"
document.write "</CENTER>"

If Hour(Now) < 6 OR Hour(Now) > 22 Then
```

```
        document.write "<CENTER>"
        document.write "<H1>"
        document.write "Sorry, we open at 6 AM"
        document.write "</H1>"
        document.write "</CENTER>"
End If

If Hour(Now) > 5 AND Hour(Now) < 10 Then
        document.write "<FORM NAME = ""MenuForm"">"
        document.write "<CENTER>"
        document.write "<TABLE BORDER BGCOLOR = ""#ffff00"">"
        document.write "<TR><TH COLSPAN = 2>Breakfast</TH></TR>"
        document.write "<TR><TD>Two fried eggs $2.95</TD><TD><INPUT TYPE
            = CHECKBOX NAME = BButton onClick = ""SetPrice
            2.95""></TD></TR>"
        document.write "<TR><TD>Two scrambled eggs
        $2.95</TD><TD><INPUT TYPE
            = CHECKBOX NAME = BButton onClick = ""SetPrice
            2.95""></TD></TR>"
        document.write "<TR><TD>French toast $2.95</TD><TD><INPUT TYPE
            = CHECKBOX NAME = BButton onClick = ""SetPrice
            2.95""></TD></TR>"
        document.write "<TR><TD>Oatmeal $1.95</TD><TD><INPUT TYPE
            = CHECKBOX NAME = BButton onClick = ""SetPrice
            1.95""></TD></TR>"
        document.write "<TR><TD>Bacon $1.95</TD><TD><INPUT TYPE
            = CHECKBOX NAME = BButton onClick = ""SetPrice
            1.95""></TD></TR>"
        document.write "<TR><TD>Coffee $.95</TD><TD><INPUT TYPE
            = CHECKBOX NAME = BButton onClick = ""SetPrice
            .95""></TD></TR>"
        document.write "<TR><TD>Orange juice $1.50</TD><TD><INPUT TYPE
            = CHECKBOX NAME = BButton onClick = ""SetPrice
            1.50""></TD></TR>"
        document.write "</TABLE>"
        document.write "<INPUT TYPE = TEXT VALUE = """" NAME = Total
            Size = 20>"
        document.write "</CENTER>"
        document.write "</FORM>"
End If
```

```
If Hour(Now) > 10 AND Hour(Now) < 15 Then
        document.write "<FORM NAME = ""MenuForm"">"
        document.write "<CENTER>"
        document.write "<TABLE BORDER BGCOLOR = ""#ffff00"">"
        document.write "<TR><TH COLSPAN = 2>Lunch</TH></TR>"
        document.write "<TR><TD>Turkey sandwich $3.95</TD><TD><INPUT
        TYPE
            = CHECKBOX NAME = BButton onClick = ""SetPrice
            3.95""></TD></TR>"
        document.write "<TR><TD>Roast beef sandwich
        $3.95</TD><TD><INPUT TYPE
            = CHECKBOX NAME = BButton onClick = ""SetPrice
            3.95""></TD></TR>"
        document.write "<TR><TD>Ham sandwich $3.95</TD><TD><INPUT TYPE
            = CHECKBOX NAME = BButton onClick = ""SetPrice
            3.95""></TD></TR>"
        document.write "<TR><TD>French fries $1.95</TD><TD><INPUT TYPE
            = CHECKBOX NAME = BButton onClick = ""SetPrice
            1.95""></TD></TR>"
        document.write "<TR><TD>Soup $1.95</TD><TD><INPUT TYPE
            = CHECKBOX NAME = BButton onClick = ""SetPrice
            1.95""></TD></TR>"
        document.write "<TR><TD>Coffee $.95</TD><TD><INPUT TYPE
            = CHECKBOX NAME = BButton onClick = ""SetPrice
            .95""></TD></TR>"
        document.write "<TR><TD>Soda $1.25</TD><TD><INPUT TYPE
            = CHECKBOX NAME = BButton onClick = ""SetPrice
            1.25""></TD></TR>"
        document.write "</TABLE>"
        document.write "<INPUT TYPE = TEXT VALUE = """" NAME = Total
            Size = 20>"
        document.write "</CENTER>"
        document.write "</FORM>"
End If

If Hour(Now) > 15 AND Hour(Now) < 22 Then
        document.write "<FORM NAME = ""MenuForm"">"
        document.write "<CENTER>"
        document.write "<TABLE BORDER BGCOLOR = ""#ffff00"">"
        document.write "<TR><TH COLSPAN = 2>Dinner</TH></TR>"
        document.write "<TR><TD>Turkey dinner $7.95</TD><TD><INPUT TYPE
```

```
                = CHECKBOX NAME = BButton onClick = ""SetPrice
                7.95""></TD></TR>"
        document.write "<TR><TD>Roast beef dinner
        $7.95</TD><TD><INPUT TYPE
                = CHECKBOX NAME = BButton onClick = ""SetPrice
                7.95""></TD></TR>"
        document.write "<TR><TD>Ham souffle $7.95</TD><TD><INPUT TYPE
                = CHECKBOX NAME = BButton onClick = ""SetPrice
                7.95""></TD></TR>"
        document.write "<TR><TD>Soup $3.95</TD><TD><INPUT TYPE
                = CHECKBOX NAME = BButton onClick = ""SetPrice
                3.95""></TD></TR>"
        document.write "<TR><TD>Baked potato $1.95</TD><TD><INPUT TYPE
                = CHECKBOX NAME = BButton onClick = ""SetPrice
                1.95""></TD></TR>"
        document.write "<TR><TD>Coffee $.95</TD><TD><INPUT TYPE
                = CHECKBOX NAME = BButton onClick = ""SetPrice
                .95""></TD></TR>"
        document.write "<TR><TD>Tea $.80</TD><TD><INPUT TYPE
                = CHECKBOX NAME = BButton onClick = ""SetPrice
                .80""></TD></TR>"
        document.write "</TABLE>"
        document.write "<INPUT TYPE = TEXT VALUE = """" NAME = Total
                Size = 20>"
        document.write "</CENTER>"
        document.write "</FORM>"
End If
</SCRIPT>

<SCRIPT LANGUAGE = VBScript>
Dim TotalCost
TotalCost = 0

SUB SetPrice(Cost)
        TotalCost = TotalCost + Cost
        document.MenuForm.Total.Value = " Your bill: $ " +
        CStr(TotalCost)
END SUB

</SCRIPT>

</HTML>
```

That's it for the self-modifying menu—and that's it for our survey of VBScript. In this chapter, we saw a new HTML control—check boxes—and worked with new properties and methods of documents. In Chapter 10, we will start working with databases on the Internet, using Visual Basic to download and manipulate them.

WEB PAGES AND DATABASES

In this chapter, we'll explore database concepts and design and find out how to use a database in an **.html** Web page on the Internet. We'll use the Data control in Visual Basic to connect our new database to a Visual Basic program. We'll also use various controls, such as listboxes and text boxes, to display the data from that database. Finally, we'll see how to create a standard **.mdb** database file (used by Microsoft Access and other database programs) from the database we've stored in a Web page. Let's start by seeing what databases are all about and how they can be useful to us.

What Are Databases?

As you might expect from the name, *databases* are ways of organizing data for easy handling. We're familiar with simple variables such as integers and long integers, but data handling can require the use of much more complex and powerful tools than these elementary forms. Consider, for example, a hospital that needs to maintain an inventory of thousands of supplies as well as maintain employee and patient records. It's clear that something powerful is needed here, and that's what databases are all about.

To see how database methods and concepts develop, let's say that we are in charge of teaching a class on Visual Basic. At the end of the class, we are responsible for sending the students' grades to the registrar of the school. We might make a table showing the names of the students and the grade each one received:

Ann	C
Mark	B
Ed	A
Frank	A
Ted	A
Mabel	B
Ralph	B
Tom	B

This seems natural enough, and tables like this one are the foundations of databases. By making a list that has one entry for each student, we've designed a database without even being conscious of it.

Placing Our Database in a Web Page

It's almost that easy to place our database in a Web page. All we have to do is to reproduce the preceding table in a Web page, which we'll call **db1.htm**. Such a page might look like this in HTML:

```
<HTML>
<HEAD>
<TITLE>DB</TITLE></HEAD>
```

```
<BODY>
<CENTER>

<TABLE>
<TR>
<TD>Name</TD>
<TD>Grade</TD>
</TR>
<TR>
<TD>Ann</TD>
<TD>C</TD>
</TR>
<TR>
<TD>Mark</TD>
<TD>B</TD>
</TR>
<TR>
<TD>Ed</TD>
<TD>A</TD>
</TR>
<TR>
<TD>Frank</TD>
<TD>A</TD>
</TR>
<TR>
<TD>Ted</TD>
<TD>A</TD>
</TR>
<TR>
<TD>Mabel</TD>
<TD>B</TD>
</TR>
<TR>
<TD>Ralph</TD>
<TD>B</TD>
</TR>
<TR>
<TD>Tom</TD>
<TD>B</TD>
```

```
</TR>
</TABLE>

</CENTER>
</BODY>
</HTML>
```

You can see this Web page in Figure 10.1. As we'll see, the Visual Basic OpenDatabase() method will read our database from this **.html** table.

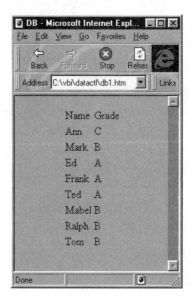

Figure 10.1 Our Web page database.

It's that easy to store our database in a Web page.

Database Design: Tables, Records, and Fields

Our table is broken up into rows and columns; in database language, they are called *records* and *fields*. Each row makes up a student's record, and each column makes up a field in the table (which can hold the student's name or grade):

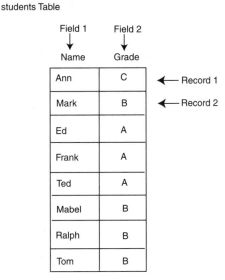

students Table

Databases can contain several such tables, and the data in each table can be related to data in other tables in ways that we'll see (such as having one or more columns, or fields, in common). That is why databases in Visual Basic are called *relational* databases. Because a database can contain several tables, we'll give a name to this table: students.

The Visual Basic Data Control

Now that we have a database to work with, let's see how to display its data using an example program that uses the Visual Basic Data control. It's easy to connect the new database in our **.html** page to a Data control in a Visual Basic program. In this example, we'll read our Web page and display the data in it.

Using the Application Wizard, create a new SDI Visual Basic project called **datactl**. Next, double-click the **Data control** tool in the toolbox; this action creates a new Data control, as shown in Figure 10.2.

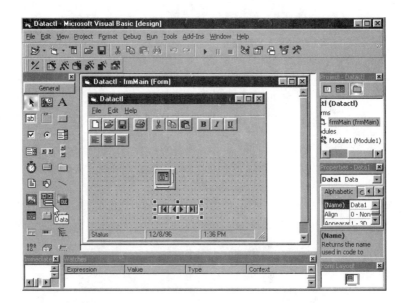

Figure 10.2 Creating a new Data control in a Visual Basic program.

Now we can connect our Data control to the database in our Web page, **db1.htm**. To do that, open the datactl project's Form_Load() event handler:

```
Private Sub Form_Load()
    Me.Left = GetSetting(App.Title, "Settings", "MainLeft", 1000)
    Me.Top = GetSetting(App.Title, "Settings", "MainTop", 1000)
    Me.Width = GetSetting(App.Title, "Settings", "MainWidth", 6500)
    Me.Height = GetSetting(App.Title, "Settings", "MainHeight", 6500)
End Sub
```

Our first step is to open the database in the **db1.htm** file, creating a new Database object, named db1, in our program. (OpenDatabase() can take the name of a local file or a URL such as http://www.server.com/bigbigco/db1.htm.)

```
Private Sub Form_Load()
-> Dim db1 As Database
    Me.Left = GetSetting(App.Title, "Settings", "MainLeft", 1000)
```

```
    Me.Top = GetSetting(App.Title, "Settings", "MainTop", 1000)
    Me.Width = GetSetting(App.Title, "Settings", "MainWidth", 6500)
    Me.Height = GetSetting(App.Title, "Settings", "MainHeight", 6500)

-> Set db1 = OpenDatabase ("c:\vbi\datactrl\db1.htm", False, False,
        "HTML Import;")
        .
        .
        .

End Sub
```

To specify that this new database is coming from a Web page, we use the keywords "HTML Import" at the end of the OpenDatabase() call. (Recall that you can both get and post HTTP data with the Internet Transfer control. This means that you can get a database from a Web page this way and, if you want to, construct a program to upload a changed version of the database.) Next, we will create a Recordset object (we will see more about recordsets soon) to hold the table we are interested in:

```
Private Sub Form_Load()
    Dim db1 As Database
-> Dim rs1 As Recordset
    Me.Left = GetSetting(App.Title, "Settings", "MainLeft", 1000)
    Me.Top = GetSetting(App.Title, "Settings", "MainTop", 1000)
    Me.Width = GetSetting(App.Title, "Settings", "MainWidth", 6500)
    Me.Height = GetSetting(App.Title, "Settings", "MainHeight", 6500)

    Set db1 = OpenDatabase ("c:\vbi\datactrl\db1.htm", False, False,
        "HTML Import;")

-> Set rs1 = db1.OpenRecordset("DB", dbOpenTable)
        .
        .
        .

End Sub
```

Finally, we connect this new table to the Data control Data1 using its Recordset property:

```
Private Sub Form_Load()
    Dim db1 As Database
    Dim rs1 As Recordset
    Me.Left = GetSetting(App.Title, "Settings", "MainLeft", 1000)
    Me.Top = GetSetting(App.Title, "Settings", "MainTop", 1000)
    Me.Width = GetSetting(App.Title, "Settings", "MainWidth", 6500)
    Me.Height = GetSetting(App.Title, "Settings", "MainHeight", 6500)

    Set db1 = OpenDatabase ("c:\vbi\datactrl\db1.htm", False, False,
        "HTML Import;")

    Set rs1 = db1.OpenRecordset("DB", dbOpenTable)
--> Set Data1.Recordset = rs1

End Sub
```

And that's itÑour Web page database table is connected to our Data control.

Cursored Database Access

You may be disappointed to find that the Data control is simply a short toolbar that contains a few buttons with arrow captions, as shown in Figure 10.2:

Where is our data from the database? If we run the program at this point, nothing will appear beyond the Data control on the form.

The reason is that the Data control is responsible only for connecting to the database we've selected and for setting the current record in that database. The *current record* in a database is the one that we are currently examining, and it's possible to have only one such record. When we make changes, it's always to the current record; when we look at a record, that record is or becomes the current record. This kind of access to the database is called *cursored* access. For example, when we start the program as it stands, the first record in our database is the current record:

Name	Grade
Ann	C
Mark	B
Ed	A
Frank	A
Ted	A
Mabel	B
Ralph	B
Tom	B

←——Current Record (points to Ann row)

If we were to click the right-pointing arrow in the Data control, we would move to the next record in the database:

Name	Grade
Ann	C
Mark	B
Ed	A
Frank	A
Ted	A
Mabel	B
Ralph	B
Tom	B

←——Current Record (points to Mark row)

The left-pointing arrow moves us back one record. The arrow key at the far left in the Data control moves us to the beginning of the database, and the arrow key at the far right moves us to the end.

In this way, the Data control allows us to move through the database record by record. However, the question remains: how do we display our data? The answer is to use data bound controls.

Data Bound Controls

Because there are many ways to display data in a Visual Basic programÑtext boxes, picture boxes, grid controls, combo boxes, and so onÑit doesn't make sense that the Data control should have only one way of displaying data. The programmer should determine just how the data is displayed. In Visual Basic, that's done with controls like the ones we've just mentioned. In fact, these controls are now designed to work easily with a Data control to do just that.

For example, let's say that our program has both a text box, Text1, and a Data control, Data1:

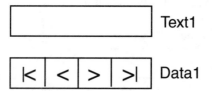

When we start our program, the Data control will be connected to the students table in our database, and we can set the current record in it using the arrow buttons. We can also display the current record using the text box. To do that, we set the text box's DataSource property to the name of the data control, Data1, like this: Text1.DataSource = Data1. The current record will be made up of two fields (Name and Grade), and we can display only one field in the text box. To display, say, the Name field of the current record in the database, we set the text box's DataField property to Name this way: Text1.DataField = Name. (We can also set the DataSource and DataField properties in the properties window at design time.)

When we run the program, the database will be connected to the Data control, and the contents of the Name field of the database's current record (the first record) appear in the text box:

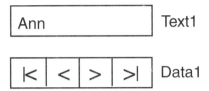

If we click the right-pointing arrow in the Data control, we move to the second record in the database, and the contents of the Name field of that record ("Mark") are displayed in the text box:

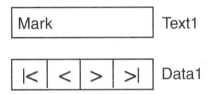

In this way, the text box is *bound* to the Data control. There are 10 controls in Visual Basic that can function as bound controls: check boxes, combo boxes, DBCombo boxes, DBGrids, DBList boxes, image controls, labels, listboxes, picture boxes, and text boxes. Each control has properties that we can set to tie it to a Data control (see Table 10.1).

Table 10.1 Data Bound Controls

Control	Properties to Set
Check box	DataField = desired Boolean field, DataSource = data control's name
Combo box	DataField = desired field, DataSource = data control's name
DBCombo box	BoundColumn = desired field, DataField = desired field, DataSource = data control's name, ListField = desired field, RowSource = data control's name
DBGrid	DataSource = data control's name

Table 10.1 Data Bound Controls (continued)

Control	Properties to Set
DBList box	DataField = desired field, DataSource = data control's name, RowSource = data control's name
Image control	DataField = desired field, DataSource = data control's name
Label	DataField = desired field, DataSource = data control's name
Listbox	DataField = desired field, DataSource = data control's name
Picture box	DataField = desired field, DataSource = data control's name
Text box	DataField = desired field, DataSource = data control's name

Table 10.1 lists three controls we have not seen before: DBCombo box, DBGrid, and DBList. Although all the controls in Table 10.1 work with the Data control, these three controls are specially designed for that purpose. Although the other controls work only with one field of one record at a time, the DB controls display that field of *all* the records in the database and indicate (through highlighting) which one is the current record. We could, for example, create a DBCombo box named DBCombo1 and connect it to the Data control and the Name field in our database. When we opened DBCombo1 at runtime, we would see all the Name fields of all the records in the database at once, and the current record would be marked. In the same way, the DBList control displays a list of the Name field of each record, highlighting the current record. The DBGrid control is even more powerful. Because it can display both rows and columns, this control displays our entire table (Name and Grade fields) and also indicates the current record by highlighting it. When you use the data control to move to a new record, the highlighted line in a DB control also moves to match, so the current record is always highlighted.

Displaying Database Data with Bound Controls

Let's put bound controls to work in our datactl program. We can add a number of data bound controls but not all of them, because some are inappropriate; for example, a data bound Image control would require a database of images, not text. Let's add a text box, a combo box, a label, a DBList box, a DBCombo box, and a DBGrid box, as shown in Figure 10.3.

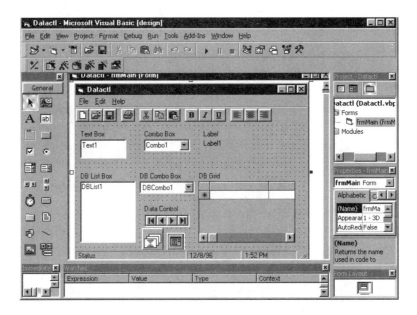

Figure 10.3 Adding data bound controls to our program.

Here's how we set the properties of the controls in datactl to connect to the Name field of our database, which is connected to the control Data1:

Text1	DataField = Name, DataSource = Data1
Combo1	DataField = Name, DataSource = Data1
Label1	DataField = Name, DataSource = Data1
DBList1	DataField = Name, DataSource = Data1, RowSource = Data1

DBCombo1   DataField = Name, DataSource = Data1,
              BoundColumn = Name, ListField = Name
              RowSource = Data1

DBGrid1   DataSource = Data1

Note that we set only one property (DataSource) of the DBGrid control; we set it to Data1. Because the DBGrid displays our entire database table, there is no need to indicate a particular field to display. Now we run the program, as shown in Figure 10.4.

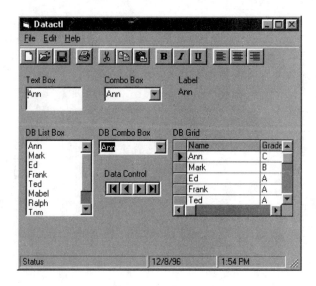

Figure 10.4 Displaying database data in a program.

Note that the OpenDatabase method has named the fields in our new table according to the captions (the top row entries in the table) we gave them: Name and Grade. The Name field in the first record in our student table is "Ann":

Name	Grade
Ann	C	←——Current Record
Mark	B
Ed	A
Frank	A
Ted	A
Mabel	B
Ralph	B
Tom	B

This field also appears in each of the data bound controls, as shown in Figure 10.4. Note also that the Name field for every record appears in the DB controls and that the DBGrid control is displaying the entire table. Also note that the DB controls mark the current record.

If we were to click the right-pointing arrow in the Data control, we would move to the next record in the database:

Name	Grade
Ann	C
Mark	B	←——Current Record
Ed	A
Frank	A
Ted	A
Mabel	B
Ralph	B
Tom	B

The Name field from that record, which contains the name "Mark," appears in each of the data bound controls now, as shown in Figure 10.5. Our program is a success. The **frmmain.frm** appears in Listing 10.1.

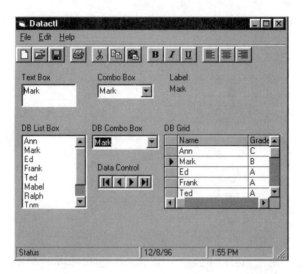

Figure 10.5 Accessing a record in a database.

Listing 10.1 (Datactl) FrmMain.frm

```
VERSION 5.00
Object = "{F9043C88-F6F2-101A-A3C9-08002B2F49FB}#1.1#0"; "COMDLG32.OCX"
Object = "{6B7E6392-850A-101B-AFC0-4210102A8DA7}#1.1#0"; "COMCTL32.OCX"
Object = "{FAEEE763-117E-101B-8933-08002B2F4F5A}#1.1#0"; "DBLIST32.OCX"
Object = "{00028C01-0000-0000-0000-000000000046}#1.0#0"; "DBGRID32.OCX"
Begin VB.Form frmMain
   Caption        =   "Datactl"
   ClientHeight   =   3945
   ClientLeft     =   165
   ClientTop      =   735
   ClientWidth    =   6090
   LinkTopic      =   "Form1"
   ScaleHeight    =   3945
   ScaleWidth     =   6090
   StartUpPosition =  3  'Windows Default
   Begin ComctlLib.Toolbar tbToolBar
      Align       =    1  'Align Top
      Height      =    420
```

```
Left            =    0
TabIndex        =    1
Top             =    0
Width           =    6090
_ExtentX        =    10742
_ExtentY        =    741
ButtonWidth     =    635
ButtonHeight    =    582
Appearance      =    1
ImageList       =    "imlIcons"
BeginProperty Buttons {7791BA41-E020-11CF-8E74-00A0C90F26F8}
   NumButtons      =    17
   BeginProperty Button1 {7791BA43-E020-11CF-8E74-00A0C90F26F8}
      Key              =    "New"
      Object.ToolTipText      =    "New"
      Object.Tag       =    ""
      ImageIndex       =    1
   EndProperty
   BeginProperty Button2 {7791BA43-E020-11CF-8E74-00A0C90F26F8}
      Key              =    "Open"
      Object.ToolTipText      =    "Open"
      Object.Tag       =    ""
      ImageIndex       =    2
   EndProperty
   BeginProperty Button3 {7791BA43-E020-11CF-8E74-00A0C90F26F8}
      Key              =    "Save"
      Object.ToolTipText      =    "Save"
      Object.Tag       =    ""
      ImageIndex       =    3
   EndProperty
   BeginProperty Button4 {7791BA43-E020-11CF-8E74-00A0C90F26F8}
      Object.Tag       =    ""
      Style            =    3
   EndProperty
   BeginProperty Button5 {7791BA43-E020-11CF-8E74-00A0C90F26F8}
      Key              =    "Print"
      Object.ToolTipText      =    "Print"
      Object.Tag       =    ""
      ImageIndex       =    4
   EndProperty
   BeginProperty Button6 {7791BA43-E020-11CF-8E74-00A0C90F26F8}
```

```
      Object.Tag                =     ""
      Style           =    3
   EndProperty
   BeginProperty Button7 {7791BA43-E020-11CF-8E74-00A0C90F26F8}
      Key             =    "Cut"
      Object.ToolTipText    =     "Cut"
      Object.Tag            =     ""
      ImageIndex      =    5
   EndProperty
   BeginProperty Button8 {7791BA43-E020-11CF-8E74-00A0C90F26F8}
      Key             =    "Copy"
      Object.ToolTipText    =     "Copy"
      Object.Tag            =     ""
      ImageIndex      =    6
   EndProperty
   BeginProperty Button9 {7791BA43-E020-11CF-8E74-00A0C90F26F8}
      Key             =    "Paste"
      Object.ToolTipText    =     "Paste"
      Object.Tag            =     ""
      ImageIndex      =    7
   EndProperty
   BeginProperty Button10 {7791BA43-E020-11CF-8E74-00A0C90F26F8}
      Object.Tag            =     ""
      Style           =    3
   EndProperty
   BeginProperty Button11 {7791BA43-E020-11CF-8E74-00A0C90F26F8}
      Key             =    "Bold"
      Object.ToolTipText    =     "Bold"
      Object.Tag            =     ""
      ImageIndex      =    8
   EndProperty
   BeginProperty Button12 {7791BA43-E020-11CF-8E74-00A0C90F26F8}
      Key             =    "Italic"
      Object.ToolTipText    =     "Italic"
      Object.Tag            =     ""
      ImageIndex      =    9
   EndProperty
   BeginProperty Button13 {7791BA43-E020-11CF-8E74-00A0C90F26F8}
      Key             =    "Underline"
```

```
        Object.ToolTipText     =    "Underline"
        Object.Tag             =    ""
        ImageIndex      =    10
     EndProperty
     BeginProperty Button14 {7791BA43-E020-11CF-8E74-00A0C90F26F8}
        Object.Tag             =    ""
        Style           =    3
     EndProperty
     BeginProperty Button15 {7791BA43-E020-11CF-8E74-00A0C90F26F8}
        Key             =    "Left"
        Object.ToolTipText     =    "Left Justify"
        Object.Tag             =    ""
        ImageIndex      =    11
     EndProperty
     BeginProperty Button16 {7791BA43-E020-11CF-8E74-00A0C90F26F8}
        Key             =    "Center"
        Object.ToolTipText     =    "Center"
        Object.Tag             =    ""
        ImageIndex      =    12
     EndProperty
     BeginProperty Button17 {7791BA43-E020-11CF-8E74-00A0C90F26F8}
        Key             =    "Right"
        Object.ToolTipText     =    "Right Justify"
        Object.Tag             =    ""
        ImageIndex      =    13
     EndProperty
  EndProperty
End
Begin VB.Data Data1
  Caption         =    "Data1"
  Connect         =    "Access"
  DatabaseName    =    ""
  DefaultCursorType=   0    'DefaultCursor
  DefaultType     =    2    'UseODBC
  Exclusive       =    0    'False
  Height          =    345
  Left            =    1800
  Options         =    0
  ReadOnly        =    0    'False
```

```
        RecordsetType   =   1   'Dynaset
        RecordSource    =   "students"
        Top             =   2760
        Width           =   1215
    End
    Begin VB.ComboBox Combo1
        DataField       =   "Name"
        DataSource      =   "Data1"
        Height          =   315
        Left            =   1800
        TabIndex        =   3
        Text            =   "Combo1"
        Top             =   840
        Width           =   1215
    End
    Begin VB.TextBox Text1
        DataField       =   "Name"
        DataSource      =   "Data1"
        Height          =   495
        Left            =   120
        TabIndex        =   2
        Text            =   "Text1"
        Top             =   840
        Width           =   1215
    End
    Begin ComctlLib.StatusBar sbStatusBar
        Align           =   2   'Align Bottom
        Height          =   270
        Left            =   0
        TabIndex        =   0
        Top             =   3675
        Width           =   6090
        _ExtentX        =   10742
        _ExtentY        =   476
        SimpleText      =   ""
        BeginProperty Panels {2C787A51-E01C-11CF-8E74-00A0C90F26F8}
            NumPanels       =   3
            BeginProperty Panel1 {2C787A53-E01C-11CF-8E74-00A0C90F26F8}
                AutoSize        =   1
```

```
            Object.Width        =    5106
            MinWidth       =    2540
            Text           =    "Status"
            TextSave       =    "Status"
            Object.Tag          =    ""
        EndProperty
        BeginProperty Panel2 {2C787A53-E01C-11CF-8E74-00A0C90F26F8}
            Style          =    6
            AutoSize       =    2
            Object.Width        =    2540
            MinWidth       =    2540
            TextSave       =    "12/8/96"
            Object.Tag          =    ""
        EndProperty
        BeginProperty Panel3 {2C787A53-E01C-11CF-8E74-00A0C90F26F8}
            Style          =    5
            AutoSize       =    2
            Object.Width        =    2540
            MinWidth       =    2540
            TextSave       =    "12:59 PM"
            Object.Tag          =    ""
        EndProperty
    EndProperty
    BeginProperty Font {0BE35203-8F91-11CE-9DE3-00AA004BB851}
        Name           =    "MS Sans Serif"
        Size           =    8.25
        Charset        =    0
        Weight         =    400
        Underline      =    0    'False
        Italic         =    0    'False
        Strikethrough  =    0    'False
    EndProperty
End
Begin MSComDlg.CommonDialog dlgCommonDialog
    Left           =    2400
    Top            =    3240
    _ExtentX       =    847
    _ExtentY       =    847
    FontSize       =    1.79117e-37
```

```
      End
      Begin MSDBGrid.DBGrid DBGrid1
         Bindings        =    "frmMain.frx":0000
         Height          =    1575
         Left            =    3240
         OleObjectBlob   =    "frmMain.frx":0010
         TabIndex        =    5
         Top             =    1920
         Width           =    2535
      End
      Begin MSDBCtls.DBList DBList1
         Bindings        =    "frmMain.frx":09C2
         DataField       =    "Name"
         DataSource      =    "Data1"
         Height          =    1575
         Left            =    120
         TabIndex        =    6
         Top             =    1920
         Width           =    1455
         _ExtentX        =    2566
         _ExtentY        =    2778
         ListField       =    "Name"
      End
      Begin MSDBCtls.DBCombo DBCombo1
         Bindings        =    "frmMain.frx":09D2
         DataField       =    "Name"
         DataSource      =    "Data1"
         Height          =    315
         Left            =    1680
         TabIndex        =    7
         Top             =    1920
         Width           =    1455
         _ExtentX        =    2566
         _ExtentY        =    556
         ListField       =    "Name"
         BoundColumn     =    "Name"
         Text            =    "DBCombo1"
      End
      Begin VB.Label Label8
```

```
        Caption         =    "Data Control"
        Height          =    255
        Left            =    1800
        TabIndex        =    14
        Top             =    2520
        Width           =    1215
    End
    Begin VB.Label Label7
        Caption         =    "DB Grid"
        Height          =    255
        Left            =    3240
        TabIndex        =    13
        Top             =    1680
        Width           =    1215
    End
    Begin VB.Label Label6
        Caption         =    "DB Combo Box"
        Height          =    255
        Left            =    1680
        TabIndex        =    12
        Top             =    1680
        Width           =    1215
    End
    Begin VB.Label Label5
        Caption         =    "DB List Box"
        Height          =    255
        Left            =    120
        TabIndex        =    11
        Top             =    1680
        Width           =    1215
    End
    Begin VB.Label Label4
        Caption         =    "Label"
        Height          =    255
        Left            =    3360
        TabIndex        =    10
        Top             =    600
        Width           =    1215
    End
```

```
Begin VB.Label Label3
    Caption         =   "Combo Box"
    Height          =   255
    Left            =   1800
    TabIndex        =   9
    Top             =   600
    Width           =   1215
End
Begin VB.Label Label2
    Caption         =   "Text Box"
    Height          =   255
    Left            =   120
    TabIndex        =   8
    Top             =   600
    Width           =   1215
End
Begin VB.Label Label1
    Caption         =   "Label1"
    DataField       =   "Name"
    DataSource      =   "Data1"
    Height          =   495
    Left            =   3360
    TabIndex        =   4
    Top             =   840
    Width           =   1215
End
Begin ComctlLib.ImageList imlIcons
    Left            =   1740
    Top             =   3120
    _ExtentX        =   1005
    _ExtentY        =   1005
    BackColor       =   -2147483643
    ImageWidth      =   16
    ImageHeight     =   16
    MaskColor       =   12632256
    BeginProperty Images {8556BCD1-E01E-11CF-8E74-00A0C90F26F8}
        NumListImages   =   13
        BeginProperty ListImage1 {8556BCD3-E01E-11CF-8E74-00A0C90F26F8}
            Picture         =   "frmMain.frx":09E2
```

```
   Key              =    " "
EndProperty
BeginProperty ListImage2 {8556BCD3-E01E-11CF-8E74-00A0C90F26F8}
   Picture          =    "frmMain.frx":0D34
   Key              =    " "
EndProperty
BeginProperty ListImage3 {8556BCD3-E01E-11CF-8E74-00A0C90F26F8}
   Picture          =    "frmMain.frx":1086
   Key              =    " "
EndProperty
BeginProperty ListImage4 {8556BCD3-E01E-11CF-8E74-00A0C90F26F8}
   Picture          =    "frmMain.frx":13D8
   Key              =    " "
EndProperty
BeginProperty ListImage5 {8556BCD3-E01E-11CF-8E74-00A0C90F26F8}
   Picture          =    "frmMain.frx":172A
   Key              =    " "
EndProperty
BeginProperty ListImage6 {8556BCD3-E01E-11CF-8E74-00A0C90F26F8}
   Picture          =    "frmMain.frx":1A7C
   Key              =    " "
EndProperty
BeginProperty ListImage7 {8556BCD3-E01E-11CF-8E74-00A0C90F26F8}
   Picture          =    "frmMain.frx":1DCE
   Key              =    " "
EndProperty
BeginProperty ListImage8 {8556BCD3-E01E-11CF-8E74-00A0C90F26F8}
   Picture          =    "frmMain.frx":2120
   Key              =    " "
EndProperty
BeginProperty ListImage9 {8556BCD3-E01E-11CF-8E74-00A0C90F26F8}
   Picture          =    "frmMain.frx":2472
   Key              =    " "
EndProperty
BeginProperty ListImage10 {8556BCD3-E01E-11CF-8E74-
                          00A0C90F26F8}
   Picture          =    "frmMain.frx":27C4
   Key              =    " "
EndProperty
```

```
            BeginProperty ListImage11 {8556BCD3-E01E-11CF-8E74-
                                00A0C90F26F8}
                Picture         =   "frmMain.frx":2B16
                Key             =   ""
            EndProperty
            BeginProperty ListImage12 {8556BCD3-E01E-11CF-8E74-
                                00A0C90F26F8}
                Picture         =   "frmMain.frx":2E68
                Key             =   ""
            EndProperty
            BeginProperty ListImage13 {8556BCD3-E01E-11CF-8E74-
                                00A0C90F26F8}
                Picture         =   "frmMain.frx":31BA
                Key             =   ""
            EndProperty
        EndProperty
    End
    Begin VB.Menu mnuFile
        Caption         =   "&File"
        Begin VB.Menu mnuFileNew
            Caption         =   "&New"
            Shortcut        =   ^N
        End
        Begin VB.Menu mnuFileOpen
            Caption         =   "&Open"
            Shortcut        =   ^O
        End
        Begin VB.Menu mnuFileClose
            Caption         =   "&Close"
        End
        Begin VB.Menu mnuFileBar1
            Caption         =   "-"
        End
        Begin VB.Menu mnuFileSave
            Caption         =   "&Save"
            Shortcut        =   ^S
        End
        Begin VB.Menu mnuFileSaveAs
            Caption         =   "Save &As..."
```

```
End
Begin VB.Menu mnuFileSaveAll
   Caption         =   "Save A&ll"
End
Begin VB.Menu mnuFileBar2
   Caption         =   "-"
End
Begin VB.Menu mnuFileProperties
   Caption         =   "Propert&ies"
End
Begin VB.Menu mnuFileBar3
   Caption         =   "-"
End
Begin VB.Menu mnuFilePageSetup
   Caption         =   "Page Set&up..."
End
Begin VB.Menu mnuFilePrintPreview
   Caption         =   "Print Pre&view"
End
Begin VB.Menu mnuFilePrint
   Caption         =   "&Print..."
   Shortcut        =   ^P
End
Begin VB.Menu mnuFileBar4
   Caption         =   "-"
End
Begin VB.Menu mnuFileSend
   Caption         =   "Sen&d..."
End
Begin VB.Menu mnuFileBar5
   Caption         =   "-"
End
Begin VB.Menu mnuFileMRU
   Caption         =   ""
   Index           =   0
   Visible         =   0   'False
End
Begin VB.Menu mnuFileMRU
   Caption         =   ""
```

```
            Index           =    1
            Visible         =    0      'False
         End
         Begin VB.Menu mnuFileMRU
            Caption         =    ""
            Index           =    2
            Visible         =    0      'False
         End
         Begin VB.Menu mnuFileMRU
            Caption         =    ""
            Index           =    3
            Visible         =    0      'False
         End
         Begin VB.Menu mnuFileBar6
            Caption         =    "-"
            Visible         =    0      'False
         End
         Begin VB.Menu mnuFileExit
            Caption         =    "E&xit"
         End
      End
      Begin VB.Menu mnuEdit
         Caption         =    "&Edit"
         Begin VB.Menu mnuEditUndo
            Caption         =    "&Undo"
            Shortcut        =    ^Z
         End
         Begin VB.Menu mnuEditBar1
            Caption         =    "-"
         End
         Begin VB.Menu mnuEditCut
            Caption         =    "Cu&t"
            Shortcut        =    ^X
         End
         Begin VB.Menu mnuEditCopy
            Caption         =    "&Copy"
            Shortcut        =    ^C
         End
         Begin VB.Menu mnuEditPaste
```

```
            Caption          =     "&Paste"
            Shortcut         =     ^V
         End
         Begin VB.Menu mnuEditPasteSpecial
            Caption          =     "Paste &Special..."
         End
      End
      Begin VB.Menu mnuHelp
         Caption          =     "&Help"
         Begin VB.Menu mnuHelpContents
            Caption          =     "&Contents"
         End
         Begin VB.Menu mnuHelpSearch
            Caption          =     "&Search For Help On..."
         End
         Begin VB.Menu mnuHelpBar1
            Caption          =     "-"
         End
         Begin VB.Menu mnuHelpAbout
            Caption          =     "&About Datactl..."
         End
      End
   End
End
Attribute VB_Name = "frmMain"
Attribute VB_GlobalNameSpace = False
Attribute VB_Creatable = False
Attribute VB_PredeclaredId = True
Attribute VB_Exposed = False
Private Declare Function OSWinHelp% Lib "user32" Alias "WinHelpA" (ByVal
hwnd&, ByVal HelpFile$, ByVal wCommand%, dwData As Any)
Private Sub Form_Load()
    Dim db1 As Database
    Dim rs1 As Recordset
    Me.Left = GetSetting(App.Title, "Settings", "MainLeft", 1000)
    Me.Top = GetSetting(App.Title, "Settings", "MainTop", 1000)
    Me.Width = GetSetting(App.Title, "Settings", "MainWidth", 6500)
    Me.Height = GetSetting(App.Title, "Settings", "MainHeight", 6500)

    Set db1 = OpenDatabase _
```

```
        ("c:\vbi\datactrl\db1.htm", _
        False, False, "HTML Import;")

    Set rs1 = db1.OpenRecordset("DB", dbOpenTable)
    Set Data1.Recordset = rs1

End Sub


Private Sub Form_Unload(Cancel As Integer)
    If Me.WindowState <> vbMinimized Then
        SaveSetting App.Title, "Settings", "MainLeft", Me.Left
        SaveSetting App.Title, "Settings", "MainTop", Me.Top
        SaveSetting App.Title, "Settings", "MainWidth", Me.Width
        SaveSetting App.Title, "Settings", "MainHeight", Me.Height
    End If
End Sub


Private Sub mnuHelpAbout_Click()
    'To Do
    MsgBox "About Box Code goes here!"
End Sub


Private Sub tbToolBar_ButtonClick(ByVal Button As ComctlLib.Button)

    Select Case Button.Key

        Case "New"
            mnuFileNew_Click
        Case "New"
            mnuFileNew_Click
        Case "Open"
            mnuFileOpen_Click
        Case "Save"
            mnuFileSave_Click
        Case "Print"
            mnuFilePrint_Click
        Case "Cut"
            mnuEditCut_Click
        Case "Copy"
```

```vb
                mnuEditCopy_Click
            Case "Paste"
                mnuEditPaste_Click
            Case "Bold"
                'To Do
                MsgBox "Bold Code goes here!"
            Case "Italic"
                'To Do
                MsgBox "Italic Code goes here!"
            Case "Underline"
                'To Do
                MsgBox "Underline Code goes here!"
            Case "Left"
                'To Do
                MsgBox "Left Code goes here!"
            Case "Center"
                'To Do
                MsgBox "Center Code goes here!"
            Case "Right"
                'To Do
                MsgBox "Right Code goes here!"
        End Select
    End Sub


    Private Sub mnuHelpContents_Click()

        Dim nRet As Integer

        'if there is no helpfile for this project display a message to the
        'user you can set the HelpFile for your application in the
        'Project Properties dialog
        If Len(App.HelpFile) = 0 Then
            MsgBox "Unable to display Help Contents. There is no Help
            associated with this project.", vbInformation, Me.Caption
        Else
            On Error Resume Next
            nRet = OSWinHelp(Me.hwnd, App.HelpFile, 3, 0)
            If Err Then
                MsgBox Err.Description
            End If
```

```
        End If
End Sub


Private Sub mnuHelpSearch_Click()

    Dim nRet As Integer

    'if there is no helpfile for this project display a message to the
    'user you can set the HelpFile for your application in the
    'Project Properties dialog
    If Len(App.HelpFile) = 0 Then
        MsgBox "Unable to display Help Contents. There is no Help
        associated with this project.", vbInformation, Me.Caption
    Else
        On Error Resume Next
        nRet = OSWinHelp(Me.hwnd, App.HelpFile, 261, 0)
        If Err Then
            MsgBox Err.Description
        End If
    End If
End Sub


Private Sub mnuEditCopy_Click()
    'To Do
    MsgBox "Copy Code goes here!"
End Sub


Private Sub mnuEditCut_Click()
    'To Do
    MsgBox "Cut Code goes here!"
End Sub


Private Sub mnuEditPaste_Click()
    'To Do
    MsgBox "Paste Code goes here!"
End Sub


Private Sub mnuEditPasteSpecial_Click()
    'To Do
    MsgBox "Paste Special Code goes here!"
```

```
End Sub

Private Sub mnuEditUndo_Click()
    'To Do
    MsgBox "Undo Code goes here!"
End Sub

Private Sub mnuFileOpen_Click()
    Dim sFile As String

    With dlgCommonDialog
        'To Do
        'set the flags and attributes of the
        'common dialog control
        .Filter = "All Files (*.*)|*.*"
        .ShowOpen
        If Len(.filename) = 0 Then
            Exit Sub
        End If
        sFile = .filename
    End With
    'To Do
    'process the opened file
End Sub

Private Sub mnuFileClose_Click()
    'To Do
    MsgBox "Close Code goes here!"
End Sub

Private Sub mnuFileSave_Click()
    'To Do
    MsgBox "Save Code goes here!"
End Sub

Private Sub mnuFileSaveAs_Click()
    'To Do
    'Set up the common dialog control
    'prior to calling ShowSave
```

```
        dlgCommonDialog.ShowSave
End Sub


Private Sub mnuFileSaveAll_Click()
        'To Do
        MsgBox "Save All Code goes here!"
End Sub


Private Sub mnuFileProperties_Click()
        'To Do
        MsgBox "Properties Code goes here!"
End Sub


Private Sub mnuFilePageSetup_Click()
        dlgCommonDialog.ShowPrinter
End Sub


Private Sub mnuFilePrintPreview_Click()
        'To Do
        MsgBox "Print Preview Code goes here!"
End Sub


Private Sub mnuFilePrint_Click()
        'To Do
        MsgBox "Print Code goes here!"
End Sub


Private Sub mnuFileSend_Click()
        'To Do
        MsgBox "Send Code goes here!"
End Sub


Private Sub mnuFileMRU_Click(Index As Integer)
        'To Do
        MsgBox "MRU Code goes here!"
End Sub


Private Sub mnuFileExit_Click()
        'unload the form
```

```
        Unload Me
    End Sub

    Private Sub mnuFileNew_Click()
        'To Do
        MsgBox "New File Code goes here!"
    End Sub
```

In this way, you can use the data bound controls to display data from a Web page database, and you can move around in that database using the arrow buttons in the Data control.

Creating a Database in Code

Next, we'll see how to read our Web page database and create a standard database (**.mdb**) file so that other programs (Visual Basic programs or database programs) can use it. We will create the table we put together earlier and save it as the file **Created.mdb**:

Name	Grade
Ann	C
Mark	B
Ed	A
Frank	A
Ted	A
Mabel	B
Ralph	B
Tom	B

To do this, use the Application Wizard to create a new Visual Basic project named **CreateDB**. Place a button on Form1 and give it the caption **Create Database**. When the user clicks this button, we will create our database, which we will call **Created.mdb**, and display the students table in a bound grid control:

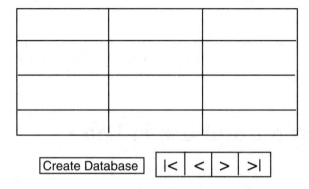

Let's start working in code now. Open the click event connected to the **Create Database** button:

```
Private Sub Command1_Click()

End Sub
```

When the user clicks this button, we want to create the **created.mdb** database file that contains the students table.

Defining a Database

Now it's time to examine some of the data access objects (DAO) available to us in Visual Basic. The first DAO object we'll see is the DBEngine object:

DBEngine

This object, the basis of database programming in Visual Basic, contains a collection of workspaces. A *collection* is like an array of objects; the collection of workspace objects in the DBEngine is named Workspaces, and the first workspace in Workspaces is referred to as Workspace(0). *Workspaces* are where we open and work with databases in Visual Basic. (This arrangement is useful, because it means that our program can have several databases open at once.)

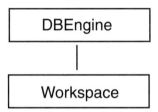

In DAO programming, collections of objects use the object name and add an *s* to the end; for example, a collection named "fields" contains objects of type field. One workspace already exists in this collection: Workspace(0), the default workspace. We will create our database as an object of type Database in this workspace:

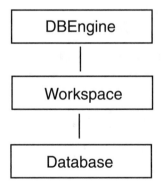

We'll use the CreateDatabase method of this workspace to create an object of type Database:

```
Set TheDB = Workspace.CreateDatabase(Filename, Ordering,
Options)
```

Here, Filename is the name of our new database, and the Ordering argument specifies how to order text records (which varies by language and may be any of the constants in Table 10.2). The optional argument Options allows us to request an encrypted database or to set the version of the Microsoft Jet database engine we want. Possible values appear in Table 10.3.

Table 10.2 CreateDatabase Ordering Selections

Constant	Meaning
dbLangGeneral	English, German, French, Portuguese, Italian, and Modern Spanish
dbLangArabic	Arabic
dbLangCzech	Czech
dbLangCyrillic	Russian
dbLangDutch	Dutch
dbLangGreek	Greek
dbLangHebrew	Hebrew
dbLangHungarian	Hungarian
dbLangIcelandic	Icelandic
dbLangNordic	Nordic languages
dbLangNorwdan	Norwegian and Danish
dbLangPolish	Polish
dbLangSwedfin	Swedish and Finnish
dbLangSpanish	Traditional Spanish
dbLangTurkish	Turkish

Table 10.3 CreateDatabase Options

Constant	Meaning
dbEncrypt	Create an encrypted database.
dbVersion10	Create a database that uses the Microsoft Jet database engine version 1.0.
dbVersion11	Create a database that uses the Microsoft Jet database engine version 1.1.
dbVersion25	Create a database that uses the Microsoft Jet database engine version 2.5.
dbVersion30	Create a database that uses the Microsoft Jet database engine version 3.0.

In code, then, we create our new database this way with CreateDatabase():

```
Private Sub Command1_Click()
    Dim TheDB As Database

    Set TheDB = DBEngine.Workspaces(0).CreateDatabase("CREATED.MDB",
        dbLangGeneral)
        .
        .
        .
```

At this point, we have an object of type Database named TheDB, which corresponds to our database. We are ready to set up one table in our database object, and that is our table named students:

Name	Grade
Ann	C
Mark	B
Ed	A
Frank	A
Ted	A
Mabel	B
Ralph	B
Tom	B

We do that by *defining* a new type of table named students using a TableDef object:

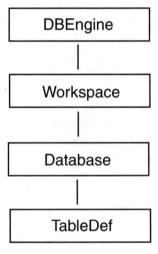

After we have designed our table definition (by specifying the fields that go into it), we will be able to create tables of that type. We begin by creating an object of type TableDef in our database object:

```
Private Sub Command1_Click()
    Dim TheDB As Database
-> Dim studentsTD As TableDef

    Set TheDB = DBEngine.Workspaces(0).CreateDatabase("CREATED.MDB",
        dbLangGeneral)

-> Set studentsTD = TheDB.CreateTableDef("students")
    .
    .
    .
```

Now the new table definition, studentsTD, is ready for us to set up as we like. In this case, we want two fields in our tableÑName and GradeÑand both are text fields. To create these fields and install them in our table definition, we will create new objects of type *Field*, using the TableDef method CreateField, and then attach them to our table definition:

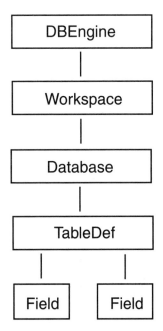

Here, we create two new fields, which we call studentsFlds(0) and studentsFlds(1), making them text fields:

```
   Private Sub Command1_Click()
       Dim TheDB As Database
       Dim studentsTD As TableDef
-> Dim studentsFlds(2) As Field

       Set TheDB = DBEngine.Workspaces(0).CreateDatabase("CREATED.MDB",
           dbLangGeneral)

       Set studentsTD = TheDB.CreateTableDef("students")
-> Set studentsFlds(0) = studentsTD.CreateField("Name", dbText)
-> Set studentsFlds(1) = studentsTD.CreateField("Grade", dbText)
       .
       .
       .
```

Note the keyword dbText, which indicates that these fields are text fields. The other possibilities are dbDate, dbMemo, dbBoolean, dbInteger, dbLong, dbCurrency, dbSingle, dbDouble, dbByte, and dbLongBinary. If we want to specify the size of the field—such as making the Grade field only one character long—we use a third argument:

```
   Set studentsFlds(1) = studentsTD.CreateField("Grade", dbText, 1)
```

At this point, we've defined our two fields. Next, we add their definitions to the table definition. We use the TableDef method Append. A TableDef object, such as studentsTD, contains a collection of fields named Fields, and we append the new field definitions to that collection:

```
   Private Sub Command1_Click()
       Dim TheDB As Database
       Dim studentsTD As TableDef
       Dim studentsFlds(2) As Field

       Set TheDB = DBEngine.Workspaces(0).CreateDatabase("CREATED.MDB",
           dbLangGeneral)

       Set studentsTD = TheDB.CreateTableDef("students")
       Set studentsFlds(0) = studentsTD.CreateField("Name", dbText)
       Set studentsFlds(1) = studentsTD.CreateField("Grade", dbText)
```

```
-> studentsTD.Fields.Append studentsFlds(0)
-> studentsTD.Fields.Append studentsFlds(1)
              .
              .
              .
```

Now we've defined a new type of table named students. The table contains two text fields: Name and Grade:

students

Name   Grade

The next step is to add our completed table definition to the collection of TableDef objects (named TableDefs) in our database object. We use the Database Append method:

```
Private Sub Command1_Click()
    Dim TheDB As Database
    Dim studentsTD As TableDef
    Dim studentsFlds(2) As Field

    Set TheDB = DBEngine.Workspaces(0).CreateDatabase("CREATED.MDB",
        dbLangGeneral)

    Set studentsTD = TheDB.CreateTableDef("students")
    Set studentsFlds(0) = studentsTD.CreateField("Name", dbText)
    Set studentsFlds(1) = studentsTD.CreateField("Grade", dbText)
```

```
    studentsTD.Fields.Append studentsFlds(0)
    studentsTD.Fields.Append studentsFlds(1)
--> TheDB.TableDefs.Append studentsTD
         .
         .
         .
```

That's it. We've defined our type of database; it contains one table (students) and that table contains two fields (Name and Grade). Now that we've set up the table definition, the next step is to create an object of that type.

Creating a Table

Now that we've defined our students table, we need an actual object of that type to work with. In older versions of Visual Basic, we would do that by creating an object of type Table; now, however, we create an object of type Recordset:

```
Private Sub Command1_Click()
    Dim TheDB As Database
    Dim studentsTD As TableDef
    Dim studentsFlds(2) As Field
--> Dim studentsTable As Recordset

    Set TheDB = DBEngine.Workspaces(0).CreateDatabase("CREATED.MDB",
        dbLangGeneral)

    Set studentsTD = TheDB.CreateTableDef("students")
    Set studentsFlds(0) = studentsTD.CreateField("Name", dbText)
    Set studentsFlds(1) = studentsTD.CreateField("Grade", dbText)
    studentsTD.Fields.Append studentsFlds(0)
    studentsTD.Fields.Append studentsFlds(1)
    TheDB.TableDefs.Append studentsTD

--> Set studentsTable = TheDB.OpenRecordset("students", dbOpenTable)
         .
         .
         .
```

This new *recordset* is what we will actually work with. We will be able to reach the Name and Grade fields in it directly and to use recordset methods such as Edit and Update. In fact, there are three types of recordsets: tables, dynasets, and snapshots.

A table is what we are already familiar with as a table in our database; to open a table-type recordset, we pass OpenRecordset() the parameter dbOpenTable.

A *dynaset* is like a table, but it can also contain tables from other databases. In addition, a dynaset's methods of searching and seeking differ from those of tables, and dynasets can perform such operations on a number of tables at once. To open a dynaset recordset, we pass OpenRecordset() the parameter dbOpenDynaset.

A *snapshot* is just like a dynaset except that a snapshot is read-only and may not be modified. Because it is read-only, operations can be much quicker with a snapshot than with a dynaset or a table. To open a snapshot-type recordset, pass OpenRecordset() the parameter dbOpenSnapshot.

It's also worth noting that we can reach the internal recordset of a Data control by referring to its Recordset property like this: Data1.Recordset. OpenRecordset() can also take a third argument, which sets various sharing and reading options as shown in Table 10.4.

Table 10.4 OpenRecordset Options

Constant	Meaning
dbDenyWrite	Other users can't modify or add records.
dbDenyRead	Other users can't view records.
dbReadOnly	You can only view records; other users can modify them.
dbAppendOnly	You can only append new records (dynaset-type Recordset only).
dbInconsistent	Inconsistent updates are allowed.
dbConsistent	Only consistent updates are allowed.

Table 10.4 OpenRecordset Options (continued)

Constant	Meaning
dbForwardOnly	The Recordset is a forward-only scrolling snapshot.
dbSQLPassThrough	The Microsoft Jet database engine query processor is bypassed.
dbSeeChanges	Generate a runtime error if another user is changing data you are editing.

We open our new recordset as a table object in our program this way:

```
Set studentsTable = TheDB.OpenRecordset("students", dbOpenTable)
```

Now our table, studentsTable, is finally ready for use. The next step is to set up the source database from our Web page, **db1.htm**. As we did earlier in this chapter, we use OpenDatabase() to open the Web page and create a database object from it. This time, we'll call that database object sourceDB:

```
Private Sub Command1_Click()
-> Dim sourceDB As Database
    Dim TheDB As Database
    Dim studentsTD As TableDef
    Dim studentsFlds(2) As Field
    Dim studentsTable As Recordset

-> Set sourceDB = OpenDatabase("c:\vbi\dbcreate\db1.htm", _
        False, False, "HTML Import;")

    Set TheDB =

DBEngine.Workspaces(0).CreateDatabase("C:\VBI\dbcreate\CREATED.MDB",
        dbLangGeneral)

    Set studentsTD = TheDB.CreateTableDef("students")
    Set studentsFlds(0) = studentsTD.CreateField("Name", dbText)
```

```
    Set studentsFlds(1) = studentsTD.CreateField("Grade", dbText)
    studentsTD.Fields.Append studentsFlds(0)
    studentsTD.Fields.Append studentsFlds(1)

    TheDB.TableDefs.Append studentsTD

    Set studentsTable = TheDB.OpenRecordset("students", dbOpenTable)
        .
        .
        .

End Sub
```

We need a recordset from sourceDB so that we can copy its records to our
new database, TheDB. We set up the source recordset, which we call
sourceTable:

```
Private Sub Command1_Click()
    Dim sourceDB As Database
    Dim TheDB As Database
    Dim studentsTD As TableDef
    Dim studentsFlds(2) As Field
    Dim studentsTable As Recordset
->  Dim sourceTable As Recordset

    Set sourceDB = OpenDatabase("c:\vbi\dbcreate\db1.htm", _
        False, False, "HTML Import;")

->  Set sourceTable = sourceDB.OpenRecordset("DB", dbOpenTable)

    Set TheDB =
DBEngine.Workspaces(0).CreateDatabase("C:\VBI\dbcreate\CREATED.MDB",
dbLangGeneral)

    Set studentsTD = TheDB.CreateTableDef("students")
    Set studentsFlds(0) = studentsTD.CreateField("Name", dbText)
    Set studentsFlds(1) = studentsTD.CreateField("Grade", dbText)
    studentsTD.Fields.Append studentsFlds(0)
    studentsTD.Fields.Append studentsFlds(1)
```

```
TheDB.TableDefs.Append studentsTD

Set studentsTable = TheDB.OpenRecordset("students", dbOpenTable)
         .
         .
         .
End Sub
```

Now that sourceTable and studentsTable are open, we transfer the records from one to the other:

We do that with a loop over all the records in our table:

```
For loop_index = 1 To 8
         .
         .
         .
Next loop_index
```

First, we create a new record in studentsTable using the AddNew method:

```
For loop_index = 1 To 8
    studentsTable.AddNew
         .
         .
         .
Next loop_index
```

Next, we copy the data in the two fields (Name and Grade) from the source table to the target table:

```
    For loop_index = 1 To 8
        studentsTable.AddNew
->      studentsTable!Name = sourceTable!Name
->      studentsTable!Grade = sourceTable!Grade
             .
```

```
            .
            .
            .
    Next loop_index
```

Then we update the studentsTable to install the new data:

```
    For loop_index = 1 To 8
        studentsTable.AddNew
        studentsTable!Name = sourceTable!Name
        studentsTable!Grade = sourceTable!Grade
->      studentsTable.Update
            .
            .
            .

    Next loop_index
```

Finally, we move to the next record in the source table to begin the process again:

```
    For loop_index = 1 To 8
        studentsTable.AddNew
        studentsTable!Name = sourceTable!Name
        studentsTable!Grade = sourceTable!Grade
        studentsTable.Update
->      sourceTable.MoveNext
    Next loop_index

    TheDB.Close
```

Now we've copied the data to the target table. At the end of all this, we close the database and write it to disk with this statement: TheDB.Close. That's itÑnow we've created **created.mdb**. CongratulationsÑyou've produced your first DAO database using Visual Basic DAO methods.

To display our new table, we add a Data control, Data1, and a DBGrid control, DBGrid1, to our program:

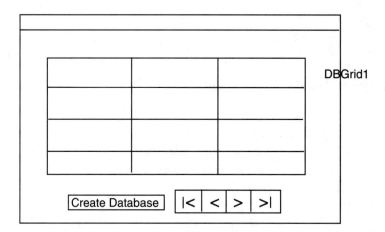

We set the Datasource property of the grid to Data1. In our program, we set the DatabaseName ("Created.mdb") and RecordSource properties (the table in our database: students) of Data1 after creating the database file. Then we enable the grid and the data control, and we refresh the data control to make it read the data from the database file:

```
Private Sub Command1_Click()
    Dim TheDB As Database
    Dim studentsTD As TableDef
        .
        .
        .
    studentsTable.AddNew
    studentsTable!Name = "Tom"
    studentsTable!Grade = "B"
    studentsTable.Update

    TheDB.Close

-> Data1.DatabaseName = "C:\VBOOK\CREATEDB\CREATED.MDB"
-> Data1.RecordSource = "students"
-> Data1.Enabled = True
-> DBGrid1.Enabled = True
-> Data1.Refresh
End Sub
```

When the user clicks the **Create Database** button, our database is created and displayed, as in Figure 10.6. Our program is a success. **FrmMain.frm** appears in Listing 10.2.

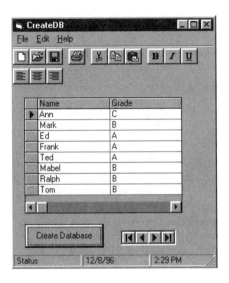

Figure 10.6 Creating a database file from a Web page.

Listing 10.2 (CreateDB) FrmMain.frm

```
VERSION 5.00
Object = "{F9043C88-F6F2-101A-A3C9-08002B2F49FB}#1.1#0"; "COMDLG32.OCX"
Object = "{6B7E6392-850A-101B-AFC0-4210102A8DA7}#1.1#0"; "COMCTL32.OCX"
Object = "{00028C01-0000-0000-0000-000000000046}#1.0#0"; "DBGRID32.OCX"
Begin VB.Form frmMain
   Caption        =   "CreateDB"
   ClientHeight   =   4575
   ClientLeft     =   165
   ClientTop      =   735
   ClientWidth    =   4335
   LinkTopic      =   "Form1"
   ScaleHeight    =   4575
   ScaleWidth     =   4335
   StartUpPosition =  3   'Windows Default
```

```
Begin ComctlLib.Toolbar tbToolBar
   Align           =    1  'Align Top
   Height          =    1080
   Left            =    0
   TabIndex        =    1
   Top             =    0
   Width           =    4335
   _ExtentX        =    7646
   _ExtentY        =    1905
   ButtonWidth     =    635
   ButtonHeight    =    582
   Appearance      =    1
   ImageList       =    "imlIcons"
   BeginProperty Buttons {7791BA41-E020-11CF-8E74-00A0C90F26F8}
      NumButtons      =    17
      BeginProperty Button1 {7791BA43-E020-11CF-8E74-00A0C90F26F8}
         Key              =    "New"
         Object.ToolTipText      =    "New"
         Object.Tag              =    ""
         ImageIndex       =    1
      EndProperty
      BeginProperty Button2 {7791BA43-E020-11CF-8E74-00A0C90F26F8}
         Key              =    "Open"
         Object.ToolTipText      =    "Open"
         Object.Tag              =    ""
         ImageIndex       =    2
      EndProperty
      BeginProperty Button3 {7791BA43-E020-11CF-8E74-00A0C90F26F8}
         Key              =    "Save"
         Object.ToolTipText      =    "Save"
         Object.Tag              =    ""
         ImageIndex       =    3
      EndProperty
      BeginProperty Button4 {7791BA43-E020-11CF-8E74-00A0C90F26F8}
         Key              =    ""
         Object.Tag              =    ""
         Style            =    3
      EndProperty
      BeginProperty Button5 {7791BA43-E020-11CF-8E74-00A0C90F26F8}
```

```
      Key                =    "Print"
      Object.ToolTipText    =    "Print"
      Object.Tag            =    ""
      ImageIndex     =    4
EndProperty
BeginProperty Button6 {7791BA43-E020-11CF-8E74-00A0C90F26F8}
      Key              =    ""
      Object.Tag          =    ""
      Style          =    3
EndProperty
BeginProperty Button7 {7791BA43-E020-11CF-8E74-00A0C90F26F8}
      Key              =    "Cut"
      Object.ToolTipText    =    "Cut"
      Object.Tag          =    ""
      ImageIndex     =    5
EndProperty
BeginProperty Button8 {7791BA43-E020-11CF-8E74-00A0C90F26F8}
      Key              =    "Copy"
      Object.ToolTipText    =    "Copy"
      Object.Tag          =    ""
      ImageIndex     =    6
EndProperty
BeginProperty Button9 {7791BA43-E020-11CF-8E74-00A0C90F26F8}
      Key              =    "Paste"
      Object.ToolTipText    =    "Paste"
      Object.Tag          =    ""
      ImageIndex     =    7
EndProperty
BeginProperty Button10 {7791BA43-E020-11CF-8E74-00A0C90F26F8}
      Key              =    ""
      Object.Tag          =    ""
      Style          =    3
EndProperty
BeginProperty Button11 {7791BA43-E020-11CF-8E74-00A0C90F26F8}
      Key              =    "Bold"
      Object.ToolTipText    =    "Bold"
      Object.Tag          =    ""
      ImageIndex     =    8
EndProperty
```

```
            BeginProperty Button12 {7791BA43-E020-11CF-8E74-00A0C90F26F8}
                Key               =    "Italic"
                Object.ToolTipText    =    "Italic"
                Object.Tag            =    ""
                ImageIndex       =    9
            EndProperty
            BeginProperty Button13 {7791BA43-E020-11CF-8E74-00A0C90F26F8}
                Key               =    "Underline"
                Object.ToolTipText    =    "Underline"
                Object.Tag            =    ""
                ImageIndex       =    10
            EndProperty
            BeginProperty Button14 {7791BA43-E020-11CF-8E74-00A0C90F26F8}
                Key               =    ""
                Object.Tag            =    ""
                Style            =    3
            EndProperty
            BeginProperty Button15 {7791BA43-E020-11CF-8E74-00A0C90F26F8}
                Key               =    "Left"
                Object.ToolTipText    =    "Left Justify"
                Object.Tag            =    ""
                ImageIndex       =    11
            EndProperty
            BeginProperty Button16 {7791BA43-E020-11CF-8E74-00A0C90F26F8}
                Key               =    "Center"
                Object.ToolTipText    =    "Center"
                Object.Tag            =    ""
                ImageIndex       =    12
            EndProperty
            BeginProperty Button17 {7791BA43-E020-11CF-8E74-00A0C90F26F8}
                Key               =    "Right"
                Object.ToolTipText    =    "Right Justify"
                Object.Tag            =    ""
                ImageIndex       =    13
            EndProperty
        EndProperty
        MouseIcon       =    "frmMain.frx":0000
    End
    Begin VB.Data Data1
```

```
    Caption         =     "Data1"
    Connect         =     "Access"
    DatabaseName    =     ""
    DefaultCursorType=    0   'DefaultCursor
    DefaultType     =     2   'UseODBC
    Exclusive       =     0    'False
    Height          =     345
    Left            =     2280
    Options         =     0
    ReadOnly        =     0    'False
    RecordsetType   =     1    'Dynaset
    RecordSource    =     ""
    Top             =     3840
    Width           =     1215
End
Begin VB.CommandButton Command1
    Caption         =     "Create Database"
    Height          =     495
    Left            =     240
    TabIndex        =     3
    Top             =     3720
    Width           =     1695
End
Begin ComctlLib.StatusBar sbStatusBar
    Align           =     2    'Align Bottom
    Height          =     270
    Left            =     0
    TabIndex        =     0
    Top             =     4305
    Width           =     4335
    _ExtentX        =     7646
    _ExtentY        =     476
    SimpleText      =     ""
    BeginProperty Panels {2C787A51-E01C-11CF-8E74-00A0C90F26F8}
        NumPanels        =   3
        BeginProperty Panel1 {2C787A53-E01C-11CF-8E74-00A0C90F26F8}
            AutoSize         =    1
            Object.Width             =    2540
            MinWidth         =    2540
```

```
        Text            =    "Status"
        TextSave        =    "Status"
        Key             =    ""
        Object.Tag              =      ""
    EndProperty
    BeginProperty Panel2 {2C787A53-E01C-11CF-8E74-00A0C90F26F8}
        Style           =    6
        AutoSize        =    2
        Object.Width            =    2540
        MinWidth        =    2540
        TextSave        =    "12/8/96"
        Key             =    ""
        Object.Tag              =      ""
    EndProperty
    BeginProperty Panel3 {2C787A53-E01C-11CF-8E74-00A0C90F26F8}
        Style           =    5
        AutoSize        =    2
        Object.Width            =    2540
        MinWidth        =    2540
        TextSave        =    "12:23 PM"
        Key             =    ""
        Object.Tag              =      ""
    EndProperty
    EndProperty
    BeginProperty Font {0BE35203-8F91-11CE-9DE3-00AA004BB851}
        Name            =    "MS Sans Serif"
        Size            =    8.25
        Charset         =    0
        Weight          =    400
        Underline       =    0     'False
        Italic          =    0     'False
        Strikethrough   =    0     'False
    EndProperty
    MouseIcon       =    "frmMain.frx":001C
End
Begin MSComDlg.CommonDialog dlgCommonDialog
    Left            =    1740
    Top             =    1350
    _ExtentX        =    847
```

```
      _ExtentY       =    847
      FontSize       =    1.65893e-37
   End
   Begin MSDBGrid.DBGrid DBGrid1
      Bindings       =    "frmMain.frx":0038
      Height         =    2415
      Left           =    240
      OleObjectBlob  =    "frmMain.frx":0048
      TabIndex       =    2
      Top            =    1080
      Width          =    3375
   End
   Begin ComctlLib.ImageList imlIcons
      Left           =    1740
      Top            =    1350
      _ExtentX       =    1005
      _ExtentY       =    1005
      BackColor      =    -2147483643
      ImageWidth     =    16
      ImageHeight    =    16
      MaskColor      =    12632256
      BeginProperty Images {8556BCD1-E01E-11CF-8E74-00A0C90F26F8}
         NumListImages  =    13
         BeginProperty ListImage1 {8556BCD3-E01E-11CF-8E74-00A0C90F26F8}
            Picture        =    "frmMain.frx":09FA
            Key            =    ""
         EndProperty
         BeginProperty ListImage2 {8556BCD3-E01E-11CF-8E74-00A0C90F26F8}
            Picture        =    "frmMain.frx":0D4C
            Key            =    ""
         EndProperty
         BeginProperty ListImage3 {8556BCD3-E01E-11CF-8E74-00A0C90F26F8}
            Picture        =    "frmMain.frx":109E
            Key            =    ""
         EndProperty
         BeginProperty ListImage4 {8556BCD3-E01E-11CF-8E74-00A0C90F26F8}
            Picture        =    "frmMain.frx":13F0
            Key            =    ""
         EndProperty
```

```
BeginProperty ListImage5 {8556BCD3-E01E-11CF-8E74-00A0C90F26F8}
   Picture        =    "frmMain.frx":1742
   Key            =    ""
EndProperty
BeginProperty ListImage6 {8556BCD3-E01E-11CF-8E74-00A0C90F26F8}
   Picture        =    "frmMain.frx":1A94
   Key            =    ""
EndProperty
BeginProperty ListImage7 {8556BCD3-E01E-11CF-8E74-00A0C90F26F8}
   Picture        =    "frmMain.frx":1DE6
   Key            =    ""
EndProperty
BeginProperty ListImage8 {8556BCD3-E01E-11CF-8E74-00A0C90F26F8}
   Picture        =    "frmMain.frx":2138
   Key            =    ""
EndProperty
BeginProperty ListImage9 {8556BCD3-E01E-11CF-8E74-00A0C90F26F8}
   Picture        =    "frmMain.frx":248A
   Key            =    ""
EndProperty
BeginProperty ListImage10 {8556BCD3-E01E-11CF-8E74-
                           00A0C90F26F8}
   Picture        =    "frmMain.frx":27DC
   Key            =    ""
EndProperty
BeginProperty ListImage11 {8556BCD3-E01E-11CF-8E74-
                           00A0C90F26F8}
   Picture        =    "frmMain.frx":2B2E
   Key            =    ""
EndProperty
BeginProperty ListImage12 {8556BCD3-E01E-11CF-8E74-
                           00A0C90F26F8}
   Picture        =    "frmMain.frx":2E80
   Key            =    ""
EndProperty
BeginProperty ListImage13 {8556BCD3-E01E-11CF-8E74-
                           00A0C90F26F8}
   Picture        =    "frmMain.frx":31D2
   Key            =    ""
EndProperty
```

```
        EndProperty
End
Begin VB.Menu mnuFile
    Caption         =   "&File"
    Begin VB.Menu mnuFileNew
        Caption         =   "&New"
        Shortcut        =   ^N
    End
    Begin VB.Menu mnuFileOpen
        Caption         =   "&Open"
        Shortcut        =   ^O
    End
    Begin VB.Menu mnuFileClose
        Caption         =   "&Close"
    End
    Begin VB.Menu mnuFileBar1
        Caption         =   "-"
    End
    Begin VB.Menu mnuFileSave
        Caption         =   "&Save"
        Shortcut        =   ^S
    End
    Begin VB.Menu mnuFileSaveAs
        Caption         =   "Save &As..."
    End
    Begin VB.Menu mnuFileSaveAll
        Caption         =   "Save A&ll"
    End
    Begin VB.Menu mnuFileBar2
        Caption         =   "-"
    End
    Begin VB.Menu mnuFileProperties
        Caption         =   "Propert&ies"
    End
    Begin VB.Menu mnuFileBar3
        Caption         =   "-"
    End
    Begin VB.Menu mnuFilePageSetup
        Caption         =   "Page Set&up..."
```

```
            End
            Begin VB.Menu mnuFilePrintPreview
               Caption         =   "Print Pre&view"
            End
            Begin VB.Menu mnuFilePrint
               Caption         =   "&Print..."
               Shortcut        =   ^P
            End
            Begin VB.Menu mnuFileBar4
               Caption         =   "-"
            End
            Begin VB.Menu mnuFileSend
               Caption         =   "Sen&d..."
            End
            Begin VB.Menu mnuFileBar5
               Caption         =   "-"
            End
            Begin VB.Menu mnuFileMRU
               Caption         =   ""
               Index           =   0
               Visible         =   0   'False
            End
            Begin VB.Menu mnuFileMRU
               Caption         =   ""
               Index           =   1
               Visible         =   0   'False
            End
            Begin VB.Menu mnuFileMRU
               Caption         =   ""
               Index           =   2
               Visible         =   0   'False
            End
            Begin VB.Menu mnuFileMRU
               Caption         =   ""
               Index           =   3
               Visible         =   0   'False
            End
            Begin VB.Menu mnuFileBar6
               Caption         =   "-"
```

```
            Visible        =    0   'False
        End
        Begin VB.Menu mnuFileExit
            Caption        =    "E&xit"
        End
    End
    Begin VB.Menu mnuEdit
        Caption        =    "&Edit"
        Begin VB.Menu mnuEditUndo
            Caption        =    "&Undo"
            Shortcut       =    ^Z
        End
        Begin VB.Menu mnuEditBar1
            Caption        =    "-"
        End
        Begin VB.Menu mnuEditCut
            Caption        =    "Cu&t"
            Shortcut       =    ^X
        End
        Begin VB.Menu mnuEditCopy
            Caption        =    "&Copy"
            Shortcut       =    ^C
        End
        Begin VB.Menu mnuEditPaste
            Caption        =    "&Paste"
            Shortcut       =    ^V
        End
        Begin VB.Menu mnuEditPasteSpecial
            Caption        =    "Paste &Special..."
        End
    End
    Begin VB.Menu mnuHelp
        Caption        =    "&Help"
        Begin VB.Menu mnuHelpContents
            Caption        =    "&Contents"
        End
        Begin VB.Menu mnuHelpSearch
            Caption        =    "&Search For Help On..."
        End
```

```
        Begin VB.Menu mnuHelpBar1
            Caption        =   "-"
        End
        Begin VB.Menu mnuHelpAbout
            Caption        =   "&About CreateDB..."
        End
    End
End
Attribute VB_Name = "frmMain"
Attribute VB_GlobalNameSpace = False
Attribute VB_Creatable = False
Attribute VB_PredeclaredId = True
Attribute VB_Exposed = False
Private Declare Function OSWinHelp% Lib "user32" Alias "WinHelpA" (ByVal
hwnd&, ByVal HelpFile$, ByVal wCommand%, dwData As Any)


Private Sub Command1_Click()
    Dim sourceDB As Database
    Dim TheDB As Database
    Dim studentsTD As TableDef
    Dim studentsFlds(2) As Field
    Dim studentsTable As Recordset
    Dim sourceTable As Recordset

    Set sourceDB = OpenDatabase("c:\vbi\dbcreate\db1.htm", _
        False, False, "HTML Import;")


    Set sourceTable = sourceDB.OpenRecordset("DB", dbOpenTable)


    Set TheDB =
DBEngine.Workspaces(0).CreateDatabase("C:\VBI\dbcreate\CREATED.MDB",
dbLangGeneral)


    Set studentsTD = TheDB.CreateTableDef("students")
    Set studentsFlds(0) = studentsTD.CreateField("Name", dbText)
    Set studentsFlds(1) = studentsTD.CreateField("Grade", dbText)
    studentsTD.Fields.Append studentsFlds(0)
    studentsTD.Fields.Append studentsFlds(1)


    TheDB.TableDefs.Append studentsTD
```

```
        Set studentsTable = TheDB.OpenRecordset("students", dbOpenTable)

        For loop_index = 1 To 8
            studentsTable.AddNew
            studentsTable!Name = sourceTable!Name
            studentsTable!Grade = sourceTable!Grade
            studentsTable.Update
            sourceTable.MoveNext
        Next loop_index

        TheDB.Close

        Data1.DatabaseName = "C:\vbi\dbcreate\CREATED.MDB"
        Data1.RecordSource = "students"
        Data1.Enabled = True
        DBGrid1.Enabled = True
        Data1.Refresh

End Sub

Private Sub Form_Load()
    Me.Left = GetSetting(App.Title, "Settings", "MainLeft", 1000)
    Me.Top = GetSetting(App.Title, "Settings", "MainTop", 1000)
    Me.Width = GetSetting(App.Title, "Settings", "MainWidth", 6500)
    Me.Height = GetSetting(App.Title, "Settings", "MainHeight", 6500)
End Sub

Private Sub Form_Unload(Cancel As Integer)
    If Me.WindowState <> vbMinimized Then
        SaveSetting App.Title, "Settings", "MainLeft", Me.Left
        SaveSetting App.Title, "Settings", "MainTop", Me.Top
        SaveSetting App.Title, "Settings", "MainWidth", Me.Width
        SaveSetting App.Title, "Settings", "MainHeight", Me.Height
    End If
End Sub

Private Sub mnuHelpAbout_Click()
    'To Do
    MsgBox "About Box Code goes here!"
```

```
End Sub

Private Sub tbToolBar_ButtonClick(ByVal Button As ComctlLib.Button)

    Select Case Button.Key

        Case "New"
            mnuFileNew_Click
        Case "New"
            mnuFileNew_Click
        Case "Open"
            mnuFileOpen_Click
        Case "Save"
            mnuFileSave_Click
        Case "Print"
            mnuFilePrint_Click
        Case "Cut"
            mnuEditCut_Click
        Case "Copy"
            mnuEditCopy_Click
        Case "Paste"
            mnuEditPaste_Click
        Case "Bold"
            'To Do
            MsgBox "Bold Code goes here!"
        Case "Italic"
            'To Do
            MsgBox "Italic Code goes here!"
        Case "Underline"
            'To Do
            MsgBox "Underline Code goes here!"
        Case "Left"
            'To Do
            MsgBox "Left Code goes here!"
        Case "Center"
            'To Do
            MsgBox "Center Code goes here!"
        Case "Right"
            'To Do
```

```
            MsgBox "Right Code goes here!"
        End Select
End Sub


Private Sub mnuHelpContents_Click()

    Dim nRet As Integer

    'if there is no helpfile for this project display a message to the
    'user you can set the HelpFile for your application in the
    'Project Properties dialog
    If Len(App.HelpFile) = 0 Then
        MsgBox "Unable to display Help Contents. There is no Help
        associated with this project.", vbInformation, Me.Caption
    Else
        On Error Resume Next
        nRet = OSWinHelp(Me.hwnd, App.HelpFile, 3, 0)
        If Err Then
            MsgBox Err.Description
        End If
    End If
End Sub


Private Sub mnuHelpSearch_Click()

    Dim nRet As Integer

    'if there is no helpfile for this project display a message to the
    'user you can set the HelpFile for your application in the
    'Project Properties dialog
    If Len(App.HelpFile) = 0 Then
        MsgBox "Unable to display Help Contents. There is no Help
        associated with this project.", vbInformation, Me.Caption
    Else
        On Error Resume Next
        nRet = OSWinHelp(Me.hwnd, App.HelpFile, 261, 0)
        If Err Then
            MsgBox Err.Description
        End If
    End If
End Sub
```

```
Private Sub mnuEditCopy_Click()
    'To Do
    MsgBox "Copy Code goes here!"
End Sub

Private Sub mnuEditCut_Click()
    'To Do
    MsgBox "Cut Code goes here!"
End Sub

Private Sub mnuEditPaste_Click()
    'To Do
    MsgBox "Paste Code goes here!"
End Sub

Private Sub mnuEditPasteSpecial_Click()
    'To Do
    MsgBox "Paste Special Code goes here!"
End Sub

Private Sub mnuEditUndo_Click()
    'To Do
    MsgBox "Undo Code goes here!"
End Sub

Private Sub mnuFileOpen_Click()
    Dim sFile As String

    With dlgCommonDialog
        'To Do
        'set the flags and attributes of the
        'common dialog control
        .Filter = "All Files (*.*)|*.*"
        .ShowOpen
        If Len(.filename) = 0 Then
            Exit Sub
        End If
        sFile = .filename
    End With
    'To Do
```

```
                'process the opened file
        End Sub

        Private Sub mnuFileClose_Click()
                'To Do
                MsgBox "Close Code goes here!"
        End Sub

        Private Sub mnuFileSave_Click()
                'To Do
                MsgBox "Save Code goes here!"
        End Sub

        Private Sub mnuFileSaveAs_Click()
                'To Do
                'Set up the common dialog control
                'prior to calling ShowSave
                dlgCommonDialog.ShowSave
        End Sub

        Private Sub mnuFileSaveAll_Click()
                'To Do
                MsgBox "Save All Code goes here!"
        End Sub

        Private Sub mnuFileProperties_Click()
                'To Do
                MsgBox "Properties Code goes here!"
        End Sub

        Private Sub mnuFilePageSetup_Click()
                dlgCommonDialog.ShowPrinter
        End Sub

        Private Sub mnuFilePrintPreview_Click()
                'To Do
                MsgBox "Print Preview Code goes here!"
        End Sub

        Private Sub mnuFilePrint_Click()
```

```
        'To Do
        MsgBox "Print Code goes here!"
    End Sub

    Private Sub mnuFileSend_Click()
        'To Do
        MsgBox "Send Code goes here!"
    End Sub

    Private Sub mnuFileMRU_Click(Index As Integer)
        'To Do
        MsgBox "MRU Code goes here!"
    End Sub

    Private Sub mnuFileExit_Click()
        'unload the form
        Unload Me
    End Sub

    Private Sub mnuFileNew_Click()
        'To Do
        MsgBox "New File Code goes here!"
    End Sub
```

That's it for our Web page database handling—and that's it for our book! We've come far in this book. We've talked about how to handle FTP and HTTP protocols, the Hyperlink object, and VBScript. We've explored composing, sending, and receiving email and discussed the ins and outs of secure Web links. We've studied ActiveX controls and ActiveX documents, explaining how to download FTP and HTTP text and binary data. You've learned how to write a Web browser, including the details of history and hyperlinks and how to register users through email. We've covered MAPI controls and synchronous and asynchronous transfers. We've explored how to add methods, events, and properties to ActiveX controls and how to distribute ActiveX controls on the Internet. You've learned how to use the Setup Wizard and digital signatures as well as initialize Web pages and handle passwords with VBScript. We've also looked at self-modifying Web pages—and more. All that remains is to put all this programming power to work for yourself. Happy programming!

INDEX